Hustlers & Con Men

AN ANECDOTAL HISTORY
OF THE CONFIDENCE MAN
AND HIS GAMES

BY JAY ROBERT NASH

M. Evans and Company, Inc. / New York, N. Y. 10017

LIBRARY OF CONGRESS CATALOGING IN PUBLICATION DATA

Nash, Jay Robert.
  Hustlers and con men.

  Bibliography: p.
  Includes index.
  1. Fraud—United States—History. I. Title.
HV6695.N37   364.1′63′0973   75-38602

ISBN 0-87131-188-7   HARDCOVER

ISBN 0-87131-376-6   PAPERBOUND

M. Evans and Company, Inc.
216 East 49 Street
New York, New York 10017

Design by Joel Schick

Manufactured in the United States of America

9 8 7 6 5 4 3 2 1

This book is for my
brothers Neil and Jack

Contents

Acknowledgments ix

1. THE FIRST HUSTLE 1
2. THE ANCIENT GAMES 21
3. MAGIC WALLETS AND PIGEON-DROPS 40
4. "DO THE MOTHS BOTHER YOU?" 58
5. THE INHERITED BILLIONS 77
6. ALL THAT GLITTERS 97
7. THE SHORT CON 110
8. SIRENS, STRUMPETS, AND SMOOTHIES 133
9. "I AM BUT A SCIENTIST" 160
10. WHEN THE SPIRITS PAID OFF 172
11. GIVING THEM THE BUSINESS 195
12. CON CLANS 214
13. CON INTERNATIONAL 233
14. THE BIG STORE 256
15. IMPOSSIBLE IMPOSTERS 270

A Chronology of Con 291
Glossary 339
Bibliography 346
Index 364

Acknowledgments

I would like to thank James Patrick Agnew, my friend and co-researcher, who toiled in scores of libraries and archives on this book's behalf. My boundless gratitude goes to an extraordinary typist, Carolyn Zozak; to Jan, for "proofing" the madcap prose; to the staff of the Chicago Public Library, especially Joseph Lutz in the history and travel department and Jimmy Downs; to Peter Weil of the Newberry Library; to Robert C. Miller, assistant director for general services at the Joseph Regenstein Library at the University of Chicago; to the staff at Northwestern University Library; to once-upon-a-time con men Joseph "Yellow Kid" Weil, John O'Hara, Jack Goose and others.

And to those who contributed so many rich anecdotes and verifiable stories—postal and police officials who prefer to remain anonymous; James Elkins; John Agnew, Sr.; John Agnew, Jr.; Patrick Agnew; Bob Connelly, who cherishes Wilson Mizner's zany exploits; Ed Crawford; Tom Buckley; Marc Davis, formerly of the *Chicago Tribune*, who remembered so well the story of Sigmund Engel; Jerrie Lynn Klein; Art Kluge; Jim Small; Curt Johnson; Norbert Blei; Hank Oettinger; Edgar Krebs, my journalistic savant in California; Jerry Goldberg; Mary and Tom McComas; and my cooperative newspaper friends Herman Kogan, Tom Fitzpatrick, Roger Ebert, Paul McGrath, Bill Granger, Paul Galloway of the *Chicago Sun-Times*, Mike Royko, Henry Kisor, Larry Finley, Robert Herguth and Barry Felcher of the *Chicago Daily News*, Mike Lavelle of the *Chicago Tribune*, and Joseph Longmeyer of the *Chicago Defender*.

Hustlers & Con Men

One

The First Hustle

THE COMING of the con man to America was as natural as the peeling back of one frontier after another. He was a woodsman, a peddler, a traveler quite ordinary. He struggled to California in the Gold Rush, plying his devious games in the mud-spattered shanty-built boom towns. His subtle grift could be found, long before the Civil War, in the thick-carpeted salons of the paddle-wheelers slurping and sloshing their Mississippi ways from Illinois to New Orleans. He rode the first rails West in comfort, fleecing his fellow passengers with a smile.

In the cobblestoned East he was a hawker, a mobile seller of wares and nostrums, a drifter of easy manner and average garb, appearing at town meetings and country fairs. He also moved, formally attired and scented, through stylish High Society, bilking, through the embryonic American business world. But for the most part he was a ubiquitous, nameless individual, employing against the naïve such simple cons as three-card monte, banco, chuck-a-luck, green goods, the gold brick, the country send, the Spanish prisoner. Sometimes he was a man of repute who risked reputation and identity in big cons (later to be termed "the big store"), protected only by audacity and will.

1

Precedent for the games of these wily wags had long been set by spectacular European harbingers. Con man and credit trimmer Richard Town had so incurred the wrath of his high-placed victims that in London, on May 23, 1712, he was hanged for secreting fifteen tons of tallow on board a ship and attempting to flee with his money, thus defrauding creditors. Town's open-air execution before a cheering multitude was highlighted by the fact that the day was his birthday. This suave con man stood coolly on the scaffold and shouted in a stentorian voice: "My friends, this is my birthday. I see you have come to help me honor it." To an attractive lady nearby he remarked: "Madam, my compliments, and thank you for coming to my adventure." True to the unruffled demeanor that was to hallmark those of his miscreant trade, Town then adjusted the cap over his head and cavalierly signaled the drop to fall.

John Law's Fantastic Bubble

After Town's fabulous demise, Europe became pockmarked by a plague of celebrated con artists. Hot on Town's heels was Edinburgh-born John Law, ugly, ill-tempered, trained in finance by a banker father, a born confidence man whose wild schemes would bring about the economic ruination of France. Branded a murderer and fugitive, Law fled England after killing a man named "Beau" Wilson in a one-sided duel over the dubious affections of one Elizabeth Villiers (later Countess of Orkney). Obtaining a directorship in the Bank of Amsterdam, Law befriended the Duke of Orleans, who was to become regent for France's Louis XV. Through the Duke, Law was appointed head of the Banque Général and later Controller-Général of France's money.

The country was then hopelessly in debt, $625 million owed for the extravagant wars and whims of the hedonistic Louis XIV, and Law's plan to solve the financial dilemma was to float paper currency—government secured bank notes—and create a national elastic monetary system. Coinage was called in and restamped with half its weight in metal without losing its former face value. To this scheme Law added, in 1717, a government-backed con history would call "the Mississippi Bubble." Law developed the Mississippi Company, the purported intention of which was to develop the vast trading riches of French Louisiana, but his real aim was to exploit the company's stock, and this he did on a level so broad that the entire country was seized by a frenzy of speculation. Blessed by the Duke, the government, and the decaying royalty, Law opened lavish offices at the Hôtel de Soissons and initiated his financial rape.

By 1720 Paris was a madhouse, jammed, it seemed, by every citizen in France attempting to buy Mississippi Company stock. Formerly poor people retired wealthy in months, purchasing Law's phony stock and reselling it to the desperate at 120 percent profit, just as Law, on a grander scale, was doing. (American confidence man William F. Miller would, in 1899, offer a 520 percent short-term increase on money invested in his bogus Franklin Syndicate; Charles Ponzi of Boston would also follow Law's Peter-to-Paul game, with variations, in 1919). Not a ship departed for Louisiana to develop its much-touted wealth of trade, yet tens of thousands kept purchasing empty stock certificates, the soaring rate of which was impossible to comprehend. In the summer of 1720 a 500-livre share vaulted to a value of 18,000 livres.

The boom made everyone artificially rich. Living space was at such a premium that houses renting for $200 a year rocketed to $4,000 a month. A cobbler retired after renting his narrow stall to brokers for 200 livres ($40) a day. And apocryphal or not, one report had it that a "hunchback made a small fortune by standing still at various points in the almost inconceivable crush and allowing the use of his deformed back as a desk for a reasonable fee."

Unprepared and overextended the nation was stunned at the exposé revealing Law's stocks to be useless; there simply was no Mississippi Company. John Law, dressed as a beggar, escaped to the border and disappeared. His departure at the threat of public lynching was so hasty that he thoughtlessly left behind sacks of accumulated gold and jewels, an enormous fortune, and vanished as penniless as he had made France.

In that same year, 1720, another highbinder, Robert Harley, Earl of Oxford and Mortimer, who had been made Chancellor of the Exchequer and Lord High Treasurer, almost brought England to ruin in an identical scheme (hatched in 1711) with the collapse of the phony South Sea Company. American John Morris would duplicate the "bubble" con game with the corrupt Louisiana Lottery, begun during the Civil War and surviving exposure for thirty years. The Mizener brothers, Wilson and

Addison, con men supreme were to blow the Florida real estate bubble to fantastic proportions, and reap fortunes before its explosion in the mid-1920s.

The Humbugging Humberts

Another redoubtable European con artist was a French peasant woman, Thérèse Dauignac, whose fake claims of inherited millions in the late 1870s brought her $14 million in glittering wealth (a swindle copied thirty years later by the American con woman Cassie Chadwick, who made arcane claim to being Andrew Carnegie's illegitimate daughter). Married to Frederick Humbert, Thérèse announced in her poverty-bare Paris home that she had been left $20 million by an American industrialist, Robert Henry Crawford, whom she had nursed back to health while he was in the throes of a deadly disease.

Madame Humbert slyly enlisted the French courts as her accomplices, instituting false claims and counterclaims by fictitious people avariciously seeking the Crawford fortune. She created Crawford's two nephews (as, indeed, she had Crawford), Robert and Henry, who were, in reality, her two brothers Emile and Romaine. Posing as the American millionaire's relatives, these two actually obtained a court order that sealed a large safe in which the Crawford money allegedly reposed. The safe stood, adorned with the colorful legal seals of France, in the middle of the Humbert salon for thirty years while Madame Humbert blithely borrowed millions against its contents. She and her clan were careful to continue to wage bitter warfare in the courts over the Crawford money, until the estate became an interminable legal web that confounded lawyers and judges alike. No one dared, once the official governmental seals were placed on the safe, to challenge its contents, and creditors in legions showered the Humberts with wealth at highly usurious rates.

Unlike the traditional portrait of the French temptress, Madame Humbert was, according to an acquaintance, "short, stout, yellow-skinned, obese, she looked the typical French cook." She was uneducated, spoke with a lisp and a thick Provençal accent, and repelled and alarmed the most solicitous (and probing) visitors to her salon. Her iron nerve never faltered through the three decades in which she gave the most lavish parties, balls, and dinners in Paris. The *crème* of French society delightedly attended her baroque fetes, and these social lions were, when possible, eventually exploited or compromised by the Humberts on behalf of their incredible claims.

The dazzle, dash, and spectacle of the Humbert clan popped to nothingness in 1902, when creditors got a court order and forced open the legendary Crawford safe. Inside was found, not the $20 million in securities, but a little more than $1,000 in negotiable bonds, an empty jewel box, and some brass buttons. A dozen Humbert creditors committed suicide the next day, but the extent of the punishment meted out to the family was short jail terms, such was the grudging French admiration for Madame Humbert's long-lived con.

Watering Stock with Daniel Drew

Americans, in typically pioneer spirit, were quick to emulate the confidence games so boldly practiced by their European forerunners, and one in particular led the way at the beginning of the nineteenth century, the notorious robber baron rascal Daniel Drew, whose ill-gotten financial empire was built upon one con game after another. Drew, a towering, rail-thin, lean-faced individual, began fastidiously small, but would later connive to steal millions, and like many a money potentate before and after, attempt to exculpate his deeds by public thrusts at piety and charity. (He founded Drew Seminary and headed several religious committees in New York, one of which, in 1852, purchased and razed the Old Brewery, a charnel house where hundreds of murders and vile crimes had been committed.)

Crafty Daniel Drew, who began by watering livestock and ended watering stock certificates. (UPI)

One of Drew's first victims was Henry Astor, John Jacob's brother. In 1815 Drew was scrounging his living as a chief drover of Ohio cattle herds, a comic figure wearing a huge, floppy hat and baggy pants and urging his gaunt cattle forward with a battered umbrella. En route to Astor's New York cattle station, Drew ordered his men not to let the cattle drink water for three days, further dictating that salt be liberally mixed with their feed. Shortly before arriving at the Astor station, Drew allowed the half-mad cows to drink their fill. Hours later the herd, each animal enormously bloated, were weighed, while Astor made the astonishing remark, "Drew, that's the finest-looking herd of cattle I've seen."

Collecting his cash for the watered stock, Drew vanished, leaving Astor cursing the following day as he inspected a stockyard full of sickly, rib-thin cows.

Drew, a man who never learned to write, realized that if he could water stock for a huge profit, he could do the same with securities and bonds. He invested his cattle-fraud monies in sawdust- and meat-packing firms, broken-down inns, and a shoddy ferry line allegedly designed to compete with Commodore Cornelius Vanderbilt. The boat service was a ruse designed to get Vanderbilt to buy the line out. The Commodore paid an exorbitant fee to eliminate Drew's line, only to discover that the competition consisted of one paddle-wheeler, the *Water Witch*, a jumble of patched-up splinters that would not bring salvage money.

With glee, Drew, fast becoming America's first illiterate tycoon, continued to prey on the surprisingly gullible Vanderbilt, a rogue in his own right, who kept coming back for more, a classic mark in the annals of con. The Drew-Vanderbilt financial battles were really jousts between con men extraordinary. Vanderbilt's prosaic plans always called for the same tactic—buy, consume, own. "What do I care for the law?" he once proclaimed. "I got the power, ain't I?" He put his faith in money and drew his meager philosophy from *Pilgrim's Progress*, reportedly the only book he ever read in his eighty years of covetous life.

Gould and Fisk, the First Super Con Men

Drew plotted Vanderbilt's end with two cunning con men of expansive ambitions, the calculating and unconscionable Jay Gould, who loved nothing but wealth and gardening, and the slothful rake Big Jim Fisk. Both men qualified as Drew's protégés. By the age of thirty-three Gould had cheated two partners out of a successful leather goods factory and become an expert stock manipulator on the New York Stock Exchange. Fisk, once a circus barker, had bought and sold cheap war contracts and made a fortune as a carpetbagger in the financially crippled South following the Civil War. In 1867 Daniel Drew appointed these two suave crooks directors of the Erie Railroad, in which he owned large blocks of stock, and which he knew Vanderbilt lusted to add to his own New York Central line.

The plot hatched by Drew and his pernicious lieutenants was uncomplicated. They would simply con Vanderbilt into believing that by buying up enormous chunks of Erie stock he could corner the market. But there would be no end to the stock.

Vanderbilt immediately purchased the first blocks of Erie as they appeared on the market. Several million dollars later the Commodore, knowing he had bought up enough shares to corner the market on the railroad, suspected that Drew and his henchmen were selling short, borrowing certificates from other stockholders with the intention of buying them back at deflated prices from the lenders once they had broken Vanderbilt.

Examining the situation, Vanderbilt belly-laughed: "Why, I've got more shares than were ever issued on this company." He planned to resell the shares to Drew, but at $1 million a share, which would break old Daniel. On the floor of the Stock Exchange, bedlam took over when Vanderbilt's corner was made known. Erie stock skyrocketed, but to Vanderbilt's astonishment, thousands of shares kept appearing on the market, none of which were released by him; he would never foolishly break his own corner.

The appearance of this extra stock was due to a watering process dear to the heart of Daniel Drew. Fisk and Gould had bought a small printing press and were simply running off thousands of extra shares. The massive, gaudily dressed Fisk was quoted as saying: "If this printing press don't break down, I'll be damned if I don't give that old hog [Vanderbilt] all he wants of Erie!" The trick worked. Erie's value raced upward to $57 million before a broker on the Exchange floor fainted when the ink on one of the railroad's certificates smeared under his thumb pressure. Fisk and Gould had been printing the stock so fast the ink hadn't time to dry. The discovery threw the Exchange into a panic never before seen in American history. Not only Erie stock but almost all others plummeted to the bottom, and as one writer reported, "High above the bedlam sounded the mad roars of Commodore Vanderbilt, who was said to have lost $7 million in fifteen minutes."

Old Daniel Drew had not broken Vanderbilt, but he had certainly bilked millions out of his pockets, and in the process had established the rogues Fisk and Gould as super con men of enormous wealth. As directors of the debunked line, they first fled melodramatically, escaping process servers in the middle of the night, with $6 million in cash stuffed into their pockets, aboard the New Jersey ferry, owned, ironically, by Vanderbilt. Next, Gould traveled incognito to Albany, New York, where he blatantly bribed the state legislature into legalizing the extra Erie stock dumped on the hapless Vanderbilt, plus much more, enough to keep Gould on as a director of the railroad. Such Machiavellian moves were then possible; there were no state and federal restrictions to hamper wholesale bribery.

Gould not only survived legal attempts to jail him for his part in the Erie War, but with his new fortune he attempted, two years later, on September 24, 1869, to corner the gold market. There was then about $15 million in gold in nationwide circulation, and with the help of his con pal Fisk, who worked diligently on President Grant to involve him in the scheme by ordering Federal gold reserves off the market, Gould squeezed the price of gold upward.

When Grant learned of Gould's corner, however, he balked and ordered the Treasury to step in and sell off government gold. Through well-paid spies in the government, Gould learned of Grant's move and sold off his gold stock, netting about $20 million. His scheme worked, and with his gains this phenomenal con artist then bought New York City's "El" lines, Western Union, and the Union Pacific Railroad, the latter "already floating on a sea of watered stock." Yet Gould managed to gut it further, reaping huge profits. Fisk fared equally, buying the Grand Opera House and involving himself in innumerable cons with political boss Marcy Tweed. (He would be shot to death by another schemer, Ned Stokes, on January 6, 1872, in a passionate dispute over Fisk's mistress, Josie Mansfield. Fisk's wife Lucy kissed him on his deathbed, murmuring, "he was a good boy.")

Master manipulator Drew stopped chortling over his successful cons in 1873, however, when a selling panic ruined him in the Exchange, leaving him with listed assets of about $500. These included a "seal-skin coat, watch and chain, bibles and hymn books." Though his mentor had collapsed on bad times, Gould went on to further successful skullduggery, his coffers brimming until he met another confidence man more than equal to his own cunning.

Robber baron Jay Gould (left) and his partner and fellow stock-rigger Big Jim Fisk. (UPI)

Gordon-Gordon Cons a Con Man

This nemesis first appeared mysteriously across the Atlantic, in the form of an elegantly attired Edinburgh gentleman named Lord Glencairn. In the winter of 1868, Lord Glencairn, preceded by his valet-secretary, who wore a large cockade in his hat representing a royal commission held by his master, sauntered into the glittering jewelry salon owned by Marshall and Son, Edinburgh's leading dealer in rare jewels. On this first visit, Glencairn selected several gems, paying for them with an impressive check, which cleared and thus established his gilt-edged credit. For months he bought more jewels, but on credit. The owners became alarmed in early spring, 1869, when they discovered Lord Glencairn owed them more than £25,000 for his purchases. Failure to pay their many bills caused Marshall and Son to summon the police, but their investigation proved fruitless. Lord Glencairn and his gewgawed secretary had vanished, taking with them baubles valued at close to $100,000. A thorough check revealed that no such Lord Glencairn existed, and the young, handsome con man posing as same was thought to have exited for America.

Two years later, in 1871, this individual—his true name was never learned—surfaced, of all places, in Minneapolis, Minnesota, this time under the bogus title of Lord Gordon-Gordon. He quickly established his stately English background and wealth by registering at the best hotel and depositing $40,000 in the leading bank. He announced to Colonel John S. Loomis, land commissioner of the Northern Pacific Railroad, that he intended to buy up vast tracts of railroad land on which to relocate his impoverished tenants in Scotland. Such a land boom, he quietly announced at a banquet of the state's leading citizens, would, no doubt, greatly enrich Minnesota.

Lord Gordon-Gordon was a meticulous con man, tall and slender, his garb the height of fashion. A new silk hat adorned his head, and patent-leather gloves covered manicured fingernails. Starved for social status, the Minnesotans eagerly became his easy marks. The homes of the rich were thrown open to him en masse, although he was careful to attend only the most important parties.

Businessmen organized an expedition in which Lord Gordon-Gordon could inspect the rich lands adjacent to the railroads, particularly the Northern Pacific, which footed the bill. For weeks Gordon-Gordon was pampered, traveling in private rail cars and surrounded by caravans of wagons filled with servants and luxuries. One historian reported that "two palatial wall tents were provided for his exclusive use, in one of them, with silver and the loveliest china, were served to him viands that would have enraptured Epicurus. Fruit was brought from Mexico for him, curaçao from the Spice Islands, dry Monopole from its fragrant home. His table was like Montezuma's."

After three delirious months of fetes and balls, the magnificent noble, having selected hundreds of thousands of acres upon which he would build bright new cities, carefully pointing out to the pious Minnesotans where the churches and schools would be, departed for the Èast to arrange transfer of his funds from Scotland in payment for the land, which had already been marked sold.

Gordon-Gordon moved, carefully and in style, toward New York City and his intended victim, crafty Jay Gould. He and a retinue of servants made leisurely stops along the way, establishing his identity in the press and in quarters of High Society. His coming was well publicized, and in February 1872 Gordon-Gordon, with much pomp, took up residence in the finest suite of rooms the fashionable Metropolitan Hotel had to offer.

As he had with Marshall and Son in Scotland and with the prominent citizens of Minneapolis, Lord Gordon-Gordon sent off forged letters of introduction from impeccable British leaders, containing glowing recommendations of the millionaire lord and asking one and all to treat him with the respect and honor commensurate with one of his noble bearing and background. One of these delicately worded missives was delivered to journalistic oracle and *New York Tribune* editor Horace Greeley, who, eager to please the mighty in the knowledge that he would soon be a candidate for the American Presidency, scurried to the Metropolitan to pay homage.

Upon Greeley's arrival, Lord Gordon-Gordon's manservant presented him with another letter, a glowing report on the nobleman's magnanimity and his staggering purchases of Northern Pacific lands, written by the already duped railroad commissioner, Loomis. The editor was awed by Gordon-Gordon's display of wealth, his liveried servants, his monogrammed silverware and napkins at a sumptuous feast. They were soon fast friends, and the lord finally, with a great display of discretion, revealed to Greeley that he and his English associates had quietly bought up millions of shares of Erie Railroad stock—enough, it appeared, to take control of the line at the next election of the board of directors. Greeley was delighted when the Right Honorable Lord told him he wanted the line "cleaned up," that its horrible reputation was no doubt attributable to the activities of one Jay Gould, its president and manager. "I've heard that he's an impossible rascal, dear me," fluttered Gordon-Gordon. "That simply won't do, will it, Mr. Greeley?" He dropped the matter as obviously repugnant to the tastes of a cultured gentleman, but allowed after several more meetings with Greeley and other important stockholders of the line, his so-called ideas for "reform" to be literally pried out of him.

Daubing his powdered cheek with a lace handkerchief, Lord Gordon-Gordon mumbled something about such an "unpleasant topic of conversation," but with a sigh admitted that he and his British associates felt it would be best for the railroad's tarnished image, not to mention its stock value, if Mr. Jay Gould would resign as the director of the line. Greeley, Colonel Thomas A. Scott, and other honest stockholders were gleeful at the prospect, but Gould, who employed Erie as a buffer and front for his many other cons, was terrified.

One of the most accomplished con artists of his day, Gould, through the bona fide information passed along by Greeley, Scott, and others, sincerely believed his ouster imminent, and desperately sought to head off Gordon-Gordon's move. After applying pressure through friends, Gould arranged a meeting with the hesitant lord in his suite of rooms. Gould came right to the point.

"What's your interest in Erie?"

Gordon-Gordon sipped his tea and whispered over his cup: "I presently own thirty millions of the stock, my friends another twenty millions. You see, we control the whole."

The soft-speaking lord then added that he thought it best that Mr. Gould step down from his post as president, thus completing what latter-day con men would term "the stall," establishing conditions apparently to prevent the mark from making his money—in Gould's case, to prevent him from continuing to gut Erie and through its prestige other interests—a direct challenge that compelled the mark to overcome any obstacle looming in his path on his way to the riches.

The robber baron was shocked, white faced, fist clenched and speechless—but only for seconds. Gordon-Gordon then implemented the stage of the classic con known as "the hurrah" and invited Gould, with ever so friendly gestures and words, to "talk it over" while they shared the lord's ample breakfast.

Back-peddling, Gordon-Gordon proceeded to strengthen his position by detailing his background to Gould as if merely making social conversation. This subtle con man talked candidly of his career and family, telling the uneducated Gould that he had taken his seat in Parliament at the age of twenty-two as the youngest member of the House of Lords, that he was a confidant of Queen Victoria, bless her heart, and had accomplished scores of secret missions on her behalf, one of which involved sensitive negotiations with that war-mongering Bismarck. The lord smilingly told of the Queen's undying gratitude for his diplomatic pacification of the German warlord.

At that moment, previously arranged and scheduled by Gordon-Gordon, Horace Greeley was shown into the suite, and entered the conversation about Gould's resignation from Erie, an unwitting witness to the imposter's proposals. Gould was told by Gordon-Gordon that he might reconsider his staying on as the railroad's manager if he would institute honest policies laid down by the lord.

Gould gushed promises to do so.

"I'm afraid," intoned the lord, "it requires more than mere words. You must show me by satisfactory proofs that what you state to me is true."

"If you will aid me," Gould stated, "I will be most happy to place my resignation in your hands, to hold and activate should I fail." Further, Gould, in his desperation to appease this holier-than-thou Englishman, tried to convince Gordon-Gordon to buy more Erie stock with him.

The Englishman blanched, and in a great act of recovery, declined the suggestion, haughtily retorting, with bristling indignation: "My dear Gould, I am not in the habit of having my credulity and my pocket tested at the same time!"

Withering under the testy rebuke, Gould stammered: "Please excuse me . . . I don't mean it that way . . . I will carry the stock both for you and myself."

Lord Gordon-Gordon leaned back in his chair, a portrait of pensiveness; then, with measured words, he agreed to allow Gould to remain in his lofty position, adding that he could see reason in accepting Gould's shares, 20,000 at $35 a share in all, and holding these and Gould's written resignation as a sort of security that he would act ethically on Erie's behalf. He went on to point out that he had spent more than $1 million in gathering together his English investors, lobbying for legal security in Albany and various "investigations." This paltry sum, Gordon-Gordon calmly stated, could be properly charged against the company, since it was expended on behalf of Erie.

The suggestion did not take Gould aback. He was more than familiar with milking his own company, and he happily agreed to cover half of the lord's expenditures by placing in his hands, for safekeeping only and as a measure of his own good faith, the tidy sum of half a million dollars. As Gould angrily testified later in court: "In view of the fact that he had made these advances personally and that the success of the new plan would depend very much on my good faith and his cooperation, I agreed to deposit with him securities and money to the extent of about one-half of his expense, or about five hundred thousand dollars. This pledge was not to be used by him, but was to be returned to me on my carrying out my part of the agreement."

Gordon-Gordon was satisfied, his fears for Gould's honesty abated when the shares were delivered. Hours after receiving the securities, however, Gould received a note from the lord pointing out an "error in the footing." Afraid to raise the Englishman's displeasure, Gould quickly delivered another $40,000 in stock, and to quiet any further tremors the lord might have concerning his character, a package containing $200,000 in cash, which was to be held in escrow.

"I would appreciate a receipt," Gould said. "A formality."

Gordon-Gordon, on the brink of accomplishing the final stage of the game—"the sting," as it would later be known—showed marvelous nerve, willing to turn his back completely on the suavest confidence game of the nineteenth century, a game that had taken him months of elaborate preparation and moves. Without an eyelid fluttering, he shrugged, and more or less threw the money and securities back into Gould's trembling hands. "Gould, the thought that *my* word is inadequate security in any business transaction is both insulting and intolerable." With that the plucky Englishman went to a chair, sat down, and with an unconcerned air began to read what appeared to be confidential reports on Erie.

Wily Jay Gould, for the first time in his nefarious life, was nonplused. He headed for the door, then stopped halfway, turned, and walked to a table, where he gently placed the stocks and money. The financial barracuda meekly stated to Gordon-Gordon, who refused even to look in his direction, "I always ask for business receipts as a matter of form but—" and he must have come close to choking on the words—"in your case, Lordship, your word, of course, will be more than sufficient."

Gould was stung, and Gordon-Gordon wasted no time in disposing of the stocks, selling blocks in Philadelphia. When the sales were made known to Gould, he exploded and demanded the return of the cash and securities. Greeley acted as a bewildered emissary and delivered these to Gould, who immediately realized he had been short-changed by more than $150,000. He swore out a warrant for the Englishman's arrest and filed suit, employing the distinguished lawyers David Dudley Field and Elihu Root. But Gordon-Gordon was not ready to give up the pretense. He would battle the robber baron in court, he announced, and Gould's old enemies scrambled to the lord's defense. Vanderbilt, still seeking revenge for the watered Erie stock caper, put up Gordon-Gordon's bail of $40,000 through his son-in-law Horace Clark. One-legged General Daniel Sickles, hero of Gettysburg and an Erie stockholder several times bilked by Drew and Gould, rushed to court to become the Englishman's legal counsel.

Gordon-Gordon's appearance in court the first day of the trial was amazingly aloof, and he succeeded in convincing everyone save the

Gould faction of his sincerity. That night, however, Gould went near mad with delight as his dozens of cables inquiring of British authorities as to Lord Gordon-Gordon's veracity were answered. He was an unknown imposter, came the word. Triumph grinning in his face, Gould entered the courtroom the following day, but he, along with everyone else, waited for Gordon-Gordon's appearance in vain.

It was time, the imposter resolved, after the first day of legal battle, to flee. It was only a matter of time, he knew, before his pose would be pricked by English officials. He left with his $150,000 loot, in the middle of the night on a fast train bound for Canada.

Gould offered $25,000 for his capture. The bilked firm of Marshall and Son sent investigators on his trail from Scotland. Even the Minneapolis citizens, more angry over being duped socially than over losing money to this scoundrel, streamed across the Canadian border in search of the fabulous imposter. Gordon-Gordon took refuge in the distant outpost of Fort Garry, Manitoba, where he successfully fought off extradition through authorities gulled by his handsomeness and charm. Several attempts by Minnesotans to kidnap him and return him to the United States were fouled by Canadian police (Five Americans—two of whom would become governors of Minnesota, the other three congressmen—were jailed for attempting the kidnapping.)

Thomas Smith, the clerk at Marshall and Son who had sold Gordon-Gordon jewels in Edinburgh, then arrived at Fort Garry, and on behalf of his firm identified the con man and swore out a warrant for his arrest. He obtained an order for "Lord Glencairn's" return to Scotland to stand trial. He was not believed by the Canadians, who had fallen in the sway of Gordon-Gordon's charms, but Smith prevailed, and, surprisingly, the Englishman agreed to return to Britain to quash these "foolish charges."

A great ball was given in his honor, a going-away party, by one of Fort Garry's leading citizens. At 3:00 A.M., weary of the festivities at which he was the witty, affable core of attention, Gordon-Gordon beamed his good-nights and closed the door of a guest room. Moments later a shot echoed. He was found sprawled dead on the floor, a bullet through his temple. Thus ended in high drama, as Gordon-Gordon intended, one of America's first truly Big Cons.

The Hustler of Early High Society

Gordon-Gordon was not the first imposter-con to tread American shores in search of guile-gotten riches, but of the early pioneers in the field he was one of the most spectacular. Predating Gordon-Gordon was Colonel Novena whose games were, albeit less ostentatious, certainly no less original in that golden age of gullibility. He was a high-society con man who moved with ease in and out of the splendorous homes of the rich. His real name was Julian Cinquez, but he was known to his blue book admirers at various stages of his career as General Alverosa, Count Antonelli, Sir Richard Murray, and his own favorite alias, Colonel M. Novena, under which his debut was made in 1859.

Migrating from Havana, this necromancer was to become one of the first business con men in America. His charm was boundless, and his manner and looks elevated his image to that of any cultured gentleman he wished to be. A retired, obscure member of the American Secret Service, George S. McWatters, writing in an equally obscure tome, *Detectives of Europe and America; or Life in the Secret Service*, described Novena, in his rather florid style, as "no small man in his way. He was a handsome man, too, possessing a finely shaped face, with large, dark, not quite black, eyes and eyelashes, such as would rouse the enthusiasm of the master painters and which gave to those eyes that sweet alluring expression so irresistible to women; or when reflecting the light of anger from them added a twofold horror to their expression, enough to make the strongest man quail, for the man seemed then a very demon." Standing five feet ten, considerably tall for that period, he was well built, finely proportioned, a perfect ladies' man of the type so popular in the ante-bellum South, where grace, dignity, strength, and charm counted for everything. George McWatters added admiringly: "Novena was as lithe and flexible as a cat, or better, perhaps, a tiger."

The faultlessly dressed Colonel was a wonder at imitations. He could assume the dulcet-toned pose of the literary savant or the harsh stolidity of a Dutch judge. Equipped with a stunning portfolio of letters from famous Americans that he had collected over the years, he was invited to the most lavish parties of the era.

One of the first mandatory stops in his roaming was Washington, D.C. Access to the President and other dignitaries in the White House was then a fairly easy matter. No American President had been assassinated as yet, and few guards bothered to ask the business of any visitor. Novena simply walked in one day and chatted with President Buchanan, who so much enjoyed his cordial company he invited the bogus Colonel to dine many times.

Letters from Buchanan, as well as from Andrew Johnson, General John C. Fremont, Chief Justice Taney, and Secretary Seward, soon swelled Novena's brief, and all of these special letters were made known to the socially prominent who invited the Colonel into their homes. While the women were doting upon the suave Novena, he borrowed money, considerable sums, from their husbands with no intention of repayment. "It's only until I can draw upon my New York account," he would say, or "till my manager in Havana forwards my dividends in plantation interests."

This ploy soon wore thin, but no legal action was taken. Though some wealthy men lost thousands to Novena in this manner, they dismissed him as a mere adventurer who brought a chuckle and a smile. "Novena? That rogue? Ah, well, his company was worth the price," one lender pooh-poohed.

The good Colonel, after exhausting social welcomes in Baltimore, Richmond, and Philadelphia, suddenly appeared at receptions in the smarter homes along New York's Fifth Avenue. All barriers were down to him, and this time he chose not to borrow a dime. His scheme was brighter. Once socially established, Novena optioned ten or twelve adjoining lots in a distinguished but underdeveloped section of the city, publicly announcing that this would be the site of an architectural wonder, the Novena Building. Producing architects' drawings, the Colonel displayed on paper an eye-popping structure of magnitude and magnificence. It would, however, only take up the three corner lots, plans for the others remaining a mouth-watering mystery.

Rich land speculators in 1859 found Novena's reluctance to let them in on the project unnerving, and began to offer him sums ten, twenty times the value of his optioned land, property Novena had not paid for. Just as reluctantly he sold off the surrounding lots, even the land the wonderful Novena Building itself was destined to sit upon. The Colonel

Sophie Lyons was a pathfinder in American con; she later became America's first gossip and society columnist. (UPI)

then departed New York, his architectual plans and plentiful profits jamming a carpetbag. None of his options were ever picked up, of course, but, ironically, many of his original sites were developed into thriving business areas.

Novena is credited with being the innovator of this real-estate con game, the first in American criminal history to employ it successfully. But he was only the first of many firsts in the ever-increasing army of confidence men (and women) who would mulct millions out of the pockets of the American public.

One of Novena's hard-working peers was Sophie Lyons, considered by most to be America's first important con woman, an enterprising harlot who graduated from whoredom to hustle after wedding master bank burglar Ned Lyons. A squat five feet two, matronly Sophie managed, from 1862 when associated with the cream of New York's underworld—Marm Mandelbaum, Adam Worth, Mark Shinburn (later "Baron" Shinburn, who retired with his stolen loot to the French Riviera)—to her retirement in the 1890s to steal, according to Pinkerton Detective estimates, more than $1 million in confidence games. Sophie embarrassed and humbled every police department on the East Coast when, in 1897, she went to work for the *New York World* and became the nation's first society columnist.

The Fleecing of Oscar Wilde

In the late 1860s, such flamboyant confidence men as "Hungry Joe" Lewis emerged to fleece the mighty. Hungry Joe plied his trade, usually banco—even then an ancient con, and from whence the word "bunko" came—for twenty years, making big scores. He, Tom O'Brien (who murdered the originator of the gold brick con, Reed Waddell, in Paris in March 1895), and Charles P. Miller, known as "King of the Banco Men," specialized in taking wealthy suckers, the more notable and reputable the better, as these gentlemen were less apt to admit to police they had been conned.

In 1882 Hungry Joe struck up an acquaintance in New York with Oscar Wilde, when the English author was on an American lecture tour. Posing as a struggling writer-painter, Hungry Joe dined several times with Wilde at the Hotel Brunswick, always as the author's guest. He suggested a game of chance to Wilde, who, then in his cups, jovially agreed, following Lewis to an old brownstone on Seventeenth Street, not far from where Wilde was staying. In an all-night sharper's game, Lewis, Miller, and O'Brien fleeced the naïve poet out of $1,500 in cash and his personal check for an additional $5,000. Wilde staggered home, a physical and mental wreck, while the confidence men headed for the bank.

Regaining his senses and realizing he had been conned, Wilde raced to the Park National Bank, upon which he had written his check, and stopped payment just as Hungry Joe and his friends arrived. Spotting Wilde, a large man with hamhock fists doubled, jaw jutting in anger, Hungry Joe beat a quick retreat, content with the $1,500 in cash.

Bilking with Bathos

Confidence men grew up with America, from high rollers like Hungry Joe, whose annual take for twenty years, by his own average, was more than $100,000, to the lowest con artists, like "The Crying Kid." The nineteenth century was much less demanding of the innovative and inventive. The Crying Kid, who operated in the 1870s, said of his near simpleton marks: "Even when they've been taken, they'll come back for more. They're the sort of hick you can sting twice in the same place and get away with it."

The Crying Kid, a horse-race slicker, easily demonstrated his theory by touting horses to rubes inside pool rooms, knowing the nags would lose and betting with other sharpers against the marks' bets. When a victim learned his horse had lost, he would walk angrily from the pool room looking for the Kid, not unreasonably desirous of jamming the Kid's "inside tip" down the con man's throat fist first. To the sucker's chagrin, he would find the Crying Kid waiting for him outside the pool-room, earning every letter in his moniker. The Kid would hang his head pathetically and lament with near-hysterical sobs: "I'm through! Every nickel I had in the world was on that dawg's nose. I steered you wrong, pal, but I played it straight . . . right alongside you. Everything is gone now . . . I'm gonna bump myself off, that's what I'm gonna do, and I'm gonna spend my last quarter for a bottle of carbolic . . . So long, friend . . ."

In almost every instance, the victim was so moved by the Crying Kid's performance that he quickly reached into his pockets and gave the con man more money, to prevent his suicide as well as to feed his nine mythical children. The Kid took the money reluctantly, sobbing fitfully and choking out his gratitude, and the sucker departed, feeling much better. "It eased their conscience a good deal," the Kid remarked, "to know they had saved me from self-destruction," not to mention forgetting the bum steer he had given them in the first place.

Early American con men—Jimmy McViccor, Joe MacDonald, Billy Knight, Buck Boatright, Ben Marks, George Pole, John Henry Strosnider, Charley Gondorf (his name was changed to Henry, as was his place in history, in the movie, *The Sting*), Willie "The Sleepy Kid" Loftus, Big Joe Turley, Charley Drucker, the Honeygrove Kid—developed, modified, and streamlined the confidence game into society's most sophisticated criminal act. In the 1920s the allegedly retired con artist W. C. Crosby knowledgeably stated that "confidence is a business, and, like all business, changes and conforms to conditions . . . con takes rise from the conditions of life about it and adapts itself as does social life. And con plays an invariable chord in the human make-up—good, old earthy greed. But this greed must be played upon according to the times and circumstances . . . con is perennial . . . con grows constantly greater. . . ."

Two

The Ancient Games

OF THE OLDEST con games in America, front runners have to be the shells and three-card monte, a toss-up for the historic first. The shell game, practiced on rubes at country fairs and circuses, was popular up and down the Mississippi in the early 1830s. Most expert at this con was Jim Miner, King of the Shell Men, who was also known as "Umbrella Jim."

Miner carried an umbrella with him rain or shine, ergo the sobriquet. Astonishingly fast with his hands, he moved the small rubber ball, or sometimes a pea, under three metal or wooden cups or shells with such dexterity for thirty years that his fortune was said to be more than $1 million when he retired.

Umbrella Jim would attract his suckers at station landings or on board luxurious riverboats by waving his parasol in a circle and chanting doggerel that was to become more than familiar to the thousands he duped over the decades:

> A little fun, just now and then,
> Is relished by the best of men.
> If you have nerve, you may have plenty;
> Five draws you ten, and ten draws twenty.
> Attention given, I'll show to you,

How Umbrella hides the peek-a-boo.
Select your shell, the one you choose;
If right, you win; if not, you lose;
The game itself is lots of fun,
Jim's chances, though, are two to one;
And I tell you your chance is slim
To win a prize from Umbrella Jim.

As a crowd assembled, one, sometimes two, cappers (also called "steerers" or "shills") would step forward boldly and bet heavily that he or they could outguess the deft Miner. These accomplices always won. The suckers were then primed, and stepping up gingerly, convinced that Miner could be beaten as the shills had demonstrated, plunked down their money and immediately lost everything to the fast-talking, mercurial-handed Miner.

Three-Card Monte

It took incredible naïveté to play into the hands of a shell game expert, but most early citizens west of the Alleghenies were ripe for just such an unsophisticated con, and many came to do the plucking. At about the same time a Spanish con game imported from Mexico became the most popular frontier game that offered no hope at winning for any suckers. This was three-card monte, a game, completely controlled by the con artist, in which players bet against the dealer, who, with flourish of hands and spiel of tongue, never failed to draw large crowds. The "tickets" or cards displayed by the operator were usually two aces and a queen, which would then be thrown face down and quickly manipulated. It was the object, as in the hoary shell game, to locate "the old lady." Also, as in the shells, cappers were used to prove to the spectators that the dealer could be beaten.

The capper or steerer would, unlike the shell game, whisper in the ear of some prosperous-looking rube that the dealer in his frenzied shuffling had slightly bent the corner of the queen, aligning himself in avarice with the mark, a conspiracy against the operator which could not fail to reap profits. The capper would then prove this to the mark

"Canada Bill" in action, fleecing suckers.

by guessing the queen several times. When the mark's turn came, he would usually bet a large sum of money, wait for the three cards to fall face downward, and select the one with the bent corner. But behold —the card was an ace. The dealer had merely thumbed the queen flat and bent up the edge of the ace when shuffling for the rube.

As in all confidence games, the mark seldom if ever complained to authorities that the dealer cheated, for following that statement would surely come the disclosure that the victim was attempting to cheat the dealer.

Early pioneers of this historic grift were George Devol, William Jones (better known as "Canada Bill"), Ben Marks, Tom Brown, and Holly Chappell. Devol is generally credited with instituting three-card monte on board the Mississippi riverboats as early as 1840. At sixteen Devol was one of the most glib con men working the Rio Grande Steamboat line, his success lining his pockets with $3,000 in his first year. One historian estimates that more than $2 million passed through his hands before his retirement in 1887. His old-age poverty was due to his obsession with faro, a game in which he was a perennial loser. He would earn huge amounts playing three-card monte on the swanky riverboats, only to lose it in land-based faro games. His sometimes partner, Canada Bill, was afflicted by the same passion, also spending his three-card monte profits on faro games he knew were rigged.

It was Canada Bill who, in the 1850s, provided the gambler's most classic quip. Devol found Bill playing faro in Baton Rouge and drew him aside.

"Don't you know this game's crooked?" Devol asked him.

Canada Bill, who was as sloppy and unkempt as Devol was fastidious, shrugged his shoulders and croaked: "I know, but it's the only game in town."

Bill eventually quit the paddle-wheelers in search of more lucrative quarry, feverishly plying three-card monte on railroads heading West. He fairly looted hundreds of thousands from gullible travelers before his death, in 1877, in Reading, Pennsylvania.

Another three-card monte protagonist was Ben Marks, who journeyed from Council Bluffs, Iowa, to Cheyenne, Wyoming, in 1867. Marks was so successful at three-card monte, considered a "short con," that he opened a store in Cheyenne to better handle and fleece the home-steading and gold-seeking hordes moving West. His simple innovation established a new genre in confidence games that would be known as "the big con" or "the big store," because of the gigantic profits it reaped. Classic con men like Joseph "Yellow Kid" Weil would become masters of this swindle.

Maurico's Slippery Handkerchief

By 1870 three-card monte was passé, too crude a game, especially in the East, to gull even the rawest of suckers. This ancient flimflam is revived periodically, however, and even meets with some success. As late as 1958, seventy-two-year-old Maurico Eiman, a con man for fifty years, was cheating marks at three-card monte. Eiman was also a master of the old con game, the Spanish prisoner, but with variations. His was really the Spanish handkerchief game, but the principle was the same: the victim, in order to earn quick money, had to put up earnest money of his own.

In Eiman's game, he would approach a wealthy-appearing Spanish gentleman in mid-town Manhattan—New York was his beat—and speaking Spanish, ask directions to the nearest airline ticket office. At this moment an accomplice would appear, and also engage in conversation. Seemingly worried, Eiman acted out the part of the confused foreign visitor. He would then explain that he had miserably failed his dying father, a well-to-do businessman in South America. His mission was to deliver $8,000 to a man his father had cheated years ago. The old man wanted to make restitution before meeting his Maker, but, Eiman related sorrowfully, he had been unable to locate this hapless soul. Failing to find the once double-crossed business partner, Eiman was to donate the money to worthy Spanish charities. "The trouble is, gentlemen," Eiman would whine, "I don't know what charities my father had in mind." There would be a quick flash of a fat bankroll inside a handkerchief, a hundred-dollar bill on top, play money rolled inside. "And I have no time to locate such charities. My good father is dying and I must fly to his bedside."

At this mournful moment, the roper would offer to aid the pressed-for-time Eiman, who in turn offered *both* men a $500 fee, as compensation for their efforts.

Then Eiman would add, half apologetically, "I'm sure you gentlemen are responsible citizens, but I would like to be able to assure my father that you are men of substance. Would you mind showing me that you have some money?"

Without hesitation, the roper would nod and say: "That's only fair," and produce a thick wad of greenbacks. The victim, by then totally committed to either helping Eiman from a humanitarian standpoint or obtaining a quick $500 and still retaining an easy conscience, rarely balked at offering to draw money, usually $500, from his bank to show his good faith. Eiman would then suggest meeting the two men later in a Manhattan church.

It was in the deep shadows of the church where Eiman's quick hands would go to work. Taking the mark's $500, he would place it on top of his own fat roll, the alleged $8,000, as well as the earnest money offered by the roper, and stuff it into the victim's pocket, appearing for all the world a simple, trusting human desperate to do his saintly father's bidding. He would then depart, naturally with all the money, which he had palmed, leaving the mark with shredded newspapers.

Up to 1958, Eiman's average income from this ancient con was about $30,000 a year. His last score prior to his arrest by New York detectives was $1,800, which he took from a wealthy Cuban psychiatrist. The artful old confidence man sat smoking a cigar in police headquarters and admitted proudly, "I used some psychology on the psychiatrist."

The Most Ancient Flimflam

The Spanish prisoner game, operating now for close to 400 years, since the time of Sir Francis Drake, is, perhaps, one of the oldest bunko games in the business. Although it requires considerable earnest monies doled out of a mark's pocket, it appeals to the American sense of adventure and chivalry, making the participant feel equated with, at least, Captain Blood, Lancelot, Robin Hood, or some other dashing figure of noble spirit. And yet, as one writer put it, the game "is so fantastic, shallow and crude that it should be an obvious mess of malarkey to almost anybody."

It begins with a wealthy U.S. citizen receiving a letter from a foreign country, written by someone ostensibly jailed, and quite unjustly, because he has a vast fortune secreted in the United States. The jailers or prosecutors, you see, are after the money. The letter's recipient is told in highly confidential terms that if he will aid in recovering the secreted fortune, he will share in it, but he is expected to provide for the prisoner's attractive young daughter. The prisoner is usually incarcerated in either Spain or Mexico in a remote, almost unreachable bastion.

A plethora of confederates are employed in the Spanish prisoner swindle but since one group of con men handle as many as 5,000 suckers each year, there is plenty of loot to spread around. (As late as 1952, the U.S. Post Office estimated that gullible and very fanciful Americans lose $600,000 each year in this game.)

Dating back to 1588, the first letters written by the sharpers who inaugurated the game appealed for money to ransom those unfortunate Spanish sailors captured and imprisoned in English dungeons after the breakup of the Armada. The ransom angle was soon discarded for the secreted treasure, which, on the Spanish galleons of the Armada, were bountiful. Long after the invading Spanish prisoners were dead, the letters continued to flow to suckers, describing by that time the imprisoned plight of fabulously wealthy grandsons and great-grandsons of the original Spanish prisoners. (Alexander Dumas, well aware of this universal con, borrowed some of its technique for his adventure yarn, *The Count of Monte Cristo.*)

Intricacy and intrigue are, perhaps, the most convincing factors of the Spanish prisoner routine. By the turn of the century, the Spanish prisoner became the Mexican prisoner, with letters by the thousands —postal authorities received 1,431 prisoner letters in 1900—sent out to prospective dupes. The pitch was always the same. The writer was usually a banker who had been thrown into jail over a bankruptcy, but before his incarceration he had managed to ship across the border to the United States anywhere from $250,000 to $500,000 (depending upon the inflationary aspects of each era) in a false-bottomed trunk.

Two suitcases with secret compartments held both the key to the trunk, which was with the unknowing daughter, a rare beauty, and a certified check ranging in amounts from $25,000 to $50,000. This check, the prisoner pointed out, was made payable to the bearer. Unfortunately, the suitcases had been impounded by the Mexican courts, which had sentenced the banker to several years in prison and levied a burdensome fine against him. The prisoner then deadlined the deal by informing the receiver that the suitcases with the key to the fortune, as well as the certified check, would be sold at public auction if the fine and court costs, normally about $10,000, were not paid two months from the date of the letter.

How the banker got the mark's name in the first place was easily explained by the miserable prisoner, who had befriended an American in jail, a friend of the letter's recepient who, naturally, had to remain nameless to protect his family's good name.

In return for paying his fine, the letter writer promised, the mark could keep the certified check, worth about three times the American's investment and have half of the fortune, which had been converted into greenbacks, around $150,000, if he would also see to it that the banker's "darling, beautiful eighteen-year-old daughter" was well provided for. Along with the letter was a picture of a sexy, well-endowed young woman.

With the appeal of an easy fortune and a beautiful woman luring the reader on, the writer then explained that should he undertake this humanitarian mission, he must "tell no one why you have come to Mexico and wait for the contact man." The contact man, usually the letter writer himself, would put the American in touch with a prison guard whom the prisoner had also befriended, and this man would arrange for the impounded suitcases to be released to him.

Preposterous as the whole affair may seem, thousands of duped U.S. citizens—curiously, many doctors are prime suckers for this con—travel with all speed to Mexico and take up residence in the prescribed city and hotel. After several mysterious phone calls and a period of anxious waiting, a nervous contact man arrives and begins the game, a series of clandestine meetings with surly-looking desperado types, at which times a lot of hurried whispering and nervous glances take place. The whole act is designed to unsettle the mark, and by the time the contact man has led him, in the middle of the night, to the gray-walled prison outside of town to meet the friendly guard, he is a nervous wreck.

The prison guard, an accomplice in uniform, also appears close to trauma, explaining to the American that the authorities have found out about the plot to help the prisoner and that they are looking for him. He, the American, cannot therefore show up in court and pay the prisoner's fine and court costs, but the crafty guard has taken care of that little matter. He has broken the seals of the suitcases, retrieved the claim-check stub that will release the trunk stored in the United States, and has the certified check for $35,000. He, the guard, will see to it that the fine and court costs are paid so his own actions will go undetected.

By this time the mark realizes that he is a wanted man in a foreign country, the ironic result of his charitable mission. In almost every instance, the American has forked over the $10,000, pocketed the claim-check stub and certified check, and raced for the border while horror and fear grind at his stomach. He then flies to the city where he has been told the daughter lives and the trunk awaits only to discover that the daughter is myth and the trunk invisible. When he attempts to cash the certified check to recoup his own losses, he discovers it to be bogus.

Few victims ever complain to authorities, let alone tell relatives, about being suckered in the prisoner game. As businessmen, which most marks are, such admissions would certainly reveal their much-vaunted acumen to be shoddy. Wounded pride, and a glaring inability to judge character, are other potent factors that induce the victim to keep a closed mouth. Those who do protest are immediately themselves labeled avaricious crooks, eager to take advantage of a get-rich-quick scheme.

Some marks do complain. Rev. Edgar Allan Lowther of San Francisco, who traveled to Mexico with his family, lost $3,500 in 1940, but none of his accusations proved fruitful; no identities of the Mexican con men could be established. The prisoner ring that had fleeced Lowther also took $4,000 from Victor E. Borden, a Seattle meat packer. Robert Wood, an industrialist from Mississippi, was also played by the ring but was stopped short by the ironic comments of a Mexican bank teller who was changing some money for him.

"I suppose," the teller told Wood humorously, "you're another victim of the Spanish prisoner game." Wood blanched and then went to the Mexican police, who put him in touch with James E. Speake, an inspector for the U.S. Post Office who had been working on the swindling of Reverend Lowther. Both Wood and Speake, through ingenious meetings and moves of their own, met with the leaders of the prisoner ring, and Speake managed to take their pictures with a small camera hidden on his person.

Identified were Juan Barrena, who had acted the part of the contact man and was an office manager for several rings of con men working the Spanish prisoner game, and Camilo Lopez Vasquez, a hatchet-faced individual whose hulking appearance was guaranteed to scare the wits out of any mark. Vasquez had usually played the part of the phony prison guard.

Extraditing these two extraordinary con men from Mexico to the United States (they were indicted by a San Francisco grand jury) proved frustrating, since no extradition based on mail fraud then existed between the two countries. Mexican police officials, long plagued by the prisoner con, distributed leaflets at all border crossings warning of the fraud. And two public-spirited policeman finally delivered Vasquez and Barrena to San Francisco authorities.

The extradition was considered extralegal by the Mexican press, and several newspapers exploded the incident to international proportions, claiming that con men Barrena and Vasquez had been kidnapped.

The newspaper *Excelsior* pointed the finger at the American dupes as being out-and-out miscreants themselves, and lauded the Mexican con men as working toward equalizing an uneven international money system: "If you study the problem purely and strictly from the point of view of justice, Vasquez and Barrena are nothing more than two patriots—two ingenious helpers of morality. . . . They worked to level the balance of exchange so perniciously weighted in favor of the powerful speakers of English. They are helpers of morality because they dedicated themselves to the noble task of punishing all secretly immoral persons —defaulters without courage."

These incredible words could serve as the true apologia for all con men everywhere, and as the theme basic to the defense of any confidence game, an attitude the con man banks on in a share-the-guilt criminal profession. However, the Mexican press notwithstanding, Barrena and Vasquez received stiff sentences in the United States.

Mailing the Spanish Prisoner

Not all the prisoner letters were in-coming to the United States. An enterprising con artist named Celedonio Sevilla operated for years out of the Empire State Building in Manhattan. His firm sent out thousands of letters to wealthy South American marks employing a fake priest, Father John Miller, as the author of a prisoner letter that described the fate of a bank embezzler named Nelson Lawrence Watkins, and detailed the predicament identical to the ancient Spanish or Mexican prisoner, except that the mythical daughter was about fourteen years old. Sevilla reasoned that South American men preferred younger ladies.

Mail response to Sevilla's con was channeled through a New York church, the pastor of which had been requested to send on the bogus Father Miller's letters. Sevilla and confederates explained that Father Miller was a South American citizen traveling in the United States. The request was simple enough, and the enormous amount of mail from Latin and South American countries was forwarded to a sparsely decorated office on 42nd Street.

Sevilla was a master at prisoner letters, dangling before the eyes of the mark treasure so vast as to make him drool deliriously. One of the more artful missives signed by the indefatigable Father Miller elaborately cautioned the gullible to

> have care in taking the lining from the trunk, and separate the double walls so as not to deteriorate what is there. Among the contents are: one thousand $100 bills, eight hundred $500 bills, four thousand pounds sterling, railroad and oil shares worth many thousands of dollars. Also in the trunk are the jewels of Kathlene's [the "poor, darling fourteen-year-old daughter"] mother: a pearl necklace valued at $10,000, a diamond diadem, which—that her mother may rest in peace—Kathlene must wear on her wedding day, worth $35,000. There is also the mother's wedding ring worth $5,000, a gold bracelet with the mother's name in rubies and emeralds, and some odd jewelry. There are two checkbooks on the National Bank of Argentina, with two deposits—one amounting to $16,000, the other $36,000. The little girl carries the key to the trunk on a little gold cord hanging about her neck.

Sevilla was undone before he could reap his rewards, however, by a suspicious secretary hired blind to receive and process the prisoner letter responses. She went to the postal authorities and Sevilla got seven years.

Not all recipients of the Spanish prisoner letters are intrigued, roped in, and financially seduced. Postal authorities revealed one letter from a Florida resident sent to con men operating the ancient swindle that read:

> Dear Señor:
> Your letter of August 20th received, and I am surprised to hear that someone who knows me had spoken highly enough of me for you to trust me in this very delicate proposition. It couldn't have been anyone who knows me well. But I would like to thank you just the same, and assure you that I cannot get away at this time.
> I'd like to reciprocate with an amazing offer of my own to you. Naturally, I cannot give definite names and places in this letter, as it might fall into the hands of others. My proposition is as follows:
> Years ago, a certain ship, headed across the water from one country to another country, was sunk with a large treasure aboard.

Now I know what ocean this happened in. If you will come . . . with as large a boat as possible and two deep-sea divers with complete outfits, I will give you the name of this ocean. (It is necessary for you to keep this offer quiet.)

By the way of compensation for your trip, I will give you all three thirds of whatever you are able to salvage.

I cannot sign my own name, for reasons you will understand, but you can refer to me as Sucker. Even if you can't make it up here, I surely hope you get out of jail soon. It must be annoying to have a suitcase full of money just around the corner and be unable to get at it.

Yours very truly,
Sucker

The Sealed Green Goods

Avarice, not honor, was the strict appeal made by the green-goods con man who operated this ancient racket in the United States for approximately fifty years, from about 1869, when the game began to flourish in New York City, to the mid-1920s, when U.S. postal agents began to crack down on operators. The notorious gold-brick salesman Reed Waddell was one of the early leading con men who gleaned fortunes from the green goods swindle (also called "the sawdust game"), which was nothing more than offering through boldly printed circulars sent through the mails the sale of "perfect" counterfeit currency without really delivering the goods.

Waddell and his successors obtained the names of likely suckers from lottery subscription lists, bookmakers, and betting parlors. These persons, the confidence men aptly reasoned, would be most prone to buy up "queer" or phony money, either to bet it or make up for losses that had to be kept secret.

A typical mailing piece from a green-goods man in 1890 read:

Dear Sir:

I will confide to you through this circular a secret by which you can make a speedy fortune. I have on hand a large number of counterfeit notes of the following denominations: $1, $2, $5, $10, and $20. I guarantee every note to be perfect, as it is examined carefully by me as soon as finished, and if not strictly perfect is immediately destroyed. Of course, it would be perfectly foolish to send out poor work, and it would not only get my customers into trouble, but would break up my business and ruin me. So, for personal safety I am compelled to issue nothing that will not compare with the genuine. I furnish you with my goods at the following low price, which will be found as reasonable as the nature of my business will allow:

> For $ 1,200 in my goods (assorted) I charge...$100
> For $ 2,500 in my goods (assorted) I charge...$200
> For $ 5,000 in my goods (assorted) I charge...$350
> For $10,000 in my goods (assorted) I charge...$600

These blatant circulars were then followed up with letters and even booklets that displayed photos of real bank notes, which potential clients were told were counterfeit. Those who responded were led to several meeting places, to give the mark the idea that extreme caution against being followed was mandatory. The operator, with hasty over-the-shoulder glances, whirligigged the sucker in a quick exchange of the mark's real money (usually wrapped in a plain brown package, according to the con man's instruction) and a carpetbag containing either cut newspaper or sawdust.

There was never any attempt at counterfeiting; the green goods swindle was merely a "come-on" con, its success riveted to the ability of the operator to create a maze of imperative meetings and desperate exchanges of goods. In his travels, Major Arthur Griffiths of Scotland Yard became fascinated by the green goods game, and launched a full-scale study of the con. His most valuable information came from a celebrated New York police inspector, Thomas Byrnes. Together they concluded that the swindle had been originated by James "King" McNally, shortly after the Civil War. McNally, who operated un-hampered for thirty years, took advantage of the confusion arising from the newly issued government treasury certificates and bank notes, which displaced longstanding specie.

Another highly successful green goods man was Timothy Moore, alias J. E. Breen, who operated throughout the East for twenty-five years, his end coming in 1899 in New York when he was arrested at age sixty-two when trying to dupe F. M. Snively into buying $13,000 worth of green goods for $1,000. Snively answered one of Moore's circulars and was sent a genuine $1 bill as a sample of his goods.

A series of meetings was then set up, Snively traveling from Cuba, Illinois, to Buffalo, New York, and then on to Fishkill, New York, where, in Flannery's Hotel, the goods were to be exchanged for Snively's thousand dollars. The sucker, however, had been mulcted before in this game, and had contacted postal inspectors, who, on agreement, shadowed Snively to Fishkill. As they waited across the street from Flannery's Hotel, they saw Snively throw open a window and frantically wave to them to come up. Running into the mark's room, they found self-styled vigilante Snively holding a pistol on Timothy Moore and pointing angrily to a carpetbag brimming with sawdust. "Well," Moore said lamely, "what did you expect? The McCoy?"

Those who complained about green goods swindles often came under heavy legal scrutiny themselves. In late 1898 J. P. Williams, a businessman from Nashville, Tennessee, was bilked out of $2,000 by Big Joseph Barnett, a long-time green goods man. Traveling to Flushing, New York, after several tiresome ferry rides and meetings, Williams was taken by Barnett to a room over a saloon and there watched bug-eyed as the con man placed what appeared to be $30,000 in green goods into two tin boxes. Barnett then walked Williams to the ferry, and before departing wagged a warning finger and stated: "Now don't open those boxes until you get all the way back to Nashville." Incredibly, Williams waited out his long trip home before opening the tin boxes and finding four $10 and three $1 bills neatly placed over packages of paper cut to currency size. He kept his mouth shut, but on July 27, 1899, when he read a story of Barnett's swindles, Williams rushed to New York and informed authorities that he had been taken by Big Joe. His testimony at Barnett's trial helped to send the con man to jail, but then the prosecution initiated such a probe of his own business affairs that Williams and his small company came under suspicion and eventual public embarrassment, thus proving the risk any citizen makes when exposing a con man.

One of reformer Anthony Comstock's much-hooted coups was the nabbing of con man George Lehman, alias Nigger Baker. A man named

Gates received one of Lehman's circulars from Allentown, Pennsylvania, then a center for a thriving green goods ring, in early 1901. Gates passed this on to Comstock, who advertised himself as a one-man army against vice and corruption (and who was responsible for condemning as lewd and obscene the innocuous painting "September Morn," a hazy portrait of a seminaked woman bathing, which immediately vaulted its mediocre creator to dizzy heights of prominence). Comstock turned Lehman's green goods circular over to postal inspectors, and one of them, posing as Gates, attempting to purchase $20,000 of queer money. Lehman was trapped, and Comstock delightedly sat day after day in court, reveling in his victory, until the con man was convicted for green goods swindles for the sixth time since 1896.

"Why don't you go straight when you get out, George?" Comstock asked the prisoner before he was led away.

"Don't be silly," Lehman replied. "When you got a profession, you stick to it. It's the only way to get ahead."

Lehman's entrapment led to the capture of confederate Joseph Hoffman and the breaking up of the Allentown green goods gang, also known as the "Mike Ryan" or "Westchester Depot" gang, one of the last effective con rings dealing in green goods.

The Banco Game

Predating green goods by more than a decade, the chestnut con of banco first emerged in the western United States about 1855, introduced by an English sharper who adapted the British game of eight-dice cloth. Banco was described at various times by writers as "Buncombe" or "bunkum," and these were eventually bastardized to "bunco," a word now descriptive of any and all types of con games.

Along with the shell game and three-card monte, banco proved to be one of the first popular con games of the Old West. Played with either dice or cards, there was, of course, no way in which the mark could win. The deck was always stacked, the cards marked, the dice loaded, yet verdant rubes flocked to the banco tables. If dice, a cloth with fourteen spaces was used; if cards, a cloth with forty-three spaces was employed. In cards, the banco cloth had one blank space and forty-two numbered spaces, thirteen of which had stars. Prizes from $5 to $5,000 could be won on twenty-nine of the numbered spaces. Each player received eight cards numbered from 1 to 6, the total of his hand signifying the number he had won on the cloth or board. If a player drew a prizeless star number he was allowed to draw once more, providing he upped his original ante.

The mark was encouraged by the operators, who allowed him to win up to $5,000. At this crucial stage a hand totaling 27, the conditional number, was dealt to the sucker. The conditional number was, in con parlance, the hurrah, for once drawing this number in banco there was no turning back. The condition demanded that the player put up an equal amount to that owed him, usually about $5,000, which was no problem to the gold-rich miners of the West, and draw a final time. Naturally, in this highly rigged game, the player lost by drawing a blank or star number.

To lessen the horrifying suspicion of being fleeced, operators always employed a capper or steerer, who played hand for hand alongside the mark, his fortunes equally rising. When the sucker lost, so did the capper, and before the sucker could protest, the capper went berserk with rage, upstaging any genuine protest the sucker could register. It was a case of misery loves company, and the resultant, highly staged fistfight between a capper and his employer, the operator, was usually enough to distract any big loser from complaining.

Banco was strictly for the gullible, which no doubt shortened its life as players became more sophisticated. Charles P. Miller, the previously mentioned "King of the Banco Men," so successfully operated a banco game in New Orleans after the Civil War that he migrated to New York with $35,000 in his pockets and opened a lavish banco room in the Astor House, which reaped him several fortunes.

Peddling the Gold Brick

For cretins and hayseeds only was the eternal nineteenth-century con game called "the gold brick," which was given birth during the California Gold Rush of 1849. In its crudest form, this game was performed by a con man posing as a miner who had struck a fabulous mother lode in the West and was stranded. He was compelled to sell one of his gold bricks at an absurdly low rate to alleviate his dire poverty.

Reed Waddell, born of a good family in Springfield, Illinois, was the most successful gold-brick artist during the life span of this early con. When he sold his first gold brick, for $4,000 in New York in 1880, it was the first marketed in the East, although prior to this time thousands of lead bricks painted gold and with a plug of real gold inserted in it to convince the sucker of its genuineness had been sold in the western states. Waddell's technique was simple. After gaining the confidence of a somewhat greedy merchant, he would offer his gold brick for sale, stating that he hated to part with it but he was penniless and had to return to his Colorado gold mine, taking what losses were forced upon him.

To convince the sucker the brick was solid gold, Waddell led him to what appeared to be a U.S. Assayer's office, and there an accomplice, posing as a government assayer, would elaborately weigh and estimate the chunk of bullion, pronouncing it worth at least $10,000. Those who were still doggedly skeptical were told to take a sample of the brick to their own jeweler. Waddell had other appointments with prospective buyers for his gold brick and could not, unfortunately, go along with the mark to see his jeweler. He also had to hold onto his brick for other buyers to examine, but he would offer to give the mark a small piece of the brick for examination. With that he would quickly dig out the painted-over plug of real gold and send the sucker on his way. The victim would come panting back from the jeweler, his money in hand, having ascertained the worth of Waddell's sample.

Waddell reportedly made $250,000 in operating the gold-brick swindle before branching out into the green goods racket in Europe. His spoils in the green goods game were enormous, but he didn't live to enjoy them. In 1895, at one meeting in Paris with confederates, a hot argument over spoils ensued, and banco con man Tom O'Brien drew a pistol—unheard of by confidence men, who take pride in going unarmed—and shot the engaging Waddell through the heart (his least vulnerable spot, acquaintances later scoffed).

James Blackwell, a transcontinental con man of many aliases—Cameron, Fisher, Stanley, Saunders—was considered by most as the man who inherited Waddell's gold brick mantle. He and his erstwhile backup man, Frank Smith (also known under the aliases of Cameron Bostetter, "Red"

Adams, and Big Charlie White) took in, according to their meticulously kept record book—neither man trusted the other, so they both agreed that everything had to be in writing—$110,524, minus expenses, in the seven years from 1893 to 1900. The expenses included additional accomplices, who usually played the part of the man with the gold brick.

Blackwell's gold-brick con differed from Waddell's in that he did not bother to insert a genuine plug of gold into the brick. He and Smith devoted their efforts to rural districts, conning rich farmers. On a fine spring day in 1900, in Feeding Meadows, Massachusetts, a few miles from Springfield, Smith hailed a prosperous farmer named David Leonard, greeting him as he moved down the steps of his church. The con man explained that they had met at a county fair years earlier and he had decided to take up Leonard's invitation to have dinner. Leonard, shuffling, stammered out an apology for not remembering Smith, but invited him to dinner anyway. Smith later showed up at Leonard's farm, and acting puzzled, stated he had met an Indian in the woods who had two gold bricks he wanted to sell.

"What do you think they're worth?" Leonard asked.

"I don't know, says he got them from some prospector."

The two men went to a nearby woods, where they were met by a dark-skinned man carrying two gold bricks. The Indian, of course, was a confederate, who helped Smith and Leonard to take borings from one brick. Smith, acting dubious about the entire affair, told Leonard not to purchase the bricks until checking with a jeweler. The three men drove into Springfield, and while Leonard and the Indian waited outside, Smith entered a jewelry shop with the brick shavings. He returned quickly, saying that the jeweler was too busy to make the examination but had directed them to a U.S. Assayer who was located in the hotel across the street.

The trio entered the assayer's room and there met James Blackwell, who impersonated the government official. After much folderol weighing and eyeglassing the bricks, Blackwell looked up with arched eyebrows and blurted: "Why, it's nearly pure gold, worth a fortune." He turned to the Indian and said: "I'll give you five thousand dollars apiece."

Smith, the roper, jumped in. "Now just a minute. This here Red Man offered to sell those bricks to Mr. Leonard for four thousand each, and that's what's known as a prior agreement in my business."

The passive Indian made a slight movement in Blackwell's direction, as if he were about to sell the con man his own bricks.

Receiving a furtive look from Smith, Leonard took the bait and fairly leaped across the room to block the Indian's path. He quickly pulled out the $8,000 he had withdrawn from the bank when the three men first got to Springfield and offered this sum with outstretched hand. "Cash in hand and on the barrelhead."

The Indian blinked, took the money, and gave Leonard the painted-over lead bricks. Leonard whistled all the way to the bank—where he was informed of his valueless purchase. By the time the enraged farmer could swear out arrest warrants, Blackwell and Smith were on board a train for Dallas, Texas. They fleeced a cattleman there of $8,000 with the same con and raced on to Danville, Quebec.

In Danville, Blackwell and Smith had convinced a father and son named Gordon to buy several gold bricks, but their scheme was foiled by an alert clerk who called police when the Gordons appeared at their bank to withdraw a large sum. The con men fled, but two of their confederates were caught, and in the pocket of one was found a letter to a former Blackwell victim telling him to keep quiet over the swindle lest he be publicly ridiculed. This letter and the confessions of the confederates led police to Blackwell's home in Manhattan, where he was arrested. Smith was caught a few days later in Hogansburg, New York, where detectives easily spotted him walking down the street. He was bent almost in half as he struggled with a suitcase holding twenty painted lead bricks.

Both men received long sentences, and although the gold brick game staggered on through the 1910s, Blackwell, Smith, and associates were the last big-time operators to see heady profits from a swindle that died of widespread infamy and the absurd premises on which it was based, which even the greenest sort of jake came to recognize in a moment.

In reality, the gold brick con became just too good to be true; the sucker progressed keenly beyond it, the confidence man skipping slightly ahead to devise new methods that would take the apparent con out of con, making it more difficult for the mark to get at the bait, let alone swallow it. At least that was the business theory of William Elmer Mead, a teetotaling con man known as "The Christ Kid." He gave everybody the business, along with his wallet.

Three

Magic Wallets and Pigeon-Drops

HE WAS a thin, wispy man, balding, a pince-nez perched at the end of a long nose, dull, gray eyes blinking nervously behind the glass. Known under half a hundred aliases in his long career as a confidence king, William Elmer Mead was the originator of one of the cleverest cons ever concocted: the magic wallet. The game, according to police and FBI estimates, netted Elmer, as he preferred to be called by confidants, a cool $2 million over forty successful years of playing it with suckers.

Born in Springfield, Illinois, in 1875, Mead was orphaned at two and then adopted by an Iowa farming couple, rigid fundamentalists. He lived the simple, rural life of hard, daylong labor and Bible-reading nights. At fifteen he ran away and never returned, but his strict religious background no doubt influenced him to forsake liquor, smoking and chewing tobacco, even swearing. Throughout his long criminal history, Mead attended church every Sunday. His pretentious piety earned him the paradoxical monicker, "The Christian Kid," or "The Christ Kid."

Like most other con men, Elmer began small, learning the tricks of card sharps in the saloons and gambling dens where he took odd jobs. He graduated from swamper to gambler before he turned twenty, and gleaned an impressive income as a "stake player" in poker, splitting with any gambling house that would back his bets. As Elmer's pockets filled, his donations to national religious groups grew larger, until he was a life member in several.

In 1897 Mead fleeced the wrong sucker in California and was sentenced on a charge of grand larceny to three years in San Quentin. He escaped from guards on the way to prison, was reapprehended, and subsequently served almost two years before being released. The jail stint apparently reformed Elmer, for he soon married and settled down, working at various jobs for four years. Then the old tingle crawled up Elmer's spine again. What happened then, about 1903, in the middle of what is considered the heyday of the American con, was best described by an old-time confidence man and oftentimes Elmer's sidekick and backup man, Will Irwin: "Sometimes I see a stranger who looks like easy money. Sometimes a fellow with 'good thing' printed all over him struts into my hotel. Then the old feeling rises up under my vest and makes me itch to get at him. Perhaps I can make it clear to you in this way: You like hunting? You know your sensation when a buck steps out of cover and you lift your gun to cover him? Well, it's like that, only a hundred times stronger. There's no hunting in the world like hunting men."

Mead deserted his wife and was off conning the gullible. He hunted both animals and men, especially after marrying (on hearsay evidence that his wife had divorced him) a woman known alternately as "Frisco Kate" or "Klondike Kate." The couple would retreat to resorts and mountains cabins after pulling capers, and occupy sun-filled days by hunting and fishing, Elmer's favorite pastime other than exercising his considerable flimflam.

Elmer and Frisco Kate visited every national park and attractive resort in the West. The con man even bought a ranch in Oregon, which later served as a hideout. And as his fortunes grews, so did his legitimate holdings. He bought land in several states and several apartment buildings in Chicago. Safe-deposit boxes, all under aliases, in a dozen cities held his securities, stocks, cash.

A disgruntled William
Elmer Mead, whose
magic wallet con finally
landed him in jail in 1936
after decades of
successful grift. (UPI)

Fixed Foot Races

One con game that kept Elmer in the chips was the fixed foot race. These races were then quite popular, and Mead was more than familiar with the fact that viewers loved to wager on them. His grift was fairly simple then. He would approach a larcenous sheriff in a small town, and offering a slice of the take, bribe the lawman into first allowing the race to be held and then fake a raid to arrest the betters.

Mead and a few confederates—he rarely associated with the same partners-in-crime more than once, preferring to lone-wolf it—would then check the background of some wealthy, gambling-prone resident nearby and lure him to the town where the race was to be held. Elmer would convince the sucker that only one man could possibly win the race, and a large bet was accordingly made on the sure thing. They would then join other inveigled yokels at a secluded spot, feigning great alarm lest the sheriff show up and arrest the lot of them.

Scowls cracked the faces of Elmer's cappers as they watched his selected winner pull twenty, thirty, forty paces ahead of the pack. Elmer's confederates had, of course, bet $50,000 to the sucker's $10,000 that the sure-thing runner would not win. The race half over, the sucker was beside himself with mouth-watering anticipation; he was about to pocket the $50,000. The racers scrambled forward, and then, almost at the moment of victory, tragedy struck. The racer who had been fixed to win suddenly clutched jerkily at his chest, coughed, spat, foamed at the mouth, and then fell to earth, his body quaking spasmodically as if he were in the traumatic throes of an epileptic fit.

At this crucial time, Elmer, who always acted as stakeholder and the sucker's confidant, would spot the sheriff and his men swooping down on the gamblers. His normally tremulous voice would quaver upward to a high shriek as he shouted, "My God, run! It's the sheriff and his boys!" And run they would, Elmer dragging the almost petrified sucker along to the train station, where he would be put aboard a train with nervous promises that he would be met in the next town. The mark was more than happy to escape the embarrassment of being thrown into jail, and momentarily disregarded the money he had given Mead to hold.

A distinctive Mead touch: the victim would receive a telegram in the next town down the line that invariably read, "All is lost. The racer is dead. Keep on going." The sucker, gripped with terror lest he be involved in a death over gambling, kept on going, and never looked back for either Elmer or his money.

By 1910 Elmer Mead was one of the most successful con men in the business, operating more or less out of Denver, Colorado, a center for such criminal activities. Denver in those days was known to sharpers as "the big store," and any con man could cool off there, protected by Lou Blonger and his enormous ring of confidence men. The local police were bribed almost to a man. At about this time, Elmer, who had always played the old established games, hit upon the scheme that was to prove a Golconda. Some say Mead stayed in bed for an entire week, thinking the flimflam through before knotting the end of every string, staring constantly at his wallet, flat and empty on a bureau. No doubt Elmer mused, in his money-depleted doldrums, on the many cons he had employed over the years, and perhaps he thought of one of the more successful, the one he had worked in Missouri and Iowa in the late 1900s known as "the country send."

The Country Send

This was a simpleton's version of a simpleton's game, old three-card monte—or as Elmer called it, "California euchre," but it worked on wealthy farmers for years. After introducing himself as a well-to-do businessman eager to buy a farm for his retiring spinster sister, Elmer invariably worked the farmer into a three-card monte game with a passing sharper Elmer and the farmer would accidentally encounter on the back roads while Mead was being shown his prospective farm. Naturally, the sharper was Mead's associate. Elmer and the farmer would proceed to fleece the dealer, who had already shown them a carpetbag full of greenbacks, $7,000 worth to be exact. The sucker's winnings usually totaled more than $5,000, as would Elmer's, but the dealer, naturally, refused to pay off. Had the gentlemen indeed intended to pay him, he would ask suspiciously, if he had won? Of course, Elmer piped, and produced a wad of bills. The farmer was not in the habit of keeping large sums at home but he would prove his good faith before being paid off by withdrawing and producing $5,000 from the local bank, to which place the trio immediately retired.

Before entering the bank, Elmer would caution the farmer that the game of chance the threesome had played that afternoon was illegal; it would be better all around if the dealer waited in a nearby hotel. Elmer would stay with him just to keep things honest. The farmer came running in minutes, his outstretched hands clutching $5,000. The dealer would grimace his okay, take the money from the farmer, and appear to place it inside the carpetbag. He would then disappear, after handing the bag over to the farmer. Elmer, too, made his excuses to leave, promising to return to the farm he intended to buy the following day. With that Mead and his partner vanished from the county, leaving the farmer literally holding the bag—filled with cut newspaper, of course.

Financing the End of the World

Elmer Mead's new creation involved only one aspect of the old country send, the most important in his magic wallet scheme. The actual showing of the cash brimming the carpetbag was the key, and it was this factor that became all important in Mead's new game.

To launch his new con, Elmer used the most spectacular event of the decade, Halley's Comet, which caused wonder, fright, and alarm across the country in 1910. Its impending arrival was heralded everywhere by religious fanatics, who broadcasted the end of the world. Newspapers were headlining the exhortations of prophets predicting Judgment Day.

In Cleveland, Elmer posed as a judge, mixing in gentlemanly company and befriending a rich contractor. Casually, Mead suggested they talk over the possibilities of building an extravagant house he, the judge, had long had in mind. They went to lunch and there discovered, under a chair, Elmer's magic wallet. Inside the sucker found out only money, but a wad of impressive checks and papers that indicated the owner was the important builder and proprietor of baseball parks and sporting arenas in the United States, if not the world.

By chance, the wallet's owner appeared, and Elmer and the sucker returned it to him. The magnate joined them for lunch. He would buy.

It was the least he could do. Mead's house was soon forgotten as the ball-park tycoon beamed gratitude.

"I want you to make an estimate," the ballpark impresario said to the contractor, "on the largest sports stadium ever built in America." The contractor was overwhelmed. "It's going to be built anyway," the tycoon said. "Why shouldn't you do it? After all, you're honest. You proved that when you returned my wallet and saved some very precious documents." The contractor eagerly accepted, conjuring a vast fortune from such a commission. The judge, Elmer, thought it a grand opportunity.

Before the contractor could bring himself to ask for some sort of advance on his future labors, the ever-thoughtful arena mogul visibly registered an inspiration. "Wait a minute! How silly of me! There's an important factor I've almost overlooked. While you're estimating such a gigantic job, you'll require considerable funds. I was just thinking of how to arrange that . . . hmmmmmmmmm . . . I have it! With the baseball season over, my parks are empty. For a small stipend, let's say ten thous-sand dollars, I would be willing to lease every park and arena across the country to you."

The contractor was stunned. "But, what for?"

Withdrawing a newspaper that blared the coming of Halley's Comet and told of the thousands of religious sects about to gather on Judgment Day, the tycoon cried, "why, for the end of the world! Think of it. The greatest spectacle in the history of man. Don't you read the papers?"

The contractor nodded and stared at the doomsday warnings in the newspaper spread before him.

"He's right!" Elmer almost shouted. "Why, you will fill those grand-stands with tens of thousands of people!"

The concept was so bizarre it immediately appealed to the duped con-tractor; he was covered from any serious loss by virtue of the enormous building contract dangling before him. He accepted, wrote out a check for $10,000, and was given a lease to fifty ballparks and stadiums. Going their separate ways, the judge and tycoon departed. Elmer and his con-federate hurriedly cashed the check and left town. The Cleveland con-tractor first busied himself with promotion schemes to lure the doomsday fanatics into the arenas. Only later did it occur to him to check an in-town park. His phony lease and claims evoked laughter from the park managers. He was out $10,000 and a lot of pride.

Mead worked this big con with different associates through the year until Halley's Comet arrived and departed without sending so much as a single soul to eternity. The event was over, he concluded, but the device had worked perfectly and he was a con artist who could readily adapt to change.

Toiling for Tolls

Remembering the cons of old where the Statue of Liberty and the Brooklyn Bridge had been sold for handsome profits, Elmer concentrated on rural areas where road and bridge construction was flourishing. In one Missouri city in 1912, Elmer, again playing the part of a judge, befriended a country squire type and treated him to several lavish dinners and sporting events. The judge, quite by accident, found a wallet containing important contracts and checks made out for staggering amounts. A contractor arrived and claimed the wallet, and the trio became close friends. The grateful contractor offered to sell the judge and the farmer an interest in his newly constructed viaduct.

The judge thought for a while, doodling figures on a tablecloth. "Why, that bridge will be the most used one in the city. The toll of, say, twenty-five cents an auto and fifteen cents a horse-drawn wagon would reap us a handsome income, my friend." The farmer agreed, and both wrote out checks for $10,000 for third ownerships in the viaduct.

Days later, after Elmer and his associate had departed with the farmer's $10,000, the viaduct was closed at dawn and homemade signs erected at both entrances. The farmer patrolled one end of the viaduct with a shotgun, demanding his tolls from reluctant citizens, their cars and wagons accumulating for blocks.

One man almost came to blows with the farmer, screaming: "You moron! This is no toll bridge. The city owns it!"

The farmer leveled his shotgun. "That's the bunk! I own it. I paid ten thousand dollars for this bridge, and you pay your toll or get out of the way so the rest of these good people can get along."

Several burly policemen arrived, disarmed the farmer, and took him along to headquarters, where the confidence game, by then familiar to most law officials, was explained to him.

Elmer and his partner, Joe Furey, later dragnetted in a 1922 en masse roundup of confidence men in Denver, worked this variation of the magic wallet for several years, but Elmer habitually exchanged Furey for other accomplices. When Furey proposed they work the con exclusively, Mead declined.

"I know, you've always been a lone wolf," Furey later remembered telling Mead, "but we could make a lot of dough together. When they take the bait from you, boy, they swallow it."

"Yes, I know," Elmer responded. "But I'm not going to be a sucker myself. I figure that any gang of confidence men that runs together very long gets caught. I'd rather dip in and out. It's safer."

Helpmate of the President

Elmer dipped in at Cheyenne, Wyoming, in 1917 at the beginning of America's involvement in the First World War. At that time the Allies were desperate to obtain horses for the western front, these being extensively used to draw cannon and field kitchens and to mount cavalry. Enlisting an entirely new group of con men from the center of confidence-game activities, Denver, Mead ordered his accomplices to spread throughout Wyoming, ostensibly to search for horse herds among the many big ranches. "You want to buy all the horses in the world, remember," Elmer reminded them. "Flash your rolls, inspect the stock, and locate the most well-to-do ranchers, people with cash, gentlemen."

Two associates located a wealthy widow woman who owned a sprawling ranch outside of Cheyenne. They had government contracts, they told her, to buy up every animal on her land at top dollar. She agreed to talk over the purchase during lunch at a Cheyenne hotel. As she sat down in the dining room, her hosts flamboyantly flourishing courtesies, the widow woman felt the discomfort of something lumpy immediately under her posterior. She stood up, and lo and behold, a long black leather wallet, thick with money and papers, was on her chair. This time the contents of Elmer Mead's magic wallet took on the importance of state secrets.

Following a natural impulse, the widow carefully examined the wallet to learn the owner's identity. She found a large wad of crisp, brand-new

$100 bills, enough to buy every horse in the West. There were checks, too, astronomical amounts written on them. The widow's eyes widened as she unfolded letters addressed to a Professor Graystone. Upon these, the widow gasped in recognition, was the seal of the U.S. Treasurer's Office. One letter to "My dear Professor" from the Treasurer of the United States relayed the President's warm regards, and went on to ask for the President how "their little deal was getting along."

"Why, this Professor Graystone is a personal friend of the Treasurer and President of the United States," the widow woman whispered to Mead's confederates, both men staring at the letters open mouthed, awe in their faces.

"But that makes sense," one con man put forth. "Isn't President Wilson an ex-professor, or something?"

"Sure," the other accomplice jumped in. "Wilson was a professor at some eastern college, Princeton or Harvard."

The wealthy widow woman was hardly halfway through the shock of this incredible find when a thin, fluttering-eyed man adjusting a pince-nez came into the dining room, glancing about nervously, long fingers a-tremble. One of his associates gave him a signal and the man came up to the table.

"Is this your wallet?" the con accomplice asked innocently.

"Oh, Lord, yes," Mead answered in his best dithering voice. Pocketing the wallet, he sat down, more absent-mindedly than nervous. "What a relief! I am *so* grateful. How can I ever repay you?"

Elmer started by buying lunch. The widow woman, enthralled at meeting a personal friend of the President, in those days a distant, Godlike figure in remote, powerful Washington, D.C., was more than happy to accept the professor's invitation to dinner the following evening. There were several more lunches and dinners, at which time Mead conducted himself in a most professorial manner, reciting lines from classic poetry, outlining the works of Stendhal, Ibsen, Chekhov. One evening, no longer able to control her curiosity, the widow inquired about the letters from the Treasurer.

Professor Graystone was at first hesitant, but then, gropingly, as if trying to tip-toe verbally through a delicate secret, he quietly informed the wealthy rancher that the President and Treasurer were, indeed, his close friends, and "the little deal" referred to in one of the letters he carried involved confidential favors he was more than happy to bestow upon America's leader. Moreover, it was his duty as a citizen to aid such men in their times of need. In one breath, Elmer had elevated his status from friend of the mighty to unflinching patriot. He went on to explain carefully that the President and the Treasurer didn't really have much to live on except their miserable salaries, and that their expenses in a hullaballoo town like Washington were enormous.

"As you know, dear lady," Mead said, "everybody in Washington must do as the President and Treasurer say, so whenever they are short of expense money, they simply order the Government Printing Office to print a new batch of hundred-dollar bills for them. Of course, they must exercise caution in spending these new bills lest someone become suspicious. Prudently, they have selected several men like me to help them out."

With that, Elmer flipped out his magic wallet and flicked his thumb over a thick wad of new $100 bills. Further, he stated, it was his mission to sell this new money at 50 cents on the dollar. In this way the public at large would also benefit, and the President and Treasurer would then have ready cash for their important expenses. "It's the old money they need, so as not to arouse any suspicion. It's nothing new . . . done all the time—for years—since Abraham Lincoln."

"Imagine that? Abraham Lincoln, too!"

Mead then resumed his air of gratitude, saying that since the widow and the horse buyers had proven themselves such honest people, he had

John H. "Jackie" French (left), a sometime roper for Mead; (right) French's girlfriend, the gun-wielding Buda Godman, alias Helen Strong, who sometimes steered for Mead and was an expert at the badger game.

selected them to share in the bonanza, offering all three $100,000 a piece at a substantial discount, even less than the normal 50 percent.

"My cash is in a Denver bank," the widow replied.

"Curious," the professor replied, "I am traveling to Denver on the morning train."

They agree to go together, along with the horse buyers, who were more than happy to help President Wilson out of his financial bind. The professor, with much fanfare, informed the trio that they were such nice people that he would let them have $100,000 each for a measly $35,000 from each person. The widow woman, upon arriving in Denver, hastily withdrew $35,000 from her bank account, paid the professor, and received, as did the accomplices, sealed packages. He warned the recipients that they should wait until getting home before opening the boxes. "Discretion, discretion. We don't want to embarrass President Wilson, now do we?"

Elmer Mead and his confederates were soon fleeing in different directions, each with a share of the widow's loot. She went home with a package of cut newspapers, discovered the swindle—and kept quiet. She was afraid, she later told friends, that the President would find out. So, thoroughly duped, the rancher continued to think she had helped the nation's Chief Executive, whose dire circumstances had, no doubt, increased, compelling him, through Professor Graystone, to take drastic measures such as not paying off. For years this gullible woman considered her flimflammed cash "a loan to the government."

The magic wallet continued to gush forth its cornucopia of wealth for several years. Mead wintered in Miami, Florida, making scores in nearby cities. He took a Jacksonville resident for $11,600 in 1921, but slipped up by using the mails as part of his fraud. Postal detectives were soon on his trail, with an accurate description of him. He was identified in the 1922 roundup in Denver a year later and sentenced to Canon City Penitentiary for ten years for a Colorado caper. After serving almost three years, he was released, but federal marshals were waiting for him as he stepped through the prison gates. On trial for the Jacksonville swindle, Elmer put up a large bond and skipped. It would be ten years before federal agents again located him.

During that span of time, Mead wandered through several states, keeping his magic wallet fat. In 1932 he took a Missouri contractor for an estimated $200,000, the largest sting in his lifetime of con. In Beverly,

Massachusetts, also in 1932, Elmer clipped a businessman named Barker for $59,000. He flimflammed a man named Harrison in Jefferson City, Missouri, in 1933 for $50,000. Then a Jacksonville, Florida, merchant named Martin fell for his magic wallet in 1934 for a mere $11,360; the depression was beginning to take its toll of his victims. Profits dropped so drastically that Elmer contemplated the development of a new con, but postal authorities caught up with him in early 1936 and sent him to prison for two years at age sixty-three. The last stretch finished him, broke his spirit, especially when he received word that the authorities were preparing a tax evasion case based on his delinquency in not paying $60,000 for a period of eight years, 1921–28, on the staggering profits he had garnered from his magic-wallet con.

"Somebody talked," he moaned in his cell. "I should've figured it out so I could have done it all alone. Partners! It's disgusting."

Entertaining an Englishman

Mead's tongue-wagging confederates spread the news of his inventive and lucrative magic-wallet game over the years until it was wholly institutionalized in the confidence world. By 1922, when Elmer was rounded up with other confidence men in Denver, the ploy was being used by hundreds of con artists. A trio of flimflammers—William Kent, James Christian, and David Sherman—were fleecing an average of five suckers a week with the lost-and-found wallet routine in Manhattan. They specialized in travelers like James Fortney, a real estate dealer from Melbourne, Australia.

Fortney, who had been touring the United States with his family, was staying at the Hotel Woodward, preparing to leave by boat for England. A stranger, William Kent, with a "decidedly English accent" befriended Fortney in his hotel lobby one June afternoon, and over cocktails informed the Australian that he, too, was sailing for England and they both might as well go to the Cunard Line offices to pick up tickets. They took a limousine, thoughtfully provided by Kent, to the pier.

The victim later related his amazing experience to police: "On the pier the stranger found a wallet containing English currency, American money, and personal papers bearing the name of a man stopping at the Park Avenue Hotel. He suggested that we go to the hotel and return the wallet. When we reached the hotel we found the owner of the wallet [James Christian], and he appeared to be glad to recover it, not so much for the money it contained . . . but for the 'priceless' papers.

"The owner of the wallet was so grateful that he offered to take me and my friend to a poolroom, where they could clean up on a sure thing he would give us. All three of us went to the poolroom, where there was great activity. More than a dozen men were engaged in answering telephones, and the place was handsomely furnished [this type of betting parlor was the universal setting for the big-con game].

"My English friend was told by the proprietor [David Sherman] that it was a rule of the house that he put his money up on the good thing, but my friend pulled out his wallet and found that he was short fifty-four hundred dollars to make the cleanup. I hurried in a taxicab to my hotel, obtain the fifty-four hundred, and returned to the poolroom, where I gave it to the man I met in the hotel lobby."

In what must have been the fastest exodus of any cluster of con men in history, Fortney, emerging from a rest room in the betting parlor, found the poolroom completely deserted, his erstwhile friend gone, and his money lost. The trio of con men were later arrested on the corner of Forty-Seventh and Broadway with dozens of loaded wallets on their persons, but they were released days later when the embarrassed Fortney failed or refused to identify them.

The Wallet's Secret Code

Ten years later, in 1932, William P. Hunt of Fort Lee, New Jersey, was gleaning almost as much from the magic-wallet con as its inventor, Mead —$300,000 in a five-year span, he admitted to police who arrested him for mulcting $25,000 from William Loeterie, a Long Island, New York, butcher. As Elmer Mead had so cleverly demonstrated, the magic wallet was a come-on device that was almost foolproof in producing the pigeon's earnest money. Hunt, said to be a one-time sidekick of Mead's, understood this fact all too well.

A man calling himself Kello entered Loeterie's Long Island butcher shop on January 15, 1932, and without mincing words offered to buy his business for $10,000. He counted out the money and repocketed it. Loeterie wasn't so sure he wanted to sell. Several meetings later, in a mid-Manhattan hotel on February 4, Kello "accidentally" found a wallet containing $50, a coded message, and the address of one William P. Thompson, who was really Hunt. Kello convinced the butcher that not only should they return the wallet, but that he understood the coded message to mean that Mr. Thompson was, no doubt, a very successful gambler, the code indicating that the wallet's owner certainly had "genuine inside information on the hottest horses races" available. The butcher accompanied Kello to the Lexington Hotel, where Thompson was given his wallet.

The flushed gambler was beside himself with joy—not, again, for the return of the money, but for obtaining that very secret coded message. "Look, fellas," Thompson confided, "this means an awful lot of jack to me, more than you will know, and I don't mind placing a few bets for the both of you based on this information"—jabbing the numbered and lettered piece of paper—"as a way of saying thanks."

Kello, quite naturally, blurted: "I'm all for that."

Loeterie the butcher wasn't so certain; he was ordinarily not a betting man. "It's like the wallet," Kello whispered to him. "It's found money." The butcher then nodded approval, and Thompson fairly leaped to a phone and made, presumably, a series of bets with a bookie, ranting off numbers and letters from the unintelligible scrap of paper. The following day Thompson informed Loeterie that his horse had won, and should he continue to place bets for him? Sure, the butcher replied pragmatically, noting that he had not placed a dime in Thompson's hand. Day after day, the coded message recovered from Thompson's magic wallet continued to provide a winning streak in which the butcher's profits dizzily soared. At the end of the week, Thompson called Loeterie and Kello to his rooms and showed them piles of greenbacks stacked neatly on his desk.

"There, gentlemen," he said, indicating with a sweep of his arm, "is one hundred twenty thousand dollars for each of you—your winnings."

Loeterie almost fainted. "You mean all that money is mine?"

Thompson smiled affably. "Everybody wins, thanks to you and Mr. Kello returning my wallet." But as the butcher reached for his money,

Thompson raised a restraining finger. "Just one thing. I'm a little bothered by the fact that neither of you gentlemen has put up any money for possible losses." He withdrew a note pad and scribbled quickly. "I've figured here that if the code had broken down, you would have owed about twenty-five thousand dollars each. Not that you lost anything, but I feel honor bound to ask you to produce that much each to prove to me that you would have assumed your responsibilities."

Kello didn't hesitate. "I'll be back in half an hour," he said, and the butcher followed him into the lobby. "What are you going to do?" Loeterie asked Kello.

"Do? My, God, man, I'm going to run all the way to my bank, withdraw twenty-five thousand dollars and claim my winnings."

Loeterie wasn't so sure, he said. The whole thing sounded crazy to him.

Then came the hurrah. Kello looked determinedly at his victim and said: "All right. I can withdraw fifty thousand instead and pick up the whole quarter of a million." He moved toward the door.

"No you don't, Kello," Loeterie barked. "Nobody's taking my winnings. I'm going to my own bank and I'll be back here in ten minutes." With that he dashed out the door and ran down the block. Kello walked across the street, bought a cigar and waited.

Within minutes Loeterie and Kello were again in Thompson's suite, showing their $50,000 earnest money. Thompson ushered Loeterie into a side room, closing the door. He took the butcher's $25,000, counted it out carefully, and placed it into a tin box next to the stacks of money on his desk. "Would you send in Mr. Kello, please," Thompson told Loeterie. "I'll be right with you. And between you and me, I really don't trust that man. I'm going to make damned sure that he has his twenty-five thousand before I turn over any winnings to him."

"You're right to think that way," the butcher concurred. "He's a clever one. Why, that guy was gonna take all the winnings for himself; he told me so. But he's not that fast for me."

"I'll settle with him," Thompson said conspiratorially, "and then we'll conclude this transaction."

Loeterie stepped from the room. Kello entered and closed the door. The butcher waited and waited and waited. After an hour, he walked into the room to find Thompson, Kello, and all the money gone. They had slipped out a side door hidden behind a drape. Loeterie went to the police and spent days lookinging through rogue's gallery photos, finally identifying a picture of William Hunt as the man called Thompson. In September 1932 police located Hunt in New Jersey, and he was quickly brought to trial for grand larceny, his seventh such arraignment. He was subsequently sent to prison, but Kello, his loquacious accomplice, as well as the butcher's $25,000, was never located.

Pulling the Pigeon's String

Elmer's magic wallet got more mileage than most Model T Fords in the first half of this century. The con spawned several other offshoot games, and inspired the revival of similar archaic cons that continued to line the pockets of sharpers, the most notable of which is "the pigeon-drop." It has many variations, and is known also as "the drag game," "dropping the leather," and "dropping the poke." Some criminal authorities claim that it originated in China more than a thousand years ago and was brought to America's western shores by immigrating Chinese about 1850. Crime writer John Kobler contends that "home-grown swindlers, chiefly Negroes, adapted and perfected it. The pattern employed seldom varies by a word or gesture; it has been handed down in writing from generation to generation. Yet the drag remains the most prevalent as well as one of the most lucrative of all con games."

Essentially, the con is worked by two confederates who, after spotting an apparently well-off person—middle-aged women prove to be the best suckers for this racket—conveniently find a pocketbook stuffed with money. It is a deftly handled proposition. The pocketbook or purse is discovered in such a way that the victim is also in on the find; the purse is usually retrieved inches away from her foot. Following much exclamatory babble about windfalls and Dame Fortune, the two con artists solicit the advice of the sucker as to what to do with the bonanza.

The honest person usually suggests turning it over to the police, even though no means of identifying the owner is possible. (Invariably, in the pigeon-drop there is never a shred of personal identification such as driver's license, credit cards, home address—just the money.) The con

From Baltimore to Cleveland, Oakey Jackson, shown here testifying before a senate subcommittee on juvenile delinquency in 1956, was known as the dean of pigeon-droppers. (UPI)

man or woman (this is usually a woman's con) pishtushes the notion of turning it in to the authorities. The coppers will only pocket the money and have a good laugh at our naïveté, one of the accomplices states. We might as well divide the money, the other con artist concludes. That's the fair way to settle it.

To calm the pigeon's fears that someone will be looking for the money, one con artist suggests that the pigeon hold onto the wallet and money for, say, a month or two. If no one steps forth to claim the find, it will be divided. But one of the flimflammers has second thoughts. After all, we've all just this moment met in the street. There must be some way of guaranteeing the honesty of the sucker. There is, one of the accomplices says. The pigeon will put up earnest money, a paltry $1,000, which will be turned over to the two con artists to show good faith. It's no risk at all, considering the fact that the purse or pocketbook contains ten times that amount.

The earnest money is usually handed over to the con artists within a short time and they depart, reassured that their mutual discovery is being protected by a veracious individual. The pigeon departs with the money-stuffed wallet, only to discover later, horrified, that it contains wads of paper cut to currency size.

The pigeon-drop is known as a "short con," for the aim of its perpetrators is to capture a quick but small amount of money without the elaborate preparations entailed in such Big Cons as Mead's magic wallet, where considerable and genuine up-front money must be expended and displayed. In recent years, the pigeon-drop has proved to be one of the most vicious cons practiced. Con artists, concentrating on elderly women, quickly gut the senior citizen's bank account, which can sometimes so depress victims as to lead them to suicide, as in the case of the sixty-year-old schoolteacher in Glendale, California, who lost $7,740 to a band of con women.

Some Notable Pigeon-Droppers

One of the more successful pigeon-drop sharpers was Oakey Jackson, a colorful black patriarch of the game who taught it to several generations of flimflammers in the Cleveland area. Jackson reputedly made the biggest score in the game's history, $20,000, before his semiretirement and purchase of a flea-ridden thirty-three-room hotel in Cleveland, which became a hotbed for con game instruction. Oakey could not resist an easy score, even in his advanced age, and was indicted in the 1950s four times for pigeon-drop swindles in Pittsburgh, eventually evading conviction. Another Cleveland con man, Emmet Cobb, adorned himself with red fez and golden earring piercing the left ear lobe, and instructed a host of black girls in the wiles of the pigeon-drop. A self-styled "Moslem educator," Cobb told authorities that "my teachings stress highly moral principles according to which I live."

The granddaddy of all pigeon-drop artists was "Boss" Harvey Caldwell, who sported ankle-length vicuna coats and rode in $10,000 cars. A cocaine addict, Caldwell made tens of thousands on the pigeon-drop, and publicized the fact that in his old age he had become deeply religious. He admitted to his many dedicated years of conning the gullible, but none of that seemed to interest him toward the end. "Fancy clothes, women don't mean a thing," he was quoted as saying before his death. "What counts is everywhere I go, I'm loved." This from one of the most scabrous pigeon-drop con men in the business. He took to writing letters to the slightest of acquaintances, sermonizing and lecturing on the spiritual life. He even wrote some of his former victims, the word goes, telling them that their own gullibility robbed them, not "Old Man Caldwell," who had merely fended off poverty by the only means at his command, the pigeon-drop con, which was imparted to him before he was a teen-ager. His letters were convincing though paradoxical, and they never lacked confidence.

Pigeon-dropper Emmet Cobb in 1937, when just beginning his con career.

Caldwell used the mails to exonerate himself, a curious selection of communication in that the U.S. mails had provided a system through which enterprising con men had reaped millions in halcyon days before laws leaped up to snare them and suckers got savvy.

Four

"Do the Moths
Bother You?"

SINCE 1872, the U.S. Post Office has waged war against some of the most enterprising con men in the business; it was in that year that stringent postal fraud laws were enacted, and during the century since the birth of these laws, thousands of fraud orders were issued. Woefully, only a fraction of those confidence men prosecuted for mail frauds went to jail, while millions of dollars each year were pocketed by ingenuous flimflammers. (The U.S. Post Office estimated that for one year, 1911, con men took in $77 million from duped investors in mail-order schemes; of the 572 indictments in that year, only 184 convictions were secured.) On the con man's part, all it took to get rich quick was up-front capital to finance fairly inexpensive ads in newspapers and buy postage stamps.

Before 1872, American con men had a field day with a gullible public that responded by mail to advertisements for mining rights, real estate, securities, inventions, and medicines. Too distant to seek reparation, almost all postal suckers were helpless, and suffered their loss with only teeth-gritting indignation.

Con by Nostrum

The first victims purchased out of terror. In the colonial era, peddlers mailed out medical broadsheets that offered nostrums and medicines guaranteed to cure anything. One group of early peddlers sold a weird concoction of mustard, elm bark, and pepper, in the form of a poultice, which was supposed to cure diptheria, then called "throat distemper." This mess was applied to the throat and, of course, was useless. Another nostrum was "snail water," which was a mixture of snails and worms ground together in a mortar. Dissolved in water, children suffering any sort of maladies were expected to get well after gulping down great volumes of this swill.

Rattlesnake Root, offered by Dr. John Tennant of Virginia, guaranteed to remedy pleurisy. Another pre-revolutionary wonder drug sponsored by an unknown early con man was a mysterious white powder that promised positively to do away with any toothache, gout, cancer in all forms, snake bites, and labor pains. A man named Perkins in the early 1800s sold, through the mails, two shiny rods he called Metallic Tractors, which would be passed over the ailing victims and redirect his "electrical" currents in a manner that would cure him of any disease. Perkins came to believe so intrinsically in his own swindle that, upon contracting yellow fever, he disdained all medical attention; his Metallic Tractors would do the job. For three days cronies passed the rods from his head to his toes. Then he died.

Bezoar Stone, an ordinary rock allegedly treated with herbs, was claimed, in the 1820s, to cure any type of snake bites. And a typical newspaper ad promoting useless cures was one that appeared in the *Connecticut Courant* in October 1834:

MOORE'S ESSENCE OF LIFE

A safe and efficient remedy for whooping cough
Sold by appointment at the sign of the
Good Samaritan

The Essence of Life was nothing more than colored water. Many bogus doctors and pharmacists offered only one product, but that medicine was claimed to cure almost any ailment known to man. Turlington's Original Balsam promised to remedy fifty-one deadly diseases. A so-called Dr. Spear offered through newspaper advertisements his magic Balsam of Life, which Dr. Spear insisted would cure consumption almost overnight. The quack con man who offered Brandreth's Pills went a lot further in one ad that ran for years in newspapers. It stated:

> Remember in all cases of disease no matter whether it be cold or cough, whether it be asthma or consumption, whether it be rheumatism or pleurisy, whether it be typhus fever and ague, or bilious fever; cramp or whooping cough or measles; whether it be scarlet fever or small pox Brandreth's Pills will surely do more than all the medicines of the Drug Stores for your restoration to health.

In 1850 one of the most popular quack medicines was Tuscarora Rice, the maker of which positively promised to cure consumption. This remedy for tuberculosis was nothing more than ground corn.

The era of the patent medicines took over about the time of the Civil War. Con men by the score moved into the field, and the ridiculous cure-all medicines continued to be advertised and sold by mail long into the twentieth century. There were nostrums to turn blacks white, to change the kinky hair of Negroes straight and blond, to restore total manhood to octogenarians. Mormon Bishop Pills promised faithfully to cure tuberculosis. (They came in three colors—patriotic red, white, and blue.) Also a claimed cure for tuberculosis, John Hampton's Vital Restorative was a two-pill medicine. One pill, the first the victim was directed to take, contained methylene blue, which would turn the sucker's urine bright green and badly frighten him into taking the second pill, which was made of licorice and saw palmetto.

The Brainwaves of J. H. Kelly

One of the most blatant medicine con men was J. H. Kelly of Nevada, Missouri, who claimed through full-page newspaper ads that he could cure anyone of any illness no matter where they were. He could, he insisted, perform such miracles through a "practical scientific system" that, when explained, boiled down to his own home-grown telepathy dressed in gobbledegook. If the victim cleared his mind of all problems at the appointed time, Kelly, the modern Merlin, would concentrate upon his illness and together they would successfully "think it away." This charlatan became a millionaire many times over with his medical con, gleaning by 1900 between $1,000 and $1,600 a day from the three thousand letters flowing into his office, where a staff of secretaries were employed for the exclusive purpose of slitting envelopes and withdrawing cash, checks, and money orders. Each victim would receive a postal card telling him the day and hour to clear his brain and thus achieve his cure. (Kelly was diplomatic enough to add that he and his "scientific system" had nothing whatever to do with Christian Science.)

Although brought to trial several times by postal authorities, Kelly managed to squeeze through a number of legal battles, and the Magnetic School lingered for a decade longer, until his claims of long-distance healing became laughable.

Hayes's Sex Salve

Another con man extraordinaire in the field of medical quackery was Edward Hayes, who for years promoted Man Medicine, which Hayes insisted would provide the recipient "once more with gusto, the joyful satisfaction, the pulse and throb of physical pleasure, the keen sense of man sensation." It was a simple laxative, yet Hayes bilked millions from insecure, easily duped males. Brought to trial by the Postmaster General and fined $5,000 for fraud in April 1914, Hayes promised the courts to desist in promoting such wild schemes. But months later he was advertising a new miracle product, Marmola, a foolproof cure for obesity. And fat men fell across the land by the tens of thousands for that sham, too.

Sure Cure for T.B.

Probably one of the most vicious of the medical con men, Charles Aycock, marketed, with no personal medical background, a product named Tuberclecide, claims for which centered about a complete cure for tuberculosis, especially in children. From 1918 to 1928 Aycock sold his "medicine" (creosote carbonate) to thousands of parents desperate to aid their stricken children. Hauled into court a number of times, Aycock slipped through legal loopholes to continue his licentious practice. Scores of doctors testified as to the effectiveness of his product, and their widespread indecision allowed this culprit to evade conviction until 1928, when a federal court determined Tuberclecide was useless. The number of deaths attributed to the sole use of this so-called miracle drug remained undetermined. Aycock himself played the innocent, mailing with his product a pamphlet in which he stated: "I am like Jesus Christ opening the eyes of the blind, and when critics asked how it was done he said: 'I do not know, I was blind but now I see.' That is all I can say. I took it and got well. Others took it and got well. That is all I know."

Ordering the World

The mail-order medical racket was only a small segment of the ad-and-mail con rings. Some sharpers made their loot the other way around, by ordering tons of goods as samples. Two enterprising con men, Henry Morgan and R. Klein of New York City, were arrested in their Manhattan offices for mail fraud. They had set up a dummy firm, Lyon & Co., to purposely confuse their operation with the successful Lyons & Co., and then proceeded to order, on a trial basis, every conceivable product made in the United States. When arrested in 1897 for fraud, police uncovered carloads of bicycles, cotton, and brooms stored in their warehouses, all scheduled for resale to reputable firms at cut rates. As the two were being led out of their sparsely furnished offce, a messenger arrived with bills of lading to be signed. It was another shipment of bicycles from a midwestern firm. "One moment, officer," Morgan said as he stepped forward and signed the bills. "Business is business."

A Portrait of President Garfield, Cheap

When the mail-order cons reached their peak, their perpetrators seemed to take a perverse delight in not only mulcting suckers but pouring salt into their wounded pocketbooks as a way of amusing themselves. The process took on an "I dare you" attitude that challenged the gullible to protest. One classic nose-thumber in 1882 advertised in more than two hundred newspapers, offering what appeared to be a rare portrait of President Garfield, whose assassination the previous year had evoked widespread grief.

> I HAVE SECURED the authorized steel engravings of the late President Garfield, executed by the United States Government, approved by the President of the United States, by Congress and by every member of the President's family as the most faithful of all the portraits of the President. It was executed by the Government's most expert steel engravers, and I will send a copy from the original plate, in full colors approved by the Government, postpaid, for one dollar each.

To each person remitting the dollar, the con man mailed an engraving of President Garfield, a U.S. five-cent postage stamp.

Fifteen years later a money-clutching wag offered an unusual recipe by which annoying household bugs could be eliminated quickly:

> DO THE MOTHS BOTHER YOU?—If so send us fifty cents (50¢) in stamps, and we will furnish a recipe CERTAIN SURE to drive the pests from furs or rugs or any other old things.

A few weeks after the mark had remitted her 50 cents' worth of postage, legal tender, she received the foolproof recipe, the reply reading:

Dear Madam: Dampen the article in question in kerosene thoroughly (to soak it is even better) and add one lighted match. If the moths do not disappear your money will be cheerfully refunded.

Yours truly, THE BUNCOMB COMPANY

Rural Rubes

Farmers are perennial victims of mail-order flimflammers. For nearly fifty years one of the quickest swindles was offering rural folk an easy way to grow mushrooms. Remittance for the spawn averaged $4 to $5, which really cost the sender about 10 cents, and the recepient almost always found the process of growing the mushrooms so tedious he discarded the project in short order.

During a particularly devastating beet season in which blight devoured most of this vegetable crop, the government assigned experts to study the problem. Their efforts were attended by a glut of publicity, and when they admitted their inability to find a cause for the crop failure, this timely advertisement appeared:

HOW ABOUT YOUR BEETS?—If you have experienced trouble with them, send us $1 for printed instructions how to raise them.—WE KNOW HOW!

Desperate, farmers by the thousands answered this ad and were rewarded for their naïveté with a return card reading: "Plant your feet firmly, take tight hold of the tops, and pull!"

Every aspect of day-to-day living was examined by the con man. His eagle-eyed come-ons promised to banish the smallest of problems. One schemer offered to provide "A Perfect Substitute for a Razor," and sent to those mailing $2 two-cent pieces of pumice stone. A sharper offered an astounding formula "to make your mustache grow," and for each 60 cents in stamps he received, he returned a card that advised the reader to "lather thoroughly and shave hard, at least once a day." Thousands of members of New York's best social clubs received in 1905 an elegantly printed offer to provide, for the small stipend of $1.50, "a bottle of our best whiskey and one of our best wine." To the thousands of those remitting, all thinking the new firm eager to cultivate high-class clientele, each received two bottles, both no more than two inches high, filled with whiskey and table claret. One man offered to make short men taller and took in more than $50,000. The device he widely advertised turned out to be a torture rack copied from the medieval original.

Costly Love Letters

Love was not ignored in the schemers' blind ads. At the turn of the century one of the more successful mail-order cons received tens of thousands of dollars in response, all from lovesick young ladies. The ad read:

> EVERY GIRL, who is fond of the society of young men is anxious to make an impression. But modesty, lack of training, the feeling that she is not pretty or lacks refinement or a knowledge of the world, makes it difficult sometimes for a girl to know how. We can tell every girl How to Make an Impression That Has Never Failed and we will send it to her, sealed, for $1 in a blank envelope.

The response read: "Sit down in a pan of dough."

A Professor A. H. Thole of McCook, Nebraska, wrenched a fortune from the lovelorn by placing the following ad in hundreds of newspapers in 1904:

> THE GREAT SECRET. How you can make your lover or sweet-heart love you; they just must love you; they can't help themselves. This secret is based on scientific principles and cannot fail. Send 25 cents in silver to Prof. A. H. Thole, McCook, Neb.

Answering the clammy-handed youth who had eagerly sent along his quarter, the all-knowing professor's card read:

> Your letter of recent date at hand, and in reply will say that to win the woman you love you must constantly think with your whole soul's intensity that you want her to love you; in addition to that you must not drink. Keep clean and neat in your dress. Be polite and attentive to her. Be generous, for women hate stinginess

in men, but dearly love generosity. Be brave, for women hate triflers. Walk with your head and shoulders well thrown back; be dignified; be courteous, and every inch a gentleman. Flattery goes a long way to win a woman, but don't overdo it. Don't be bashful, as women hate bashfulness in men, but love bold men.

Yours for suckers, Prof. A. H. Thole.

Doubling the Mark's Money

Get-rich-quick schemes were and always will be the most appealing confidence game applied through the mails. These cons have ranged from the absurd to the intricately complex. In 1908 one artful dodger placed the following advertisement in scores of eastern-based newspapers:

HOW TO DOUBLE YOUR MONEY

This is not a fake—it does not ask you to speculate, to gamble, nor to canvass. You can do it at home. Five dollars becomes ten—ten dollars becomes twenty dollars. It is absolutely sure, and if you do not prove it true to yourself within a week after we send you our secret we will return your money. The wealthiest men of the country have tried it and succeeded. For two dollars ($2) we will send your our secret. Remember, if you find it fails within a week you can have your two dollars back.

To the many thousands who sent in their $2, each person was sent this message with which, in truth, no one could take any issue: "Convert your money into bills, and fold them."

From the small hamlet of Belfast, Maine, a con man advertised that his "business was peculiar" in that he had a "money-making method" that involved the acquiring of several types of money, stating in his ad that all of this was achieved by deft exchanges of bills for coins and vice versa. For $2 he would provide the remitter with money representing $50. He returned to the sender a Confederate $50 bill.

A duped man in Minneapolis who answered this phony ad got an idea and took out space in newspapers in which he offered "40 for $1—not

Confederate." Those who responded to the Minnesotan's pitch were sent a booklet that gave directions for the removal of "kinks" from hair, instructions on how to make "obesity soap," and a host of other inane "secrets." The pitchman added that his pamphlet "contains $50 worth of information and schemes, so you get what we stated."

A Sucker Strikes Back

One sucker who had been duped dozens of times by the get-rich-quickers, Will MacMahon, decided in 1913 to strike back, but he found himself, in a seemingly endless web of con men, being bombarded by counterproposals to make him wealthy. He answered three ads. The first stated:

I MADE $50,000 in five years with a small mail-order business; began with $5. Send for my free booklet. It tells how to do likewise. Peacock.

The second advertisement read:

Do not be an underpaid, overworked clerk. Here is a chance for you to make $40 to $60 a week with a mail-order business of your own. No experience needed. Small capital. Huge profits. Beanse.

The third plea was a screamer:

I WILL MAKE YOU FABULOUSLY RICH IN THE MAIL ORDER BUSINESS! With an idea and a bank roll of only one hundred dollars, I built a business that brought me six hundred and fifty thousand dollars in eighteen months selling merchandise by mail. I dare you to let me start you to quick fortune making. Queerham, America's Greatest Mail-Order Marvel.

MacMahon wrote to all three sharpers. The first response came from the booklet-offering Peacock:

Dear Sir:
All I need to know is: Do you intend to work for wages all your life? No! Then send me $3 for my unbeatable mail-order business

instructions on how to make the $50,000 in five years. Use the enclosed strong envelope for remitting purposes.

Hot on the heels of this urgent missive, Mr. Beanse's letter appeared in MacMahon's mailbox:

Dear Friend:

I am a manufacturer and make no charge of any kind whatsoever for my mail-order business lessons. It is an enterprise that can only be learned by actual experience. Theory is useless. Do not pay something for nothing. I have no fake instruction books or correspondence courses to peddle. You simply buy my agent's cooperative plan for $21.08. It includes all necessary catalogues and stationery for the trade, with your name neatly printed thereon; also a shoehorn for your own use, (Free). Send me in the very next mail $2 to place a trial newspaper ad for you and I will prove that I am a money getter. Remit currency, stamps, postal or express money order, just as you wish.

Queerham's pitch followed in short order:

My dear friend:

I am Opportunity! You shall be enriched in health and wealth by the mail-order business if you act now. Grow a spine—and the overloaded postman will wear a deep path to your door. My course of instructions is $100, but I only ask you for $15 down. I will trust you for the other $85. A splendid future summons you to the battle of betterment. I say to you, my dear friend: Rise, Go On and Up! Send your remittance preferably in cash, registered.

Before MacMahon could decide which of the three con men he would again contact, the marvelous Queerham sent along a follow-up letter. It read:

My very dear friend:

I have been waiting, watching and wondering! Is it possible that you think me a mercenary monster, seeking to wring from you your hard-earned dollars? Heaven forbid! Now, I have decided to throw down the bars to you, my friend, and offer as sincere a heart-to-heart talk and brotherly opportunity as was ever offered a fellow man in this cold, grab-it-all workaday world. Send me just

$5 and I will trust you with the other $95. Promise me that this confidential arrangement between you and I [sic] shall be kept a sacred secret. Remit within ten days or I will be forced to the sad conclusion that you are allowing a mere trifle to foolishly stand between you and a glorious life of liberty and luxury instead of the sickening yoke of the slavish stipend!

MacMahon was struck by the replies of all three con men to respond with a devilish impulse of his own. As the whim urged, he sent copies of the letters from Queerham and Peacock to Beanse, begging him to give his opinion of their integrity. With lightning speed, Beanse responded:

I want to again sincerely congratulate you for writing me. The first named of the mail-order business teachers is a Cunning Hog; the other is a Lyre Bird. Please send, in any form convenient to yourself, the $21.08 for my generous agency plan.

MacMahon then sent Beanse's letter to Queerham for his appraisal and received the following:

The alleged manufacturer mentioned in your kind letter of inquiry sells his agency plan to anybody, everywhere. That is how he avoids prosecution; he wouldn't last a day if he sold exclusive territory. There probably is an army of men in your locality all stuck with the same worthless outfits. Incidentally, that plausible faker, without a moment's rehearsal, would make a fine model for a corkscrew. Send me $10.54 and I will not only duplicate his $21.08 proposition, but let you have my $100 instruction for $2.50 additional. This is trusting you with $97.50, you observe.

Peacock, too, had some not too kindly remarks to pass along to MacMahon regarding Beanse's business ethics:

I'm not naming anyone, but being as you've asked—that confidence man merely is a four-flushing jobber. Regular stores sell his line cheaper than he charges inexperienced agents. Send me $1, cash or stamps, and I will place more advertising for you than he does for $2.

With the con men viciously vying for his business and turning upon each other with alacrity, using up considerable postage in so doing, which was not beyond the plan of the once-bilked MacMahon, the would-be victim fired off Mr. Peacock's letter to Mr. Queerham and vice versa. Peacock wrote back first:

> That slick individual merely is my imitator! He originally tried manufacturing and failed. His specialty was a fake face cream, made of Vaseline and talcum powder, but called the Dorothea De la Vere Peaches-and-Cream Complexion Beautifier. He was run out of the business for making bearded ladies of his customers. Send me $1.50 and I will forward you a complete copy of his so-called "instructions" gratis.

Queerham's labored response ended MacMahon's odyssey through the mail-order con games, but it proves even today to be a masterpiece of wheedling, conniving con to gain his customer's trust as well as a penetrating view of a tenacious con man more than willing to put across his scam and claim his mark at the risk of destroying every other con man in his slippery business. Queerham mustered every bit of eloquence at his command when he wrote:

> Watch out for your pocketbook! That half-baked vegetable nearly went into enforced retirement for mixing goose grease and alcohol, highly perfumed, and calling the compound the Millicent Montressor Magic Hair Auxiliator. It bred dandruff until the fair user looked like a miller's bride. I am the only legitimate, broad-gauge, and open-minded instructor in the mail-order business. The American people lose fully one hundred millions of dollars ($1,000,000) annually on fakes. Many newspapers and some magazines are simply a-crawl with advertising vermin. Here are several choice examples:
> —"A genuine engraving of George Washington, suitable for framing, 10 cents." For your dime you get in return an uncanceled one-cent postage stamp.
> —"How to draw a tooth, molar or bicuspid, absolutely without pain. Complete outfit and instructions by mail for 25 cents." A quarter-dollar remittance beings you a small pencil, nicely sharpened, and a blank sheet of drawing paper. The only purchaser with a fighting chance for redress would be one afflicted by a severe case of writer's cramp.
> —"I will give you $10 for the names and addresses of ten sick

persons in your locality. Send me only 50 cents for my valuable symptoms chart and modus operandi." If the half dollar comes from a Southerner, the advertising quack demands a list of sufferers from snow blindness; if from the North, victims of the hookworm. There. I have made my point by exposing the unworthy who venture to compete with me. Now send me the names of ten neighbors, men beyond reproach, and I will trust you with my entire $100 course without a cent down. Then you can commence a series of joyous trips to the bank with the proceeds from stacks and stacks of moneyed mail steadily streaming into your hands. Ah, my dear friend, you will think it all a perfect dream.

Willis B. Powell, editor of the newspaper in Lacon, Illinois, became so fed up with the plethora of get-rich-quick schemes advertised in newspapers that, as early as 1875, he wrote and published his own scheme obviously intended as satire—although suckers by the droves answered his zany offering. Powell's ad read:

GLORIOUS OPPORTUNITY TO GET RICH

We are starting a cat ranch in Lacon with 100,000 cats. Each cat will average 12 kittens a year. The cat skins will sell for 30 cents each. One hundred men can skin 5,000 cats a day. We figure a daily net profit of over $10,000. Now what shall we feed the cats? We will start a rat ranch next door with 1,000,000 rats. The rats will breed 12 times faster than the cats. So we will have four rats to feed each day to each cat. Now what shall we feed the rats? We will feed the rats the carcasses of the cats after they have been skinned. Now get this! We feed the rats to the cats and the cats to the rats and get the cat skins for nothing.

Phony Jobs for Real Dupes

The bunkum was and is endless. Those earnestly seeking jobs were duped and bilked with such easy regularity that many of the small ads appearing in most newspapers half a century ago were fraudulent. A Chicago firm advertised in neighboring weeklies that restless young men from small towns would have no trouble in finding "excellent work. Good men are wanted, the pay is good." The firm was made up of retired philanthropists, the ad stated, who were eager to see young men get ahead, and if they would send $2 to cover advertising and mailing expenses, they would receive "a classified list of hundreds of places where prompt, well-paid situations awaited mere choice." Those suckered by this scheme found in their mailboxes a page ripped from a daily newspaper, the classified want ads.

For years one man took in thousands by advertising "an inexpensive bicycle" for sale, and when receiving $3 from each victim, sent along a very cheap watch charm in the shape of a bike. I. Weinstein advertised nationally in the 1920s for girls to type copies of letters at home on something called the Baby Typewriter, a product that had to be purchased from Weinstein's firm for $20. The girls were to make $10 an hour typing the copies, so the investment seemed realistic. Those thousands of tenement girls responding signed a contract to type X number of letters each day, but upon receiving the typewriter, a cheap rickety instrument, found that the keys would jam, the roller would not roll, and the machine generally fell to pieces before the first letter was typed. When the disillusioned typists asked that their $20 payments be refunded, Weinstein wrote back:

> It is evident that you did not observe the proper care in operating a machine constructed on such delicate lines as the Baby Typewriter. We have nothing to do with that. Your failure to turn in the contracted number of letters has caused us much annoyance and has exposed you to a claim for breach of contract by us. If the typewriter is returned at once, however, by express prepaid, we are willing to overlook this and will make you an allowance of two dollars on the damaged machine.

Invariably, the shop girls who had sought to add pittance to their normally miserable incomes returned the machine and gladly suffered the loss of $18 each, fearful of being brought into court. Weinstein would then rewire the useless Baby Typewriter and send it out to the next sucker answering his advertisements.

A similar con was immensely successful for almost twenty years, from 1905 to 1925. This New York-based organization of con men did not wait, however, as did Weinstein, for its flimsy device—a tin hand instrument that was fastened to the edge of a table—to break down. Suckers answering this firm's ads were promised a new Soezy Sewing Machine after selling several packets of the company's product, washing blue. When the Soezy machine arrived, the firm took great pains to include a notice that, more or less, headed the victim off at the pass, as well as took stern and imperious umbrage at the sucker's much-anticipated rage, second- and third-guessing the victim's very thoughts. It read:

We have your letter, and would advise you to keep cool and not make any rash statements before you are sure as to what you are saying. You seem to think we agreed to send you "an up-to-date, high-grade sewing machine, with all the latest attachments." If you can show us in our advertisement where we made any such agreement, we will send you such a sewing machine. We will go over the advertisement with you, word by word. You will note the first word is "FREE." That means that something is given away. Next we see, "AN UP-TO-DATE, HIGH-GRADE SEWING MACHINE, WITH ALL THE LATEST ATTACHMENTS, COSTS FROM $30 TO $40." This is simply a plain statement of fact, telling you what such a sewing machine would cost you if you went to buy it in a store. We show a picture in the advertisement of the kind of a sewing machine that would cost from $30 to $40. Then we say, "DON'T THROW YOUR MONEY AWAY." This, you will admit, is good advice. It simply means that you should not waste money on high-priced sewing machines. Now, having given you this good advice, we go on to say—

"BUT TAKE ADVANTAGE OF OUR GENEROUS PROPOSITION;" and now you are ready to see what the generous proposition is. Next we say, "IF YOU WISH TO OWN A SEWING MACHINE THAT WILL DO EXCELLENT SEWING, SEND US YOUR NAME AND ADDRESS, AND AGREE TO SELL ONLY 30 PACKAGES OF OUR WASHING BLUE AT 10 CENTS A PACKAGE." You have accepted our proposition; you have sold the blue, you have sent us the amount received from the sale thereof—$3, and fulfilled the terms of our proposition. You will find, upon reading the advertisement further, that we distinctly agreed, on our part, after you had sold the blue and sent us our money, to simply send you our new AUTOMATIC TENSION SEWING MACHINE, as a reward for your efforts in introducing our blue among your neighbors and friends. This is exactly what we have done, as you or anyone with a grain of common sense must readily admit. We hope you will sit down and write us a letter and apologize for insinuating that our object was fraud. [This in light of the fact that the victim had not yet complained of the piece of junk sent her.] You have hurt our feelings very much. We would advise you not to answer any advertisement again until you are absolutely sure you understand it.

It was unlikely that any mark ever took action after receiving this saber-rattling missive. The conning of these suckers was, indeed, "Soezy."

This is Hugh B. Monjar, who reaped millions in the 1920s through his mail order scams. (UPI)

The Big Shots of the Mail-Order Flimflam

Until postal inspectors ultimately caught up with them, several millionaire mail-order con men ran rampant. Hugh B. Monjar was making $3,000 a month in 1927 from only one of the many white-collar clubs he had organized. Monjar charged members $20 each initiation fee and $2 monthly dues to belong to one of his Mantle Clubs, which supposedly protected special interests but, in reality, did nothing but bank all incoming money. Before being sent to a federal penitentiary for mail fraud, Monjar's income in his last year of operation was a bulky $7,666,631.

William J. Cressy was another mail-order mogul whose cons netted him burgeoning fortunes. Cressy began in 1934 by offering through newspaper advertisements $75 for Indian head pennies dated before 1910. Those who responded to the bait wound up receiving four-page coin catalogs at 10 cents each. Stopped by a postal fraud order, Cressy, operating with a partner, Jennings B. Momsen, then offered in 1935 a flying career to novices. He wanted men "willing to work for $75 monthly while training to become aviators." It took little, during the depth of the depression, to encourage phalanxes of suckers to answer such a tempting, glamorous offer. They sent in $1 and received razor-thin pamphlets, abridgments of Army Air Corps publications that outlined pilot training. Cressy was finally bound over on federal indictment for a scheme that brought 861 complaints, and his career was stopped in midstream.

Like Monjar, the dapper, Malacca-cane-carrying A. C. Bidwell of the early 1920s organized a club on a grand scale and reaped enormous income. His was the International Automobile League, which was low yielding on dues but mammoth on the sale of cheap by-products.

Bidwell first advertised for members, promising them the best auto accessories available through his league at basement prices. He cleverly provided several prominent citizens in many large cities with genuine top car accessories, obtaining from these distinguished personages letters of testimony. The bulk of his membership, however, received bottom-of-the-barrel products, and when they brought Bidwell to court, he was ably supported by those customers to whom he had shown favored service. His portfolio of testimonial letters was so impresive he eluded judgment for years, until Richard E. Lee of the Vigilance Committee of the Associated Advertising Clubs tracked him to earth with one hundred unfavorable depositions from suckered clients for each endorsement the con man could provide. He subsequently faced trial and, histrionically, pleaded guilty.

For mail-order cons, it was hard to beat the offer of one William John Madone, who, in the late 1950s, widely advertised his pamphlet entitled *How to Sell Your Business and Beat the Con Men*. He, like the legendary Queerham almost five decades before him, exposed the methods of sharpers, including his own.

A Black Prince Promises Ivory

One of the most unusual mail-order cons came from a fellow named Prince Bil Morrison, who claimed to be of noble birth in dark Nigeria.

The black prince wrote to several American daily newspapers, pleading for pen pals. So moved were the newsmen by his appeals that they published his address, free-of-charge. Following several exchanges, the prince asked his pen pals in the United States to send him $4 and an old pair of pants. In return he promised to send them ivory, emeralds, diamonds. A considerable amount of money as well as hundreds of pairs of old pants were sent to the Nigerian prince, but no rare jewels were forthcoming. When the post office received complaints a fraud order was initiated, but officials delayed legal action. The prince was an impoverished fourteen-year-old boy, and con man or not, his age prevented the compassionate authorities from prosecuting.

Deluge for an Inheritor

One young man, Edward F. Dougherty, a one-time office boy in Wall Street who inherited $150,000 in 1931, during the depression, probably holds the record for receiving more pitches from con men through the mails than any other single victim. His inheritance was extensively publicized, and as a result, dozens of sacks of mail began to appear regularly on his doorstep.

The Hell Gate Bridge in New York was offered to him for a paltry $20,000. Another sharper wanted to sell him a fourth interest in the Holland Tunnel for $62,000. That was all that remained, the pitchman apologized; the other percentages had already been purchased. A group of con men sent in dozens of letters, framed in glossy prose, attempting to induce Dougherty to buy part of a state reservoir. Others tried to sell him a quarter interest in an oil gusher for $5,000. There came an offer from an alleged deep-sea expedition to salvage coal underwater for only $6,000. A nonexistent dude ranch was offered for sale to the youth for $25,000. Con men sent pictures of Long Island mansions purportedly for rent at a mere $3,000 a month.

Dazedly, the youth complained: "They all wanted cash, and each one, as he saw that his scheme was not working, tried to get at least a small down payment. . . . It seems as if they were determined to get it [the money] one way or another . . . you are never safe as long as you have money." Dougherty the inheritor might not have been safe, but a fellow named Oscar Hartzell from Iowa made mountains of money from an inheritance that never existed and was safe only as long as gulled yokels continued to believe that the distribution of one of the world's greatest fortunes was imminent. Against that moment Oscar worked with Trojan dedication, becoming, in spite of his absurd postures and incredible statements, one of the true kings of con.

Five

The Inherited Billions

LEGEND DIES HARD, and almost never in England. Elizabethan con men, only months after hearing of the death of British buccaneer Sir Francis Drake on board his ship *Defiance* off Nombre de Dios on January 28, 1596, began to spread the rumor that the sailor's staggering fortune was for the taking if only certain investments were made by "shareholders" to wrest the treasure from the government. Drake's looting of Spanish ships—"singeing the beard of the King of Spain," he called it—had produced for Virgin Queen Bess's empty coffers riches beyond calculation.

This wealth, early flimflammers hawked, belonged rightfully to Drake's heir, the illigitimate son born to the commissioned pirate and none other than Queen Elizabeth, a scandalous progeny produced during one of their many clandestine trysts. Con men approached wealthy but naïve persons with his canard and created, over the span of three hundred years, an ever-widening gullery of victims who believed their investment in the fight to free the Drake billions would replenish their extended capital a hundredfold.

The Drake inheritance con was operated in the United States as early as 1835. In the 1880s the American ambassador to the Court of St. James, Robert Todd Lincoln, alarmed at the number of marks stung for large amounts in this swindle, issued public warnings that "shares" in the so-called Drake fortune were nonexistent and that the treasure was mythical. Still, little prevented scammers from bilking thousands of folk named Drake who were enamored of inheriting an overwhelming chunk of the great boodle. Even those whose names were not Drake were approached and told that they, too, for a small investment toward defraying legal expenses to free the Government-suppressed estate, could participate and glean thousands of dollars.

Hurrahing the Hartzells

One of these, in 1919, was a farming woman named Hartzell who lived in Madison County, Iowa. She was approached one sweltering summer afternoon by two modest-looking strangers who appeared on her front doorstep. Though they gave different names, the earnest-faced couple presenting themselves were two accomplished con artists. Mrs. Sudie Whiteaker and Milo F. Lewis. As Mrs. Hartzell and her two sons, Oscar and Canfield, sat quietly listening in their sparsely furnished living room, the couple proceeded to unravel the Drake inheritance proposal, telling Mrs. Hartzell that for "every dollar you invest to help free this treasure, a hundred will be returned to you."

The allure of wealth was emphasized subtly as they chitchatted through the evening, the Hartzells growing more eager to learn of their glittering future. Mrs. Hartzell became so intrigued with buying "shares" in the Drake estate that she ordered her son Oscar to retrieve the family funds, secreted in a tin box in the attic, and doled out $6,000 to the sharpers, who wrote out an elaborate receipt, departed with handshakes and a respectful tipped hat, and promised to contact the family shortly and inform them of the legal progress in the case. Of course, Mrs. Hartzell never saw the pair again, but Oscar, the semiliterate, shrewd, intuitively suspicious son made it a point to force another encounter with the swindlers.

One-time Iowa farm boy Oscar Merrill Hartzell (center), here under arrest in 1933, suckered thousands in his fabulous Sir Francis Drake inheritance swindle. (WIDE WORLD)

Oscar Taps In

The day after his mother was gulled, Oscar journeyed to Sioux City, which boasted the nearest library, and rummaged through every book dealing with the English freebooter, Drake. Though unschooled, this ploughboy, who had given up tilling the land to become a deputy sheriff, was possessed of astute senses and a unique craftiness that would have been the envy of any self-enriching Borgia. Steeped in the adventuresome Drake past, Oscar boarded a train for Des Moines. Through his connections with law enforcement officials, he had quickly discovered that Mrs. Whiteaker and Lewis called that city home, and he located them there as they were about to fleece a hardware merchant.

"Oh, we were about to send you a letter about the inheritance," Sudie told him.

"Cut that," Oscar bellowed. "I know all about *that* inheritance!"

The couple did not protest when he suggested they talk it over in a nearby hotel. The pair admitted, upon Oscar's accusations of swindle, that they had conned their way through Iowa in two months and had reaped $65,000. To their amazement, Oscar Merrill Hartzell laughed uproariously. The hayseed farm boy who would later be described by a postal inspector as "heavy-joweled, florid, shifty-eyed, crude, vain, hot-tempered, and ignorant" told them they were "rubes at your own game." Oscar went on to tell them that "this field is untapped. You took small pickin's. Why, my mother still believes your scheme will come through. So does everyone else I talked to who fell for your line. Thousands! Hell, there's millions in this racket. But you can't go sneakin' around like alley rats. You gotta come out in the open. Make it respectable, legitimate. Open an office. I even got a name for the operation."

So he did. In a week Sudie, Milo, and Oscar were joined in partnership under the business banner of the Sir Francis Drake Association, and this old dodge went into high gear.

At first the trio fanned out through Iowa, Missouri, and Illinois, contacting only persons named Drake, telling them that a Missouri man, Ernest Drake, was the true heir to Sir Francis's fortune but that they, too, would prosper when the inheritance was finally settled in England. They quickly, however, discarded the exclusivity of the Drake name and included any and all investors, who would share pro rata in the distribution of the fortune.

Hartzell, all the while, took careful measures not to involve himself directly with the suckers falling for the inheritance routine. He acted as a sort of advance man who set up the marks. Sudie and Milo followed up with the collection, it falling to them to write out receipts and send out letters to prospective investors. While studying the extensive backgrounds of Drake and Queen Bess, Oscar had paid careful attention to the postal laws, and would have nothing to do with the mails. If the U.S. Post Office authorities ever contemplated arresting him for fraud, he reasoned, he would never be the party to provide them with evidence to convict him.

For two years Oscar traveled the rube circuit, a comical figure whose brown hair slipped forward in wisps over bulbous, staring eyes. His garb was intentionally hayseed. He wore tight-fitting pants that were too short, exposing old-fashioned high-topped, broad-toed shoes. He snapped red-striped galluses when he talked in his blustery, instantly believable manner. "I want to look just like them," he confided to Sudie, "not like some slicker from the city."

This was the same approach Hartzell had employed when selling seed and farm equipment with his brother Canfield through Iowa, Illinois, Wisconsin, Nebraska, and the Dakotas. Now he wandered through the same territory selling the worthless shares in Drake's imagined fortune, and along the way he picked up a hard-core group of shifty lieutenants, who, under his tutelage, spread out across the farming states scooping up suckers. From his native state, Oscar chose fellow Iowans Harry Osborne, A. L. Cochran, C. A. Storla and C. C. Biddle, all traveling salesmen in their middle years who were tired of their tedious lives and unhappy with meager profits from their ancient short cons. Another disciple, perhaps the most important in the vast scheme Oscar slowly unraveled to them, was Otto G. Yant, a bleak little man who had once been a barber and was then the cashier in the Mallard, Iowa, bank. It became Yant's job to supply the group with lists of wealthy suckers, which he obtained by surreptitious correspondence with tellers across the state and throughout the Midwest.

Thus armed, Oscar and his minions—he had also roped in his *non compos mentis* brother Canfield—whirlwinded their ways through "blue river land" (the locale in which marks fell with difficulty for the con), drawing thousands into their absurd but titanic swindle.

So brazen was Oscar that, after holding a town meeting in Quincy, Illinois, he and his cohorts signed up every adult in the city as "donators" to the struggle to free the Drake billions, 2,000 persons in all. The chamber of commerce in a North Dakota town endorsed Hartzell's impossible scheme, and 2,500 persons there religiously donated their life savings to "the cause." Profits mounted. Oscar began to count out $1,000 a week for himself after paying his people their handsome commissions.

Will the Real Drake Heir Please . . .

In 1924, to further enlarge his glossy bubble, Oscar was suddenly inspired with the urge to travel to England. At his regular weekly meeting in a Des Moines hotel room, he told his accomplices that Ernest Drake, the so-called heir to the Drake fortune living in Missouri, was "a fake." Hartzell added, in hushed tones: "I have learned who the real heir, is and he lives in England." After disposing of Mrs. Whiteaker and Milo Lewis (Hartzell claimed that they were "a couple of crooks who have been reneging on donations and secretly lining their pockets with our honest collections"), he announced he would leave for London immediately to take charge personally of freeing the Drake Estate from the greedy clutches of the British government. Oddly, Mrs. White-aker and Lewis departed without complaint; Oscar had them sign pledges never to reveal the nature of his operations.

Indeed, Oscar and his agents stressed "silence, secrecy, and non-disturbance" with all who invested their money in the giant fraud. Further, he and his confederates instructed all who participated in his zany scheme that no word of "the deal" could ever reach law officials lest the investor risk Oscar's wrath, which amounted to his "red-inking" their names from the muster rolls in line for the fortune.

Stating that he "must have $2,500 a week," Oscar was off to England to track down the missing Drake heir and free the fortune for his American investors. He made elaborate arrangements for the delivery of the money to him. He instructed his aides to "never send letters to me, only cables, all letters will be refused." Hartzell further directed them to send his weekly $2,500 for expenses to his brother Canfield, who would reside in New York. Canfield Hartzell, in turn, would travel each week to Canada and send the weekly payments as American Express money orders to Oscar in London.

Hayseed Hustler in London

When Oscar Hartzell arrived in London, he posed as an oil-rich Texas millionaire and promptly discarded his country bumpkin style. He rented a luxurious suite of rooms in London's fashionable Basil Street and immediately had a hundred suits meticulously tailored by the finest haberdashers along Saville Row. Only the best restaurants sufficed for his daily meals, and season tickets to the most important shows were habitually tucked into his vest pockets.

Wenching became a devout pastime for Oscar until he caused one buxom blonde barmaid to get in the family way. Her father showed up at his rooms and remonstrated with Oscar to "do the right thing." Hartzell not only turned on the back-country charm but let loose his herculean pitch, convincing the Cockney father of his fabulous Drake heir story to the point where the old man rushed to the bank, withdrew his savings, and invested \$2,600 in the scheme. Oscar then stopped seeing the girl.

Within months Oscar had made himself over as the "Premier Duke of Buckland," a title he conferred upon himself, and hired a faithful valet, W. J. Stewart, whom Hartzell passed off as "one of the Royal Stuarts of Scotland." But with all his acquisition of pretentious mannerisms and bogus titles, Oscar never once let up the bombardment of his con associates back home.

First, Oscar cabled that he was in hot legal pursuit of Drake's \$22 billion. He subsequently stated that the treasure was more like \$400 billion. In one cryptic cable, intended to be read at secret meetings with suckers, he stated: "I am going to tell you all something I have never told you before in regard to the amount of the whole affair. If you had over and above one billion pounds sterling, which is equivalent to five billion dollars, if you had all above that amount, you could buy the whole city of Des Moines and build a fence around it."

Actually, Oscar's erratic computation of the alleged Drake fortune meant whatever his agents wanted it to mean. To some investors, it meant a return of 500 percent on their money; to others it meant that 1,000 percent would be paid to them on each dollar donated.

Oscar's dopey but loyal brother Canfield Hartzell, who fronted for the Drake swindlers in the United States while Oscar was in Europe. (WIDE WORLD)

Con Through Cable

If there was any letup in the weekly \$2,500 payments from America, Hartzell would dash off a frenzied cable to brother Canfield, and his stern sermons would be filtered to the faithful as before. The more the fortune grew in his own imagination, the broader based his claims became. In 1925 his vision of wealth stretched far beyond the purchase of a single town in Iowa. A cable read:

> As you know I have never said very much about the amount for to be perfectly candid with you I don't think any of the people in America capable of grasping the magnitude of the whole affair. The way they have all done and treated me, they have made a very bad enemy of me [those who missed their payments to him], now I am going to give you a shock about the amount. Figure up all the

land in the state of Iowa of an average of $125 an acre, and all the bank stock, and all bank deposits in Iowa, and railroads and cities combined. I could buy the whole lot and put a fence around the whole state and then have more money left than you ever thought of.

These wild claims were mixed with overt threats to "red-ink" any sucker from the investors' rolls who did not come up with additional "legal" expenses, which caused the money orders to flow unimpeded to Oscar's London address. But while Oscar's colossal swindle was reaping great profits, he himself fell victim to the wiles of a subtle South Kensington con artist, Miss St. John Montague, a parchment-skinned clairvoyant who took him for thousands. Answering an ad, Oscar attended one of Miss Montague's crystal-ball seances and was entranced with her glossy predictions of his future. Hartzell began visiting her three times a week.

Slickered in a Seance Setup

Miss Montague, sizing up Oscar's showy figure, immediately put a private detective, Tom Barnard, on his trail to estimate his worth and determine his income. Barnard, who frequently prepared secret reports on Miss Montague's clients, arranged for an "accidental" meeting with Hartzell in one of his favorite bars. Oscar, for all his blustering poses, was not a man who could hold his liquor, and once in his cups, spilled his swindle to Barnard, who, in turn, relayed the information to Miss Montague.

The medium cleverly told Hartzell in thinly veiled terms of the Drake fraud, parceling out in not-too-delectable morsels each aspect of his con. Armed also with Barnard's uncovery of the pregnant girl Hartzell had so unchivalrously left in the lurch, the sham mystic more or less blackmailed the con artist into paying huge amounts of hush money as fees, an estimated $50,000 over a five-year period.

This, of course, was but a pittance of what Oscar accumulated from the American boobs drawn into the Drake scheme by his ropers. His yearly income while he resided almost nine years in England averaged $150,000, and most likely a lot more. But the marks were becoming uneasy about their hard-earned savings; thousands had taken out loans, some had mortgaged their homes and farms, to make their investments. So by 1927 Hartzell began sending to the dupes frantic cables that heralded the end of their financial travail. One read: "Settlement delayed for a month. Estate will be handed over with as much speed as His Majesty can conveniently allow. Waiting for the King to put his golden seal on the papers."

Hartzell's agents became caught up in Oscar's frenzy of impending great events, seasoning his ridiculous reports with the announcement that the Drake heir, who was still nameless, had unaccountably signed over power of attorney to Oscar Hartzell, who, in turn, had complete authority to dispense the inestimable fortune. The "King," however, proved reluctant to okay the deal. Some unforeseen snag held up the settlement. In June 1928 Oscar cabled:

> They were going to settle May 29, but one of the principal powers was ill and could not be on duty. The new Lord Chancellor who succeeded Lord Cave had to go thru the papers to complete the deal. The new Lord Chancellor discovered an error which means $1,200,000 to me. Plainly understand it does not make any difference whether it is ten million pounds for me or against me, it has got to be correct, according to the Lord Chancellor's decision.

Everybody Gets in the Way

His jabbering, almost incoherent excuses, when coated with real events and living persons, seemed to mollify Ocar's vast American gullery. Hartzell, realizing this and the naïveté of his marks to worldwide conditions, then seized upon any and all political upheavals the world over, loudly interpreting these acts for his rubes as part of an enormous conspiracy to prevent the settlement of the Drake Estate.

Oscar's fertile conjuring knew no limits. He spread the story that he had unearthed evidence that in 1919 (the year, if one will remember, Hartzell's mother had been fleeced by Drake swindlers) President Woodrow Wilson had been driven insane by the threat of international disclosures concerned with the Drake Estate. A British "secret ecclesiastical court" was attempting to prevent the settlement. In 1928, Oscar claimed, President Herbert Hoover, in league with Andrew Mellon, exerted pressure against British authorities "in the highest realms" not to release the Drake Estate in order to keep the billions out of America, fearful that such an influx of funds would upset the already spiraling economy. "I'm working on Hoover," Hartzell cabled.

A major setback, Hartzell told his "donators," was the stock market crash of 1929. Only weeks before this economic American disaster, he had arranged for the transfer of Drake funds to the United States. Highly placed money powers had gotten wind of the imminent settlement and had, he charged, caused the crash to prevent its dispersement. Now, it would take months, possibly years, to work the money free again, but he vowed not to stop prying it loose. Huey Long, the volatile "Kingfish" of Louisiana, was reported by Oscar and his agents to be battling secretly to free the fortune; he was a heavy investor, they said. Just about the time when the Hoover Administration had been properly "soaped" to allow the estate to be probated, President-elect Roosevelt and his New Dealers came to power, financed by American business leaders desperate to stop the deal. Hartzell became a master of twisting facts and statements. When Great Britain went off the gold standard, Oscar informed his more than 50,000 investors that the impending settlement of the ancient fortune had caused such drastic measures. He turned a fishing trip to the Bahamas by the President into "a secret meeting with British financial figures." He cleverly misquoted President Roosevelt's inaugural address to make it seem he was blocking the settlement.

As the dead years of the depression dragged on, Hartzell's countless postponements drove his dupes into frenzied reinvestments. His exasperating excuses only resulted in increased purchases of Drake stock. Thousands took out second mortgages on their farms, borrowed money, cashed in life insurance policies, liquidated crops and stock, all positive they would have more than enough to pay off their debts when they received their share of the forthcoming Drake treasure.

The Law Looks in on the Drakers

For years, postal authorities had been vaguely aware of a gigantic swindle afoot in the Midwest but inspectors always seemed to draw a blank. So entrenched with secrecy were Oscar's phalanxes of suckers that federal agents could not get them to reveal significant details of the scam. Inspectors were told that there was some fantastic business deal "abroad," but investigations invariably dead-ended at that point. One sucker who had been taken for more than $30,000 refused point blank to discuss his involvement, fearful of Oscar's threat to "red-ink" anyone who broke his vow of secrecy, merely stating: "I can't talk about that. Even to a government man."

W. H. Shepherd and his wife Ada (maiden name Drake) were typical investors. They had plunked down $5,000 in front of one of Oscar's representatives, who, by that time, had taken more than $170,000 from other Iowans. When postal inspectors told Shepherd of the swindle, he went into nervous convulsions and a subsequent breakdown rather than reveal his participation in the fraud.

Iowa's attorney general, John Fletcher, publicly denounced the Drake deal as a fraud and was immediately swamped by letters from thousands of irate citizens demanding that he shut up and not "queer" the deal. Some of Oscar's confederates were arrested under postal fraud charges and signed pledges to quit the racket, but their places were quickly taken by other sharpers. For the Post Office it was a maddening situation.

In England Scotland Yard was asked to investigate "Baron" Hartzell, and several inspectors visited him in his lavish Basil Street suite. Oscar played the gracious host but would volunteer no information, especially the identity of the "sole surviving heir" of the Drake Estate.

Oscar's demeanor was self-assured and expansive. When one of the inspectors inquired as to the whereabouts of the Drake Estate, Hartzell waved a meaty arm and said: "Oh, it's all over the place."

"There is some question whether or not this estate exists at all," one of the inspectors volunteered.

"But it's positively true." Oscar squinted through the thick lenses of his glasses. "I suppose you have been hearing stories from the United States?"

The man from Scotland Yard admitted he had read some newspaper accounts of a massive swindle regarding the Drake claims.

"There are dangerous elements in America that will stop at nothing to prevent my affairs from being completed," Oscar explained.

Another detective asked why Hartzell, an American, was so involved in the settlement of a British estate. Oscar blinked, smiled, and blurted: "Why, I'm almost British. A party in your home office has brought it all about, and when this affair is concluded you will see that my name will become Drake and that you have been talking to a British subject all along."

Confused, the detectives left, one of them remarking: "That man is insane."

His bubble was bursting; Hartzell began to dash off a series of cables that were no more than wrathful diatribes, in which he berated his investors. One exclaimed:

> If you expect Oscar Hartzell to respect you in the end, respect him now when he needs your assistance. Stand your ground—fight for your rights, do not believe the lying newspapers . . . I will force the highest powers that be over there to furnish everyone that has crossed my path with free board and lodging.

If payments relayed to him by his brother Canfield in New York were late even by a day, Oscar flew into violent rages. His cables became more vengeful and chaotic. His threats, like those in a cable to Canfield, knew no limitation:

> I have the chain around the neck of every official on your side from the highest to the lowest that has crossed my path in this matter. Remember that the disturbance that the American people have made me has caused delay and a big loss to me. Parliament has nothing to do with the date. I expect and must have $2,500 each week until I notify you of the finish. Please make up last week's shortage immediately.

Oscar Up Against It

Postal authorities stepped up their campaign against the Drake swindlers but lacked important evidence against Hartzell. The State Department was called in, and through its offices Oscar was deported from England as an undesirable alien in January 1933. The man who sauntered down the gangplank in New York was no longer a country bumpkin but was dressed in well-tailored clothes and affected a British accent. His substantial image, however, made little impression on those federal agents who arrested him dockside and instantly trained him to Sioux City, Iowa, to stand trial for postal fraud.

A laborious federal case had been building up against Oscar for several years. Postal investigators had enlisted the aid of British authorities, and Hartzell's well-paid lawyers were stunned when one inspector took the stand and related his meticulous studies of the alleged Drake Estate in England. He had spent weeks pouring over ancient records in Somerset House, a vast storehouse of English historical documents. A yellowed parchment found there revealed in court Latin the properly probated estate of Sir Francis Drake. Other experts picked apart Oscar's claim that a "secret ecclesiastical court" had hidden the Drake treasure. Documents found in the British Museum, carefully copied and entered as evidence against Hartzell's fantastic claim, included reports of the Inquisition at Lima, Peru, where Drake's young nephew, Francis, had been extensively questioned, and it was then determined that the romantic swashbuckler never had any children. Further, another record of contest between Drake's widow and brother, Thomas, proved there was little value in his estate at the time of his death.

A statement was read from the holder of the Drake estate in Amersham, one Edward Thomas T. Drake, who said he had never heard of Oscar Hartzell. (The legitimate Drake heir went on to report that he had four daughters and no son, which he ascribed "to a curse inspired by the mother of a cabin boy whom Sir Francis killed in a fit of rage.") It was also pointed out by a British legal expert who traveled to the Sioux City trial from England that the English statutes of limitation on probate expired after thirty years, and no case could be reopened following that period of time.

Oscar squirmed but felt confident he would escape conviction. He had never sent a letter or received one, for that matter, his lawyers carefully pointed out, during the nine lucrative years in which his will-o'-the-wisp operated, a period in which he and his aides had scooped up almost $2 million from more than 70,000 suckers in a dozen states. (Hartzell's take was almost $1 million.) But Oscar had overlooked the fine print in the postal regulations. It was also illegal to "cause others" to send letters through the U.S. mails in perpetrating a fraud. Oscar was convicted and sentenced to ten years in Leavenworth, but his con went blithely along, his agents continuing to reap enormous amounts from marks.

Oscar's bail and defense fund of $78,000 had ben provided by the myriad dupes who had so blindly invested in his scheme. They felt, almost to a man, that he had been "railroaded." A respected member of Chicago's Board of Trade implicitly believed Hartzell's claim, reasoning that Scotland Yard would never have allowed him to operate for almost a decade had he not been honest, and put up $21,000 for Oscar's legal fees. Suckers pumped an additional $350,000 into Hartzell's Chicago office during the trial.

One More Mulcting for Drake

While free on bond, Oscar appeared in several small towns, where he gave brow-sweating harangues to hosts of suckers, demanding they scrape up "every available dime to protect your investments." Just outside of Spencer, Iowa, where almost every resident was involved in the scheme, he mounted a wagon in front of a barn, and in the weird glow and flicker of hand-held torches, exhorted those assembled to "dig! dig! dig!" for his legal expenses. "Are we going to let the interests rob us? Take the money right out of our pockets?"

A roar of "No!" rolled back to him.

Hartzell bellowed accusations against political powers in Washington who, he said, were conspiring with London business leaders to suppress the distribution of the Drake billions. "Do you know who is behind this absurd indictment of me? I'll tell you who. None other than the King of England, that's who! But we're going to fight 'em all, and we're going to win!" As he raved on, Oscar's lieutenants scurried through the crowds with large hats that were soon stuffed with money. Before departing the near-hysterical throng, caught up as in a rivival meeting, Oscar jumped on the hood of his car as it was inching away and shouted: "I'm going home and load this car with corn and then I'm going to draw money on it and take those long greenbacks and put 'em all in on our deal!"

He exited Spencer that night with cheers echoing in his ears, but the encouraging tumult faded following his conviction. On the last day of the trial, a further insult was offered him in the form of a letter from an Englishwoman. The missive was read aloud in court. In part it declared: "I know Hartzell quite well. He swindled me out of most of my jewelry. It was right after Hartzell was made Premier Duke of Buckland in a private investiture by His Majesty."

Oscar erupted from his chair. "That lady is a confidence woman!"

Hartzell entered Leavenworth in November 1933, but his confederates were undaunted. They sent out a message (written by Hartzell) to their mulcted suckers that read:

> I will say our deal is going fine. This last stunt of taking him away is all in the play. We have been advised all along that the outside world would think this is a fraud. If the papers came out and said the Drake Estate thing was okay, we would be run to death by agents and grafters, and some of our heavy donors possibly would have trouble with kidnappers. This way no one will ever know we got the money. As to Hartzell he is not where the papers say, even though he left Chicago with officers. We know where he is and we know the reason.

The Chicago branch of Hartzell's octopus operation continued this conspiracy charge in all its communications with marks but the furor of his agents was silenced on April 8, 1935, when detectives raided the offices and arrested Otto Yant, Lester Kirkendall, Joseph Hauber, and Delmar Short.

Hauber took the detectives aside and said: "Look, I'm not with these people. I invested in this rotten scheme and arrived before you did to investigate. I was going to turn the whole bunch over to the police."

Iowa banker Otto Yant in custody; he provided Hartzell with rich sucker lists in the fabulous Drake scam. (WIDE WORLD)

Short overheard Hauber's inane plea and shouted: "That's a lie! He's been in it for years all along, just the same as us. Tell 'em how you impersonated a Scotland Yard inspector and a Secret Service agent who was supposed to be supervising the settlement. Tell 'em that, while you're at it, Joe." Hauber was taken into custody along with the others. Another thirty-seven con artists in Oscar's well-oiled ring were also rounded up, and they, including Hartzell, who was brought to Chicago to stand trial for a second time, faced postal fraud indictments.

Great pains were taken in selecting the jury for this trial, and all the jurors eventually picked claimed they had never heard of Hartzell or the Drake Estate. One man was excused from duty because he lived in Chicago's Drake Hotel. Prosecutor Austin C. Hall assembled scores of witnesses against the con clan. When testifying, these witnesses trembled with anxiety as they displayed the receipts they had been given in return for the money invested in the swindle. Anxiously, they called out to veniremen handling the receipts: "Careful of those, please, they are very valuable."

Defense lawyer Edward J. Hess, an authority on postal law and once an assistant U.S. attorney, knew Hartzell and Yant were beyond saving. He tried to excuse many of the other defendants, pointing to the fact that they had been dupes. "Whatever may be the truth about the Drake Estate," Hess intoned, "these people not only believed in it, almost as in a holy cause, but they put their money in it. Take the case of Charlie Jones. He put in from three thousand to five thousand dollars that he inherited from his father. Can he be guilty of fraud? Take the case of an engineer in Wenatchee, Washington, and a barber in Texas. The Drake Estate was a matter of social interest in their communities. It was talked of at picnics, church socials, bridge parties. People were convinced that it was the way to wealth. . . . They got these people to pool their money and ship it by railway express to Chicago."

Prosecutor Hall was brief in his summary. "Every representation of the defendants was false, and they know it."

Hartzell was convicted again and returned to serve out his full ten-year sentence in Leavenworth. Canfield Hartzell, Yant, Lester Ohmart, Delmar Short, Emil Rochel, and Joseph Hauber received a year and a day in prison; the others in the mass trial were freed.

Oscar Hartzell refused to give up his bizarre claims, and ranted so loudly and repeatedly in his cell about what he would do to those who had imprisoned him that he received a psychopathic examination in December 1936 and was adjudged mentally incompetent, with delusions of grandeur. The millionaire Iowa con man was removed to the U.S. Medical Center for federal prisoners in Springfield, Missouri, and spent the rest of his days mumbling his way through the hours, dying on August 27, 1943. His passing went almost unnoticed by a national press that had once found it incredible that 70,000 suckers could be bilked by Oscar's sometime promise of 5,000 percent return on every dollar.

The Baker Estate Con

Not as long-lived but certainly as enriching as the Drake swindle was the Baker Estate case, which was fully exposed the year Hartzell was convicted in his second trial and permanently entered Leavenworth, a red-letter year for revealing inheritance cons. Begun in 1866 in Ontario, Canada, the Baker inheritance swindle centered about one Colonel Jacob Baker, who died in Philadelphia in 1839. Perpetrators of this con insisted Baker's heirs were entitled to 2,000 acres of land, including downtown Philadelphia, an estate variously estimated to be worth $1 to $3 billion. The legacy, sharpers pointed out, encompassed dozens of hotels, banks, government and office buildings, Independence Hall, the Pennsylvania Railroad Station, the Liberty Bell, and Benjamin Franklin's grave.

Unlike Hartzell's any-and-all gullery, those swindled in the Baker Estate con had to be named Baker, Becker, or Barker, but there were enough of the above-named for operators to rake in millions from suckers by the mid-1930s. The most serious outbreaks of the Baker con occurred in 1902 and in 1936, the latter year a heyday for three con rings dealing out of Altoona, Johnstown, and Pittsburgh, Pennsylvania. More than 3,000 persons had been roped into "investing" in the Baker Estate fortune, again one of those difficult matters of probate that had to be pried loose from tenacious state and federal authorities. Postal inspector Alfred T. Hawksworth worked for more than twenty years to nail the three Baker Estate rings, snaring twenty-eight operators in the 1936 roundup, notably the conniving William Cameron Morrow Smith,

The seventy-year-old William Morrow Cameron Smith, perpetrator of the Jacob Baker estate con; he mulcted more than 3,000 persons of millions. (WIDE WORLD)

seventy, who had taken in millions on the fraud over a thirty-year period.

When the evidence against these rings first appeared shaky, a Pittsburgh newspaper lamented: "What a nice mess it'll be if the courts acquit these folk! What the hell will happen to the Liberty Bell and old Ben Franklin's bones?" Quick convictions, however, allayed such fears for national monuments.

The Happy Dupes of the Edwards Scam

Cleveland, Ohio, gave birth to another exceptional inheritance con man, one Dr. Herbert H. Edwards, who insisted fanatically in the 1880s that he was a descendant of Robert Edwards, a colonial merchant who left to his heirs sixty-five acres of Manhattan Island in the middle of which towered the Woolworth Building.

The Edwards Heirs Association was handed down from father to son, and raked in an annual $26 from each member desirous of "aiding" the family in their involved legal battles. Those who joined the association would, naturally, share in the staggering settlement that was imminent, always imminent.

Hundreds of association members met each year at a massive fete—the con men graciously paid for the food—and rejoiced at the profits to come. Some wag had composed a song especially for this merry crowd of dupes, which was lustily sung:

> We have rallied here in blissful state
> Our jubilee to celebrate.
> When fortune kindly on us smiled,
> The Edwards Heirs now reconciled.
> Our president deserves our praise,
> For strenuous work through dreary days,
> In consummating our affairs
> And rounding up the Edwards heirs.
>
> We're Robert Edwards' legal heirs,
> And cheerfully we take our shares.
> Then let us shout with joy and glee
> And celebrate the jubilee.

None of the so-called Edwards Heirs ever saw a dime from their investment, but when the Post Office finally broke up the schemes, suckers could, at least, look back fondly on several decades' worth of uproarious annual outings.

Savage Investments

Indians have long been the target of many con schemes involving legacies, a particularly severe rash of cons descending upon several tribes in the late 1930s. Indians were told by sharpers they would receive $1,000 each for their deceased tribe members at the next session of Congress if they would but pay $5 apiece for "expenses." One group of hustlers almost convinced North Dakota Congressman Usher Burdick to introduce just such a bill (the sharpers knowing it would be defeated), but he realized that he, too, was being duped and withdrew the measure.

The Dancing Rabbit Treaty of 1839 with Mississippi's Choctaw Indians served as a source of profitable con for Neshoba County sharper Odie Moore, who maintained that the treaty had been broken and that the original tribe members and their descendants were owed millions by the federal government. Since there had been wide intermarriage between whites and Choctaws in Neshoba County, Odie had little difficulty in rounding up thousands of suckers who invested heavily to receive "$1,000 for every dollar." Moore's bogus association, begun in 1930, was still going strong to the day of his death in 1945, members continuing to believe that settlement was "just around the corner."

The Family Money Tree

Though inheritance cons of magnitude have for the most part become dormant, subtle con men still play the family-tree angle. One fellow has made several fortunes over a period of forty years by putting together ridiculously manufactured genealogies of nonexistent families, such as the Cook family. Printing cheap volumes that claim to trace the Cooks back to heroic roles in the American Revolution, this con man offered each portfolio for $10 to every Cook in the phone directory, and usually sold every sucker he approached. As a bonus, he included bits of maudlin doggerel about the family and a song, composed by himself, entitled "The Battle Hymn of the Cooks." When that name was financially exhausted, he moved onto another.

Today astute con artists slink their ways through probate court and discover, when possible, heirs of estates who live in distant locales. Traveling there, the sharper tells the sucker that he has inherited a good deal of money, and for an agreed-upon price, bound by a signed contract, he will be kind enough to tell the rube in which state his fortune awaits him.

Many who operate this racket today insist that what they collect from a sucker is merely a "finder's fee," but what they have truely found is a mark and what they realistically collect is the traditional score. Making the same claim in 1871 were two flamboyant flimflammers named Philip Arnold and John Slack, and what they found, or claimed they found, produced one of the most fascinating frauds in the colorful history of American wheeling and dealing.

Six

All That Glitters

THE LURE of precious stones and metal secreted beneath the earth by the centuries is irresistible to suckers. Con men have long labored selling rubes the shafts in which alleged piles of gold, silver, and priceless gems await plucking, dangling the fortune and letting greed take the bait.

Sometimes the mark has only to be shown a hole in the ground or a freshly sheared-off cliff to be convinced of the existence of a mother lode. Such was the case in the 1930s when four con men spotted half of a hillside carved away at a road construction site near Yonkers, New York. Overnight the foursome printed hundreds of authentic-looking gold-stock certificates, and then bussed dozens of rubes to the construction area, making much of the silent steam shovels and impressive grading machinery, pointing out that the location would yield the richest gold dust in the country. In a flurry the con artists collected more than $135,-000, signing over their useless gold certificates to the dupes, all before the road gang returned to work on Monday morning.

"Wanna Buy a Park?"

Such gross naïveté is not hard to accept when one remembers the Italian immigrant who paid a handsome fee to a con man to convert the information booth in Grand Central Station into a fruit stand (the pathetic produce peddler was ejected from the station before selling one pomegranate), or the Polish immigrant, one George Sokolowski, to whom sharpers sold Cleveland's Brookside Park, lagoon, and zoo for $1,500 in October 1925. (Sokolowski spotted a policeman when looking over the city's lakeside property, and was told that the officer was included in the transaction; when the con men departed, the dupe told the cop that he, as the new owner, would keep him on to guard his property. The officer hurried Sokolowski off to headquarters, where the swindle was patiently explained to him.) Marks have bought anything and everything, including the Brooklyn Bridge, the Statue of Liberty, and the Eiffel Tower in Paris, which super international con man Victor "The Count" Lustig managed to sell *twice*.

Of course, such blatant mulcting was exercised best with foreigners, but in matters of precious metals and gems, no amount of prestige, intelligence, or wealth prevented con men from hustling the citizen "in the know."

Newspapers of the day depicted Philip Arnold and John Slack, perpetrators of the colossal diamond mine swindle, as treacherous vipers.

Phony gold and silver mines were initially most appealing to suckers. Specialists in selling bogus gold certificates at the turn of the century were New York sharpers Chappie Moran, Larry Summerfield, and Sam Giroux. George Fawcet specialized in promoting useless shares in mythical zinc mines. To bolster their fabulous claims, these classic con men would often-times resort to salting abandoned mines in the West in elaborate big-con or big-store games, but only when the sucker was sufficiently hooked and immense scores were assured.

The Classic Diamond-Mine Swindle

In the annals of American con, however, the only two grifters ever to salt a diamond mine successfully in the United States were Philip Arnold and John Slack, prospectors emeritus, who not only gleaned a fortune from their fraud but took special pride in the fact that they had conned the world's most powerful financiers.

In the summer of 1871 these two scruffy-looking fellows appeared in the offices of a mining promoter, George Roberts. "The bank ain't open and we was wond'rin' if you'd do us a favor?" Arnold inquired.

Roberts noticed a sack slung over Arnold's arm and asked what he wanted.

Arnold held out the bulging burlap bag and said: "We'd take it kindly if we could store these here valuables in your safe until the bank opens tomorrow." Expecting to find gold dust or nuggets, Roberts took the sack to a counter and spilled out its contents. He gasped. Before him in glittering piles were diamonds, emeralds and rubies.

Roberts excitedly grilled prospector Arnold, the miner responding in a hesitant, guarded manner. After dodging some direct questions, Arnold conspiratorially told Roberts that he and Slack had just returned from eastern Arizona, a dry, fierce area infested by the savage Apache and had, through the help of a friendly Indian, located a field, sparkling beneath the hot sun, where enormous diamonds, rubies and emeralds were spread about like sawdust on a barroom floor.

When pressed for details, Arnold hedged and then refused to specify the area of the diamond field. Without asking, Arnold was then offered help by the stunned Roberts. He knew, Roberts told them, that they could not afford to mount an expensive expedition into hostile country to lay claim to such a staggering find, and insisted the two prospectors allow him to help. Slack said nothing—Arnold always did the talking— and at Roberts' suggestion he only grumbled a few words, then jerked his thumb toward the door and marched out with his partner.

Seconds after Arnold and Slack ambled from his office, Roberts nervously made his way to the lavish manor home of William C. Ralston, an enormously wealthy speculator, head of the Bank of California, and a man whose every waking moment seemed dedicated to accumulating the riches of the earth. This is exactly what Philip Arnold, who had planned his original con with perspicacious vigor, knew Roberts would do. Arnold was not a man to leave minutiae out of his scheme.

The Making of an Early Con Man

As he and Slack whiled away hours playing faro and emptying a bottle of red-eye, Arnold could look back confidently on every well-developed detail of his ingenious plan. Born in Hardin County, Kentucky, in 1829, Arnold's background suggested nothing as flamboyant as the scheme he was about to unravel. Initially, his was the simple life—a small farm, family, phlegmatic tilling of Kentucky soil. But at age thirty, just before the outbreak of the Civil War, he contracted the special fever that had afflicted most frontiersmen of his day: gold. Deserting his wife and children, Arnold traveled to California, and teaming up with the dyspeptic John Slack, worked a claim for several years near Marysville, California, for about $50,000. Banking this, Arnold moved on to San Francisco, where he obtained a job with the Diamond Drill Company, a position he desired so much that he offered to work for less pay than what his bookkeeping chores normally demanded. It was an education, not a job, Arnold was really seeking.

Long hours after his bookkeeping work was finished, Arnold hung around the firm's offices and pestered officials about the diamonds used in the drilling bits manufactured for the large gold and silver mine owners like James Fair, George Hearst, Darius Mills, and the redoubtable Mr. Ralston. He carefully studied the industrial diamonds on hand, pocketing a few of these flawed gems for further examination. Arnold also devoured every book and article available that was concerned with rare jewels. After two years Arnold was probably the most knowledgeable man in the United States regarding diamonds and other precious stones. He also knew who didn't know what he knew. He quit his job, and with his savings, traveled circuitous routes to Europe, where he purchased, inexpensively, a large number of gems considered worthless except for industrial use.

It was some months later, in 1871, that Arnold, his old partner Slack at his side, turned up in Roberts' office with his bag of jewels. Now all he had to do was wait. Greed would take care of the final stages of his plan.

Then prominent in the news were the fabulous diamond strikes in Golconda, India, and those of South Africa. As far as any mining expert knew, the vast, arid stretches of the American West were of a similar geography, which could possibly yield the greatest diamond fields yet.

Greed Takes a Hand

As Arnold knew he would, Roberts took the jewels to his friend Ralston, who, in turn, called in a local jeweler. This man, having no real knowledge of the gems' worth, placed their immediate value at $125,000 (Arnold had paid about $12,000 for them in England). Ralston jumped at the bait. He had Roberts introduce him to the two sharpers and then asked if they would sell their claim.

William C. Ralston, president of the Bank of California and the first sucker taken in by Arnold and Slack.

"Not controllin' interest," Arnold insisted. "But we could use a grubstake to work the field."

Ralston was no fool, and told the prospectors so. He would stake them, all right, if they first proved their claim to be genuine. Take a qualified mining expert into the field for a first-hand look, Ralston propositioned, and if the claim was legitimate, he would back them. The two men grumbled something about "bein' taken by Frisco slickers" and then agreed to the examination, but there was a hitch. The miners would take the expert to the site of their diamond field, but he must be willing to be blindfolded until they reached the area.

Ralston balked.

"It's the only way we kin protect our rights. If one man knows where our claim is, you'll all know."

The financier capitulated and assigned David Colton, a highly respected mining authority, to accompany Arnold and Slack to the field. The trio set out on a fast Union Pacific flyer heading East, getting off at Rawlins, Wyoming. When Colton asked why they were not heading for Arizona, Arnold merely smiled. He blindfolded the inspector and led his horse into the back country. For several days the three men rode in crazy-quilt routes. Colton, of course, had no idea where he was when Arnold finally removed the blindfold. Though it seemed they had ridden more than a hundred miles, they were only about fifty miles north of Black Butte, Wyoming, and never more than twenty-five miles from the Union Pacific tracks.

Showing the Goods

Atop a sandy plateau, Colton blinked in wonder. The entire area glittered under the sun, and he quickly dismounted and walked over to a place containing several ant hills. These were covered with diamond dust, and the mining expert excitedly began to kick the ant hills over, uncovering one precious stone after another, dozens of diamonds and even a few rubies and emeralds. Colton was aghast at the incredible deposits. At times Arnold helped him probe the earth with his knife; Slack merely sat on a rock, smoking a battered pipe and saying nothing. In a matter of hours Colton had filled a sack with jewels, but his investigation was cut short by Arnold, who told him they had to get out fast; he thought he had spotted Indians. The trio rode away from the field that day, Colton once again blindfolded.

Upon their return to San Francisco, the newly unearthed gems were once again studied by Ralston's jeweler and once again an inflated evaluation was given. Colton described the far-reaching field in mouth-watering terms, saying that it appeared endless and that there were so many diamonds and other rare jewels at the claim as to dwarf the South African and Indian strikes. Coupled to this was Ralston's unbounding optimism, which infected the many fellow speculators he innocently roped into the scheme. One of these was General George M. Dodge, a sagacious type who suspected mankind as a whole of possessing a malefic character. He would deal with this fellow Arnold, he promised Ralston, and had a "serious talk" with the prospector. Then, emerging from a hotel room filled with cigar smoke, Dodge told Ralston: "I will stake my life on that fellow's integrity."

The Rich Rush In

Other financial high-rollers, William Lent and Asbury Harpending, who had been called from London by Ralston to give his opinion and promote the field, nodded approval. There was still in California a universal feeling that the West had unlimited wealth spread on and under its wilder-

ness acreage, a heady philosophy held over from the impressive Gold
Rush days. No man who had witnessed hordes of impoverished miners
becoming millionaires overnight would challenge the existence of any
kind of El Dorado. In that innocent era, as historian Herbert Asbury
pointed out, "no man of authority would have been brash enough to
say dogmatically that there were no diamond fields in the United States."

Harpending was first informed of the discovery by Ralston. He received a cable while in London, and his first reaction when talking
with several European tycoons was that Ralston had lost his senses. If
not that, he was being conned. At that moment one of the richest men
in the world, Baron Rothschild, stepped forward, talking thoughtfully
with what appeared to be amazing foresight. "Don't be too sure about
that," he cautioned Harpending. "America is a very large country. It
has furnished the world with many surprises already. Perhaps it may
have others in store." Rothschild was so interested in Ralston's cable
that he instructed his Pacific Coast representative, A. Gansl, to investigate and possibly invest. That was enough for Harpending, who took
the next ship to the United States. (He was to become the so-called
Ralston Mine's most public promoter, drawing a grand array of distinguished businessmen and politicians into the scheme, for which he
would later be made a pariah and branded "an ingenious rogue.")

By the time Harpending reached San Francisco in early spring, 1872,
feverish claims were being made about the fabulous diamond fields.
Inept jewelers and strutting experts had convinced Ralston that the
gems he had been given by Arnold and Slack were worth more than $1.5
million when, in truth, their real value did not exceed $20,000. To be
absolutely sure, Ralston and other potential investors demanded that the
two prospectors accompany them to New York, where Charles Lewis
Tiffany, proprietor of the most respected jewelry emporium in the
country, would evaluate the gems.

*Financial promoter
Asbury Harpending
unwittingly lured scores
of millionaires into the
diamond swindle that
eventually wrecked his
reputation.*

The Planned Payoff

Arnold and Slack bristled. It seemed, they said, the financiers were trying to sucker them. To allay their fears, Ralston Roberts and Lent gave

the miners $100,000 and placed another $300,000 in escrow for them. They also promised a final payment of another $300,000 when the deal, which would give them a half interest in the field, was completed. The two sharpers agreed to travel East. They were an incongruous looking pair, dressed in their stained and seedy-looking clothes and wedged on a private rail car between the elegantly attired millionaires.

The meeting in New York was a regular who's who of American society, held in the sprawling mansion of General Samuel L. Barlow, a famous corporation lawyer who represented Ralston's Bank of California. In attendance were August Belmont and Henry Seligman, esteemed bankers; General Dodge; Harpending; Lent; General George B. McClellan, the Union Army's "Little Mac" of Civil War fame; and General Benjamin F. Butler, who had been known to Confederates as "Beast" Butler for his harsh occupation of New Orleans. It was Butler's job, as a member of Congress, to herd along legislation that would turn the public lands (wherever these would subsequently be pinpointed) over to the privately held diamond monopoly, which is exactly what he did. Also in attendance was editorial gadfly and *New York World* mentor Horace Greeley, who, ironically, had just recently been involved in the Lord Gordon-Gordon swindle.

While these titans of finance closed around a table where Tiffany examined the jewels, Arnold and Slack, who had not been invited to the party, toured New York City, prudently spending a few of Ralston's dollars on simple pleasures. The two con men were unconcerned with Tiffany's examination. His scrutiny, they were sure, would be faulty. Neither he nor his lapidary knew how to affix a real value to the stones. Tiffany, however, quickly pronounced the gems worth a fortune.

Baron Rothschild, one of the richest men on earth, sent representatives from England to invest in the nonexistent diamond fields.

The Convincer

But there would be one more test.

Before paying the balance of $300,000 for their half of the diamond field, the financiers insisted on mounting another investigative expedition that would once and for all clear up any doubt of the field's genuineness. Arnold and Slack were called in, and not before a great deal of carping and resentment, agreed to the final test. While the tycoons began their search for the proper examiner and jockeyed for corporate position in the yet unestablished firm, Arnold and Slack stated they were going to the West and would leave the jewels with the investors for safekeeping. Instead, they boarded ship in New York and sailed to Europe. There, using the funds advanced by Ralston and others, they purchased the most flawed and marketless gems Antwerp and Amsterdam had to offer, sacks of them, for which they spent about $50,000. The con men, too, knew how to parlay, and returned to America, traveled West, and again salted the 6,500-foot Wyoming mesa before contacting the investors.

Waiting for them was Henry Janin, considered the best mining expert in the country. A suspicious, circumspect individual, Janin was no Colton. He vowed to go over every square inch of the field; no man could bamboozle him. Yet the con men appeared indifferent, and in the words of A. J. Liebling, "only a Philip Arnold would have led a Janin to a salted mine. The prospector had the intuition of a great poker player for an opponent's foible. For the fact was that Janin had never in his life seen diamond land and he was disarmed in advance by the high appraisal of the sample stones."

Following the same procedure as they had with Colton, Arnold and Slack led Janin to the field. Also in their party were General Dodge, Lent, Harpending, and Alfred Rubery, who had traveled from London with Harpending to get in on the great financial adventure.

The two prospectors led their prey once more through a series of canyons and mesas until they were properly confused and then into the forty-acre diamond site. Astounded, the investigators, Janin leading the way (he had examined more than six hundred gold and silver mines and had never once been wrong in assaying their worth), began kicking over anthills, digging with knives, and overturning boulders and rocks to find not only great quantities of diamonds, but rubies, emeralds, and sapphires.

For eight days the party dug up about a ton and a half of dirt, their harvest of gems amounting to almost $10,000, according to Janin. (Slack and Arnold did no digging, but looked up occasionally from their blanket rolls and sometimes suggested where to look.) Estimating the return from this small amount of superficial spading, Janin was

Alfred Rubery was accused of masterminding the diamond swindle by the London Times; he sued the paper and won.

more than convinced of a real find. Claiming about 4,000 acres for the investors, Janin told them they now possessed the richest field in mining history, that the area pinpointed should yield $5 million an acre. "With a hundred men and proper machinery, I would guarantee to send out a million dollars in diamonds every thirty days." Janin's incredible statement was the final hurrah of the con, one he unwittingly performed for Arnold and Slack. (He would later sell the 1,000 shares of private stock in the field he received as payment for his examination to Harpending and Lent for an unrecoverable $40,000.)

On the group's return to San Francisco, Ralston and the others frenziedly put together a $10 million corporation of private investors to exploit the field. First Arnold and Slack were gotten rid of, both told that they would certainly be fleeced by the energetic money moguls if they continued to insist on shares in the field. They argued, but feebly, against this position. Ralston and his powerful associates were unrelenting in their demands, and finally the two prospectors gave in and accepted the promised balance of $300,000, signing over all rights to the field, including those gems already in Ralston's possession. Oddly, it never occurred to the tycoons that for the prospectors to do so, what with Janin's glowing report on hand, was lunacy. Perhaps, they figured the two grubstakers were naïve, simple men willing to settle for comfortable cash payments—more money, in fact, than they had ever had in their lifetimes. Whatever, Arnold and Slack left California almost immediately.

Blowing Off

Arnold traveled to his homestead in Kentucky, where he was reunited with his family and quickly began several small and successful businesses. Slack disappeared completely and forever.

When word of the fabulous new El Dorado got out, thousands of anxious miners traversed the empty expanses of Nevada, Arizona, and California. Nobody, of course, knew the location of the field except Ralston's private investors, and these men opened luxurious offices in San Francisco and New York, where large topographical maps soon adorned the walls, depicting such exotically named areas of the claim as Diamond Flat, Ruby Gulch, and Sapphire Hollow.

While millions poured into Ralston's venture to develop the diamond fields, three government geologists, Clarence King, Allen D. Wilson, and S. F. Emmons, hearing of the diamond strike, decided to investigate. After scouring approximately 150 miles surrounding Black Butte, King located the field, noting on the way a distinct absence of geological formations conducive to diamonds. He and his companions quickly stomped through Arnold's salted diamond field, kicking over ant hills to discover the planted gems. Under one boulder they found a ruby, a sapphire, an emerald, and a large diamond. They plucked out a diamond they found wedged between the limbs of a small tree. This bore the obvious marks of a lapidary's tool.

Traveling to Fort Bridger, King sent a wire to Ralston, telling him that he had been swindled. Unwilling to believe at first, Ralston sent a committee to investigate the field once again. King and the other geologists took them on a quick tour of the terrain, pointing out that Arnold and Slack had made the ant hills, sprinkling them with diamond and emerald dust. The stunned investigators were also shown how easily the con men had stuck industrial diamonds between rocks and how, with an iron rod, they had punched out holes in the ground, dropped the gems inside, scooped back the earth, and then let the wind and rain reshape the ground to natural appearance.

Investigators soon revealed Arnold's purchase of the raw gems in Europe. Chagrined, the money men convened and agreed to dissolve the newly formed San Francisco and New York Mining & Commercial Company. Ralston was the heavy loser, with an estimated $2 million lost to the con artists and subsequent useless development operations, and his Bank of California failed two years later, in 1875. Harpending, Lent, and General Dodge also lost undisclosed amounts; some said their losses amounted to an aggregate $8 million. Everyone was reluctant to admit exact amounts. There was much speculation about others being part of the swindle, and the London *Times* went so far as to accuse Harpending and Rubery of complicity in the con. (Rubery sued and won £10,000 in libel damages.)

Though no one could ever locate John Slack, the whereabouts of Philip Arnold was no secret. Living in Elizabethtown, Kentucky, his once-skimpy farm having blossomed to a country-squire estate, Arnold moved about openly. The only one of the suckered millionaires to claim grievance was William Lent, who traveled to Kentucky and angrily brought suit against Arnold to recover $350,000. Arnold screamed persecution and pointed out the glowing reports of Charles Tiffany, Colton, and Janin, copies of which, along with Ralston's signed releases, he had prudently kept on hand. "Those California sharks are tryin' to ruin a good and hard-workin' man," he bellowed publicly.

Lent's suit never came to trial, and most agree that he would have lost to Arnold, who was in the bosom of his home country and surrounded by friends. The prospector-turned-sharper, however, decided to settle the matter and repaid Lent $150,000, retaining more than a quarter of a million from his diligent scam. However, he lived only a few months to enjoy it.

Arnold's ambition got the better of him when he decided to compete against a pernicious banker by opening his own bank. In late 1873 his rival emptied a load of buckshot into his back, and while recuperating, the bedridden Arnold caught pneumonia and promptly died, distinguished to this day as the only con man to ever successfully salt the one and only diamond mine in the United States.

A Talented Diamond Pirate

A more contemporary diamond-mine con man was Jean Pierre Lafitte, who claimed direct ancestry from the Lafitte pirate brothers. His career was somewhat more spectacular than the plodding Philip Arnold's. For one thing, he worked on both sides of the law. In a forty-eight-year span Lafitte was arrested twenty-three times for bunco games and fraud, but he also worked as an undercover man for the FBI. (In the mid-1940s, about to be deported, Lafitte was detained at Ellis Island, and there approached by some of Vito Genovese's gangsters, who were about to be shipped off to Sicily. They asked him to deliver a message to New York hoodlums, but he took the information to the FBI and became an informer; his work helped to build concrete cases against Genovese and others who were sent to prison.) Added to his adventures was a short stint in the French Foreign Legion in the 1920s.

In 1957, in Kittery Point, Maine, Lafitte surfaced as one Louis Romano, and soon ingratiated himself with Ralph Loomis, a wealthy speculator. Taking a $30,000 fee from Loomis, allegedly to arrange some deals with the Securities and Exchange Commission, Lafitte further double-talked Loomis into heavy investments in two nonexistent diamond mines in South Africa. For months, reports that told of huge deposits were forwarded by a confederate from the diamond fields. Lafitte pocketed $300,000 of Loomis's investment capital, and was prepared to go underground once again, but federal agents moved faster and arrested him on fifteen counts of mail fraud and transportation of stolen property. The high-living Lafitte calmly posted $25,000 bond and then skipped on December 3, 1963.

His trail vanished for six years, but in December 1969 FBI agents located the con man in New Orleans and placed him under arrest. He was found working as a master chef for the Plimsoll Club, where his famous crêpes Suzette and Dover sole had brought him the gushing gratitude of Governor John McKeithen, who made him an honorary Louisiana colonel; of New Orleans Mayor Victor Shiro, who officially welcomed him to the city; and of the visiting Mrs. Lyndon Baines Johnson, who later sent him a letter from the White House praising his cuisine.

At the time of his arrest newsmen overheard the seventy-four-year-old Lafitte murmur the con man's lament to his wife: "Just when we have everything, it looks like we'll have to run again."

Seven

The Short Con

TAKING A SUCKER'S MONEY without elaborate build-up and time-consuming stings as seen in the big store or big con is, in essence, the short con. The game is usually completed in a single day, with no more than a few meets betwen bunco man and mark. It is the tactic of a hit and run. Usually, the hustler will settle for what the victim has in his pockets, and although the con man may use ropers and sometimes disappear, his general aim is to keep the mark fixed in one spot. In con parlance, the short con is a "one-liner."

Mizner's Midget

Before he and his brother Addison turned fecund talents toward larger promotions, such as the Florida real estate speculation of the 1920s, Wilson Mizner proved himself to be a master of the short con. On one occasion Mizner scooped up several thousand dollars at Atlantic City when he and some sporting types, while strolling along the beach, did a double take at spotting the most gigantic feet they had ever seen protruding from a closed beach tent.

Mizner suggested a friendly wager on the height of the unseen vacationer. All the gentlemen gamblers bet that the enormous feet belonged to a fellow well over six feet. Mizner rubbed his chin, chomped his cigar, and said: "Something tells me that character is no taller than five feet one inch." Throwing back the tent flap, everyone, including Wilson Mizner (who was a fine actor), sucked in deep breaths. Before them sprawled a dwarf no more than four and a half feet in length. Mizner quickly collected his winnings and ambled off, wondering, no doubt, how else to employ the undersized carnival character he had picked up in New York a month previously just for the beach-and-foot scam. (Mizner's sense of humor was best illustrated when he heard that fighter Stanley Ketchell, whom he had once managed, had been shot to death. Wilson commented: "Well, all you have to do is get someone to count over him and he'll get up by the count of ten.")

Hustler with humor Wilson Mizner, shown with nightclub diva Texas Guinan in 1926. (UPI)

The Distance Between Two Points is a Sucker

Mizner was best on board ships; he preferred fleecing his suckers leisurely on warm-weather cruises. One of his favorite and consistent short cons involved betting with other well-to-do passengers as to the whereabouts of the ship and the distance it achieved each day of the voyage. It was uncanny, said the tourists who lost every day to Mizner, how the fellow could be so accurate, for at the end of each day Mizner's calculations always tallied the closest with reports from the bridge. Of course, Mizner and his associate ropers had fixed the captain, bribing him $1,000 a day to correspond the ship's performance with their calculations. According to Alva Johnston, the system only backfired once, when, approaching the captain's cabin and knocking loudly on the fourth straight day of such betting and attempting once again to pay off the skipper, they heard the loud shout: "Get out of here, you bastards! I'm four hundred miles off my course now!"

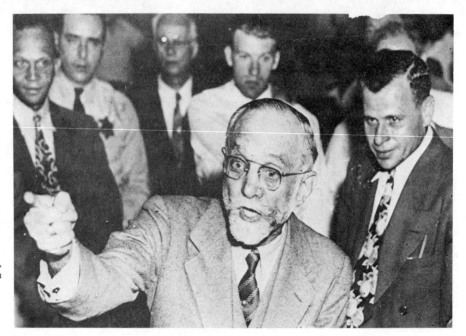

The colorful "Yellow Kid" Weil, Chicago's dean of confidence men, creatively departed from traditional con games; shown here in 1951 talking his way out of court. (UPI)

Oh, You Yellow Kid!

Another accomplished hustler—some say the greatest con man of his day—who pulled countless short cons of high invention was Joseph "Yellow Kid" Weil. Chicago political sachem "Bathhouse John" Coughlan named Weil in 1903, when he noticed the apprentice con man lounging at his bar and reading a popular cartoon strip called "Hogan's Alley," in which the Yellow Kid was a major character.

Weil, born in 1877, the son of a German barrel-maker in Chicago, unlike many other con men of his era never worked at anything in his long life but the con (he is still alive at this writing). His schemes were always complex and varied. For the most part, the Yellow Kid disdained the traditional short cons (the smack, the hot seat, the wipe, the money box, the tat, the big joint, and others). He preferred to invent his own scams, and took great pride in their originality.

Spectacular Spectacles

Graduating from selling a vile potion known as Meriwether's Elixir, which he peddled for $1 a bottle and claimed would kill off any parasitic tapeworm, Weil came up with the magazine-and-spectacles short con just after the turn of the century. Traveling through rural areas, the Yellow Kid would pretend to sell copies of a then popular magazine, *Hearth and Home,* each subscription priced at 25 cents per year. The magazine was a setup. Weil had had a printer run off several pages of very large type, and he cleverly inserted these into the magazine. Approaching a dim-sighted farmer, Weil would go into his magazine spiel and also mention that he had found a very expensive pair of glasses, which he wanted to return to the owner.

In the course of their conversation, Weil would show the glasses to the farmer who, naturally, would try them on. At this point, the Yellow Kid would abruptly turn the magazine pages to the large type and the farmer would think his vision had suddenly been greatly improved by the spectacles. Invariably, the farmer would give Weil $3 to $4 for the glasses—they looked expensive, having what appeared to be solid-gold rims—promising to return them to the owner if he could be found. The glasses were worth about 15 cents apiece, and Weil pushed these off on dupes by the gross.

The Yellow Kid's only full-time partner in flim-flamming, Fred "The Deacon" Buckminster, in 1938; he wound up teaching mathematics in Michigan State Prison. (WIDE WORLD)

The Priceless Pooch

One of Weil's favorite short cons was the pedigreed dog swindle. This he worked successfully for years with his friend and fellow hustler, Fred Buckminster.

Weil would enter a saloon in all his sartorial splendor—winged collar, cravat with diamond stickpin, cutaway coat, striped trousers, spats, patent-leather shoes. Placing his homburg on the bar, he would tie to the railing an expensive-looking leash at the end of which was a groomed and scented dog. Suddenly withdrawing a solid-gold watch from his brocaded vest, Weil would slap his forehead and exclaim: "My Lord, I have an urgent business meeting." He would glance furtively toward the dog, murmuring, "A great deal of my future depends upon this conference . . . and Rex here is not permitted in the bank offices I am to visit."

The bartender would look down at the dog, and Weil would then ask him to take care of the animal while he kept his appointment.

The Yellow Kid quickly produced pedigree papers and a blue ribbon emblazoned with the words "First Prize."

"Look," Weil stated, "this dog is extremely valuable. Here's ten dollars for watching him. Please take care of him until I return from my appointment."

Affably pocketing Weil's ten-spot, the bartender promised to treat the dog with kingly deference. Minutes after Weil had walked out, Fred Buckminster strolled into the bar. Seeing the dog, he choked on his beer and then sputtered: "Oh, my God, I've been looking for that breed of dog for five years." Laying $50 on the bar, Buckminster asked the saloon keeper to sell him the animal immediately.

"I can't, mister. The animal belongs to a stranger who only left him here for an hour or so."

Buckminster stared longingly at the canine. "I've got to have that dog," he said resolutely. Turning to the bartender, his voice rose to a demand. "I'll give you a hundred dollars for him." The saloon keeper shrugged helplessly. "Okay, okay, no more bickering," said the hustler, "I'll make it three hundred."

With that Buckminster shoved the $50 into the bar owner's hands. "Here's a down payment on the animal. My room number in the Atlantic Hotel is five-oh-seven. Call me as soon as you can persuade the owner to sell." Buckminster would then depart, after making a great show of affection for the animal.

Not more than half an hour would elapse before the Yellow Kid returned to the bar, appearing crestfallen, his countenance dour.

Solicitous, the saloon keeper, who had, by this time, secretly vowed to obtain Weil's dog, would ask: "Gee, what's the matter, mister? You look like you lost your best friend."

"Worse," the Kid would moan. "The deal fell through and I don't mind telling you, pal, that I'm financially up against the wall."

Realizing his perfect opportunity, the saloon keeper immediately offered to buy Weil's pedigreed dog.

"Oh, no, I could never part with Rex."

"Look, I'll make it good with two hundred dollars. My kids were in here just a few minutes ago and they fell in love with that dog, and it'll break their hearts if I don't get the animal for them."

"Well, I could use the money after today's setback. But two hundred dollars." The Kid shook his head. "That's not much for a grand champion."

At this point the saloon keeper usually did some quick figuring. He had already pocketed $10 from Weil and $50 from Buckminster. If he bought the dog for, say, $250, and resold it to Buckminster, his profit would be $110.

"I'll tell you what," the bar owner would volunteer sympathetically. "I'll make it two hundred fifty—I guess the pooch is worth that."

"Pooch?"

"I mean the grand champion."

Weil would stare pensively into his beer and then, with biting lip and tightly closed eyes, nod approval. Taking the $250, the Yellow Kid would hug his canine friend and sadly depart. Of course, Buckminster was not to be found by the avaricious bar owner in room 507 of the Atlantic Hotel or anywhere else. He and Weil had pocketed a profit of $190 with an investment come-on of a mere $60, all in about an hour's work. The dog, of course, was a mutt from the street or dog pound, and Weil and Buckminster managed to hustle saloon owners into buying an average of ten dogs a day until the territory got too hot, a tidy $5,000 weekly scam for each con man.

Weil went on to fleece an estimated 2,000 suckers (his own count) over a forty-year period, gleaning from $3 to $8 million in mostly big-store cons, depending on whether you believe the Kid's chroniclers or his own claim. He would pay the penalty five times out of twenty-five arrests, residing in federal and state prisons for his swindles. In the end, he mused: "Men like myself could not have existed without the victims' covetous, criminal greed."

Smack Goes the Sucker

That greed also made Buck Boatright, a train conductor turned sharper, into a rich man. A contemporary of Weil's, Boatright was the originator of the smack, a short con prevalent at the turn of the century. Boatright, with his knowledge of train schedules and types of well-fixed passengers, made Kansas and Missouri railroad depots his working quarters. He would pick out a prosperous-looking fellow waiting for his train and tell him he was also headed for the same destination, and would the mark care to walk about the town before train time to see the sights?

The lonely visitor more often than not agreed, and while the two were making their turns, a confederate would stop them and ask directions to some business office. In the course of conversation, Boatright would appear to inveigle the confederate into matching coins, throwing them into the air and then smacking them onto the backs of their hands (ergo the name "smack"). As the roper, Boatright would wink at the mark and tell him that whatever the toss, "you call heads and I'll call tails," thus preventing the confederate from winning in any event. Boatright would win, then the mark, but mostly Boatright, who intimated that he and the victim would split the profits later. In the course of the game, which never took more than fifteen minutes, the mark, thinking he was in on a good thing, fleecing some rube, genially lost to the man he had befriended in the train station. Boatright would collect from both men and then inform his confederate that he had a train to catch. The mark and Boatright would then retire to a nearby store or restaurant, and as they were about to divide their winnings, which sometimes amounted to as much as $200, half of the money being the victim's and the other half the confederate's, Boatright's associate would appear and denounce both men as con artists.

"Why, I just met this man in the train station," the mark would invariably and truthfully claim. And just as honestly, he denied any collusion with Boatright.

"I don't mind losing fairly in a game of chance," the confederate would say through a grimace and squint, "but you two will have to go your separate ways to prove you're not in together, and I'm gonna stand here and watch you fellows go."

Boatright would whisper to the sucker that they would meet later on the train and divide the spoils of their scam. Nodding, the mark would walk off in one direction while Boatright ambled in another, the confederate, hands on hips, watching them depart to assure their honesty. Naturally, the victim boarded his train, and after methodically checking each car, realized Boatright was not aboard and he had been bilked.

There are scores of short gambling cons such as the tat, which is worked by an inside man and a roper who ingratiate themselves with out-of-town visitors, and then "accidentally" find a pair of dice, one with the normal markings of one through six, the other with fives on four sides and sixes on two sides. The two con men simply bump bets and wedge the suckers between such bets while using their crooked dice.

The money box has long been popular as a short con, with hustlers building bank rolls to finance big-store or big-con games. One of the most adept money-box men was the redoubtable Victor "The Count" Lustig, who certainly rivaled any cons scored by Yellow Kid Weil, Boatright, and the Gondorf brothers.

Taking Big Al

Born in 1890 in Prague, Czechoslovakia, Lustig taught himself to speak English, German, Italian, and French while still a boy, and embarked upon the life of a con man at an early age. Through various gambling cons, Lustig worked his way to the United States in the early 1920s. Finding himself in Chicago, he fearlessly looked up the top resident gangster, Al Capone, and promised that he could double Capone's money—$50,000 was required to pad out what he himself would invest—if the racket czar was willing to put up the funds.

Such a sum was paltry to millionaire Big Al, but he didn't spend his money loosely, and while counting out fifty thousand-dollar bills to Lustig, Scarface growled: "Okay, Count, double it in sixty days like you said." This is exactly what the Count expected, and he quickly placed Capone's $50,000 in a safe-deposit box and then returned to New York to attend to some of his on-going schemes. Returning in about two months, Lustig went to Capone's headquarters and was shown into Al's coliseum-like offices. Capone motioned the bowing, derby-carrying Lustig to a chair while several blue-jawed goons surrounded him.

"You said you'd double that fifty thousand dollars of mine. What about it?"

The Count smiled apologetically. "Please accept my profound regrets, Mr. Capone. I'm sorry to report to you that the plan failed . . . I failed."

Capone's florid face reddened, his hamhock hands doubled into menacing fists. "Why, you—"

Calmly, Victor Lustig reached into his coat pocket, withdrew Capone's

A federal prisoner in 1936, Victor "The Count" Lustig bilked fortunes from marks in his money-box game. (UPI)

$50,000, and placed it on the broad mahogany desk before him. "Here, sir, is your money, to the penny. Again, my sincere apologies. This is most embarrassing. Things didn't work out the way I had thought they would. I should have loved to have doubled your money for you and for myself—Lord knows that I need it—but the plan just did not materialize."

The jowly gangster stared incredulously down at the neat stack of money on his desk, his mouth open, his fists unclenching. He sagged back in his chair. "I know you're a con man, Count," he finally managed in a weak voice. "I expected either a hundred thousand dollars or nothing. But this . . . getting my money back . . . well . . ."

Lustig stood up, airily brushing his lapel. "Again my apologies, Mr. Capone." He started to leave.

Scarface's massive forehead wrinkled and he pumped his portly frame upward with one thrust of his bearlike arms. "My God, you're honest!" he shouted, surprised at his own voice. Capone reached for his money. "If you're on the spot, here's five to help you along." He counted out $5,000 and gave it to the hustler. Lustig appeared startled, and then, mouthing his gratitude, pocketed the amount and departed. The $5,000 or something thereabouts is what Victor Lustig had been after all along, and all he had to do, he reasoned, was to play the role of an honest man, even though he felt nothing but contempt for such individuals. He was once quoted as saying: "Everything turns gray when I don't have at least one mark on the horizon. Life then seems empty and depressing. I cannot understand honest men. They lead desperate lives, full of boredom."

The Count's Fabulous Money Box

When exercising his considerable talents with the money box, life was anything but boring for the Count and his victims. The Count's money box, similar to almost every other machine used by hustlers in this short con, was a simple affair, a small box with a crank at the side. Lustig lured suckers to hotel rooms, where he displayed his marvelous machine, stating that it made perfect copies of twenty-dollar bills—and it did. He would place a genuine twenty on top of a stack of paper evenly cut to the same size. The mark was quietly informed that, because of the special plates and inking solution inside the box, one had to wait overnight before the new twenties "took." Special paper, Lustig carefully advised, used by the Treasury Department was available from a contact he had there.

Following a sweaty twenty-four hours, Lustig and his money-flushed sucker would begin to crank the money box, and *violà*—ten to fifteen twenty-dollar bills were spat out through a slot in the machine. These bills had been planted by Lustig in the box's false bottom, and when the crank was turned, the plain paper on top was carried to the false bottom and the bills to the top. Not once did Lustig fail to sell his device for less than $4,000 to the awed mark. (The box cost the Count about $15 to make.) This short con is often referred to as "the green-goods game," but as shown in a previous chapter, it is not; the green-goods con is a dexterous switch of parcels containing paper cut to the size of money.

An idea of what Lustig took in on his money box in one year is demonstrated by the following scores: Two merchants in Chicago paid $10,000 for the box; a businessman in Kansas City forked over $25,000; two pool-room owners in Butte, Montana were suckered for $43,000; several New York gamblers bought a box for $46,000; and a banker in California handed the Count a cool $100,000 for his useless machine. In that same year, 1927, Victor Lustig set up the wrong sucker in Crown Point, Indiana, taking the victim for $10,175 on the money box. Before he could escape the city limits, however, the mark tested the machine, found it a phony contraption, and soon had deputies putting the collar on the fleeing Lustig.

Thrown into the Crown Point jail, from which John Dillinger was to make a spectacular escape seven years later, Lustig hired a lawyer and tried to bargain with the victim, but the irate sucker, he learned, would press charges, intending to go the distance. The Count saw no other way out except to escape, and this he did by sawing his way through some cell bars (the file thoughtfully provided by his legal counsel, most said).

Treasury agents often attempted to arrest Lustig for his money box routine, but since he was really producing genuine bills, counterfeiting charges could not be brought against him. Success in this short con, however, led Lustig to counterfeiting, and that was the con man's downfall. His making and passing "the queer" eventually led to his arrest and permanent imprisonment.

Again it was the short-con money box that had proved so profitable to Lustig that propelled him into what he knew to be the highly dangerous crime of counterfeiting. "A smart boy never goes to the queer," he once said, but in 1930 he went against his own inclinations.

A Sheriff Sees the Light

At that time Lustig was a resident in a small Texas jail presided over by an avaricious sheriff named Q. R. Miller. The Count had been caught fleecing a sucker, and while awaiting trial discovered that Sheriff Miller was also the county tax collector.

It took little talking to interest the drooling Miller in Lustig's money box. Miller arranged the Count's release, and the two immediately retired to a hotel room, where Lustig demonstrated his money-making device. The sheriff, using county funds, paid off the hustler with $25,000 and scurried home to start cranking out his fortune. Miller was more than discouraged when nothing but blank paper came out of the slot. Screaming oaths and shaking his fists, he set upon Lustig's path, revenge flooding his mind.

Several months later, Miller found the Count living his usual luxurious life in Chicago and trapped him in his hotel suite. Drawing his six-shooter, the sheriff barked: "Talk fast, you eel. I'm gonna drill you for sure."

Lustig hurriedly went into another spiel. "Don't get excited," he cautioned Miller. "The only reason I took you for the twenty-five thousand was that I was desperate for cash to put over one of the biggest deals in my life—a deal that will make us millions!" The Count sighed as Miller lowered his pistol.

"Keep talking," the sheriff said, and sat down with the pistol still in his hand. Lustig explained that he had used Miller's money to buy a set of plates stolen from the U.S. mint, and all he needed now was enough money to buy a printing press to run off millions of dollars. The con man then blatantly pitched Miller for more money.

"All I need is another sixty-five thousand. If you can raise this, I'll make you my equal partner. What do you say?"

The already stung sheriff didn't hesitate. "I'm in." Miller returned to Texas, withdrew the $65,000 from county funds, and sent it along to Lustig, who exchanged the genuine money for $100,000 in counterfeit dollars. The blockheaded sheriff then proceeded to deposit the queer money in his own bank account, and was promptly arrested by Treasury agents and charged with counterfeiting. Miller stood trial and went to prison without implicating Lustig, but told a fellow inmate that he would "personally settle the score with the Count" when he got out.

The U.S. Treasury Department settled it for him. Lustig, convinced there was more cash in actually counterfeiting money than pretending to with his short-con money box, teamed up with an expert engraver named William Watts from Hutchinson, Kansas, and they quickly produced what federal agents thought was "some of the most skillfully executed queer ever encountered," in amounts from $5 to $100. For five years (1930–35) Lustig fenced $2,340,000 in counterfeit bills through a far-flung ring of passers. In May 1935, however, federal agents, through a tip, picked Lustig up on a Manhattan street corner. He was carrying two suitcases, and in one the agents found a key that led them to a storage locker in a subway station. Piles of counterfeit money and the original plates made by Watts were discovered, and Lustig was convicted for the first time in his twenty-seven years as a super con man.

He escaped from the Federal House of Detention in New York but was captured four weeks later in Pittsburgh. Sentenced to Alcatraz for twenty years for counterfeiting and breaking jail, Victor "The Count" Lustig never saw the outside world again. He died in Leavenworth in 1947, where inmates addressed him for years as, simply, "King Con."

Another money-box hustler was Wilson Pittsford. His machine, according to Secret Service agent U. E. Baughman, "was a handsome, wooden box which, when opened, exposed to view an elaborate-looking engine. When turned on, this machine made an impressive display of whirring gears, ringing bells, and flashing orange, green, and purple lights." This gizmo brought Pittsford enormous profits before federal agents mounted a conclusive case against him and sent him away for a long stretch.

Wishes for Sale

Obsolescence has overtaken such short cons as the hot seat, and the wipe. (See Chapter 2), but con artists are forever inventive. One hustler in Georgia made a fortune selling wishes. For $5 this character promised to make three wishes come true. His was a street approach for years, and he pried enough money from suckers to buy two houses, an office building, and a country retreat. Not until he decide to broaden his scope of operations via the U.S. mails was his scam exposed. The federal agent of the U.S. Post Office Inspection Service who arrested him outlined what this unusual con man promised to do for suckers: "He had a pot in which he burned the wishes [written down in a letter]. He said he had a four-motor airplane and he took the pot up forty-five thousand feet and burned the wishes up where the elements were not subject to the influence of the earth's movement. He could barely write his own name, but he owned a lot of property."

A Hollywood bunco operator made $5,000 in the space of about a week by bilking dozens of movie stars. He sold them "foolproof hangover pills." In the 1960s Los Angeles truck driver Richard Spencer sold degrees on the street from a mobile diploma mill, introducing himself as "chancellor of the Commonwealth, Research and Searchlight Universities" and "the don of Oxford Institute." He glommed thousands of dollars, but was finally arrested when, after receiving $700, he handed over several osteopathic degrees to a police investigator.

Begging Routines

Myriad methods are applied by hustlers working the short con. Begging is one of them. Today several sharpers work the large cities as well-dressed businessmen who have lost their wallets, victims are told, and require commuter fare home. Home is usually some distance, and a five-spot is not uncommonly rendered the spic-and-span type putting on the touch. The hustler, in turn, offers his business card and carefully writes down the sucker's name, promising with sincere gratitude to repay by mail that evening. One individual working this short con averaged $10,000 in a good year.

Children are often employed in begging cons. A young black boy whose acting talents certainly equaled anything Hollywood ever offered ingeniously mulcted customers in front of several distinguished Chicago nightclubs and restaurants for years. His take was in the hundreds, peaking in the 1969–70 season before his boyish appeal was snuffed out by adolescence.

The boy's approach was simple. Crying great tears, which ran pathetically over cherubic cheeks (like the Crying Kid a century before him), the boy, through his sobs, explained to well-dressed patrons that he and his six brothers and sisters had journeyed far from home to see a movie in the Loop. His little brother had lost the money entrusted to them by their widowed mother. Now the little family was not only out their simple, long-awaited entertainment, but had no way of returning home. Sympathetic nightclub patrons about to treat themselves to an expensive night on the town seldom could resist the boy's pitch, and handed over $5 with a smile. And it was not unusual for one of the boy's suckers to see this scamp pitch another person with the same spiel moments later; most (the author included) were delighted to be flimflammed by such a clever little fellow.

The Professional Fit-Thrower

Probably the most spectacular con man working the begging routine as a short con was George Gray, who, by his own figuring, took in about $10,000 a year for several years at the turn of the century. Gray's gimmick was to feign either an epileptic fit or a heart attack, usually in front of the residence of a well-to-do Manhattan citizen. Known as the "professional fit-thrower," this hustler, himself from a wealthy Brooklyn family, had the strange ability to simulate the bodily quakes and writhings of a man in the throes of an epileptic attack, and according to doctors at Manhattan's Presbyterian Hospital, he was "also a curiosity of nature in that he possesses the power of accelerating or retarding his heart action at will."

Gray's prosaic short con involved hurling himself to the pavement, shakily groping for a convenient stick, which he then inserted between his teeth while the alleged grand mal sent him into grotesque convulsions. This horrifying act usually brought forth the terrified resident of the house in front of which Gray had chosen to perform. He would be taken inside and restoratives applied to him, and minutes later money for transportation and medical treatment would be pressed upon him by the rich samaritan. Often as not, Gray feigned heart attacks with an equally convincing performance.

Gray did not confine his oddball operation to New York but plied his short con in Buffalo, Boston, New Haven, Newark, and several other East Coast cities.

New York's Police Department, however, had dozens of reports of him (victims described him as young, wearing an army hat, and missing a front tooth) and sought him for three years. Finally, in March 1902, overexposure ruined Gray's act.

As businessman Jesse L. Strauss was leaving his home on East Sixty-ninth Street in Manhattan, he saw a young, blond-haired man fall to the pavement, apparently stricken by some sort of seizure. Running up, Strauss and a business acquaintance, Milton Einstein, heard the prostrate man shriek: "Heart failure! Digitalis! Quick! I'm dying!"

Just as they were about to carry him inside, a curious bicycle police-man standing nearby, one Walter Leazenbec, walked over, and spotting the army hat and the cavity in the pathetic heart attack victim's open mouth, at once recognized from previous police descriptions con man George Gray.

"Okay, fellow, enough of that nonsense!" bellowed the cop. "Get up. You're under arrest for fraud."

Einstein was flabbergasted, and reproached officer Leazenbec. "Are you insane? This poor man is having a heart attack."

A doctor who had been summoned looked up and said: "Yes. His pulse is one hundred two."

Leazenbec frowned. "Yeah, I know all about that. But he's faking. He can do it. C'mon now, young fellow. Get yourself up and come along to the station."

To the amazement of the crowd gathered around him, Gray suddenly stood up, brushed off his clothes, and smiling faintly walked away with Leazenbec. After serving nine months for his short con, George Gray, the "professional fit-thrower," disappeared forever from the annals of con.

The Broken-Neck Con

Another bizarre hustler specializing in nature-faking short cons was Edward Pape, who engineered his broken neck, which resulted from a childhood injury, into a $75,000-a-year asset by 1907. Though offered kingly sums by circuses, sideshows, and dime museums, Pape preferred to fall off trolley cars, pretend to have sustained a broken neck, and then settle with the transit system for staggering amounts. According to one report of the day, "Pape can so alight from a trolley-car, slowing to stop, that he will suddenly fall and go rolling toward the gutter. Instantly, there is excitement, and a group of men to pick up the prostrate form of the injured man." Hurried to a hospital a set of x-rays would reveal Pape's broken neck, and, rather than stand the suit Pape immediately threatened to file against the trolley company, the firm would offer a huge cash settlement. A week after receiving this sum, Pape, using various aliases, would be off to another city, falling off another trolley car.

A detective for the New York City Transit System finally exposed Pape's con, and he was quickly convicted and sentenced to prison. From his cell, the talkative Pape described the difficulties inherent in his scam: "There was one time over in Philadelphia that was hell. I'd just finished my fancy fall, and they got me into the sickhouse and rigged out most to kill. They put hip-boots on me there in bed with their soles fastened to the footboard, and a rubber bandage under my chin and over my head. They put seventy-five pounds in weights on a cord and pulley-jigger to that bandage, and it nearly killed me all day long. At night I used to wait until it was dark, and then I'd haul the weights and put them under the blanket with me. Otherwise, I don't know how I'd'a got my sleep."

Con Down on the Farm

Farmers have been eternal victims of the short con. One of the most successful was the sex determiner sold by hustlers to farmers for half a century. The simple twine and lead device was simply held over an egg, and if it swung one way it was a hen, if it swung the other, a cockerel. Phony seed deals are still lucrative short cons for the enterprising hustler, and Indiana farmer George D. Rowlett was a typical victim. Rowlett was approached one spring day by two con men with a "personal recommendation" from a neighboring farmer. Should Rowlett purchase their extraspecial soybean seeds, which were extremely high priced, they, in turn, would buy his entire soybean crop at 75 cents above the market list at the Chicago Board of Trade. The prospect of a guaranteed income on an unharvested crop is impossible for any farmer to resist, and Rowlett was no exception, giving the two hustlers several hundred dollars for sixty bushels of soybean seeds and additional bushels of wheat seed, this crop also guaranteed at a top price. The seeds, to be delivered a month later, of course never arrived.

"If I'd met the man who sold me that seed," Rowlett later said, through gritted teeth, "after I'd just come in from plowing at three A.M., I'd have broken his neck."

The most ridiculous farm con ever conceived occurred at the time Mussolini was sending his enthusiastic Black Shirt troops against Haile Selassie's pathetically equipped Ethiopians. A con man in Alabama widely advertised the fuzzy fact that he was starting a "frog farm to grow froglegs for fighting fascists." The hustler pocketed thousands of dollars invested by patriotic suckers before going on to another con.

A Golf-Links Hustler

A distinctive master of the short con was Alvin Clarence Thomas, better known under his alias, "Titanic" Thompson. Thompson was on board the *Titanic* in 1912 with a group of sharpers who were fleecing passengers. When the ship sank, Thompson, the Hashhouse Kid, Indiana Harry, and Hoosier Harry managed to slip into some of the lifeboats and survive. Following their rescue, Thompson and the others not only put in maximum claims for lost baggage and valuables, but collected the names of those who had perished for fellow hustlers, so that they, too, could put in claims.

Thompson shared the dubious honor (along with "Nigger Nate" Raymond and William "Hump" McManus, Polly Adler's one-time boyfriend) of attending the last poker game played by gambler Arnold Rothstein before the "Big Bankroll" was murdered in 1928. Titanic was particularly adept at mulcting marks on the golf links. He was a superb player who convincingly feigned clumsiness on the course, betting heavily with unsuspecting golfers and losing. He would then mumble something about "getting even," double his bet, and then turn on the talent and win. Seeing his partner a bit vexed at losing, perhaps upward of $1,000, the con man would appear conciliatory, casually stating: "Look, I'm a fair man. I'll play you another round left handed, double or nothing."

The sucker, by this time, was certainly convinced that Thompson was impetuous, and maybe a little crazy. During the play of their first round, Titanic had made such zany bets as that he could knock a sparrow from a telegraph line with a golf ball or get his ball onto a green after thoroughly burying it in a sand trap. And after the victim had lost a round for a sizable amount of cash he was more than willing to take up Thompson's offer of left-handed play. Leaping at the bait, the mark and Thompson would begin all over again and Thompson would win handsomely, being a natural southpaw.

Though the golf courses in Texas were Thompson's usual stomping grounds, he and an unknown but gifted amateur once, in 1938, took two internationally famous golf pros on the links at Portsmouth, Virginia, for $10,000 in an single game. Until his death, Thompson averaged $250,000 each year in his incredible golfing short cons.

Dapper con man "Titanic" Thompson; he specialized in bilking wealthy golfers. (UPI)

Flimflamming Fatality

Of all the short cons, probably the most sinister are those dealing with death. In the world of con, this short game, repugnant to more dignified hustlers like Yellow Kid Weil, Lustig, and the Mizners, is called "selling stiffs" or "C.O.D." ("collect on death"). One of the earliest vultures operating short death cons was A. L. "Dead Man" Hicks, who is generally credited with the C.O.D. gimmicks still popular today. Hicks, scanning the death notices, especially in the rural papers (circa 1910), would spot a deceased man of means and mail off a fountain pen that bore the dead man's name in gilt letters. A letter to the man's widow informed her that her late husband had ordered the special "porographic" pen. Included in this C.O.D. package was a bill for $5. Almost always, the widow (or other relatives) felt obligated to pay for the delivery and kept the same as a remembrance. The pen, which cost Hicks about 25 cents, never worked anyway.

Fifteen years later a small army of short-con hustlers worked Hicks' pen gimmick for thousands of dollars each month, going directly from door to door where black wreaths were prominently displayed. One of the hustlers who was apprehended stated blandly: "People are so full of grief they seldom ask us questions. They rarely insist upon seeing written proof of the truth of what we say. Ordering that fountain pen was the last act of a father or brother, or whoever it was, they reflect. He had it made to suit his own tastes. It would be a pity not to take it. Sentiment makes them clutch at the bright new pen as another tie to the life that has gone."

Hicks was also first responsible for sending out Bibles imprinted with the deceased's name along with a bill for $6 (the Bible, of course, costs Hicks only a few cents; this doddering short con, though chronologically out of order, was effectively enacted in the motion picture *Paper Moon*). A plethora of C.O.D. items from good-luck charms to pianos ceaselessly flow to the doors of the dead to this day.

War Dead Cons

Particularly vicious were the short death cons flourishing during and after World War II and Korea. An Indian widow, whose husband had been killed and buried in France, was only one of thousands who received the following mimeographed letter:

Our organization, which is cooperative and nonprofit, has personal representatives stationed near all military cemeteries overseas. We can guarantee that the grave of your relative will be regularly and *personally* cared for. The initial fee is $30. After the first month, dues are $5 monthly, including fresh flowers. Give name, rank, and serial number of deceased. Send money order or cash—no checks.

The widow dutifully sent off the information and enclosed a money order for $30. After several weeks without hearing from the caretaker organization, she, like hundreds of others, wrote a letter of inquiry, which was quickly returned with the postal direction: "Not at Address Given." Gleaning thousands of dollars from their con, the hustlers had closed shop and skipped.

War-dead cons included the offer from the middle-aged, well-dressed hustler who appeared on the doorsteps of those who had lost a son, father, or brother in the war. He represented the International Photo Service, he said, and he produced samples of photos of military cemetaries and close-ups of soldiers' graves. For a mere $15 he promised to supply six photos, all from different angles, of the deceased's grave site. Taking the money, the con man left an address of his so-called studio, which later turned out to be an abandoned warehouse.

A gang of ghoulish con men were captured in Detroit shortly after World War II. In the back of a bungalow that served as their head-quarters, investigators found the flimflammers' "studio." Many mounds of earth in a row with white crosses on them had been marked with the names given the con men by war widows wanting photos of their hus-bands' graves. A Chicago flimflammer went even further by promising families, for a considerable sum, to "speed the return of your relative's body to the United States." Not one corpse was ever shipped.

Francis Gross, a one-time merchant seaman of Utica, New York, re-ceived a year-and-a-day prison sentence in June 1945 following a scam in which he promised the relatives of war dead to return the personal effects of slain servicemen, which he had allegedly obtained. After re-ceiving exorbitant fees, Gross, of course, sent nothing to the bereaved families. Judge Henry Goddard, in sentencing Gross, could not restrain his anger, commenting, "This is the lowest, meanest thing a man could do."

Reaping Nonexistent Life Insurance

One of the most energetic sharpers operating the short death con in the 1950s was Jake Max Landau. Like the swindling birds of prey before him, Landau was an avid reader of death notices, and spying a good mark, would inform widows that happy fortune had smiled upon them in the midst of tragedy, that their husbands had left unrecorded insurance policies in amounts ranging from $4,000 to $25,000. He offered these women, for a service fee of $29.75, to expedite the payment of the hidden policies. The response was overwhelming and con man Landau was soon wealthy, his only concern being how to dodge the inevitable follow-up complaints from his victims when the insurance monies failed to materialize. Landau, whose grandfatherly appearance of white hair and soft, kindly eyes hid the fact that he had once broken out of a Kentucky penitentiary, concentrated his death con in the Midwest, scoring with five hundred victims in the St. Louis area alone before his fraud was exposed and he was arrested.

A unique twist on the short death con was employed in New York in the late 1960s by an old woman from Yorkville, who traveled the state fainting on people's doorsteps. Revived by the house owner, the kindly grandmother sorrowfully produced hand-knitted pink baby clothes and told how she was en route to her granddaughter, her own child having died while giving birth to the infant. Such bathos was impossible for most compassionate victims to resist, and they usually wound up giving the nice old lady $15 to $25 travel fare to attend her daughter's mythical funeral.

"Mournful" Meeker Bilks the Bereaved

For sheer gall, nothing has surpassed in the short death con the exploits of Thomas "Mournful" Meeker, who operated widely about 1914. His business day began during the funeral of any well-to-do, middle-aged decedent. Attired in cheap but neat clothes, all in black, the lanky, cadaverous Meeker, his eyes red with apparent weeping, appeared at the home of the deceased, where the body, as was the custom then, was lying in state in a library or parlor. Mournful would softly introduce himself, as though assuming his name would be recognized as that of an old friend of the deceased.

The grief-stricken widow, son, or daughter invariably choked out something like, "Of course, I'm sure I remember Father talking about you."

His identity thus established, Meeker joined the mourners about the casket. Shortly, tears streaming down his face, moans and sobs escaping pathetically from his throat, Mournful would become the epitome of lugubriousness. No matter who in the room appeared deeply grieved, Meeker was more beside himself. His wails were louder, longer, deeper. His tears were endless. His hands quivered in grief, and his head nodded in almost uncontrollable anguish at the loss of his "dear, dear friend."

As the closest relatives of the dead man closed around Meeker to console him, he would usually blurt, through a handkerchief, his sincere apologies.

"But, my good man, why should you apologize?" he would be asked.

"Why . . . because . . . Mother . . . could not . . . attend," Mournful would stammer between sobs, appearing to everyone present to be tottering on the brink of hysteria.

Regaining his composure, but only momentarily, Meeker would explain. "Mother, as you are aware, is over seventy, and it has nearly killed her to know that she couldn't come to the funeral. I hate to tell you, but the fact is—" He broke down briefly, his sobs overtaking him, before continuing—"Mother had to sell her last good dress so I could travel here today. Neither of us have had anything to eat for over a day. Every cent we had went when my rascally partner defaulted, and I have just lost my last job trying to take care of my mother. I felt that I just had to come and explain, for I knew that you would be surprised at not seeing Mother at the funeral." Mournful would look up, screwing up his eyebrows in anguish, and wave toward the dead man: "And now he's gone and we'll never see him again!" At this juncture, Meeker would break down completely, his face buried in his handkerchief.

Moved and shocked, the kindly relatives would gently take Mournful into the next room, offering him financial aid that never dipped beneath several hundred dollars. Meeker valiantly resisted the loan, but after the usual insistence, he broke down and humbly accepted the funds foisted upon him, mumbling gratefully that it was "a temporary loan, to be repaid when I get on my feet again." He would then shuffle out in a broken-hearted manner, and once outside, check his watch and schedule and race on to the next funeral. Some reports have fixed Mournful's take in that early tax-free era as high as $1,000 a day.

Meeker's end was as dynamic as his act was melodramatic. He appeared at one funeral, told his story, and received his loan. Included among the relatives of the deceased who had listened so sympathetically to Mournful's tale was a powerful college fullback, who lost his own father a month later. And who should be at that funeral, telling the same story word for word, but Mournful Meeker. Concluding his act, Meeker once again again covered his sorrow-streaked face with the handkerchief, but instead of consolation and money, he received the shock of his miscreant life. To quote one report: "He was suddenly tackled, punted across the room, along the hall, and out the front door. Then, with a tremendous drop kick he sailed down the steps and into the arms of a passing policeman."

Arrested, Meeker was sent to prison for fraud. A kindly judge gave him a reduced sentence, so moved was he by the great tears that coursed down Mournful's face.

Eight

Sirens, Strumpets, and Smoothies

THE WOMAN-MAN STRUGGLE in the history of con is one of classic involvement. Every human emotion and psychological nuance is brought into devilish play, the victim wholly blinded by implicit trust or undying love, the hustler completely devoid of loyalty, affection, and pity.

Ellen Peck, the Vamping Con Queen

Beyond the financial and romantic intrigues of Betty Bowen (Madame Jumel); the enterprising Cassie Chadwick of Ohio, who passed herself off as the illegitimate daughter of Andrew Carnegie and lived in fat luxury until her bubble burst; Sophie Beck, of Philadelphia's Storey Cotton Company, who swindled $2 million in 1903 and lived like a queen in Paris; and the previously mentioned Sophie Lyons, the most persistent female con artist in America was the inimitable Ellen Peck. She conducted dual social life styles throughout her mature years with the dexterity of a master juggler. New York Police Inspector Thomas A.

133

The most durable con woman in history, Ellen Peck, who bilked suckers for forty years. (UPI)

Byrnes, long her nemesis, labeled her "queen of confidence women" and she painstakingly earned every letter in that regal title.

Ellen Peck was born Nellie Crosby in 1829, in the cozy hamlet of Woodville, New Hampshire. Her uneventful small town life inched to maturity and she became a schoolteacher (in the tradition of Etta Place of Wild Bunch fame).

She taught in Connecticut and then moved to New York City, where she met and married businessman Richard W. Peck. Three children later she was still a beautiful creature, once described as "demure in manner and faultless in face and form."

Mrs. Peck's First Millionaire

Moving to Sparkville, New York, Mrs. Peck spent her first fifty years in domestic tranquillity but something strangely stirred her being after celebrating her first half century of life. At fifty-one Ellen Peck suddenly packed her bags and took a trip to New York, first taking up lodging in a fashionable but sedate hotel much akin to her own personality, which one account states was "always unassuming in dress, without jewelry or expensive habits or tastes." Her figure and face were remarkably preserved, and it was these fleshly attributes, no doubt, that ingratiated her with one B. T. Babbit of Manhattan, a gullible old millionaire whose fortune had been made on the sale of soap.

Mrs. Peck contrived to meet the doddering Babbit at a social tea in the spring of 1880, and she at once became his confidante. He entertained Ellen in his mausoleum-like home on many occasions, and their dinners, each sitting at the end of a long table, were illuminated only by two candles to pierce the gloom of the cavernous manse. She visited his offices frequently, and many times was left alone in Babbit's inner sanctum while he hobbled off to attend board meetings. Mrs. Peck would occupy these empty moments by methodically rummaging through the tycoon's business papers and desk. One of her curiosity-filled searches yielded a portfolio containing $10,000 in negotiable bonds, and these she quickly slipped beneath her dress.

Days later, Babbit croaked out his agony to her. He had either "misplaced" the bonds, he said, or "some vile culprit has absconded with them." Not for a second did the ancient businessman suspect his matronly paramour. Nervelessly, Ellen, who had already sold the bonds and deposited the money in a secret bank account, volunteered her services as a detective. "I've had considerable experience in these matters," she announced brazenly. "The thief must be an associate in the firm or someone who knows, on intimate terms, an individual who has access to your office."

Disdaining the publicity that would certainly arise should he call in the police, Babbit gratefully accepted Mrs. Peck's offer to track down the guilty party. "Of course," she added, "such investigations are costly, and I must have expenses . . . I would never ask, but my widow's pension won't permit the financial extravagances of criminal detection."

"Whatever it costs," Babbit unthinkingly promised, "I will pay, even more than the bonds are worth, to catch the rogue." He wrote out a check to Mrs. Peck for $5,000 and she went about her investigation, quizzing Babbit's employees, conducting searches of his plant and offices, and according to her own report, "keeping dark rendezvous with sinister men" who might know the whereabouts of the missing bonds. The "case" dragged on for months, Mrs. Peck telling Babbit that she was getting closer each week to uncovering the bonds and the rascal who stole them. Her snooping activities cost a great deal of money, she pointed out, and funding her detective career had all but depleted her initial expenditures. Babbit wrote out another check for $5,000 and the imaginary hunt went on.

One day Babbit called on his tireless investigator at her hotel, only to discover that she had checked out, leaving no forwarding address. Suspicion poked through senility and Babbit hired some professional detectives, who ran Mrs. Peck to earth four years later in Sparkville. She was indicted for swindling and sentenced to four years in prison.

Paroled in a year, Mrs. Peck resumed her con career with a vengeance. Her next victim was another human wreck, the feeble and aptly named Dr. Jason Marks, whom she gulled for $20,000 in cash and jewelry. In 1887, then fifty-eight, Mrs. Peck had apparently not lost any of her physical charms, for she immediately employed her feminine wiles on the robber baron Jay Gould, an energetic womanizer, and hustled him for a considerable but undisclosed fortune. Police, at Dr. Marks's request, picked up Ellen and she was once again in prison.

After she was released in 1892, Mrs. Peck returned home to Sparkville and lived there quietly with her family for two years. Then the itch shuddered up her spine again in 1894 and Ellen was off to the great metropolis to seek more fortunes. Taking a suite of rooms in an elegant Brooklyn hotel, Mrs. Peck became Mrs. Mary Hansen, impersonating the wife of Admiral Johann Carll Hansen of the Danish Navy. The reputable Hansen was away on an extended vacation at the time, and during his absence Ellen Peck borrowed freely on his name from banks, some estimates of this scam being upward of $50,000, before fleeing when bank investigators appeared at her hotel.

A Doctor Succumbs

Moving into a brownstone under a different name months later, Mrs. Peck went to work on a Brooklyn neighbor, Dr. Christopher Lott, an octogenarian whose sexual appetites had apparently not dwindled with the wrinkling years. The athletic Mrs. Peck not only wore out the good doctor with her bedroom exercises to the point where he had to quit his practice, but exhausted his life savings of $10,000, which he gave to her in daily installments. Inside of a month he was a physical wreck and financially ruined. (Later Dr. Lott exclaimed: "She was the last great craving of my life.")

Exhausted by his fornicating bouts with the pulchritudinous Ellen, Dr. Lott took to bed in Mrs. Peck's own home. Ellen quickly hired a trained nurse, Miss Nellie Shea, to succor the doctor back to health, thinking there were more funds yet available in his account. Then, upon learning that Miss Shea had accumulated considerable savings, Mrs. Peck subtly developed what one report describes as "an unnatural and unwholesome liaison" with the nurse. Nellie forked over her savings, too, about $4,000.

Swindling the Diamond Merchants

Apprehended in 1897, Ellen Peck was once again behind bars, sentenced by Judge Cowing, while he himself resisted a bold proposition from the dogged con woman, to five years in Auburn Prison. Upon her release, Mrs. Peck traveled to the old homestead in Sparkville, where her husband, Richard, no doubt one of the most trusting spouses of that century or any other, welcomed her without admonishment or expressing a shade of belief in her guilt. Months later she was back in New York, hustling an elderly diamond merchant named John D. Grady. Ellen persuaded Grady that $21,000 in diamonds were not as safe in his vault as they would be in her kitchen cupboard ("After all, Mr. Grady, who would think to look in such an unlikely place as my pantry?") and quickly sold some of the gems and fled. Caught again for the Grady caper, Mrs. Peck faced twenty-five indictments, but, incredibly, this time she was acquitted. Her demeanor upon the witness stand had improved over the years, and jurors were treated to an impressive "wronged woman" act.

Days after her release, Mrs. Peck victimized a Cuban jeweler for a

$12,000 score. Her swindling net caught furniture dealers, money lenders, and bankers by the dozen. The disposal of the remaining diamonds she had conned from Grady and the Cuban presented a problem that Ellen thought she could solve simply by placing an ad in a newspaper offering them for sale. This move brought con man and convicted felon Julius Columbani and a new professional twist into her shamefully wicked career. Answering the ad, Columbani offered Mrs. Peck, in lieu of cash for her diamonds, negotiable Richmond County bonds. She accepted and then discovered that she, one of the most astute con women of her time, had in turn been swindled. The bonds had been recently stolen. Rather than risk fencing these, Mrs. Peck went to her arch-enemy Police Inspector Byrnes, the man who had tracked her down and arrested her on numerous occasions, and revealed Columbani's swindle. Byrnes and Mrs. Peck set a trap for the thief in a room over a Sixth Avenue saloon to which Ellen lured the con man on the pretext of acquiring more bonds (she had been careful to inform Byrnes that she had paid her own cash for the bonds, never mentioning the diamonds she had conned from her marks).

The rendezvous scene was luridly melodramatic. Columbani arrived and demanded more diamonds, waving bond certificates in the air. Ellen Peck nervously knocked over a lamp, a prearranged signal to Byrnes. His detectives burst through the door. Columbani drew a revolver and shouted: "You bulls will not take this man alive!"

Standing to one side as the thief kept the police at bay, Mrs. Peck opened her purse and withdrew her own revolver, which she coolly fired at the only man to ever victimize her in a con scheme. The bullet pierced Columbani's hand, and with a shriek he dropped the revolver and dove out the window, crashing to the pavement below. Policemen carried him away with arms and legs broken as Ellen Peck peered smugly from a second-story window. In moments, she had forgotten the sting of being suckered as grand new schemes, thanks to Columbani, shimmered in bright visions before her.

The con man's use of stolen bonds convinced Ellen Peck that such devices were in natural keeping with her own ideas of grift. The difference was that her bonds and deeds to expensive real estate would not be stolen but mythical. From 1895 to 1905 Ellen Peck was unusually active in working the con. "Age seemed to sharpen her wits," one report had it.

The Stinging of a Roughrider

A typical Mrs. Peck scam in this decade culminated in 1898. Working with three confederates, Mrs. Peck stung a well-known German businessman, Franz Mayer, in Astoria, New York. Mayer, who had raised a regiment of volunteers to ride with Teddy Roosevelt in the Spanish-American War, wanted to put his wealthy sign-making business in order before leaving for the front. At that time Mayer and his wife owned all the stock, but the businessman thought they should sell some of the shares to provide his family with funds while he was away at war.

Informing his company clerk of such desires, Mayer was soon approached by two businessmen, George N. Van Zand and Hugh Mason. The clerk had sent them along, they said, and without fanfare the two offered Mayer the deeds to 10,000 acres of coal and woodlands along the Big Sandy River in Kentucky, which they claimed was worth more than $50,000. Though he preferred cash, Mayer told the pair, such an exchange would certainly be to his benefit, and he turned over $46,000 in the sign-making company's stock, which was then valued at $100,000. The gullible Mayer was soon visited by another member of Mrs. Peck's gang, Miss Jessie B. Seal, who exchanged mortgages on property near Atlantic City, New Jersey, for 8,000 additional shares in the company. Days later, while Mayer was being fitted for the smart officer's uniform he was to wear into the battle at Roosevelt's side, an elderly and distinguished grande dame, carrying herself with regal bearing, was shown into his office. It was the indefatigable Ellen Peck. She was introduced to Mayer by Miss Seal, who had been introduced by Van Zand and Mason. Mrs. Peck, by then so notorious she had assumed an alias, quickly got to the point. She had heard that Mayer was exchanging stock for ideal mortgages and deeds, and since she had "always wanted to go into the sign-making business," she had confidently brought along title deeds to 8,000 acres of lush land in Presidio County, Texas. Mayer jumped at the chance to acquire such a tract of land, and quickly signed over the last 15,000 shares of his company in exchange for the deeds.

Arriving the next morning, Mayer found a tough-looking thug guarding his office door. After much arguing he was permitted inside, only to be greeted solemnly by Van Zand, Mason, Miss Seal, and Ellen Peck.

The elderly woman with the finely chiseled face stepped forward and announced: "Mr. Mayer, we shall have to ask you to leave the premises. We, as the stockholders possessing all of the shares in this firm, have voted you out."

"Voted me out?" Mayer shouted.

Upon a motion to the bozo at the door, Mayer was collared and thrown from his own plant. He raced home and began to check the deeds and mortgages the gang had passed to him. Mrs. Peck and her associates speedily liquidated the company's assets and changed the name of the firm. More than $100,000 on this flimflam passed into the con ring's hands, Ellen Peck receiving 80 percent of the score. She left on an extended vacation in company with Miss Seal, while Van Zand and Mason remained behind to milk the firm dry. The scheme was exposed weeks later, when Mayer proved to authorities that the deeds and mortgages given him in return for his company's stock were worthless. By the time Van Zand and Mason were arrested there was nothing left of Mayer's business; he was utterly ruined, not even having enough funds to pay off the mortgage on his own house.

The day Mayer declared bankruptcy, a New York newspaper reporter appeared at the sign-making plant. His path was barred by a towering, brutish-looking fellow.

"Why are you on guard here?" the reporter inquired.

"To keep that German fellow Mayer out of the place," the goon replied through curling lips.

"But the men who swindled Mr. Mayer are in prison and the women have fled."

"I don't know nuthin' about that," the strong boy said. "I'm paid to guard against that fellow and that's what I'm doing."

"Who pays you and when?"

"I get the cash through the mail every week. That nice old lady sends it."

That nice old lady went on with her far-flung cons, her last important score being the swindling of Normand, Wilson and Schubert, a New York real estate firm, of $2,400. Again she had attempted to pass off her nonexistent land in Kentucky, but she was apprehended shortly after pocketing the money and, at seventy-nine, was sentenced to twenty years at Auburn Prison.

Mrs. Peck languished behind bars for two years. An appeal for her pardon based on her advanced years was turned down in 1909 by Governor Hughes, who adamantly insisted that "old age is no excuse for crime." His successor, Governor Dix, was more sympathetic, and he granted Mrs. Peck a full pardon in 1911. The eighty-two-year-old con artist returned to her Sparkville home and her husband, still as gullible as any of her hundreds of victims had been, absolutely refused to believe in her guilt, stating that his wife, whose court trials had bled him white, was "a victim of circumstances and her own generosity." He borrowed money from friends to provide Ellen with an enormous fete to celebrate their golden wedding anniversary. Her children refused to be present at the occasion, long since having turned against their flimflamming parent.

Police Inspector Byrnes thought he had heard the last of Mrs. Peck, whose illicit earnings, secreted in distant bank accounts and never recovered, he estimated to be well over $1 million. Then came a report in 1913, when Ellen Peck was eighty-four, that she had conned a Latin American businessman aboard a steamer bound for Vera Cruz. She had compromised him, the businessman later complained, in his stateroom (which certainly attested to Ellen Peck's remarkable physical preservation and endurance). He had signed over several plantations to her before stomping down the gangplank with empty pockets. The hunt was on again, and investigators found the con woman once more at home, ill in bed. They hadn't the heart to make an arrest, nor much evidence against her, so she was merely given a lecture.

Bristling indignantly, Mrs. Ellen Peck rose on one elbow and said: "How dare you? There is nothing in my life that is tainted. Gentlemen, you are looking at a devoted wife and a hard-working mother." When she died, policemen across the land sighed in relief.

Con Lady with an Amorous Spouse

Where Ellen Peck in all her con sorties never promised marriage but companionship, marriage was the bait in the celebrated Halliott-Villiers case of a century ago. New York police had to contend with Mrs. Peck, but the ravishing con woman Jeanette Villiers became the exclusive quarry of the relentless Pinkerton Detective Agency. The pert Mademoiselle Villiers and her subtle marriage grift in Baltimore in 1868 filled many hours of Alan Pinkerton's time.

Three years after the Civil War, a wealthy old man named Willett died, leaving his entire estate to his pretty young wife. The widowed Mrs. Willett decided to live in relative comfort and moved into one of Baltimore's more lavish hotels. One afternoon at tea she was introduced to a charming French girl, newly arrived in the United States, named Jeannette Villiers. The Frenchwoman, in turn, introduced a dashing young man, Henry Halliott, alleged son of a ranking Union officer.

Jeanette Villiers, who shortly took up residence with her friend Mrs. Willett in a new house, encouraged an aggressive courtship between Halliott and the widow lady. Miss Villiers not only managed Mrs. Willett's house, but was aware of her employer's vast wealth almost to the penny; the widow kept nothing from her. The affair between Halliott and Mrs. Willett deepened until the widow's entire life seemed to center on the young man, whose attentive presence strongly suggested imminent nuptials.

Suddenly, in early 1869, Henry Halliott became seriously ill. Mrs. Willett rushed to his bedside, and to her hand-wringing horror, discovered him dying. As she held him in her arms, the handsome Lothario weakly murmured a confession, out of love for her, he said. Jeanette Villiers was really his wife, he admitted, and she was with child. Please, madam, he implored, take care of my little family.

Mrs. Willett, the soul of gullibility, never flinched from her promise to the dying Henry Halliott. Following Halliott's "death" and funeral, which Mrs. Willett did not attend (Jeanette Villiers did), the grief-stricken widow, in the company of her lawyers, turned over $10,000 in cash to the pregnant French lady. Three months later Jeanette gave birth to a boy. The generous Mrs. Willett made a formal gift of another $40,000 in government bonds to the mother and child, who promptly vanished. Mrs. Willett's lawyer thought the disappearance of Mrs. Halliott and her child suspicious, and he called in the Pinkertons to trace her whereabouts. The detectives found a clerk in a Baltimore hotel who had been fired for shady activities, and this man admitted that Halliott never died but, instead, had collected his wife and child and moved to St. Louis, where the family was living in opulence.

Pinkertons found them and tendered a full report to Mrs. Willett's lawyer, and he passed the information on to his client.

The widow's reaction to being bilked out of $50,000 by two adroit schemers of the matrimonial con was surprisingly indulgent. In fact, she prohibited any legal action against the two sharpers. Further, when the mulcted widow remarried, she and her husband were often seen socially with the grifting Halliotts. Though scorned, Mrs. Willett, like so many a mark after her, could not bring herself to admit to the frailty of her own emotions. Once touched by love for a rascal, it was impossible for her to recognize or even act upon his faithless betrayal or the ersatz bond of friendship so expertly engineered by the shrewd Jeannette Villiers.

The Feminine Fleecer from Natchez

Where Mrs. Peck was matronly and Miss Villiers sisterly, Lulu Cummings was an overt but stylish vamp. She roared into Chicago from Natchez in the mid-1920s, her arrival ballyhooed by the most rakish rogues in the city. Several long-distance calls were made to one of Chicago's swankiest hotels by a secretary who demanded the finest suite for Mrs. Cummings, and she arrived to red-carpet treatment. Adorned with dazzling jewels and accompanied by body servants, this blue-eyed southern belle was an instant hit. Her suite of rooms was full of salesmen almost from the moment of her arrival. Establishing the fact that her plantation outside of Natchez was one of the largest in Mississippi, Mrs. Cummings, a widow (naturally), made expensive purchases of gowns, jewelry, paintings, much of which was charged to her hotel account.

Chicago's toddling society embraced Lulu from the start, and she received invitations to every important social event on the calendar, making it a point to attend the charity balls and suppers. On these occasions she would choose among the gentlemen admirers surrounding her—most of whom were married men of means—and coax them into buying trinkets for her, the payment going to the poor. Moments later she would discover that her purse was missing or that she was low on cash, how foolish. Money and checks were heaped upon her, temporary loans, she insisted, but they were, of course, never repaid, and no men-

tion ever made of them by her tuxedoed escorts. Many of these gentlemen, the veritable cream of Chicago's business community, visited Lulu
in her hotel suite long after the city had gone to sleep.

In the space of two weeks, Mrs. Cummings had purchased $50,000 in
goods, furiously writing her own checks to cover payment. The cash
received from her admirers she pocketed. One of her dinner companions
was the famed lawyer Clarence Darrow, and she was also seen with the
millionaire sons of the city's industrial giants. Her whirlwind social success was unparalleled in the history of the metropolis. Lulu's famous
seductions were not scandals but news.

When her hotel bill peaked at $10,000, the manager was compelled to
ask for payment. Lulu discussed the matter over a quiet candlelit sup-
per in her suite. The manager was instantly smitten; Lulu vowed her
undying love. She would pay, she promised, but she must first make a
trip to Kentucky to cash some bonds. Leaving several trunks behind, the
Dixie vamp departed with maid, a train of luggage filled with gowns
and other loot, and never returned. The trunks she left behind as
security were found to be filled with old newspapers and telephone
books.

The manager, cursing himself for a fool, sent through Mrs. Cummings's check, which she had left in partial payment for her hotel bill.
It, like all of those scattered about the town, bounced Ping-Pong ball high.
The manager went to the hotel president, and he called in a private
detective, one Leonard Johnson, who, through long-distance phone calls
made by Mrs. Cummings, tracked the lady con artist to Louisville, Kentucky, where she was living in luxury in one of the finer hotels.

Johnson cornered Lulu, then living under the alias of Mrs. Fitzmaurice,
in her suite and demanded she pay the Chicago hotel bill of $10,000 or
he would call the police. "I'll wait in the lobby for half an hour before I
call the cops." Lulu said that was more than enough time, and in the
space of twenty minutes, responding to half a dozen phone calls made
by the comely flimflammer, four prominent Louisville gentlemen appeared. None of them saw each other, so precise was Lulu's timing.
Johnson was called up to Lulu's room.

"Here," she said haughtily, and handed him the $10,000. "I'd like a
receipt."

The detective wrote out a receipt and departed, shaking his head at the thought of the speed with which Lulu had gulled four more men into paying off, certainly a standing record in the history of con.

Marie Stanley, Always a Bride

Speed was not as essential to Marie Stanley, female flimflammer superb, who took her time fleecing suckers in five midwestern states twenty years after Lulu Cummings had faded from the scene. Rural squires were Marie's usual victims, and she often posed as a magazine or newspaper writer interviewing interesting farmers. One of her marks was a well-to-do tiller of the soil who was also a bachelor, one of the facts Marie made sure to check in advance. The victim also owned a plane, and under the pretense of interviewing the gentleman pilot, Marie Stanley went to work. After much pitching of woo, the article on flying farmers was forgotten and plans for a glorious wedding ensued.

The groom was surprised that his bride-to-be had a dowry to fatten his already considerable bank account. Marie told the sucker that she wanted to sell her dress shop (at other times it was a beauty parlor, small newspaper, or apartment building) before the wedding. A customer in Detroit wanted to buy the business for $45,000, she explained, but there was a little problem of hurry-up financing. The mortgage of $9,000 on the shop could hold up the deal, and she unhappily admitted that she had only $3,400 to pay off the bank. She would require only $5,600 to glean the $36,000 profit.

Her ploy seldom failed, and the mark thought the small investment a mere trifle in return for a loving wife and more ready cash. The sucker invariably arranged for a cashier's check, and Marie was off to settle her business, blowing kisses and promising to return soon to her future farming spouse. Of course, after cashing the check, Marie Stanley always returned to her husband and five children, who lived in a trailer camp outside of Lima, Ohio.

Marie's simple scam reaped her close to $100,000 before FBI agents picked her up on charges of fraud. (The Bureau could not enter any con case unless checks were cashed across a state line for more than $5,000.) A host of suckers fell for Mrs. Stanley's routine, which never took more than a few days to complete. In Minnesota a farmer was bilked for $5,000; a Wisconsin hog dealer sold his animals and gave her $2,450; a farmer in Illinois pressed $2,500 into her hand; and another country jake forked over $3,500 in South Dakota.

When finally apprehended, Marie Stanley staunchly maintained that she had swindled no one, that her male accusers (not all of these men testified against her, so entranced were they with her charms) had defaulted on love and that they had merely paid for her sexual favors. Though she tried desperately to con the jury into believing this hokum, Marie Stanley was trapped by her own words. When arrested, she had blurted to FBI agents, "I always told them no in the beginning, because it made them want me more."

The Many Lives of Mildred Hill

Washington confidence woman Mildred Hill mulcted hundreds of lonely men in her mail-order marriage con. (WIDE WORLD)

Probably the only matrimonial con artist to ever sucker more pigeons than Marie Stanley was a sixty-four-year-old woman jailed in Washington, D.C. According to one postal inspector, "she had so many old goats on the string that she used a mimeograph machine for her come-on correspondence." This woman was the notorious Mildred Hill, who had given birth to ten children, most of whom she later put to work in her confidence game, keeping them busy at writing love letters to the forty or fifty men always kept dangling on the matrimonial string.

Along with each mimeographed letter—none of her would-be suitors thought such letter-writing practices unusual—Mrs. Hill enclosed a picture of herself, or rather a picture she claimed was of herself. It was really a photo of her attractive twenty-year-old daughter. In her love correspondence, Mildred was always careful to mention her unfortunate need for money. Cash and checks flowed to her from cities always more distant than five hundred miles from Washington, D.C., a rule that was strictly kept by this Delilah. The money went for train tickets, clothing, food, and especially for Mildred's ailing mother, the con woman lamented. If the male suitor was pertinacious enough to come to Washington, Mrs. Hill met him and impersonated her own mother, explaining that her beauteous daughter had unexpectedly departed for Florida. She milked the sucker of more money for several days, and then showed him a telegram. Her daughter, the wire starkly announced, had eloped with a used-car salesman. The sad suitor returned to Butte, Montana, jilted and fairly broke.

For years Mildred's scheme worked marvelously. Then greed got the better of her and she began to travel, again impersonating her own mother, to the cities where potential suitors awaited her approval. Mrs. Hill's inspection was severe, and she always found prospective grooms unworthy of her daughter's hand but not before mulcting them for more money with which to pay for an alleged operation or buy a house for the soon-to-be newlyweds.

Her end came in 1945. One of Mrs. Hill's Chicago suckers called Washington to talk to his betrothed and was informed that she was in Chicago. Mildred showed up at the victim's Chicago home some hours later.

"But where is your daughter?" the suitor inquired.

"Oh, she's in Washington, poor dear," Mildred explained. "She's been ill these last few weeks and our family doctor thinks an operation might be necessary." Handkerchief-daubed tears followed. "Such medical expenses are so costly these days."

"How interesting," the client said, and asked Mrs. Hill if she would like a cup of coffee. She nodded, and the suitor walked into another room and called the police. Following a quick trial, the multifaceted Mildred Hill received a five-year prison sentence.

Con Man in Search of a Dowry

Competing with Mrs. Hill for conquests in the matrimonial con was a spry individual named Allen McArthur, alias Ashur McAvoy. This sharper fairly whirlwinded his way through scores of love-starved females eager to marry and give him anything he so desired, including their life savings. McArthur's game was to scrutinize the lovelorn columns in all the major cities, check the likely prospects, and fire off an ardent letter to his future wife. Upon receiving a favorable response, McArthur hurriedly packed his bags and was on his way to mulct another fortune. He was on a tight schedule. The con man would set up his victims by the half dozen, usually in neighboring cities, and allow himself no more than forty-eight hours to complete his swindle.

If one victim was located in Chicago, McArthur would prime another in Milwaukee and a third in St. Paul, going north by short hops and saving considerably on travel expenses. His routine never varied. The Chicago sucker, whose ample affluence was established, would meet him on a Monday. Early the next day, posing as a wealthy salesman from San Francisco, McArthur would discover his traveler's checks missing, and almost at the same moment, receive a wire (which he sent to himself) reading something like: "Your presence urgent to conclude $1 million deal." Frightfully embarrassed, McArthur had no trouble in relieving his adoring fiancée of $500 to $1,000 as a temporary loan for expenses, to be repaid when he concluded his important business conference. In two days he would be on his way to the next town and the next mark.

The con man became so successful that the U.S. Post Office, besieged by irate victims demanding McArthur's capture, had a special agent assigned exclusively to his case. Inspector Adolph Anderson started out by placing the same ad in almost every major newspaper across the country. It read:

> I am a widow, 48 years old. I have a farm and my friends say I look fifteen years younger. I have $8,000 in the bank. I will marry the right man. (Signed) Mrs. Alice R. Carroll, P. O. Box 65, Stillwater, Minn.

Anderson was inundated with responding love letters, 224 to be exact, and within that pile of gushing, mawkish prose reposed a missive, tactfully worded, from a man whose handwriting matched McArthur's. Anderson, as Mrs. Carroll, wrote back and encouraged the con man to visit her in a Chicago hotel. The meet was in a tenth-floor suite (the postal inspector wanted to make sure McArthur would not escape via the windows). An attractive policewoman played the part of Mrs. Carroll as Anderson waited behind a bedroom door.

McArthur arrived breathlessly, dismissing the first day's ritual of romance and going right into his act. As soon as the flimflammer had incriminated himself, Anderson leaped into the room and made his arrest.

The postal inspector and the police woman were startled when Mc-Arthur broke into high-pitched laughter.

"What's the matter with you?" Anderson asked.

"I knew this whole thing was fishy as soon as I walked in the room."

"Why?"

Poking a finger toward the policewoman, McArthur grunted. "This dame here was too glad to see me. Usually they are so damned coy you get sick."

Kindly George Ashley

Matrimonial clubs, though many are run along legitimate lines, have long been a hotbed of love cons, and the most flagrant of these in recent history was Life's Estate, Ltd., operated by a portly white-haired gent named George Ashley. The distinguished-looking Ashley had served two prison terms, and was wanted on a federal warrant for failure to pay a $6,000 fine (due in 1940), by the time his Los Angeles-based lonely-hearts club came into existence.

Ashley believed in advertising, and his come-on want ads soon had bevies of women signing his rolls. Males were charged $100 a year dues, but they were discouraged from joining. Ashley, who was married, was after the women. Ladies over age forty were charged $150, and those under, $100 annually. From the elaborate questionnaires these gullible females filled out, Ashley had a complete financial picture of his victims, as well as their personality traits and sexual interests, so he could gear his approach with pinpoint accuracy.

His pitch varied with each woman as did his name; Ashley was also known to many marks as M. Georges Fauyer. His expanding club, he would explain, required fresh capital to open branch offices, and wouldn't the lovely lady care to invest in a sure thing? Or sometimes he was about to buy a theater or a block of apartment houses. At times, especially with his most attractive clients, he offered himself.

"Your chart interested me so much that I decided to see you myself," he would coo to a new arrival. To some he was a gentleman with conservative tastes looking for a "life mate." To others he was a sexy aggressor who caused the heart to thump faster and the eyelids to flutter. One female smiled as she recalled how Ashley/Fauyer took her to his office, and looking her up and down, "grinned lewdly" and said, "I'd love to get my hands on you." The same woman, who gave the con man $10,000 after he promised to marry her, fondly remembered how "one day he came up and put his arms around me and kissed me."

Ashley would sell anything to his clients. One lonely woman gave him $7,500 for a half share in a nonexistent branch office of Life's Estate, Ltd. He bilked $34,000 from a seventy-two-year-old nurse. Of the 3,000 members listed in the club's files, Ashley had conned at least 750, banking an estimated $250,000 in three years. In May 1950, acting on complaints from suckered members, police and detectives from the Better Business Bureau formed a raid to close the club, only to find the lonelyhearts con man gone. Rummaging through the club's files, investigators found a manuscript Ashley had written while in prison. It was entitled: "I Wanted to Be Somebody."

Maurice Paul Holsinger, a Sharper's Swinger

The elusive Maurice Paul Holsinger, expert in the matrimonial con, tried to evade arrest dressed as a woman. (WIDE WORLD)

Another lonelyhearts money hunter, Maurice Paul Holsinger, ran a club briefly in Washington, D.C., that netted him $1,200 in only a few days. His club was mobile, and he next appeared in Philadelphia, cleaning out the purses of lovesick women to the tune of $7,500 in a week. Holsinger eluded police on his trail, which at first appeared strange. He was one of the most identifiable con men in the matrimonial racket—"He was an odd-looking creature with a head like a billiard ball," one account related —yet he always managed to slip through police dragnets. Then came a report that Holsinger had purchased a wig for $220. It was not a toupee, authorities learned, but a woman's wig with long tresses; the bald-headed Holsinger was scurrying about the country dressed like a woman. He was finally nabbed at the airport in Des Moines, Iowa.

"You brutes!" screamed the mink-clad female as agents grabbed her. With long, pointed fingernails clawing, high-heeled shoes kicking, Holsinger was taken into custody. As they neared a gate with their shrieking captive, a man held up his hand and shouted to the agents: "Stop manhandling that woman!"

With that an officer lifted Holsinger's wig to reveal to the bug-eyed Galahad a shining bald head. "Hello, sucker," Holsinger barked as he was led away.

A phalanx of con men have operated the matrimonial racket, the notoriously successful being Nathaniel Herbert Wheeler, who bilked 150 women over a period of ten years for $1 million; Los Angeles rake John Leonard Simmons, who wooed and ran from more than 50 flighty females with about half a million dollars; Joseph Levy, who ran wild through the boudoirs of the Midwest for a decade, swindling close to a million before making the FBI's most-wanted list and being captured by agents at the fifty-dollar window at Churchill Downs on April 30, 1953. But the most fabulous flimflammer of the lovelorn to date remains the unforgettable Sigmund Engel, last of the old smoothies, who went his fellow hustlers one bold and crazy step further; he actually married every woman he conned, thus becoming America's most outstanding bigamist.

Sigmund Engel, the More the Marrier

This twentieth-century Bluebeard of con, after fifty years of marrying and bilking women, particularly widows with substantial savings accounts, took his last fall in 1949 at the age of eighty (police, however, claimed he was only seventy-three, and therefore physically able to serve out a stiff sentence for his lonelyhearts transgressions). From the turn of the century to that year, Engel had married at least 200 women and bled them dry of $6 million by his own count. On the way to his last lockup, Engel, in dulcet tones through a wide, wrinkled smile, told reporters: "The age of woman does not mean a thing," adding zing to the cliché of "after all, the best tunes are played on the oldest fiddles."

Engel fiddled and diddled on an international basis throughout Europe in his twenties—his exact birthplace remains unknown—marrying his first pigeon in Vienna, Austria. He then married his way through London and Paris. After bilking dozens of women there, Engel hastily

Holsinger at the police station after his capture, his wig and fur coat removed. (WIDE WORLD)

departed for the green shores of America, half a step ahead of the gendarmes. Engel's police record, dating back to 1917 in America, showed twenty-two arrests and four prison terms; the dossiers also revealed that Engel, under many aliases, had married in the U.S. at least 40 women before 1927.

The marrying hustler worked with incredible speed. His approach seldom changed. After determining the wealth of a middle-aged unmarried woman—he preferred widows—Engel would "accidentally" meet his victim in one of the better restaurants or hotels.

Turning about in a startled manner, he would exclaim in awe: "Why, you look just like my wife!"

Any woman would ordinarily dismiss such a remark, some perhaps resenting the comparison made by a man already hooked. Knowing this, Engel would shuffle his hundred-dollar shoes a bit and then quickly append, "I mean my former wife, God bless her, she's dead these last four years."

Engel as Movie Magnate

This pitch would quite naturally lead to words of sympathy from the victim, and Engel would then suggest having lunch, at the same time, while glancing at his watch, audibly reminding himself to call Hollywood; his motion picture studio was expecting his verbal okay to continue shooting the multimillion dollar film he was making with a temperamental star. This tidbit of news never failed to arouse the female sucker's avid interest. She not only bore an "amazing resemblance" to the con man's deceased spouse, but the movie mogul was actually inviting her to break bread with him. None ever refused.

In the course of the conversation, Engel introduced himself as "Carl Arthur Laemmle, Jr.," the son of the man who ran Universal Studios. (At other times, depending on the type and tastes of his female mark, he was a millionaire businessman, an oil tycoon, a shipping magnate.) Engel's offhanded prattle over lunch would paint pictures in vivid brushstrokes of tinsel town and the sylphs and swains that swam in its glamour, always high glamour. Then would come the spiel about the rigors of having to be a movie producer, of being subject to the mad idiosyncracies of stars, the names of which changed over the years in Engel's monologue to suit the contemporary scene.

The victim was entranced. Not only did she remind this kind, thoughtful, gentle soul of his late wife, but she knew, as some stated later, that she was the right kind of down-to-earth woman this practical mogul needed. She could help him deal with the fancies of make-believe, she certainly could.

Courtships for Engel were fast and furious. He spent lavishly on his fiancées, most of whom agreed to marriage within the first few days of their meeting. The con man was careful to drop his checkbook or bank statements, always from banks in distant states, which would reveal enormous deposits, millions.

After the marriage, Engel would suggest an extended honeymoon and purchase expensive luggage and wardrobes with his new wife. As an afterthought to his plans, Sigmund, being a practical man, would remember to tidy up his bride's business affairs. "We'd better set up our joint accounts now to avoid problems later," he would say. "After all, what's mine is yours and yours mine from now on." The smitten woman, dazzled at the prospect of living the life of a movie tycoon's wife in sun-filled Beverly Hills, would not hesitate to withdraw her considerable savings, never less than $5,000, and turn the money over to her devoted husband.

At this juncture, Engel would tell his wife that he was going to the stores to pick up their new clothes and luggage, and also transfer her money to his bank and change his deposits to a joint account. The sucker's savings tucked in his pocket, Engel departed, never to return, and the mark's money did, indeed, wind up in the hustler's account, a princely sum that he used to fund further matrimonial ventures.

Engel's marks abounded with trust in him. He would call each one Cleopatra and refer to himself as Mark Antony. "Everything he did was in such good taste . . . I had no suspicions of him whatsoever," said victim Mrs. Corrine Perry of Beverly Hills; to her Engel was Eugene Walter Gordon, a corporation lawyer for eastern banks. Ruefully, Mrs. Perry added, "I wasn't foolish enough to give him the money before we were married."

Knowing this to be the main obstacle, Engel hurrahed his victims

by skipping down the aisle with abandon. He was later to emphasize
the greed of his own marks. "Don't forget," he pointed out, "these
women were trying to take me, too."

A Wary Woman Traps Mr. Bluebeard

Engel's undoing, in Chicago in June 1949, came about because he
lingered too long in the same city. Mobility had always served as an
ally, and though he later denied it, age might have slowed him down.
After swindling Chicago widow Mrs. Resada Corrigan of $8,700, a
pittance of his former scores, Engle moved to a different part of town
instead of catching the usual train. He began courting another widow,
Mrs. Genevieve C. Parro, the mother of six sons. Engel had simply
marched up to Mrs. Parro's table at the swanky Palm Grove Inn and
introduced himself as Paul Marshall, a wealthy Evanston banker living
in the Blackstone Hotel. He began his usual "you look like my wife"
routine, and this stirred a cell in Mrs. Parro's memory bank.

The intended sucker had recently read of the suave con man after
Mrs. Corrigan had given her story to Chicago newspaper reporters.
Mrs. Parro instantly identified Sigmund's pitch, but instead of calling
the police she led him on, intending to dupe the confidence man herself.
Contacting her sister-in-law, Marion Hagen, a policewoman, Mrs. Parro
was told to "string him along." Two days later, with Engel in almost
constant attendance and badgering her to marry him, Mrs. Parro leaned
lovingly over their table at the Martinique Restaurant and grabbed his
hand, saying, "I accept." She went on to make only one wedding request.
She needed new luggage for their honeymoon, and Engel happily
volunteeered to pick out "the best set we can find tomorrow."

A police trap was set up in a exclusive Michigan Avenue luggage
store, and when Engel, Mrs. Parro, and two of her grown sons (whom
she had brought along for "protection") appeared, detectives, posing
as clerks, arrested the con man.

As he was being taken to the Town Hall precinct for booking, Engel
rattled on with his con banter and persuaded detective Peter Harib to
stop off at a restaurant. Engel had not eaten that day, he complained,

and was famished. In company with two policewomen and Engel, Harib took the wily con man to a Chicago Avenue restaurant. A waitress, Miss Esther Neptune, later testified that she saw Harib go through Engel's wallet, which was stuffed with $100 bills. She also stated that the detective gave some of the hustler's money to the policewomen before the foursome continued on their way to the lockup.

The victimized Mrs. Corrigan had been notified of Engel's arrest, and was waiting for him when he walked through the doors of Town Hall headquarters. Running up to him, she shrieked: "You beast! You took my money!" With that, she struck the aging con man a powerhouse blow to the face. Engel never batted an eye, but merely tipped his hat and said quietly: "Madam, my apologies." Mrs. Corrigan broke into hysterical sobs.

Minutes later, the wronged woman calmed down and sat with the hustler at a table; he had yet to be booked or locked up. She began to smile as the con man talked to her in hushed tones. Reporters flocked about the pair and asked for a picture. Mrs. Corrigan, who minutes before had been ready to throttle the flimflammer, accepted with alacrity, putting her arm about Engel. Gently, the con man removed her arm from his shoulder and said, "I don't think it prudent, my darling."

It was a circus. Engel held court as the reporters photographed him, telling newsmen that the women he had bilked were incipient hustlers themselves. "But I'll be back in business soon," he commented.

"What business is that?" a reporter asked.

"You call it a con game," Sigmund Engel replied offhandedly.

Mrs. Corrigan was giving her own interview off in a corner, telling newspapermen about the time Engel took her to Milwaukee to visit the alleged graves of his parents. She described how the con man had knelt at his mother's grave, weeping and saying: "Mother, dear, hear me. This is the girl I'm going to marry."

Police stated that Engel was found with $455 in his wallet when apprehended, and $400 of this the con man handed over to Mrs. Corrigan in the police station, telling her that it was "payment on account." The widow went home, still vowing to prosecute.

Sigmund Z. Engle (second from left), a bilking bluebeard who married hundreds of women for their money, stands trial in Chicago in 1949, while one of his bewildered victims, Mrs. Roseda Corrigan (at right) confers with her lawyer. (WIDE WORLD)

A Loving Lockup

Engel's stay in the Town Hall lockup was one of comfort. Detective Harib provided a piano for him to play in his cell. This same detective released the con man from his cell and escorted him to expensive restaurants, where they dined on magnificent cuisine. At one point, Harib escorted Engel to the downtown offices of his lawyers, Irving L. Kruger and Harry J. Busch, to rendezvous with Mrs. Corrigan. There, Engel offered Mrs. Corrigan $5,000 in $100 bills, which he yanked from his pocket (where he got this money, with only $455 found on him at the time of his arrest, was never determined). The con man was stern, telling Mrs. Corrigan: "I'm being a good guy to give you the five thousand. They're going to let me out of jail tonight and you'll end up without a red cent. You can take it or leave it."

Mrs. Corrigan also remembered Engel confidently adding: "My lawyers are costing me five to ten thousand dollars, but they're good men who'll get me out of this whole thing right away. I gave everyone plenty to get me out of jail like this, this afternoon."

The con man, who was supposed to be locked in jail at the time, then asked Mrs. Corrigan if she wanted to go to dinner with him. She declined, and she also wasn't sure if she should take the $5,000, claiming that he had swindled her out of $8,700. According to her later testimony, everyone—the lawyers, Engel, and Detective Harib—began shouting all at once at her to take the money. Beside herself, Mrs. Corrigan took the wad of $100 bills and left. Engel was returned to his cell, where he gave another interview, telling reporters that he had been inspired by the exploits of Chicago's super con man, Joseph "Yellow Kid" Weil.

Reading this account the next day, Weil exploded and held his own conference. Then allegedly retired, Weil blasted the marrying swindler, calling Engel "stupid." The dean of living con men at the time grimaced and shook his head. "There isn't a day that someone doesn't abscond with a woman's money. Preying on the love of a woman for money is one of the most despicable ways of making a livelihood I ever heard of. [Engel] is a little ball of yarn, all wound up . . . I see he's going to write a book. I trust State's Attorney Boyle will give him plenty of time for it."

Engel had informed the press that he would shortly author three books entitled *How to Charm Women, How to Approach Women,* and *How Women Can Detect Con Men After Their Money.*

The special treatment Harib and other police officers lavished on Engel (whether or not they were paid off was never determined) inflamed Police Commissioner Prendergast to the boiling point, and he held a news conference, telling reporters: "Here is Engel, a criminal, and the police department treats him like a hero and a movie actor instead of putting him in a cell where he belongs."

But that cell was permanently reserved for Sigmund Engel. At the beginning of his trial, the spectator section was crammed with his former victims. Mrs. Ann Kubiak of South Bend, whom Engel had bilked of $5,000, was there. Mrs. Corrine Perry, who had lost cash and jewels to the con man, was sitting next to Mrs. Kubiak. Mrs. Vivien Huebler, a San Francisco widow who had lost money to him, was represented. From New York came Mrs. Pauline D. Langton, from whom Engel had taken $50,000 in jewelry (he went out the door telling her he was taking the gems to an insurance company for coverage and never returned).

Trunks and suitcases belonging to Engel were recovered, full of loot, by police in Kansas City and St. Louis. Coupled with this evidence, the testimony against the con man was brutal and conclusive. During recesses, however, Engel continued to wisecrack with reporters. The "love pirate," as the press had dubbed him, grinned and told reporters he was "afflicted with womenmania. . . . Surely they can't punish me for enjoying lovely women . . . I go for the fifty-seven varieties." As the case built up insurmountably against him, he admitted: "I'm a parlay player. I always made it a practice to spend on Mabel what I got from Jane."

At one point, following Mrs. Langton's testimony, Engel stood up as she passed his chair, took her hand gently, and kissed it, as she beamed approval. He turned to reporters, quipping: "Women dream often of chivalry, but seldom get any . . . a field in which my luster is undimmed." He swept an expansive arm in the direction of the cluster of women he had coolly deserted, then said of Mrs. Langton, "My faith in this middle-aged dame remains unshaken."

That faith was supported momentarily by Mrs. Langton, who smilingly admitted to reporters that she still loved Engel. "I thought he had money and that's why I married him . . . For twenty million dollars, why not?"

Don Juan Goes Over

Taking the stand on his own behalf, Engel attempted to pin the blame on his twin brother "Arthur," a fiction of his fertile brain. "Poor Arthur, he's a raving lunatic, you know. It was Arthur, not me, who served that time in Dannemora. I've been taking the rap for Arthur for years, and quite frankly, gentlemen, I'm a little fed up with his antics." This was a bit too much even for the con man, and he found it impossible to suppress a wide smile at his incredible tale.

The jury didn't believe it either, and Engel was found guilty of grand larceny in the Corrigan case and sentenced for from two to ten years in prison. It was the finish for the boldest love merchant of con, but Sigmund Engel parted with the press by firing a salvo of advice to apprentice matrimonial hustlers. Moments before stepping through the iron gates of the state prison, Engel handed a dos and don'ts list to reporters. It read:

1. Always look for the widows. Less complications.
2. Establish your own background as one of wealth and culture.
3. Make friends with the entire family.

4. Send a woman frequent bouquets. Roses, never orchids.
5. Don't ask for money. Make her suggest lending it to you.
6. Be attentive at all times.
7. Be gentle and ardent.
8. Always be a perfect gentlemen. Subordinate sex.

A reporter looked up at Engel and asked: "But what if some one were to follow these rules and still didn't meet with your success?"

Engel shrugged. "Above all, it's just an indefinable something. If I have a certain peculiar charm, why let's just say that I'm more fortunate than most men." He turned to step through the prison gates, then looked up. A shudder rippled visibly through his tall frame. "That goddamned Arthur," Sigmund Engel mumbled, and stepped inside.

Nine

"I Am But a Scientist"

NOTHING so fires the imagination of the sucker and tickles the itchy fingers of the grifter than the marvelous invention that will provide overnight riches. Bell proved it could happen with his telephone and Westinghouse with his air brake. The advent of the patent craze brought with it the most bizarre among hustlers and con men, their scientific razzle-dazzle spellbinding marks out of millions.

Mr. Crosby's Easy Ersatz

A pioneer in the invention con was W. C. Crosby, a trained machinist and mechanical engineer who twisted his considerable talents to create what appeared to be helpful and productive machines. In 1894, while working in Philadelphia, Crosby invented a machine that turned flour paste into coffee beans. His device molded and baked fake beans out of water and white flour, ingredients ordinarily used to make common household paste. After the crisp white beans were shot out of Crosby's machine, they were browned and then, through a crooked manufacturer, mixed with real coffee beans and sold nationwide, thus "defrauding the American breakfast table" for years, according to W. C. himself.

Will Crosby was also responsible for a host of other gadgets he sold directly to suckers, such as his automatic typewriter, which he developed some years after the bean-making machine. In essence the device was a large affair with a typewriter and a microphone attached to it. It was suppose to be guided by a voice and do away with stenographer and dictating machine. The businessman-sucker Crosby lured to his large hotel suite sat in front of a huge impressive cabinet with a microphone at the top, and on a projecting shelf, a regular typewriter. Over each of the typewriter keys was a round solenoid magnet with a central armature, or core. Crosby explained to his marks that the voice dictating into the microphone would "energize" the magnets, causing the armature to be pressed down on the keys in the proper sequence.

When the sucker expressed incredulity, Crosby simply explained that his "special mechanism" located inside the cabinet "strained" the human voice and put the pressure on the proper keys. The sucker was then encouraged to dictate a letter himself. As he carefully worded his letter, a stenographer secreted in another room, her typewriter electronically hooked up by hidden wires to the phony typewriter, began to type out the mark's message as she received it over earphones. Phenomenal, stated the prospective, manufacturer, and more often than not he gave the con man a large check for the rights to the fabulous machine.

Crosby went on to bilk hundreds of suckers with other phony devices, such as ice plants that seemed to produce ice long before such machines were really available; motion pictures that talked (a crude sort of syncopation operated by hidden phonograph records); and predating by decades the development of antifreeze, a large porcelain electric switch that was suppose to keep radiators from freezing, he insisted, to fifty below. Crosby's scams netted him at least half a million before he retired and wrote his memoirs, concluding that:

> half of the men born in America are incipient inventors and the other half susceptible to the inventions bug. Patents are the great national weakness. We have all seen the mechanical wonders created by our countrymen. We have watched some inventors pile up vast fortunes from their works, and like good human beings,

we have forgotten the others who did not . . . natural resources, triumphant speculation and inventions are the golden triplets of the popular mind.

Jernegan's "Gold Accumulator"

Full of the same pink optimism was an ingenious soul named Prescott Ford Jernegan, a one-time Baptist minister in Middletown, Connecticut, who in 1897 decided to turn to invention when down on his luck. In league with another rogue, Charles E. Fisher, Jernegan announced to the world that he had created a marvelous device guaranteed to withdraw the gold eddying about in sea water. His gold accumulator was painted with mercury and "another secret chemical" and then lowered into the ocean. Days later, before hosts of duped businessmen, the accumulator was hauled up, and behold—it was covered with gold.

These demonstrations were all-night affairs: potential investors scrupulously watched the line holding the accumulator to make sure no one tampered with it. No one did—above water. Fisher, however, an accomplished deep-sea diver, swam under water on these occasions from a distant and unseen point and replaced the mercury-coated accumulator with one crusted with grains of gold. Fisher and Jernegan took the good citizens of Connecticut for about $350,000 in cash, handing out stock certificates in the phony Gold Accumulator Company and then fleeing to Europe to live in luxury. (Jernegan later returned and repentantly paid off some of his dupes.)

Invisible Preserving Fluid

An enterprising con inventor in Chicago's early days was Harry S. Holland, whose wild scientific schemes were sponsored by Mike Mc-Donald, the city's most influential political boss and controller of almost all the gambling rackets. In 1886, through McDonald's American Stone and Brick Preserving Company, Holland "invented" and sold to the city of Chicago, via a political contract, his "secret preserving fluid." The initial recipient of this marvelous new paint was to be the Chicago Court House, and Holland and McDonald presented authorities with a bill for $128,250, which bankrupted the city treasury.

Only a few weeks after the massive structure had been painted with Holland's magic preserving fluid, a heavy downpour revealed it to be no more than chalk and water. Officials, aghast at the abysmally streaked Court House, immediately sought arrest warrants for several parties involved in the scam; William J. McGarigle, a Holland and McDonald crony, was the most prominent person to be convicted. Holland, however, escaped to points east to further develop his career as an inventor.

The Gizmo That Combated Melancholia

The con inventors in the 1890s were typified by one "Gas" Grosch, a Manhattan sharper whose little invention reaped him a tidy fortune in only a few years, though it sold for only $1. Grosch was a door-to-door spieler who droned the same line to each sucker: "If your gas bill iss more than one tollar in ein month, this iss for you; if not, no." The German-born Grosch then went on to explain that his gadget, when affixed to the then-popular gas jets in homes, assured his customers that combustion would be checked, light concentrated, and "actinic rays which were productive of myopia, pinkeye, strabismus, nostalgia, melancholia, and premature baldness" would automatically be extracted. His invention was nothing more than a composition tip that achieved the same effect as when the customer, for nothing, simply turned the gas jet down, but Grosch rarely failed to sell one.

Blunting Those Deadly Radio Waves

During the infancy of radio, a host of con men bilked listeners then susceptible to all kinds of "radio wave fears." One Chicago hustler insisted in newspaper ads that radio waves were doing mortal harm to listeners. The only way to undo the damage incurred by radio waves, he cautioned, was to be scanned regularly by his mind-saving invention, the Radio Opposer. For considerable cash payments, suckers—and there were scores who responded to his pitch—lined up in front of his towering black metallic machine and received "shooting, benevolent rays" shot invisibly through their bodies. Each person, whether realistically suffering from headache or hangover, was then given "radio pills" which were simple doses of bicarbonate of soda.

Keely's Energy Machine

In all the annals of con inventions, the most successful and durable proved to be the miraculous machine that would provide mankind with unlimited energy for a next-to-nothing cost. In 1872 John E. W. Keely presented to the world his mystifying hydro-pneumatic-pulsating vacue machine, which he claimed could propel a thirty-car train from Philadelphia to New York while using as fuel less than a quart of plain tap water. Keely's contraption was the first to exercise the water-into-fuel (or gas) invention con, and it fooled everyone who invested in its development.

Over the years, the Keely Motor Company of New York sold tens of thousands of dollars in stocks, money the inventor pocketed, although he bothered to display his magnificent machine only on rare occasions. Squatting in his Philadelphia plant was an exotic collection of elaborately connected metal, and when Keely fed it a pint of water, 50,000 pounds per square inch of pressure showed almost instantly on a colorful gauge. The machine's power was demonstrated when it shredded iron and sent bullets whizzing through planks a foot thick.

Of course, the machine was nothing but a whirligig, and the real source supplying such amazing power was a compressed air assembly hidden in a basement directly below. (It would be decades, however, following Keely's death before the con was revealed.)

The hustler's pitch to stockholders, boomed above the whirring, buzzing machine, was classic and eloquent gobbledygook sure to wow any legitimate scientist who dared scoff at Keely's marvel. A sample: "With these three agents alone—air, water, and machine—unaided by any and every compound, heat electricity and galvanic action, I have produced in an unappreciable time by a simple manipulation of the machine, a vaporic substance at one expulsion of a volume of ten gallons having an elastic energy of ten thousand pounds to the square inch. . . . It has a vapor of so fine an order it will penetrate metal. . . . It is lighter than hydrogen and more powerful than steam or any explosives known. . . . I once drove an engine eight hundred revolutions a minute of forty horse power with less than a thimbleful of water and kept it running fifteen days with the same water."

Two men, Louis Enricht and Walter Hohenau, went Keely one better in the next century, absolutely guaranteeing suckers that their formulas, again employing water, would provide limitless amounts of fuel for next to nothing. And for the doubtful, they proved their claims —or seemed to.

The Green Gas Formula of Louis Enricht

A gaunt, mustachioed man already in his seventies, Louis Enricht was considered by his Farmingdale, Long Island, neighbors an eccentric inventor who had tinkered away most of his life without direction, recognition, or financial success.

But on April 16, 1916, Enricht stepped from his dilapidated house and laboratory to greet the reporters he had called with the simple and startling announcement that he had discovered a new source of energy. "I have learned," he stated in a quavering voice, "to do what chemists have been dreaming of for years. I have discovered, gentlemen, a substitute for gasoline that can be made for a penny a gallon."

The skepticism of the reporters had been expected by the old man, and waving away their accusatory questions, he told them to observe a simple demonstration of his new invention. They followed him to an auto parked nearby, and Enricht grabbed a yardstick. This he inserted into the gas tank, loudly banging the hollow inside with it. "Dry as a bone," the old man said. "Take a look. There is no false bottom or hidden compartments in this tank."

Kneeling down, the reporters carefully examined the car to assert Enricht's statements. "Okay, so what?" one of their number said.

Picking up a garden hose, the crotchety inventor filled a pitcher and then asked some of the newsmen to taste it. "Water," one of them said.

"That's correct, gentlemen. Just water." With that Enricht produced a small vial that contained a bright green liquid, and this he poured into the pitcher of water. He hummed loudly as he mixed the concoction and then dumped it into the empty gasoline tank.

Ambling to the front of the car, Enricht gingerly cranked the auto. The engine kicked over. With a sweep of his hand, Enricht ushered two reporters into the car and then drove them about town for several minutes before depositing them again on his front lawn. "I'll be damned," one newspaperman shouted, and the group hurriedly departed to write up headlines that would proclaim Enricht's marvelous substitute for gasoline, which would cost no more, according to the inventor, than a penny a gallon in operating any automobile. Then as now there was an acute demand for fuel; the war in Europe was dissipating all available gas supplies, and the elderly inventor appeared to have solved a worldwide crisis. Readers across the nation, who were then paying about 28 cents per gallon for gasoline, avidly consumed every word about the brilliant Enricht.

A deluge of mail piled up at Enricht's door; he answered none of it, storing mailbags full of letters from potential investors in the many closets of his sprawling home. Though his phone rang constantly, the eccentric inventor never bothered to pick up the receiver.

Then reporters returned. They had bad news, they said. Enricht remained unperturbed as he was told that a noted chemistry professor at Columbia University, Dr. Thomas Freas, had refuted the possibility of Enricht's discovery. Freas had held his own press conference and stated: "There is no chemical that can be added to water that will make it combustible. Water may be broken up by electrolysis, but the energy required to break it up will be exactly equal to that produced on burning. That is, nothing would be gained."

Enricht simply smiled at this bit of elemental information. "What I'm about to tell you," he said to the newsmen, "is a simplification of a very complex development. My chemical has an affinity for oxygen contained in water and is able to separate the hydrogen in it, thus producing hydrogen atoms. These atoms, gentlemen, when combined with the oxygen atoms in the air about us, become extremely violent, and what happens next is an explosion of power."

A newsman put forth: "Many people say that such a reaction is not only impractical but unrealistic—not to say unscientific."

Enricht fingered the edges of his drooping white mustache. "I expected that. When something as important as what I have discovered is made public, there is always the crowds of nay-sayers to come forward."

Another newsman stepped up and told Enricht that engineers of the Automobile Club of America wanted to test his formula to determine its use. "Of course they promise to keep your formula a secret."

"I'll think that one over," Enricht replied.

"Un-huh," the reporter said sarcastically.

The inventor squinted back and then startled all present by stating: "If you want to be assured, talk to my good friend Ben Yoakum."

With this the reporters raced off to interview the esteemed financier and ex-president of the St. Louis and San Francisco Railroad, Benjamin F. Yoakum. The railroad magnate confirmed Enricht's discovery and said with emphasis: "I have confidence in his invention and I use it in my own car." (Yoakum had already secretly invested in the fuel, and lied about having used it.)

That was enough. Such an endorsement, widely publicized, brought the titans of American business to Enricht's door, all wanting to fund the development of his green liquid. Not the least of these was Henry Ford, whose representative, Theodore Delavigne, traveled to Long Island. In his pocket was a wire from Ford that instructed him to "put Enricht aboard the Wolverine Express and, rain or shine, deliver him f.o.b. at my Detroit office."

Enricht was not deliverable, and after several more requests and no response, the automobile king himself went to Farmingdale and interviewed the old scientist. Ford then announced that he was prepared to purchase the fabulous fuel formula provided it passed some rigorous tests. He ordered a brand-new car from his Detroit plant to be shipped to Enricht for further experimentation. To hype Ford's involvement, Enricht surreptitiously leaked a story that the Maxim Munitions Corporation was buying his formula for $1 million, plus a huge block of company stock. Upon hearing this, Ford did not rise to the bait but canceled further negotiations for the formula and demanded the return of his new car.

Ford, too, had been a smokescreen, it later appeared, for Enricht's prey had really been Ben Yoakum all along. It was almost a year and a half before newspapermen discovered that Yoakum had rushed in to back Enricht's National Power Motor Company, Inc., a short time after Ford and Maxim expressed their interest in the strange green liquid.

Where Enricht spent the money, estimated to be in the tens of thousands, was never fully determined. In 1918 Yoakum got suspicious that the doddering inventor was secretly "negotiating with spies and representatives of the German government" to sell his formula for millions. The financier swiftly brought legal action, obtaining a court order to search Enricht's safe-deposit boxes. Inside was found a packet of Liberty Bonds the old man had purchased with Yoakum's money. No formula was discovered because, as Enricht half-heartedly admitted later, there was no formula. The car with which Enricht had first demonstrated his green fuel did, indeed, have a secret gas tank, and in Yoakum's case, the old man had simply done some fast talking and gasoline pouring (from a hose and hot-water bottle).

When Yoakum's probe surfaced, so did Enricht's amazing background, carefully pieced together by curious newsmen. Emigrating from Germany, Louis Enricht had been conning his way through life for decades. His first known score was in Colorado, where he bilked several investors of thousands on the promise of building a railroad link between Cripple Creek and Canon City. He was indicted and convicted of using the mails to defraud in 1903, when he attempted to sell deeds to 45,000 acres in Tennessee that he claimed were inherited, through generations of his family, from Patrick Henry, a distant relative. A few years later, Enricht had fleeced a European investment group by selling them a phony process for making artificial stone.

The exposé of the zany con inventor, however, only served to stimulate Enricht and whet the appetite of his victims. A year after his fantastic fuel scheme failed, the hustler was busy selling shares in the bogus Enricht Peat Corporation, which netted him about $50,000, a conviction for grand larceny, and ten years in Sing Sing. He only served a year, being leniently pardoned to die of old age in 1922.

Hohenau's Marvelous Power Machine

Walter Hohenau, a fellow Teuton, was certainly aware of Enricht's phony fuel con. Hardly had the ancient hustler passed into the oblivion of yellowed newspaper accounts before Hohenau perpetrated the same fraud in different parts of the country. This madcap con man had already served two prison terms for fraud (the first at the age of fourteen) in Germany, under his real name, Frederick Jonas. And when he reached American shores, his lust for suckers had not diminished.

Dabbling in various short-con schemes, Hohenau appeared in Houston, Texas, in 1927. For several months he established himself in the area as a scientist of prodigious efforts, then capped his sham with a mammoth fete, to which civic and business leaders flocked, at one of the city's best hotels.

In center of the grand ballroom, Hohenau had placed his wonderful new machine—a large, gleaming metal barrel wrapped with glistening coils—which at first sight might have been mistaken for a still. The visitors marveled at the whirring, twirling, spinning gadgets—an electric engine, an ammeter, a voltmeter, and several devices that produced familiar and yet unidentifiable noises (these were door buzzers).

Hohenau explained that his device could effortlessly split oxygen atoms, which in turn provided powerful hydrogen gas. "The world will never be without power again, and it will cost practically nothing to provide fuel purely from water, all achieved with my marvelous hydroatomizer." Astonished visitors were told that within a few years every ship at sea, every automobile on the roads, every home heating system would be powered by Hohenau's invention. Flicking a switch, a hot hydrogen flame was produced by the machine (fed by a hidden hydrogen gas tank). This hydrogen flame was the source of the inventor's new energy.

Hohenau then feasted with his guests, and following dessert, stood behind a dais and humbly informed the fat-walleted throng: "I am but a scientist and know nothing of money. I am conservative by birth and by training, but I am told that more money will be made by this invention"—he snapped a remote-control switch and the hydrogen gas flame shot upward with a whoosh—"than any invention in history.

Some friends have organized for me the Hydro Production Company —and for you, my good friends of Houston, I have saved out some shares."

Bowing to thunderous applause from the grateful dupes, Hohenau then proceeded to collect more than $100,000 in payment for stock certificates in his nonexistent firm. The next stop, the marvelous scientist informed the gathering, would be Palm Beach, Florida. He and they would meet there to inspect a yacht owned by one of the inventor's friends, which had been outfitted with his device and could travel at unheard-of speeds while powered solely by sea water.

The happy delegation of Texas investors journeyed to the specified hotel in Palm Beach, only to find no Walter Hohenau either present or expected. There was little doubt in the investors' minds that they had been bilked. After a few days of futile searching, the once-smiling Houston stockholders became a cursing group of vigilantes who picked up Hohenau's trail and tracked him to Mexico City. The good Texans would have probably lynched Hohenau had they been able to get their hands on him.

But Mexican President Plutarco Elías Calles had been treated to a special demonstration of Hohenau's wonderful gadget and become immediately convinced of its lucrative promises. Calles also seriously believed that a fuel monopoly of Texans were bent on absconding with the inventor's machine (Hohenau told Calles that a group of "cutthroats" would try to kidnap him). When the incensed Houston citizens did arrive, Mexican Secret Service men ushered them away from the inventor's villa. Then, after clipping the Mexican government for a large, undisclosed sum, the hustler slipped away to sea on a tramp steamer heading for Germany.

Upon his arrival, Hohenau traveled to Malchow, where his wife, at his instructions, had set up another phony laboratory. Under his real name of Jonas, the con-man inventor welded together another one of his fuel machines. Several distinguished statesmen were lured to the lab, and the hustler readily demonstrated the hydro-atomizer. To his visitors, Jonas conspiratorially admitted that his name was Count von Hohenau, and that his identity was, by necessity, a private matter. The German aristocracy, blamed for losing World War I by the working class, was not much in favor, he explained. "Professor Jonas" was invited,

Mexico's President Plutarco Calles was suckered into believing Walter Hohenau's power machine could actually produce hydrogen gas from atoms. (UPI)

through his political contacts, not only to attend but address the International Fuel Conference then being held in Geneva.

So convincing was this charlatan at the conference that scientists from the world over rose to their feet at the end of this stirring speech and demonstration, wildly applauding and shouting kudos for his revolutionary discovery. He was inundated with requests to travel to the world capitals to sell his device—and this he did, bilking businessmen for tens of thousands in London, Paris, and Rome. Mussolini hailed Hohenau-Jonas as a genius, and gave him a fortune to develop his new power sources for Italy.

Returning to Germany, the con artist began work on the many "hydro-atomizers" sold to foreign interests and promised for quick delivery. Then, beginning to worry, he went directly to German President Paul von Hindenberg, begging protection from him against sinister foreign powers attempting to steal his device, an invention he intended exclusively for Germany. Hindenberg patiently heard him out in a long interview, at which time German intelligence officers photographed the hustler from behind a curtain and subsequently took his fingerprints from a glass. He was shortly identified as Frederick Jonas, and so was imprisoned.

While awaiting trial, hundreds of victims, reading of his arrest, implored his extradition to the United States, France, England, and Italy. No doubt preferring the German penal system, Hohenau-Jonas made a feeble attempt to escape and intentionally murdered a guard. He knew he would be quickly caught and sentenced to a German prison for this offense, and he was.

Following World War II no trace of prisoner Hohenau could be found; bombs had exploded near the jail where he was kept, and he escaped from his cell. He was last thought to be either in England or America, living in comfortable obscurity. He could look back to an era in which he had conned the most reputable scientists in the world and made money doing it.

Crafty old Paul von Hindenberg, while President of Germany, heard out Hohenau's fantastic spiel and then had the con man arrested. (UPI)

Ten

When the Spirits
Paid Off

COMMUNICATING with dead relatives, friendly specters, demons, and even God for favors from "the beyond" has proved to be a most lucrative business for flimflammers ever since the alchemist Cagliostro first thundered at a victim reluctant to hand over his gold: "Remember, I can afflict as well as heal!" He, St. Germaine, and a bevy of other notable European con men in this shadowy grift almost always got the gold.

In America, hustler activity in this area began, circa 1890, with what were loosely termed "pow-wowers," after the Indian rites performed by medicine men. Practitioners were generally middle-class, middle-aged women who told the victim's future and revealed hidden facts of his past for an exorbitant fee.

Madam Zingara Fleeces the Future

A deft and notorious spirit con was Elizabeth Fitzgerald, better known in Harlem before the turn of the century as Madam Zingara. This woman, a handsome female with deep-set eyes, had a knack for wheedling information from an unwitting victim and feeding the same data back to the sucker couched in terms of riches to come. She began as a pow-wower and then graduated to seeress and prophetess. Madam Zingara never lacked customers; one estimate had it that she fleeced an average of 200 dupes a month on an almost assembly-line basis.

Born Elizabeth McMullin in back of a blacksmith shop in 1863, the future mystic con spent a childhood watching her father shoe the horses of famous Manhattan socialites. At the first opportunity, Elizabeth ran away from home.

She surfaced sometime in 1888 in Worcester, Massachusetts, as Mrs. E. D. Sullivan, the wife of a dead merchant known in the area. In response to her claim that the body of her recently deceased spouse had been stolen (it had; Sullivan had lived as a bachelor, though, and whether or not Elizabeth had ever been his wife was never determined), Alderman D. F. Fitzgerald came into contact with—and finally married—the hustler. It was a short marriage. The couple were divorced under stormy circumstances, Fitzgerald in disgrace for indiscretions much publicized (and engineered) by his wife. "She got the money, the land. I got ruined," he later lamented.

After dabbling with pow-wowing, Elizabeth began to fleece marks in a dozen states, and even traveled to Australia, London, and Ireland before returning to Harlem in early 1898. (By then she had employed the aliases of Peet, Campbell, Byron, McClusky, and Bennett, before which she was always careful to pin the word "Madam.")

A typical Madam Zingara victim was Miss Mollie E. Burns, a teacher and part-time typist. When Miss Burns took sick on a trolley car, Madam Zingara happened along and helped her to her hotel room, discovering on the way that the young woman had left home after an argument with her mother. Secretly going to the mother, the hustler learned that the tiff had been over the ugly fact that Miss Burns had been seeing a married man. Such illicit affairs were scandalous in those days.

Next, the industrious "clairvoyant of Harlem" contacted the girl and told her that certain divinations had revealed shocking details about her personal life. Miss Burns, in fear of being discovered a scarlet woman, paid Madam Zingara several hundred dollars to keep her revelations to herself. The balance of the teacher's savings wound up in the sham mystic's hands within a week after Madam Zingara told Miss Burns that she could shield her from being named as a correspondent in an upcoming divorce. At the same time, the con artist had convinced several members of the Burns family that she had the ability to determine the future, and her crystal ball told her that the entire family could only be saved from impending disgrace in a divorce through her good offices and for $1,000. She received the cash almost immediately.

The blackmailing didn't stop there. Madam Zingara showed up at the Hotel Cecil, and after a little snooping told the steward, E. T. Harlow, that she had psychically determined that he was having an affair with Miss Burns. "Evil spirits are working against you," she informed the young man, but added that, for a price, she might exert her considerable seeress talents to ward them off. It cost him $500 for speedy exorcism.

Where the bruised Burns family kept quiet about their dealings with their guardian soothsayer, the clerk, Harlow, angrily trotted to a police station and reported the extortion. He later convinced Miss Burns and her family to charge Madam Zingara with blackmailing and the prophetess was arrested. But her bail was furnished instantly by one of her many dupes, one Henry Straus—an unemployed streetcleaner obsessed with finding gold with the madam's zesty spiritual aid.

Madam Zingara left the police station, went home, packed a bag, and fled West. M. J. Murphy, a detective for the New York Police Department, tracked her down and had her arrested in January 1899, in Chicago, for a scam she was operating there, but she again escaped after posting a large bond. Murphy caught up with her once more and escorted her to the Tombs Prison in New York. Early in 1900, Madam Zingara was convicted of fraud and received a stiff prison sentence.

A Hypnotic Hype

Another facile crystal-ball grifter in this era was Carrie Reynolds, who operated widely throughout New Jersey, practicing hypnotism on her suckers. Her end came in 1902 in Union Hill, New Jersey, when one Sarah J. Brabezon snapped out of her stupor long enough to tell police she had been flimflammed out of $735 after only a few sessions with the swami. Carrie had informed Mrs. Brabezon, a line practiced on almost all her suckers, that she was about to inherit $10,000, and for the $735 "kindness" she would add $500 when repaying the sum. Carrie Reynolds was arrested on Mrs. Brabezon's complaint and sentenced to a long jail term.

Working the Witchcraft Game

In the same year that Madam Reynolds disappeared behind New Jersey prison bars, a pair of weird witchdoctors who had been working their con along the East Coast for a decade were apprehended in Carlisle, Pennsylvania, their case the first of its kind since colonial times.

Mrs. William McBride and Edgar Zug had snared an elderly rich couple, Mrs. Susan Stambaugh and her senile husband, in a scam that terrified the marks. Mrs. Stambaugh visited Mrs. McBride and Zug to consult the spirits and their attitude toward wealthy people. Dressed in a strange ceremonial costume, Zug told her that she and her husband and all their property and money were under an evil spell. (As late as the early 1970s, this con, known as "the gypsy blessing game," was being worked successfully in Manhattan.)

"The only way to relieve that deadly spell," Zug intoned, "is to buy your way out of it. These evil spirits respect cash."

On her next visit, the badly frightened Mrs. Stambaugh brought along her palsy-ridden husband and the two of them heard Zug tell them: "I see your profiles on the side of a distant mountain . . . and through the brains of these profiles, evil spirits have thrust long needles. This was done many years ago and the needles are now rusty. When these needles break . . . a day not long off . . . you both will die."

With that Mrs. Stambaugh fainted and her husband went into a spasmodic fit. When they revived, Mrs. McBride told them there was yet hope, that Edgar Zug, the only practicing white witch doctor in America, could save them.

Zug explained that through certain secret rites he could induce the spirits to withdraw the needles from the profiles on the mountain. "It will require money," he emphasized, "a lot of money." Within a week the Stambaughs had turned over all their cash and deeds to their property, yet Zug was not satisfied. "I'm afraid you are going to die," he sighed at a later meeting, "unless you can come up with at least another five thousand." He added that it would all come back to them via a hidden treasure.

Sworn to secrecy, the duped and desperate couple began to contact friends for loans. Hysterical, Mrs. Stambaugh finally revealed the scheme to a friend and this led to the witch doctors being quickly arrested, tried, and convicted on fraud. As they were being led away, Zug shouted to a packed courtroom: "That's what I get for being kind!" His docile accomplice Mrs. McBride held aloft a small bag and opened it as she turned it upside down. From it fluttered a dozen neatly cut strips of paper. "Upon each," she said solemnly to her jurors, "you will find a name of one of the twelve apostles. Now save yourselves."

The "Gift Family"

Intervening with high powers was also at the root of the "Gift Family" con, which was operated by a ring of hustlers in Boston. Suckers were informed that through the Gift Family's mystic channels, a "divine source" would return to investors four times the amounts sent into the organization. An occasional check was sent back to marks to keep them happy and advertise the truth of the group's claims. Most suckers, irate at not receiving riches multiplied in heaven, got pacifying letters telling them to have faith. In the two years before they were exposed, these con men took in half a million dollars. By then hundreds had drained their life savings, mortgaged their homes and property, and gone to ruin in the belief that God would somehow pay them an unheard-of interest on their money.

The Fraud That Was Divine

The case of Mrs. May Jennings Bennett was an unusual switch of divine spirits benefiting the avaricious. She attributed her wholesale con games during the 1920s to a "divine psychologist."

Following her apprehension, Mrs. Bennett told police: "I met a man who advertised a sort of 'new thought.' He told me when I went to him that he could make people prosperous. I told him I wanted to be wealthy. I paid him more than a thousand dollars at different times, and he always told me to go right ahead with my schemes, and he was with me, that he could pray for their success. I was under a sort of hypnotic influence. I knew what I was doing was not right but had not the power to resist. . . . Finally, when I was indicted for grand larceny, I realized that I had been in a terrible dream and that this man who was or called himself a 'divine psychologist' had exercised a power for evil and not for good over me. I went to him to help me. He refused to aid me and appeared to be scared to death. I woke up then. I knew I had not been in my right mind."

Under the influence of this unnamed, all-powerful divine psychologist, Mrs. Bennett busily bilked dozens of clergymen. A Paulist father not only loaned her $200 he never saw again, but wrote letters of recommendation for her to influential New Yorkers. Her specialty was organizing charity teas and bazaars, and through esteemed clerics she was able to round up hordes of socialites who contributed heavily to such causes as the Red Cross. The organizations for whom the donations were supposedly intended never received a dime.

Mrs. Bennett lived lavishly off this money, renting a suite of rooms in the elegant Breton Hall, purchasing expensive wardrobes, and throwing immense parties. Her scams reaped so much in one month that, as a lark, she purchased $10,000 worth of Mexican oil stocks.

Several charitable institutions ultimately realized Mrs. Bennett's swindles and brought charges. When bail was set, several clerics whom she had bilked protested to the judge against the high bond of $3,500 he had set and then startled the court by providing the money. Convicted and imprisoned, Mrs. Bennett never did reveal the identity of the divine psychologist who had mesmerized her into miscreant deeds. Some unkind types mused that he was a figment of her tricky imagination.

The Clairvoyant Con Woman

It was an era rampant with superstition, mystics, and clairvoyants and a Mrs. M. LaRue was much in the news in the same period as the Bennett case. Operating throughout New York State, she advertised herself as "The World's Most Dynamic Clairvoyant." Her technique was to pry information from a victim and then refer him to the great Odessec de Blanco, a Hindu seeress who would solve all of the mark's problems. Odessec, contacted only by mail, was Mrs. LaRue's crafty mother, who fed back to the victim the personal information her daughter sent along to her, extracting huge fees in the process. And there were bonuses. Odessec was forever suggesting the purchase of special items to assure the "seeker" of riches. One mark was told that it was mandatory for him to obtain a certain rare crystal, which Odessec could order direct from India, and which would save his failing health. The mark sent along the demanded $300 and received a common glass ball.

Mrs. LaRue and her mother were averaging about $50,000 a year in the boom time of the mid-1920s, when greed got the better of them. After bilking one gent, the so-called clairvoyant ordered him to marry a local prostitute and depart for Denver immediately for reasons of health. While the mismatched newlyweds were away, the spirit hustler and her mother sold the victim's furniture, house, and property. The tart, in league with Mrs. LaRue, put knockout drops in his coffee on their wedding night and stole his money and clothes before disappearing. Returning to a state of pauperism, the sucker screamed copper and the flim-flammers were subsequently sent to prison.

The 1920s also raised the hollering, fat infants of revivalism and evangelism, which had been struggling along the American backwaters since the time of Chautauqua. Massively organized, the beaters of the Bible belt moved into sizable cities.

Revivalist Sister Aimee Semple McPherson took in huge "donations" with clotheslines before scandal wrecked her career; the Pattens of Oakland, California were dedicated followers, and Carl Thomas Patten turned out to be one of the wildest religious flimflammers along the Bible Belt. (WIDE WORLD)

Sister Aimee's Clothesline

Though several evangelists, from Gipsy Smith at the turn of the century to Billy Graham of the present day, operated on a legitimate level, many of the famous shouters for God were highly suspect, including the controversial Sister Aimee Semple McPherson. Calling herself "The World's Most Pulchritudinous Evangelist," Sister Aimee soared within the space of ten years, 1917–26, from a down-and-out tent talker traveling the dusty sideroads in a tin lizzie, to the spiritual proprietress of the $1,500,000 Los Angeles temple known as the International Institute of Four-Square Evangelism (which could contain 5,000 fervent followers a meeting), a $75,000 radio station, and a weekly payroll of $7,000.

Sister Aimee's fanatical legions coughed up enormous amounts of money to hear her tempestuous sermons, at which times she was robed in long, flowing white silk gowns, her golden hair marcelled and adorned with flowers. Colored lights played upon her ample, curvy body as she shouted her special hosannas. Though crowds swooned and fainted in religious frenzy before her, Sister Aimee was careful to point out that she was far from being a "healer . . . only the little office girl who opens the door and says 'Come in.'"

Journalist Lloyd Morris summed up this shrewd religious money-raiser in more apt terms when he wrote that she "fused economics and ecstacy, showmanship and salvation, carnival and contrition."

Despite her highly vocal denial of the riches that flowed to her, she made millions of dollars and traveled the world in luxury. "I wish I didn't have to carry on the Lord's work in such a conspicuous capacity," she once lamented. In her collections, Sister Aimee (much like her counterpart in the novel *Elmer Gantry,* by Sinclair Lewis) found the sound of coins clinking together too embarrassing and offensive, so she rigged up clotheslines to which her rabid followers pinned greenbacks. In one holy-holy session Sister Aimee cranked in $20,000 from these lines, the 5,000 spectators under hypnotic sway all but declaring bankruptcy for God.

(The fire-and-brimstone evangelist Billy Sunday, who netted about $100,000 a year from revivalism after World War I, was once challenged about his income and replied: "If there's any man here feels it's his business how much money I'm receiving, let him step forward and I'll knock his block off!")

In 1926 Sister Aimee disappeared, later showing up in Douglas, Arizona, with a fantastic story about being kidnapped. However, according to L.A. district attorney Asa Keyes, who indicted Sister Aimee for obstruction of justice, the fetching hell-raker had probably gone off on an illicit tryst with the radio operator of her Angelus Temple, Kenneth Ormiston. Though charges were later dropped, a cloud hung over Sister Aimee until her death in September 1944, from an apparent overdose of sleeping tablets.

Religious con man C. Thomas Patten and his wife, evangelist Bebe, in 1949. (WIDE WORLD)

The Pattens: Cash-and-Carry Evangelism

Some months before Sister Aimee's death, one of her most dedicated followers and a graduate of her International Institute of Four-Square Evangelism, Bebe Harrison, arrived in Oakland, California to save sinners for cash. Her husband turned out to be a super con man who would hustle evangelism out of its last cent.

Carl Thomas Patten (he used C. Thomas Patten, joking that the "C" stood for "cash") was a large, plumpish man addicted to handmade cowboy boots, a wide Stetson and gaudy ties featuring dollar signs. Born to a Tennessee bootlegger, Patten once recalled, "My daddy was baptized a Baptist in a mountain stream, but a crawfish bit on his big toe and he never went back." He was expelled from high school for operating a still in the school's basement, and in 1935 (when he "drank like a fish"), he was arrested for transporting stolen cars across a state line, receiving a suspended two-year sentence. Bebe Harrison, an attractive, statuesque evangelist met Patten in the hill country and she agreed to marry him only on the condition that he take up the evangelical trail. ("The only woman I ever saw that I couldn't get fresh with.") He agreed, and was ordained by the Fundamental Ministerial Association after Bebe spoon-fed him the Scriptures.

After ten years on the revivalist circuit, the Pattens took up residence in the rundown Elm Tabernacle in a shabby district of Oakland. The attendance was at first sparse, but through heavy advertising the couple managed to fill the small church to overflowing in a few weeks. Bebe, dressed exactly like Sister Aimee in long, flowing white gowns of silk, addressed the congregation in a stentorian voice, and Patten took up the collections, his major specialty.

A Hustler Hawks Hosannas

He minored as huckster, purchasing full-page ads in newspapers and sending out sound trucks to blare his revivalist message. "Nobody ever put over big-time religion here like I did," he once bragged. "I broke this town spiritually by spending five, six thousands dollars a week on advertising."

Crowds became so enormous that the Pattens had to move their religious show to the Oakland Women's City Club auditorium and then to the sprawling Oakland Arena, where 8,000 persons could find God at one sitting. Those who flocked to hear Bebe Patten sermonize and her colorful husband exhort the emptying of pockets answered ads that read: "Green Palms! Choir Girls in White! Music! Miracles! Blessings! Healings!"

In nineteen weeks the Pattens had collected $35,000. They then set up permanent shop at the City Club, much to the chagrin of the city's religious leaders, who had originally financed some of their operation in the hope that once they had departed the hosts of converts would stream to their churches. A highly personalized version of Pentecostal preaching is what Bebe fed her sinners, who, by the time her husband stepped forth to take up the collection, had been made limp through exhaustive and emotional bouts with the devil. His collection talks often lasted longer than Bebe's sermons.

According to writer Bernard Taper, Patten would stand before the congregation in silence, head bowed in prayer. He would then look up with a wide grin and shout: "All right, now, brothers and sisters, God says there's five thousand two hundred and forty dollars and fifty-five cents [or some such specific sum] that is here today that is to be taken up for His work, and God's word never fails. If God told me that money is here, it is *here*. That's a fact. How many say Amen? Hallelujah to His glorious name. That's a lot of money, but believe it or not, brothers and sisters, there's three people here among you going to open their hearts to the Lord and pledge a thousand dollars each. Isn't that glorious? Everybody say Amen! How many people believe the Lord is telling the truth when He says there's three people here going to give a thousand dollars each? Raise your hands! Now, who'll be the first? Somebody in the back rows? Pray for him, brothers and sisters. He's got his hand up. It's brother Lilian. Bless you, Lord, and the angels sing! Isn't that wonderful? Now there's just two more going to feel the Holy Spirit on them today, just two more . . ."

Patten's quasi-carnival spiel would singsong its way through humor, anger, passionate pleading, calm cajoling, and thunderous threats until he had raised the prescribed amount (nobody left the temple until he did). Whatever the personal needs of the Pattens, speedy collections were made to cover costs. At one time, C. Thomas told his followers that it was vital he obtain an English bulldog named Bozo, and he raised the $269.70 purchase price within minutes. Then he required a Boston bulldog named Peter and got the $150 for him, too.

Beware God

A special project once demanded a quick $3,514.60, and when Patten was able to wheedle only $1,250 out of his congregation, he exploded before them with: "God is going to slap you cock-eyed in about two minutes! This is where the fireworks start. God has been talking to one man here for five minutes. I don't know whether he is going to knock him off his seat or not. God is going to . . ." He got his money in record time.

Collections became so profitable that Patten, handling all business affairs for the congregation, purchased the City Club for more than a quarter of a million dollars, funds for which came from special collections and heavy church and bank loans. Though the Pattens owned the building and grounds jointly, it was understood by all congregation members that they were acting only as trustees, that the membership really owned the temple they had themselves paid for, a thought easily discarded by Carl Thomas Patten.

At one point Bebe told her flock: "Brother Patten and I have it fixed so that this building can never be sold. It will always belong to the people. It will be here until Jesus comes, until the hinges are rusted off the door."

Patten echoed the sentiment with "You will have it as a church long after my wife and I have left Oakland and gone back to working in the field."

The Lord's Businessman

For this unswerving dedication to their followers, the congregation gratefully filled up the collection boxes once again. The Pattens found myriad methods by which to glean more money from their gullible flock. They opened a religious school and claimed, falsely, that it was accredited by the University of California. Tuition was considerable, and Patten made some quick arrangements to have the government pay certain fees under the G.I. Bill of Rights. Further, he sold collegiate sweaters with the initial of "P" for Patten emblazoned upon them to his students by the gross. About 300 students a year enrolled, paying $20 a month tuition ($50,000 in tuition was collected over a five-year period), and miscellaneous educational expenses. One of the "extras" Patten was so fond of promoting and selling to each and every student was the Academy of Christian Education Yearbook, which was cheaply printed and netted him $5 per copy. Readers of this religious hodgepodge were treated to such revelations as: ". . . after scanning the honor role of the obedient, the eyes of God rested on the name C. Thomas Patten . . . thus was born God's businessman of the hour . . ."

The gulled student body, many of whom were religious fanatics in their sixties and seventies, were offered courses in Hawaiian Guitar, Christian Evidence, Scripture Memory, Holy Spirit, Major Prophets, Minor Prophets, Psalms, Homiletics, and Divine Healing, to name a few. (The Pattens had gotten their own degrees from a convicted con man named Denver S. Swain, who ran a mail-order degree swindle through his bogus Temple Hill College and Seminary in McNab, Illinois).

Suddenly inspired one day, Patten informed his flock that a collection should be taken up immediately for the building of a ten-story tabernacle that would be built on the highest hill of wicked San Francisco. According to one report, he raised $10,000 for this project in thirty minutes.

Of course the tabernacle was never built, but the hustler's imagination never ceased spewing forth new projects that demanded heavy donations. A hydraulically operated choir loft was proposed, along with an electronic nursery, a glass-encased baptistry, a theological seminary, a hospital, a refuge for retired evangelists, and aisle escalators to be operated by Patten himself near the pulpit, which would speedily bring members to him with their offerings. If there was any reluctance on the part of the faithful to provide a lot of cash on the spot when these ideas were put forth, Patten would become incensed, shouting: "He's going to have to put . . . you spineless cowards on the spot to do it. . . . There ain't no way out of it . . . God ain't going to back down . . . that's for sure."

Patten's Piety Dupes

For the most part, the Oakland congregation was made up of ill-educated southerners who had tasted and come under the spell of revivalism in their youth or adolescence before moving to the promised land of California to obtain lucrative jobs in defense plants and in the aeronautics industry. They were, in the words of Carey McWilliams, writing in *The Nation*, "social outcasts and urban misfits." Once in Patten's temple, these gullible souls forked over every dime in their pockets. Some elderly victims even handed over to the evangelists promisory notes for fabulous sums they would never possess but which might be unwittingly paid off as legitimate debts by their relatives after their deaths.

In time the phony evangelist abandoned all decorum, as he released the hogs of gaucherie and corn upon his sheep. One reporter was awed by "his hamhock-and-turnip-green accent, his penchant for flashy clothes, and his Western drawl. . . . [Patten] was just the man to kid the folk into loosening their purse strings. Bouncing around the stage in a tight-fitting tuxedo and cowboy boots, he would shout: "There'll be a hot time in the old town tonight!"

More and greater donations were required of the congregation, beginning to show the signs of economic anemia, when Patten told the membership that God had directly instructed him to build an orphanage. It came about this way, he explained. He was sitting in a chair, minding his own business, one summer day in 1946, and suddenly God said: "I want you to build an orphanage for Me. Will you do it?"

The hustling shepherd told his flock that he was compelled to answer God with: "Lord, I don't see how I can do it with everything else I have to do, but if You say build an orphanage then I'll build one."

Thousands of dollars more brimmed the collection boxes over. The orphanage, like the tabernacle, never materialized. Yet the collections, which were more and more like spiritual holdups, and vast tithing and pledges, under the threat of eternal damnation, continued unabated. One elderly woman handed over her entire inheritance for about $5,000 and Patten gave her an I.O.U. for half, the balance he insisted being owed for tithing and back pledges. When she later went to him needing money and showing him the I.O.U. as a gentle reminder, he took it from her and tore it up, saying nothing. The cowed woman meekly accepted the robbery as religious chastisement and kept silent in her pew.

Heaven's Rewards

Never accounting for a dime to the congregation, the donations the Pattens took in fast approached the million-dollar mark in 1947. The Pattens lived in luxury. Bebe's gowns were made by Adrian of Hollywood. C. Thomas possessed scores of tailor-made suits—his favorite was a pistachio green gaberdine—and 200 cowboy boots purchased at $200 a pair. Their expensive house was peopled by servants, and as *Newsweek* later pointed out, "two bird cages to fill the dining room with sweet sounds as the evangelists dined." God, as well as their duped congregation, appeared to have been generous.

In the summer of 1947, however, Patten committed the inexcusable.

He sold the church, school, and grounds promised to the congregation to the Loyal Order of the Moose for $450,000. This led to grumbling among the members and some actual outspoken resentment. Further trouble came from an FCC hearing in Oakland as a result of Patten's desire to operate, as had once Sister Aimee, a radio station. One witness representing the Oakland Council of Churches gave the first public outcry against the grifting evangelist: "The Patten Church meetings are highly emotional and hysterical. They are a racket dealing in mass hysteria, and a money-making device."

Policing Patten's Paradise

The flock began to break up, members resigning in droves. Support for the Patten school stopped. The district attorney, acting under complaints from bilked church members, began an investigation that caused Patten to state: "The D.A. can't prove I'm taking money under false pretenses. You can't prove that against a church. . . . All the other churches are mad because we cleaned them out. None of them get crowds like we do. We have stolen their sheep." As events proved, he had stolen a lot more than that.

The bragging zealot was indicted for grand theft, fraud, embezzlement, and obtaining money under false pretenses. A four-and-a-half month trial, beginning in February 1950, brought back memories of the Dayton, Tennessee, Scopes trial, with Patten's most ardent supporters carrying placards and signs demanding the return of religious freedom in America. Choruses of "Amens" interrupted the trial, and testimonies were punctured with words of encouragement shouted to Patten. The con man took it all with a grin. He changed his suit twice a day and his boots two or three times. He ignored witnesses and tipped his chair at precarious angles, balancing himself on two legs for the amusement of his supporters. On the witness stand he lied so fast and glibly that the jury couldn't count the strung-together fabrications.

The prosecution proved that the Patten bank accounts from 1944 to 1948 had mushroomed to $1,354,706.75 and that, considering all expenses, the sum of $691,640 was used for the hustling evangelists' private use. This was easily proved when it was revealed that the couple owned nine autos—four Cadillacs, two Packards, a Lincoln, a Chrysler, and an Oldsmobile—plus a $6,000 cabin cruiser. There was also the matter of monthly "love offerings" to Sister Bebe that ran from $3,000 to $5,000. There were the heavy gambling losses Patten had incurred in Las Vegas. When confronted with a $4,000 debt paid to a casino owner, C. Thomas mumbled, "I made a little mistake."

Try as they might, Patten's lawyers—he had been careful to publicize that a Catholic, a Protestant, and a Jew were representing him—could not overcome the damning weight of testimony.

George Lewis, an unemployed caterer, told the court that he had given Patten $10,000. "I'd go to a Patten meeting with my full pay [$125 a week] and come out with a couple of dollars. I just couldn't seem to keep from giving it . . . I never had but a few dollars to give my wife . . ."

The Patten's one-time cleaning woman, Mrs. Freeda Borchardt, wept on the witness stand as she told the jury that she and her husband had turned over their life savings of $2,800 after Patten interrupted church services to single her out in front of the entire congregation, calling her "the meanest woman in Oakland."

Patten himself had a lot to say, especially on the matter of the money he had fleeced from his followers. "People give it to me . . . I'm the man who keeps the wheel lubricated to keep the spiritual machinery moving." For days he piled obvious lie upon lie, unconcerned with the jurors' reaction.

Bebe Warns the Law

Wife and co-evangelist Bebe was not to be ignored at the legal carnival. She arrived at the courthouse in a Cadillac limousine, dressed in a blue-pleated skirt and a tight blue sweater embroidered with a gold-colored "P" above gold crosses. More than a hundred of her most fanatical students formed a guard of honor, leading her into the already overcrowded courtroom.

Raising her hands, she shouted: "We have God on our side! Glory Hallelujah! Amen!"

"Amen!" came a thunderous response from Patten's dupes.

This display encouraged C. Thomas to bolt up onto the seat of his chair and scream directly at the jury: "When you get your eyes off Jesus, you will always go down!" He turned to his chanting suckers. "How many say Amen?"

"Amen!" chorused the gullery.

Assistant district attorney Miss Cecil Mosbacher had some unkind words for Bebe as the case neared its end. "It was she," Miss Mosbacher said quietly to the jury, "who made the emotional appeal, she who set the stage upon which he operated. . . . They conspired together to defraud and deceive this community."

Stung, Bebe delivered a wrathful sermon at the close of the trial. One of her students had taken a rose from the funeral casket of a woman who had quit the Patten circus and had angrily criticized their operations. Bebe held up this flower as a symbol of revenge and lunged into vituperation: "This is just one of the many flowers that will come from the graves of those opposing us. . . . It came from the casket of that woman . . . now she has no power to change God's word. She is praying in hell tonight."

Hundreds of students and congregation members rocked in their seats, completely given over to Bebe's hysteria. Those who opposed the Pattens, she told her flock, were "sinful and ungodly . . . followers of Cain . . . God has chosen to reveal his power to those who are with him, those who are against him shall go to a premature death."

She raved on about government officials persecuting the true believers, and recalled a minister who had once opposed a Patten revival meeting in Decatur, Alabama, only to drop dead the next day. "I have always regretted that I did not live in the Old Testament days because you could have your weapons and go to war. . . . In this battle we are having right now [the trial], my prayer is that the Lord will rise up and smite someone. . . . And this outfit in Oakland has touched the spirit of God. I am looking for some people to drop dead. My prayer is: 'Lord, smite just one to encourage us—just anyone to show us you are on our side.' The Lord knows that if He had left it to us we would have done it already. I think fifty would include them all. . . . There's nothing so encouraging as to see the Lord walk into battle and slay someone. Lord, knock someone cold, no matter how unimportant, just as a sign You're on our side!"

"AMEN!"

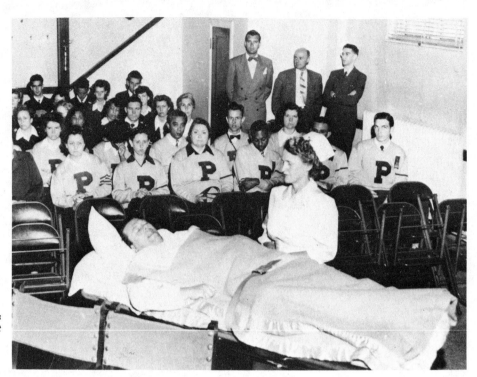

A sickly C. Thomas Patten and glum disciples seated behind him await the verdict on his religious scam. (WIDE WORLD)

Jail for a Spiritual Sharper

Con man Patten listened to closing arguments from a stretcher. After suffering an alleged heart attack, the 6-foot, 218-pound evangelist, "picking his nose moodily and getting an occasional shot of morphine from a hovering nurse," suspiciously eyed the proceedings, which had been relocated to a hospital auditorium to accommodate his condition.

When he heard the jury find him guilty of five counts of grand theft, his only reaction was to smooth down the front of his yellow silk pajamas. When he received his sentence of five to fifty years in prison, the con man, flat on his back, craned his neck about to reporters, still the cocky showman, and yelled: "There'll be a battle royal before they get me behind bars."

But there wasn't even a skirmish as the beefy flimflammer was led silently off to prison. Paroled in three years, in 1953, Patten was allowed to return to Bebe's threadbare evangelical operation, but only under one condition. He was never again to take up a collection. He never did, dying in 1959 in the kind of obscurity he had always loathed.

Baltimore's Mystical Dr. White

Con man extraordinaire in the realms of the spiritual hustle, certainly an energetic equal to the dynamic Pattens, was "Dr." Theodore White of East Baltimore, who mulcted more than 20,000 suckers out of millions of dollars in the space of two years with his mystical come-ons. He billed himself as "the greatest psychometer, telepathist, hypnotist, clairvoyant, spiritualist, mental healer, dealer in the black and white art, dispeller of evil, recuperator of fortunes, restorer of lost affections, manufacturer of love powders, importer of the Adam and Eve root, and general psychic expert."

Like the Pattens, White, too, offered a unique school for the benefit of the world. The "Correspondence College of Science" offered charms, incantations, secret prayers, and talismans guaranteed to provide any kind of miracle desired. White's mystic mail-order house sold courses to those answering the many ads he placed in rural weeklies and smaller magazines (his advertising bill alone for 1906 was $18,000, then a vast sum).

White methodically primed those who responded to his advertisements with a series of letters designed to lure the recipient into a number of purchases. The first mailing consisted of a pamphlet entitled "Blessings to All Man-kind." This was accompanied by a letter that promised to heal all disease and "symptom blanks." If the mark did not respond quickly, one of White's six fulltime secretaries initiated mailings of seven follow-up letters at intervals of a few days to lure the sucker into purchasing one of the sham spiritualist's many courses, each selling for $9 and up.

The $9 Potion Against Tragedy

Each course was merely a charm designed to provide unworldly results. For those wanting to ward off ill fortune, $9 brought them the following charm:

> Take nine drops of blood from the tail of a black cat on the first
> quarter of the moon, and the breastbone taken from a crow on the
> full of the moon, and the fork taken from the back of a frog on the
> last quarter of the moon, the shedded skin of a blacksnake, the
> roots know as Adam and Eve [the Adam and Eve root was only
> available from Dr. White at an additional price], and also nine
> strands of hair taken from the tail of a white mule. Place them all
> into a bag made for the purpose and to be worn around the body."

Other charms were guaranteed to destroy one's employer, or to
compel an unappreciative public to patronize a store, or to force
persons with huge bank accounts to pay the charm worker great
amounts of cash. One charm even promised the raising of demons
from hell ("spirits from the vasty deep," as Dr. White put it). Its
ingredients would certainly have tickled the fancy of Macbeth's caul-
dron-stirring crones:

> Take a piece of human flesh from any part of the body, preferably
> the heart; place it where it will become perfectly decayed (rotten)
> and impregnated with maggots. Take nine of the maggots, wash
> them carefully in warm water, then open them with a sharp
> instrument; take out the inner portions, leaving the skin. Place the
> skins on a plate by spreading them out. After they are thoroughly
> dry, by close observation you will find that the exact form of a
> human skeleton, especially the spine and ribs, will be seen to
> appear in the skin of the maggot. Now allow these skins to remain
> or you may place them in a row. Then take the portion which
> was taken from the inside of the maggots, mix it with sulphur and
> incense, and burn it at midnight, and you will find that there will
> be as many spirits to appear in the room as you have maggot skins.
> Again I will warn you to be careful when performing the above
> experiment.

This bit of murky wisdom cost the sucker $15. About 12,500 copies
of this charm were sold to suckers within a year, most of the purchasers
being blacks.

Healing on the Installment Plan

One of White's insidious sidelines was his "healing" course. Miss Ruth Hutchinson of Cambridge, Maryland, was a typical victim in this scheme. A paralytic since birth, she quickly answered one of White's preposterous ads declaring that he could cure any disease or physical impairment. In response to her letter and initial $9 payment, she received a needle, which White told her to insert in certain parts of her flesh (early-day acupuncture?), which would heal her. When she wrote saying no change occurred after she had carefully followed his instructions, White replied she was under "an evil spell," which he could remove for $5. Miss Hutchinson paid the $5 and much more, but the "spell" never disappeared and she remained a cripple.

"Life readings" were big money-makers for the hustler, who sold, at $7 a crack, a "spiritual planetary reading" and a "psychic and clairvoyant life reading" to those good enough to send along a lock of their hair. One report stated that this particular scam produced hundreds of replies, and "the 'doctor' always sent the same horoscope to husbands and wives, sisters and brothers, getting the same reading although their hair was as different in hue as the extremes of the rainbow." A profitable follow-up to this scheme was Dr. White's offhand discovery that many of those who sent in locks of hair suffered from dandruff and other scalp problems. He sold these unfortunates thousands of bottles of a secret hair restorer for their ailing scalps.

To those desirous of learning "the ancient rites of the Hindus and pre-historical philosophers," White offered a host of hitherto unpublished charms, but these, he cautioned, would never work unless written on "pure parchment," a type that he himself, at great effort, had obtained from India and would make available at $4 a sheet to his students. He made thousands on this flimflam, and when he was later brought to trial, it was proved that the good doctor was paying about 13 cents a yard for his "pure parchment," which was nothing more than tracing paper used by commercial artists.

White's Beholding Beauty

Mirrors were big items in Dr. White's collection of spiritual artifacts. One woman testified at White's trial that he had sold her a "magic mirror," guaranteed to make her beautfiul, for $450.

A workman was then put on the witness stand and told how he made "magic mirrors" for Dr. White. Each cost him $1.50 to make, he stated and he sold them to the con man for $3.50 each. "If I knowed he was making that much off 'em, I would have charged the old boy five dollars a copy."

White's mystical masterpiece was his Adam and Eve root, the best-selling item in his long list of bogus potions, charms, and herbs. Allegedly obtained from the west coast of Africa by White, sent to him by a witch doctor of long acquaintance, the Adam and Eve root promised to "restore lost love, reunite the separated and overthrow all evil." At $5 a root it was a steal.

Once obtained, the root was to be placed in a running stream, river, reservoir, etc. The incantation the purchaser was obligated to recite was fairly simple. To get back his runaway wife or her catting husband, the sucker was to say: "What God hath joined together, let no man put asunder. And as God didst not join thee, I put thee two asunder, ye workers of iniquity."

Following White's conviction in Baltimore for fraud, in which he received a three-year prison term and a $1,500 fine, the "doctor" turned to hundreds of the "students" who had graduated from his wacky college, paying $15 each for a "degree," and who had flocked to see their private miracle worker. White, manacled, called out to them: "Do you all have your diplomas?"

Dozens of rolled-up pieces of paper were waved majestically above the marks' heads.

"Then you are free spirits," White said, nodding, "full of eternal magic."

A guard leading White away looked over his shoulder at the waving diplomas and said to the hustler: "Why don't you give those poor boobs a break . . . tell 'em you're a fake."

White shook his head knowledgeably. "They wouldn't believe me."

Eleven

Giving Them the Business

THE AMERICAN BUSINESSMAN, from middle-class shopkeeper to industrial and banking mogul, is and always has been the primary mark of the accomplished sharper. Like the not-too-fictional George F. Babbitt, he believes that "nothing suceeds like success," and to that end no prospective killing is overlooked, no promising client ignored and no investment offering quick return shunned. The gullibility of such investors lusting for quick, big returns on their money was intimately known to William Franklin Miller. He was of the same stripe as the thousands of suckers he bilked in the wildest stock scheme ever perpetrated.

A failure at thirty-six, Miller had struggled along on a clerk's wages of $5 a week, desperately gambling on miserable stocks and losing. In the sweetly innocent year of 1899, Miller suddenly decided to ensnare his fellow man in his own dilemma. Many persons in his Brooklyn neighborhood, an area populated by frugal German, Swedish, and Dutch immigrants, knew Miller had worked in a brokerage office, and his talk of "inside tips" through which fortunes could be made had established him as a mercantile savant, someone to be trusted, someone whose word stood for smart business sense. Not an imposing figure, the five-foot five-inch Miller, sporting a thick black mustache, wore a threadbare overcoat and white Alpine hat and looked much the same as anyone else in a neighborhood of hard-working, penny-counting citizens.

520 Percent Miller Goes Into Action

In January of that last year of the nineteenth century, Miller let it be known to a dozen or so fellow members of his club that he knew of a way to provide investors with 10 percent interest on their money each week, an astounding 520 percent each year. The suckers jumped at the bait, and each of the twelve confidants foisted $10 each upon the sharper.

"Each of you will receive $1 a week interest on this money, and the principal shall be returned to you within ten weeks." He departed in search of more marks. They weren't hard to find; in fact, they found him before he sought them out.

Miller's plan was not unusual for his day. The scheme was known as "the discretionary game," and many had been active in it. It was played with bonds, stocks, corn, etc. The agent simply took the investor's money and employed it at his discretion, limited only by the promise of returning huge profits. In Miller's case he played with blue sky, hurling the game to its most fantastic distance when he promised, because of his "inside tips," to provide 520 percent on invested money per annum. Of course, Miller had no inside tips, and he never invested a dime given to him by his depositors. It was simply a matter of Peter-to-Paul, a method by which Boston flimflammer Charles Ponzi would reap millions twenty years later.

Renting a two-story brownstone at 144 Floyd Street, Miller quit his job and began to spread the word about his fabulous 520 percent offer. First, word of mouth brought in thousands from neighbors. Then a massive advertising campaign was launched under the banner of The Franklin Syndicate. Miller employed his middle name and a picture of the august Ben Franklin in his scheme. He printed thousands of newsletters, which touted his offer. One read: "My ambition is to make the Franklin Syndicate one of the largest and strongest syndicates operating in Wall

Street, which will enable us to manipulate stocks, putting them up or down as we desire, and which will make our profits five times more than they are now."

Cornucopia for a Con Man

The money poured in so fast that the vaults Miller had installed in the syndicate building could not hold all the cash, so he busied himself most days by lugging satchels full of bills to several banks, where he opened personal accounts, depositing tens of thousands of dollars. The jamming crowds, wildly waving their investments, compelled Miller to put fifty clerks to work collecting and dispersing money. Investors lined up around the corner, their numbers stretching three and four deep for several blocks. The wooden stairs leading up to Miller's offices broke under the weight of the suckers, and had to be replaced with an iron stoop. An average daily take for the Franklin Syndicate was about $80,000, and the withdrawals, through cleverly staggered payments, much less.

The process was simple enough. Investors, once lucky enough to get inside Miller's offices, lined up before a wooden railing, behind which were two roll-top desks. They deposited their money with Miller or with one of his clerks and received a certificate stating that they would get 10 percent on their money within seven days. To the right of this large parlor was an enclosed area with a small glass window, and here depositors lined up to surrender their certificates and receive each week's dividends.

Miller lived in a modest apartment nearby with his wife and child. He indulged himself by buying so many suits from expensive Fifth Avenue tailors that he lacked the room to store them. He did not, however, set up new, lavish offices, feeling that his marks would better trust a firm as thriftily furnished as were their own homes. He pointed out in one of his newsletters: "Your money buys neither mahogany desks nor oil paintings. It is put to work for you at ten per cent a week. Our running expenses are small, our profits enormous and sure."

Miller's Currency Come-on

He took particular delight in setting up his offices in such a manner that new depositors had to pass the glass window where investors were lined up to receive their dividends. As one reporter for the *New York Times* put it: "The alluring sight to the intending depositors of piles of crisp bills, gold and silver, as they passed the little window, served in hundreds of instances to make the profit-crazed patrons all the more anxious to get their wealth in the syndicate's hands."

Business became so good that Miller opened a large branch office in Boston. His newspaper ads and newsletters brought money and checks by the sackful from Chicago and points west. The volume of money he trafficked in was so great that Adams Express wagons, about six a day, showed up at his offices to deliver dozens of bags of letters from investors, about $50,000 a day. A newspaperman inquiring about Miller's phenomenal success was told by one express driver, "This chap is doing a great business. I've invested myself and have made the money he promised."

Mailmen were so awed by the deliveries they made to Miller that 125 letter carriers turned over about half of their weekly earnings to him. Also down on Miller's books were 150 policemen and detectives who had deposited money with his bogus syndicate. The sight of uniformed policemen and firemen drawing interest from their investment, flashing rolls of bills and counting same in front of new depositors, had a soothing effect on suckers. One dupe later pointed to policemen drawing their interest at the height of the run on Miller's syndicate and scoffed at rumors of bankruptcy, stating, "If these officers are not afraid, why should we be?"

Fear came to Miller, however, when E. L. Blake, an editor for a financial newspaper, sent flyers out to his subscribers warning them about Miller's discretionary methods and "to give the Franklin Syndicate a wide berth."

Alarmed by this note, one of Miller's suckers in Media, Pennsylvania, wrote to him, asking what Blake's attack meant. Miller wrote back that Blake was "a blackmailer and deputy sheriffs of three counties have been unable to locate him or his office."

Enter Robert Adams Ammon

When Blake threatened to sue for slander, Miller panicked and sought the aid of Robert Adams Ammon, a well-established lawyer and professional con man who had been involved in discretionary stock scams for a decade, his most recent mulcting escapade being the defunct E. S. Dean Company, a bucket shop that had taken in half a million before it declared bankruptcy. "Colonel" Ammons, as he was known in financial circles, had managed to squeeze out of fraud convictions in the swindle, and Miller thought him to be an excellent prospective partner.

Ammons recognized Miller's Peter-to-Paul operation immediately; he himself had operated it successfully for years. (A duplicate con operated in Spain in 1876, run by a charmer named Dona Baldomera Larra who offered suckers 20 percent a week return on their money and gleaned $80,000 before being closed up; in the United States, shortly after Miller's scam took off, the less notorious Washington Syndicate run by John G. Agnew and a third by sharper Charles D. Hughes flourished briefly; beginning in 1927 a Philadelphia con man, Robert Boltz, acting as an investment counselor to a dozen or so wealthy clients, bilked $2,500,000 in the Peter-to-Paul game over thirteen years.)

Where Miller was a shadowy little figure, Ammons was a robust extrovert exuding confidence. Under his direction, Miller took a train to Boston and staunched a flow of outgoing monies when there was a run on his branch office there; $28,000 later the withdrawals stopped, and it was back to Peter-to-Paul.

Handling Blake and other snooping reporters was another matter. Ammons told Miller to refrain from any public statements, but Blake had been sufficiently incensed by Miller's remarks to file a $50,000 lawsuit for slander. Miller knew that such a legal battle would lay his scamming operation naked. He began to pack his bags. His Boston manager had already fled to Europe with more than $150,000 in two trunks. (This sharper, Edward Schlesinger, would live regally on the Riviera for several years before dying of a gastronomic attack as a result of gorging himself on caviar and turkey.)

On November 23, 1899, Miller turned over about $180,000 to Ammon and asked him to take care of his wife and child while he fled to

Montreal, Canada, to await results. Ammon promised to take care of Miller's family and keep the syndicate operating until "it all blows over," but the shrewd lawyer knew full well that Miller's scheme was all but through; warrants had been issued for his arrest.

Marks Who Would Not Quit

The die-hard Franklin Syndicate investors, however, maintained their belief in the firm far beyond its last quivering moments. With Miller in flight and the police on his trail, thousands continued to queue up before the Floyd Street offices, many waving money they eagerly wished to deposit. A reporter at the scene of the financial bedlam wrote:

> Miller could not have selected a better neighborhood in which to work his wonderful scheme. . . . It is safe to assume that nearly every man [in the Floyd Street area] had money saved. Thousands of dollars of these savings have gone into the capacious pockets of the Franklin Syndicate and the most remarkable thing of all is that Miller, during his two years residence in the neighborhood, had gained the confidence of all his depositors.
>
> Nothing could shake it. Though the syndicate was regarded by some in the nature of a "gamble," they had received their original investment back, or something near it, and most of these were content even up to the last evening to leave the money on deposit and prove to the skeptical ones that Miller was the man they always thought him—honest, upright, and one who knew how to make money for all.

The first run on Miller's syndicate occurred the day after he fled to Canada, although his departure was a secret. About $15,000 was paid out by his furiously working clerks, but when depositors saw crowds emerging with cash, they changed their minds and began redepositing their money. By noon, Miller's strongest supporters, small businessmen and their wives, arrived and began to pump cash back into the shaky firm.

Newspapermen hovered about the crowd like locusts, interviewing. A woman in a sealskin coat put $200 into the firm and waved her deposit certificate in the face of a reporter. "Why, Mr. Miller has never failed us," she emphasized. "He's always paid dividends. I put in a hundred dollars six weeks ago and have taken sixty out. It is these newspapers and bankers that are causing this trouble. Nobody believes the papers. It's envy. They'd like to make the money themselves."

A druggist named H. M. Uhlig told everybody in the crowd who would listen to him that Miller's syndicate was "the best one that ever happened," and doubled his investment. The owner of a livery stable seconded Uhlig: "Miller's all right. He can have anything he wants in this section. We'd send him to the Legislature if he wanted to go."

In the waiting lines of investors there were all manner of confident suckers. Carl A. Preuss, a cripple, proudly showed receipts for $350, hobbling away and saying: "I'll be back Monday for my dividend." A grocer, H. D. Strunck, showed his receipt for $500. "It's money in the bank." Frank Weinstein, a confectioner who had already sunk $50 in the Miller operation, was back to deposit more, and he had brought along his cousin, J. Rosenberg of Manhattan, who invested $200. A Miss Wolford from the Bronx stood for five hours in line to deposit $50 more on top of her original investment of $100. When a newspaperman told her that Miller was probably in flight and asked her if she hadn't read the papers about the con game he had pulled off, she replied: "I don't believe those kinds of nasty reports."

August Weber, owner of a delicatessen, shook his fist at one reporter and shouted: "I got money in here! My wife has got money in here! My mother-in-law has got money in there! Go away with your rumors!"

"How much money do you have invested in this scheme?" a reporter inquired.

Weber bristled. "That's none of your business, but I tell you that if Mr. Miller wants five hundred dollars from me on Monday, he can have it."

By the end of the last day of Miller's fabulous swindle, the panic had reversed itself and the firm took in about $30,000 profit. Just as employees were struggling to close the doors at 5:00 P.M. one man broke through the crowd and forced himself inside. He knocked down several clerks in his wild attempt to get to one of the roll-top desks, and his deposit of $50 was accepted. His money was splotched with blood; the man had gashed his head getting through the door.

Exit Dividends and Miller, Too

At first, Ammon pretended to know nothing of his client's whereabouts. "I have as yet," the lawyer told police, "no official knowledge that Miller is wanted by the Kings County authorities. I do not think he has gone. It has been his habit to be away from business from Friday until Monday, and he will undoubtedly show up when it is proper."

When Ammon was told by the D.A. of Kings County that he would have to appear on behalf of his client before a grand jury, the flimflamming lawyer panicked and sent for Miller, promising that he would get him a reduced sentence. Miller returned (without the almost $2 million he took with him), and was quickly tried and convicted. His so-called "reduced" sentence amounted to ten years in prison. And though more than $2 million in claims were filed, the court reduced these, oddly enough, to $287,000, none of which was paid back to investors.

Ammon, who had secreted about a quarter of a million dollars from the scam, promised to take care of Miller's wife and child, and each week for close to two years the lawyer dutifully sent them $5 to live on. The "Colonel" was himself indicted in 1901 for receiving stolen money, and went to trial in June 1903. Miller, bitter over his lawyer's niggardly treatment of his family, agreed to testify against him.

Sick, Miller swooned in the witness chair several times as Ammon, acting as his own lawyer, badgered him. But the con man was not to be intimidated, and testified that his lawyer had absconded with more than $30,000, the initial amount Miller gave Ammon to bank. It was stolen money and the lawyer knew it, insisted Miller.

Ammon was through. He was convicted and sentenced to four years' hard labor, and was disbarred in the process. Miller was returned to jail and pardoned in 1905 for his help in sending Ammon to prison. The hustler disappeared for almost a decade. A short notice announcing his divorce appeared in New York papers in 1914.

He surfaced once more in 1920, when reporters ferreted him out in Long Island, where he ran a grocery and was known as "Honest Bill." Their action was prompted by the exposure of Charles Ponzi's Boston swindle, which was identical to that which Miller had pulled off twenty years before. "He's a piker," Honest Bill Miller mused. "And a showoff. Wearing diamond stickpins, carrying fancy canes. Big house . . . lotsa cars. Who'd trust a fellow like that?"

When reporters asked Miller what had happened to the $2 million he took away with him that black Friday so many long years ago, he smiled slightly and said: "Say, gents. Do I look like a fellow who has that kind of money?" But Billy Miller always was a frugal type, as conservative as the many thousands of suckers he had bilked. He was just the sort of man who belied the adage "you can't take it with you." He most probably did.

The Grifting Black Czar, Marcus Garvey

Just as Miller played upon the ethnic dupes of his community, realizing their grudging confidence in one of their ilk could be established only by operating on their level, Marcus Aurelius Garvey preyed upon his fellow blacks in one fabulous swindle after another. His message was simple and his role exalted. He would lead 7 million blacks back to Africa and total freedom—for a price.

(A Chicago dentist, one Howard Givin, had promised fellow blacks the same things a few years earlier. He intended to ship blacks to Dakar on Cunard liners in thousand-person contingents but suddenly decided to march all the blacks in the Midwest to the sea and commandeer ships in eastern ports. As Chicago police attempted to disband Givin's group on Archer Avenue, the dentist, who by then had dubbed himself "Prince Ephraim," drew a sword and pistol and charged the officers on horseback, killing two of their number. Givin was later hanged for the murders.)

Garvey arrived in the United States in 1914 from England, where he had received an extensive education. Setting himself up in Harlem, he announced to the black community that he was the Provisional President of the African Republic, Admiral of the Black Star Line, President General of the Universal Negro Improvement Association and African Communities League, Inc., Commander of the Nobles of the Sublime Order of the Nile, Knight of the Distinguished Service Order of

Con man Marcus Aurelius Garvey, shown here in 1922, bedecked with ribbon and plumes in one of his many self-styled "admiral's" costumes. He bilked his fellow blacks for millions. (WIDE WORLD)

Ethiopia, and Representative of the Black People of the World.

This title-burdened hustler preferred the role of admiral, and donned a garish uniform replete with medals, ribbons, golden epaulets, buttons, and chevrons. He wore a plumed commodore's hat on most occasions, and his game was to sell his fellow blacks stock certificates in the Black Star Line. It was this shipping firm, Garvey pointed out through advertising and countless meetings, that would provide transportation for America's black community back to "the promised land." More than 40,000 mostly uneducated blacks purchased stock in the nonexistent line.

To thwart any government move to charge him with fraud, Garvey purchased an unseaworthy excursion boat tied to a Hudson River pier. It never went to sea. (If it had, in all probability it would have sunk immediately.) Garvey held torchlight meetings three or four times a week on the boat, his fund-collecting speeches accompanied by blaring jazz bands. To this swindle, which netted the con man about half a million dollars over a six-year period, Garvey added the scheme of the Negro Improvement Association. Members—almost 4 million of them—forked over dues of 35 cents a month. In return, Garvey promised to set up a "lusterious black kingdom" in Africa. Of each monthly due received, Garvey pocketed 10 cents, a staggering $400,000 a month.

The millionaire's life style became as expansive as his titles. Garvey purchased several mansions, dozens of open-air carriages, a hundred elegantly groomed horses to pull them, more than a thousand tailor-made uniforms aglitter with gold braid, and newspapers and magazines, the latter used to spread his scam ever wider and deeper into the black communities across the face of the land. Needing more money for his blossoming enterprises, Garvey imperiously announced an additional $1 across-the-board charge per annum for members; those who did not pay promptly would be eliminated from the rolls of future ship sailings to Africa. The suckers happily sent in their dollars.

The power Garvey wielded on behalf of American blacks was so awesome that, in 1921, he was invited to speak before the League of Nations, and this the hustler did with great flair, full of demands for his future African "republic." While Garvey wowed the European capitals with his global plans for blacks, investigators for the U.S. Post Office began to prepare a mail-fraud case against him. Their work was rewarded in 1924, when the sharper was indicted and tried. He acted as his own lawyer in a carnival-like trial, which resulted in his conviction and a five-year prison sentence in Atlanta Penitentiary.

Before surrendering to federal custody, Garvey, free on a massive bail, hustled up enormous "appeal" funds at his elaborately planned Fourth Annual International Congress of Negro Peoples of the World (the first three had never occurred). He regaled his hooting throng with promises of riches to come, and took in tens of thousands of dollars from marks he ceremoniously appointed "dukes, duchesses, knights and ladies of the Black Republic."

In Atlanta Garvey was all but forgotten for two years. His publishing and steamship empires, hollow as they were of assets, collapsed. His associations disbanded. Upon his 1927 release, the "Admiral" was deported to Jamaica, the land of his birth, where he spent his time in lonely splendor—he had stashed several million away for just such a fate.

It suddenly occurred to Garvey that European blacks needed a savior, and he was off on a heavily financed tour of the Continent, capping his crusade with a speech at London's Albert Hall, which he expected 10,000 persons to attend. But, like the reaction throughout Europe, the lecture was a fizzling flop. Only a few hundred curious people showed up to see the colorful Garvey. At the end of his talk, no applause of support hammered into the "Admiral's" ears. One spectator loudly demanded his money back and shouted to the stage: "You're as crazy as a loon!"

It was all over for Marcus Aurelius Garvey, the most enterprising black flimflammer on record.

Oil Leasing with Cox and Cook

With the boom of Wall Street in the 1920s, slickers other than Garvey moved in on the gullible stock purchaser, thousands of them. One of the most proficient bilker of marks in fake stock sales was Seymour Ernest J. Cox, called the "arch pirate" of oil promotions. Cox had worked hard at his apprenticeship in con. At fifteen he had served a sentence in Illinois for forgery; he was arrested and fined in Michigan in 1911 for fraud; and in 1914 he was again arrested and fined for using the mails to defraud. Leaving the Midwest at the time of the wildcat oil boom in Texas and Oklahoma, Cox methodically bilked 16,000 stockholders for $7 million in phony potash and oil company swindles, dozens of them, before 1920.

A devout aviator, Cox was an inventive hustler in that he was the first (if not the only) one to scout his prey by flying over the Texas oil fields, normally barred from public inspection, and noting special activity in expansion and new "gushers." Cox put this information to use through a deluge of letters he wrote to stockholders enmeshed in oil promotion.

To a prospect in St. Louis, Cox wrote: "Are you sure that you would like to own an oil-well? Are you absolutely certain you care to assume the responsibilities of becoming a millionaire?"

Cox was assisted in his grand schemes by a dozen or so confederates. One of these was the tragicomic figure, Dr. Frederick A. Cook, a hunter of fame who claimed to have scaled Mount McKinley and attempted to rob the thunder of American hero Robert Peary by insisting that his Arctic expedition had discovered the North Pole first.

These sharpers were masters of the eloquent missive, inducing thousands of shareholders in defunct and penniless oil firms to exchange their certificates plus cash for equally worthless stock created by a series of confusing company mergers. The system was known in con circles as "stock reloading," and it paid off in the millions.

Authorities in Fort Worth, Texas, intercepted a batch of letters sent out by the con men and convinced several victims to file complaints. Cox, Cook, and eleven others were brought to trial in late 1923, their sensational activities fully exposed. It was the first major legal strike against high-rolling stock con men in an age spellbound by Wall Street.

Federal Judge John M. Killits sentenced Cox to eight years in prison and fined him $8,000, but he reserved his special wrath for the sly adventurer Cook, who got a $12,000 fine and fourteen years and nine months in jail. When Cook protested and insisted that he address the court on his own behalf, Judge Killits held up his hand.

". . . you can say nothing," Killits raged. "You have come to the point where your peculiar personality fails you. The twentieth century should be proud of you. History gave us Ananias and Sapphira. They are forgotten, but we still have Dr. Cook.

"Cook, this deal of yours is so damnably rotten that it seems to me your attorneys must have been forced to hold their handkerchiefs to their noses to have represented you. It stinks to high heaven. You should not be allowed to run at large. I know that you have your ill-gotten goods put away, but your wife and daughter should not be allowed to touch them. You have stolen this money from widows and orphans. You should start another company and distribute it back to them. Cook, have you no decency at all?"

The con man only stared at that one.

"Are you not haunted at night by these pitiable figures?"

Cook blinked and put on a floppy hat, which he pulled low over his eyes.

"How can you sleep?"

The convicted sharper began to edge toward the door leading to the lockup.

"I am not going to do justice in this case," Judge Killits boomed "for I think that you will get it somewhere else. You ought to be paraded as a practical warning in every state where you have sold stock."

By then Dr. Cook, mountain climber and discoverer emeritus, had left the court, his hands manacled, his eloquence silenced.

(Left) Seymour E. J. Cox, oil stock con artist extraordinary, shown with his wife; (right) Cox's onetime partner, Dr. Frederick A. Cook, leaving Leavenworth after serving a term for mulcting suckers in phony stock schemes. (UPI)

Birrell's Baffling Bunco

Of all the many notorious hustlers in stocks, bonds, and business, the con man supreme, called by the Security and Exchange Commission "the most brilliant manipulator of corporations in modern times," was Lowell McAfee Birrell. His was an austere beginning. Remote Whiteland, Indiana, was his birthplace, and there, on February 5, 1907, he became one of five children in the impoverished family of the Reverend Birrell, a Presbyterian minister.

"I decided early I wasn't going to be poor," Birrell later told a confidant when remembering his boyhood poverty in Wilson, New York, where his family relocated and he grew up. But Birrell was considerably aided by an enormous intellect, which carried him swiftly through Syracuse University and the University of Michigan Law School, where he graduated at the top of his class. He took his doctorate in law at the unheard-of age of twenty-one and with the dean's recommendation, was soon working for the distinguished law firm of Cadwalader, Wickersham and Taft.

The 1930s saw Birrell become one of the most successful and celebrated lawyers in New York. He opened his own law firm and later formed the Greater New York Breweries, pieced together from several small breweries he had acquired. To his friends Birrell had everything —a thriving business, a luxurious personal life. But like Maxwell Anderson's avaricious character Rocco in *Key Largo,* he wanted "more . . . yeah, that's it, more."

In 1944, according to one report, a strange event took place to assure Birrell's accumulation of much, much "more." Birrell met and befriended Cecil P. Stewart, a wealthy broker and insurance underwriter. Stewart informed Birrell that he was about to die of terminal cancer; his doctors had given him six months to live. The affable lawyer pooh-poohed the verdict and told Stewart that a gentleman of his acquaintance had survived the same dire fate by allowing a doctor from Peru, whose practices were not endorsed by the AMA, to help him. Stewart consulted the same physician and later told Birrell that, because of the mysterious Peruvian's ministering, the cancer had "shriveled up."

The grateful broker couldn't thank Birrell enough but he did insist that Birrell assume directorships in all of his many firms. Stewart then retired to his estate, where he promptly died five months later, as his doctors said he would. Birrell, meanwhile, had been named executor of his will, and began wheeling and dealing.

Within thirteen years Birrell had, like Cook and Cox before him, purchased several reputable companies with loans, emptied their coffers to repay the loans, and then merged the once-sound firms with corporations of thin value and shallow stock. He created perhaps the most confusing (to SEC investigators, not to mention the layman investor) maze of corporate organizations ever in U.S. history. Through inter-corporate firms that had interlocking directorates, foreign nominees in Cuba and Canada who acted for banks assigned stock but unnamed as company registrants, and anonymous bank accounts in foreign banks, Birrell kept his financial maneuverings secret for a decade.

Stock swindler Lowell McAfee Birrell, in police custody after arriving from Brazil in 1964. (WIDE WORLD)

Birrell Bleeds Swan-Finch

The once-respected Swan-Finch Oil company was a typical Birrell operation. After acquiring the firm, he increased its shares from 43,000 to 3 million. Switching the sound assets of one firm to another company on the verge of collapse, the hustler would then promote the watered-down original company. He would appear at the close of a trading day at the Stock Exchange and purchase small packages of stock in his own firm and thus create a small upward trend the following day. When the stock inflated to bursting, he would quickly sell, pricking the bubble that burst over hundreds of dupes.

Always a showman, Birrell glad-handed his way through New York's nightclubs, cultivating friendships with gossip columnists, many of whom boosted his hollow firms in print. He seldom slept, but gave round-the-clock bashes at his lavish Bucks County, Pennsylvania, estate. There esteemed con men like Serge Rubinstein, an expert at stock rigging (who was mysteriously murdered by a strangler in his lush Fifth Avenue home in 1955), wined and wenched with $100 call girls imported from Mickey Jelke's harlot harem, including the much-touted tart Pat Ward.

Businessman turned hustler Virgil Dardi was caught up in Birrell's schemes and went to jail; he is shown here having his picture taken by movie star Elissa Landi in 1935. (UPI)

Stock Cons Galore

The companies kept crashing. Doeskin Products, Inc., United Dye and Chemical Corporation littered the floor of the stock exchange with worthless certificates. A powerhouse business victim was Virgil David Dardi, who got caught up in Birrell's muddled empire in 1953 after meeting the "ruthless looter of companies," as *Time* labeled him, at a Manhattan cocktail party. Birrell thought Dardi an excellent front for his newly acquired United Dye firm, and made him chairman of the board. Under Dardi's direction, assets from United Dye—$2 million worth—were transferred to several Birrell firms. After the assets had been disposed of, Birrell sold his 38,500 shares in United Dye. Dardi and another swindler named Alexander Guterma subsequently merged United Dye with Handridge Oil Company, which was controlled by Guterma and Las Vegas gamblers Irving Pasternak and Samuel Garfield. Then they floated more stock, which was pushed to quick sales through seven boiler rooms, and after siphoning off $5 million in profit, left the once-wholesome firm a wreck, its value per share reduced from $15 to $1. Dardi's take was a miserable $150,000, which hardly made up for the conviction and seven-year prison sentence he received. (Three of the boiler-room captains went to jail for from four to six years; Guterma, who turned state's evidence against Dardi, received a five-year prison term.)

Where Dardi, Guterma, and others created a labyrinth of their business dealings, those of Lowell Birrell were utterly Byzantine. His incredible machinations were so misleading and confusing that investigations into his records would go on for a decade. He was certainly proud of his ability to razzle-dazzle the public, his investors, the press, and the SEC (he once pointed out the weaknesses of the Security Exchange Commission rulebook to its officials, discrepancies they were compelled to admit).

The boldness of the con man was clearly demonstrated one night while Birrell was dining in one of his favorite nightclubs. He overheard a richly attired gentleman at the next table tell a friend that he had just invested heavily in a Birrell firm. Birrell, half drunk, suddenly drew himself up and said haughtily to the investor: "You put money into one of my companies? That was a mistake, sir. Nobody makes any money in any of my companies except me."

Flying Down to Rio

And that money, at least $3 million out of the $14 million bilked from stockholders, according to New York district attorney Frank Hogan, went into several suitcases hurriedly packed by the sharper in October 1957. Some months before, Birrell had received a subpoena regarding an investigation into his shadowy financial world, and the con man, no doubt, took the hint. Spreading the word that he was suddenly "under the care of a physician," the 5-foot 8-inch, 205-pound Birrell, at age fifty-two, skipped across an unknown border and was for years rumored to be variously in Guatemala City, Havana, Paris, and Caracas. Actually he was residing in that unassailable haven for American businessmen avoiding probes into their affairs, Rio de Janeiro, Brazil, which then had no extradition treaty with the United States. (A year later, baby-faced Pittsburgh sharper Earl Belle, accused of mulcting banks and stockholders of more than $2 million, permanently ensconced himself in Rio, vowing "never" to return to the United States, commenting apologetically: "I guess permanent exile is punishment enough.")

Birrell's expatriation lasted more than six years. Then, surprisingly, he reappeared, a Brazilian police officer escort at his side, in New York and was seized by authorities. With eight indictments against him for fraud, embezzlement, and evasion of income tax involving $25 million in missing funds, the hustler faced cameras with a meaty smile and unquenchable confidence.

His voluminous, crazy-quilt records—fifty-six four-drawer filing cabinets, six cartons, a bureau, and a strongbox full—had been seized in, July 1959 by police officers, but Judge Inzer B. Wyatt ruled at Birrell's first, long-drawn-out trial that the search warrant authorizing this seizure was too vague, broad, and general and the search therefore illegal and the records inadmissible.

The pudgy fifty-eight-year-old Birrell rejoiced. "The Constitution still prevails!" he exclaimed to lawyers. He would discover, after another seven years fraught with agonizing legalities, that it certainly did. On July 30, 1970, the majestic corporate flimflammer was sentenced to two years in jail on charges of fraud. Apparently Birrell had overlooked some details of his minor swindling, and dogged prosecutors proved his unauthorized use of stock certificates in getting a $5,000 loan from the First National Bank of Cincinnati. This time appeals did no good; the Supreme Court upheld Birrell's conviction on January 11, 1972, and the con man's career ended behind the bars he had so cleverly evaded for decades.

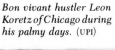

Bon vivant hustler Leon Koretz of Chicago during his palmy days. (UPI)

Lovable Leo Koretz

Though Birrell's saga of stock hustling is a landmark con and his ostentatious methods leave one stunned, no man ever displayed more gall than Chicago stock hustler Leo Koretz. (This odd schemer, a golliwog in appearance, would commit the most bizarre suicide in the history of crime anywhere. While awaiting trial for his single $5 million swindle, Koretz persuaded one of his many sweethearts to bring a five-pound box of candy to his cell. He solemnly ate every one of the chocolates and then keeled over dead, being a hopeless diabetic.)

Whether out of contempt or humor, Leo Koretz in the early 1920s sold millions of dollars of oil stock in nonexistent Central American wells to the top 500 tycoons of Chicago and then threw a party to celebrate the scam. The 500 dinner guests, dressed in tails, sat down to a sumptuous banquet at the Congress Hotel. Sitting next to a beaming Leo Koretz was William Randolph Hearst's right-hand editorialist and fellow newspaper czar, Arthur Brisbane, who had also invested heavily in Koretz's con.

During the happy fete, a bevy of newsboys raced through the hall, loudly hawking extras and shouting: "Extry, extry, read all about it —Leo Koretz Oil Swindle! Con Man Koretz Exposed! Millions Lost in Swindle!"

Before the bug-eyed investors could stagger dumbfounded to their feet and throttle the hustler, a grinning Arthur Brisbane rose. He had faked the story as a party jest, and Koretz had obligingly helped by writing out all details of his enormous swindle for the phony extra.

Holding up his hands, Brisbane said through hearty guffaws, "It's a joke! We did it just for a lark! Mr. Koretz is a great and honorable financier!"

The explanation having soothed the suckers, who would learn the lark's grim truth days later, Brisbane put his arm about the con man and drew him up next to him at the speaker's table. Brisbane waved a spoon with his free hand and then led the entire banquet hall of dupes in singing, to Leo Koretz, a rousing rendition of "For He's a Jolly Good Fellow."

Twelve

Con Clans

Joe Furey was worried. Never in his long career as a con man had a sucker reacted like J. Frank Norfleet, who, for four agonizing years, chased him and his clan of hustlers across the country, seeking vengeance for being mulcted out of $45,000. Furey, who had been successful as a con man for thirty years in Texas and the western states, found it impossible to believe that one man could so disrupt the largest, most lucrative confidence ring ever established in the United States. But he had, and with alacrity, unraveled in his search the secret operations of the 500-man con ring headed by Furey, Lou Blonger, and Adolph W. Duff, better known as "Kid Duffy."

Denver's King Con

Lou Blonger, a French-Canadian who had migrated to the mining camps while still a youth and then settled in Denver, Colorado, had started it all in 1880. With his brother Sam tending bar, Blonger opened in that year a rowdy saloon replete with wide-open gambling (all of the

214

games from roulette to faro were rigged) and dance-hall hussies available to customers for $5 a night. As law and order swept Denver clean of the more obnoxious public vices, Blonger first got rid of the girls, then the gambling. But his suffering saloon was soon revived when he instituted wholesale bunco games, tightly protected by local police who were in Blonger's secret employ.

For almost forty years Denver was Blonger's town; he operated his hustles without any interference from the law, and his clan of con men broadened until, in 1922, more than 500 sharpers were on his payroll or split 50 percent of their monies with him for being allowed to operate in Denver.

This large, red-faced, fat con artist was *the* "fixer" in the history of American con, and for several decades a private phone line ran from his office above the saloon directly to the office of the city's chief of police. As "King of the Denver Underworld," Blonger could and did order the arrest or release of any man in Denver. It soon became the capital of con, and such master hustlers as Jefferson Randolph ("Soapy") Smith began their career there, comfortably fleecing suckers while under Blonger's protective umbrella, lining the fixer's pockets with half of the take. Smith's bunco racket was as simple as any other in that gold-brick era. Working with a roper, suckers would be inveigled into purchasing bars of soap from the hustler when they were told that under the wrappers of several were $5 bills. This was demonstrated when the roper purchased a bar of soap, peeled back the wrapper, and shouted "Eureka! A five-spot! The man's honest," or some such drivel for the naïve rubes crowding around. Of course, no other bars of soap containing the alleged $5 bills were sold.

First Ask the Fixer

Blonger's power at the fix was surprisingly flexed one day at the turn of the century when Dick Turner, a deputy sheriff from a remote Colorado town, showed up in Denver on business. Minutes after registering, he was approached in the Albany Hotel by a con man newly added to Blonger's ring. Turner sidestepped the swindle the hustler

Lou Blonger, the Denver "Fixer" and head of the largest con ring in history; he died in prison at 73.

attempted to pull and went to the police. A detective accompanied Turner back to the hotel, and there, after collaring the con man, who was in the act of hustling another victim, ran into Lou Blonger.

"What's all the fuss about?" the fixer asked the detective.

The officer shrugged and said: "Nothing much, except one of your boys is running a little wild."

After hearing Turner's story, Blonger's face flushed scarlet. He had long established the rule that con men were to lure suckers to Denver and bilk them there, but that they were never to fleece local people. The attempt to mulct Turner was sacrilege. Blonger turned to the sharper and exploded: "You were recommended to me as a first-class bunco artist, and the first thing you do, you damned bastard, is to pick up a deputy sheriff. What the hell are you tackling the law for, anyway? Don't you have sense enough to let Colorado people alone in Denver? I paid your transportation to Denver and put you to work. Now you walk back, and start now."

With that the two lawmen, Blonger, and the con man drove to the city limits in a taxi, and Blonger tongue-lashed the hustler again before sending him drooping along the road into the far county. Banishment from Denver was a mild rebuke for breaking one of Blonger's dictates. Many were beaten senseless for breaking his rules. Nobody defied him, not even police chief Mike Delaney, who was on his payroll and was available for orders from the con chief on a twenty-four-hour basis. For twenty years, not one con man working for Blonger went to prison.

Kid Duffy Runs Things

Lou Blonger's Denver con clan became so unwieldy that in 1904 he took in a rough character named Adolph W. Duff, "Kid Duffy," as a partner. It was Duffy's job to make open contact with the phalanxes of hustlers operating in and about Denver, provide protection for their scams, and collect Blonger's cut of each score. Lou craved the respectability befitting his boss status, and Kid Duffy was to be his front for two decades.

Kid Duffy had once been part of the old Mabray Gang, a con ring operating in Council Bluffs, Iowa, which included the "Waco Kid," Byron Hames, and Fred "Deacon" Buckminster, Yellow Kid Weil's one-time partner, who had migrated from Chicago. He later joined the Webb City Gang and trimmed tourists in fixed foot races in the Garden of the Gods. An apprentice pickpocket and occasional opium addict, Kid Duffy soon proved his worth to Blonger by raking in about $10 million a year for Blonger from the many organized cons practiced each week in Denver. The ring became so large that out-of-town suckers were fleeced in the city only during the summer. During the winter months groups of con men, many directly under orders from Blonger and Kid Duffy, led raids into the warm vacation climates of Florida, Louisiana, and Texas.

Adolph W. Duff, better known as "Kid Duffy," Blonger's Denver con ring manager.

One of these, in 1920, was led by Joe Furey, a one-time partner of William Elmer Mead of the magic-wallet con. He had achieved so much fame that he commanded his own squad of con men, whose moves were loosely planned by Blonger. Furey's subgang of con men included W. B. Spencer, E. J. Ward, Charles Gerber, and Reno Hamlin, all experienced sharpers. Fort Worth was one of their many winter stops, and in a hotel there in 1920, employing Mead's magic-wallet trick, the group roped in a sucker named J. Frank Norfleet, a Texas cattleman who owned a sizable Texas ranch.

The Fleecing of J. Frank Norfleet

The "financier" who got back his wallet from Norfleet was so grateful that he offered Norfleet $100 as a reward. The cattleman refused the money. The financier (Furey) insisted on investing the $100 on Norfleet's behalf. The next day Norfleet was given $3,000, the return on the stock deal. He was told that he could keep it, return the next day and that he could borrow call money with it. The following day he was told that he had made $200,000. This fabulous sum, the hurrah, was placed before the Texas rancher, and according to one report, "he had the money stacked up on his arm in bills and was preparing to leave the place when the next step in the procedure was introduced." This was the convincer.

The convincer was a simple matter, Furey and the others explained. Norfleet would have to show earnest money, that he would have been willing and able to pay for any losses the "investment" group might have incurred on his behalf if their deal had collapsed. Norfleet, extremely gullible for a man who had long been a sheriff, put up $20,000. The gang was prepared to accept this score and leave when a Fort Worth law officer, who was in league with the con men and who had offered them protection over the years, insisted that a second score be made against Norfleet. The rancher was told that his earnings had soared to double the original sum and that an additional $25,000 was required as earnest money. Norfleet gutted his bank account and paid this amount, too, a total of $45,000. The con clan then pulled the "envelope switch," leaving the rancher with newspaper clippings while they divided the take and split up, each running in a different direction.

Norfleet's Manhunt

Furey first went to his family living in Denver, but decided, once he heard that Norfleet was on his trail, to hide out with his second family —Joe was a devout bigamist—in Los Angeles. In almost all cons of this sort, the victim seldom complains of being taken in, but J. Frank Norfleet, a wiry fellow who stood only five foot four and sported a bushy mustache, was a determined man. He reported the swindle to the Fort Worth police and was told there was little hope of retrieving his money. The Pinkerton Detective Agency and William Burns, head of the Bureau of Investigation, told him the same thing.

"Then I'll go after those people myself," Norfleet told Burns. "I'll get them, too, even if it takes the rest of my life."

Thus began the great hunt for the most notorious con clan in America. His wife Mattie took over the ranch, and Norfleet opened his campaign by giving his story to the press. Newspapers across the country printed it, along with descriptions of the hustlers. A sucker in San Francisco who had been mulcted by Gerber and Ward turned them in to police after reading about Norfleet's bilking. The ex-sheriff traveled to San Bernadino, California, and there identified both con men, who complained bitterly about Norfleet's manhunt. Ward then committed suicide in his cell rather than face an extended prison sentence.

The dogged Texan then sleuthed out Reno Hamlin in a Montana whorehouse, roped him like a calf, and dragged him through the mud of the main street of the town to the jail. He moved through seventeen states and even took brief trips to England, Canada, Mexico, and Cuba in search of Spencer and the elusive Joe Furey. Following leads and spending more than $17,000 in his pursuit, Norfleet arrived in Montreal in late 1923, going to the Hotel Windsor, where Spencer was allegedly residing.

In front of the hotel, Norfleet looked about a crowd gaping at a human fly, a then-popular species of daredevils, climbing the building. There stood his quarry, Spencer, watching the climber in awe.

"Spencer!" Norfleet yelled, and grabbed the con man by the neck.

"What? You?" Spencer broke away and threw a powerhouse punch that flattened the tough sheriff. The hustler then ran wildly through the crowd and dashed into a movie theater, Norfleet on his heels. They fought and struggled up aisles, and the chase ended in the balcony, where the con man disappeared out an exit door. Weeks later Norfleet discovered Spencer hiding out in Salt Lake City but by the time he arrived there the con man was under arrest. He had turned himself in rather than face Norfleet's wrath.

The Texan glared at him through the bars of a cell. Spencer shook his head and said: "None of us has had a minute's peace since you got on our trail." Norfleet only grunted satisfaction, then set out to capture Joe Furey.

He had received a wire from a Western Union official whom Norfleet had paid to inform him of any communication between Furey and his Los Angeles wife. Mrs. Furey had received money from the con man from Jacksonville, Florida, and Norfleet was soon on a train speeding to that city. After obtaining a warrant for Furey's arrest from the governor of the state, the Texan located the hustler in a restaurant and dove across the table at him. Grabbing Furey by the neck, he threw him to the floor and then jumped on him feet first.

"Help! Police!" Furey cried out. "This fellow is after my jewels!" A waiter stepped in and cracked a bottle over Norfleet's head, but Norfleet would not get off the prone Furey. He merely reached out and

J. Frank Norfleet (left) tracked down a con clan after being bilked for $45,000 (UPI); he is shown here with members of the Blonger/Duff con ring. Row one (left to right): A. H. Potts, George Leon Kelly, Robert "Big Nose" Knowles, Arthur B. "Tex" Cooper. Row two (left to right): Walter Byland, John J. Grady, Leon Felix, Roy Coyne.

drew the waiter's legs inward, sending him to the floor. A customer then attacked the waiter, shouting: "So that's the way you treat patrons, huh?" Waiters and other employees of the cafe then joined in battle with fist-swinging patrons, and throughout the donnybrook, Norfleet sat on Joe Furey's chest, grinning.

Police arrived and arrested both the con man and his victim. When Norfleet produced his warrant, Furey was turned over to his custody and returned to Texas and a prison sentence. On the long train ride back from Florida, Furey, manacled to Norfleet (who kept a pistol in his pocket aimed constantly at the con man's heart), offered the Texan $20,000 to let him go.

"Not a chance," Norfleet told him. Then the ex-sheriff asked him: "Why have you never reformed, an intelligent man like you, a man who could have been something in the legitimate world?"

Furey thought about that for a long while and then stated: "I don't know why I did not. It would have been far better if I had. Somehow, the excitement had become necessary to me. I had to keep on from one thrill to another to keep from remembering all the things I had done."

"Like what you did to me?"

"You and a lot of others. . . . Memory is a luxury that only those who go straight can afford. I believe that three months with no new thrills to quiet my memories would have driven me screaming 'bug house.' I had to go on."

220

Norfleet deposited his con man with the Texas authorities and returned, broke, to his ranch, which after four years of neglect had failed to yield a profit. But the con men that he had so ruthlessly followed and captured had exhausted their monies, too. Furey, Spencer, and the others had paid out more than $28,000 to lawyers and lawmen for protection against and hideouts from the con hunter.

Not content with capturing the con men who had hustled him, Norfleet went to Denver, and there, with the help of the few local law officials not on the con clan's payroll, eventually exposed Blonger, Kid Duffy, and about 500 other con men, scores of whom were sent to prison. Blonger's bunco ring was through, and the Texas sheriff, whose odyssey certainly equaled some of the exploits of Wyatt Earp, went back to raising mules.

The *New York Times* commented: "Just because a man is born a sucker is no sign that he may not turn into a tiger before his earthly course is run. J. Frank Norfleet made the evolutionary jump almost overnight."

The Buncoing Burr Brothers

Rivaling the Blonger con clan of the West was the Burr brothers ring in New York. The bunco games played by the Burr brothers, however, were restricted exclusively to selling fake stocks. Hundreds of sharpers worked for them in dozens of cities, selling the most ridiculous stocks ever perpetrated by con men, and yet Shelton and Eugene Burr took in more than $50 million before their activities were halted in 1910. The names of the companies they claimed to represent should have tipped off the thousands of suckers they bilked immediately, but their promise to double investments in a matter of weeks was apparently too enticing. The Burr brothers offerings included Rawhide Tarantula, Montezuma Mining and Smelting, and Golden Fleece Mining.

Another band of con men was headed by the Kaadt brothers of Indiana, who sold a "diabetes cure" for a number of years and took in millions of dollars. Out of one group of seventeen who subscribed to the Kaadt cure, twelve went into diabetic comas and five died.

Mike McDonald ran things in Chicago for thirty years, protecting swarms of con men beneath his political umbrella.

Chicago's Mike McDonald and Friends

The con clan that ruled Chicago for half a century was headed up by Mike McDonald, gambling impresario and political bigwig. Under his direction, confidence men made the Windy City the capital of con before the turn of the century. Some of the most celebrated hustlers in the rackets first began as "Mike McDonald's boys," and these included sharpers like Red Adams, Lou Ludlum, Tom and John Wallace, George W. Post, Snapper Johnny Malloy, the Gondorf brothers (Charley and Fred), Charley Drucker, Kid Miller, Snitzer the Kid, Jim McNally, Red Jimmy Fitzgerald, Tom O'Brien ("king of the bunco men") Dutchy Lehman, Dutch Bill, Boss Ruse, and Black-Eyed Johnny.

McDonald ran his con fiefdom with a pocketbook bulging with payoff money. In return for 40 percent of all scores, he provided bail bonds, paid off policemen and politicians, hired friendly witnesses, and fixed juries. He provided lists of easy, wealthy marks that he purchased from an army of tipsters in his employ. It was a con man's heyday in Mike McDonald's time, and millions could be made by a subgang each year. Tom O'Brien, before retiring to Paris, mulcted a dozen or so suckers with four ropers for $500,000 during the five months of the Chicago's World's Fair in 1893. Naturally, McDonald got his 40 percent.

A grim example of McDonald's clout can be taken from a chapter in the life of John Turner (alias Hank Davis), who was one of the boss's most enterprising hustlers. In his subgang of sharpers worked Ross Saulsbury, James Fay, and Billy Brush. Saulsbury's wife, a college graduate who had once been in the employ of a Niagara Falls whorehouse madam, acted as the roper for this clan. When her husband went to prison in 1874 (a rare event for one of Mike McDonald's boys), she moved in with Turner and set up dozens of scores for him. The couple's social status, even among the thieves and brothel keepers, was frowned upon, and when saloon owner Charles D. Whyland refused to have the pair in his wife's house for dinner, Turner drew a revolver, and in front of dozens of witnesses, pumped three bullets into the piety-bound bar man, killing him.

Awaiting the gallows, Turner told reporters: "It was an unfortunate scrape, and I can't blame anything but drink." McDonald used his influence only hours before the hangman was scheduled to make his appearance, and Turner's sentence was reduced to twenty-one years in the state prison. He served only a few years, and was soon back on the streets of Chicago, hustling.

The con clans of Chicago diminished in stature and political clout following McDonald's death on August 9, 1907 (he died of a broken heart, some said, when his second wife, burlesque queen Dora Feldman, thirty-five years his junior, shot and killed her reluctant lover Webster Guerin). Yet the con rings of Chicago struggled for existence alongside the bullying gangsters of Al Capone, their numbers sizable enough in 1933 to permit a convention in one of the posh hotels. The purpose of this meet, attended by "more than a dozen of the higher minds among the confidence profession," was to seek ways of extracting hustlers from the ranks of the gun-toting mobsters and to clean up their trade.

Courtney Riley Cooper, criminal historian, quoted one of the con enclave leaders, perhaps Yellow Kid Weil, as saying,

> . . . there's that Earl Christman [who had joined the Barker gang], a good confidence man as long as he stuck to his racket. But no, he's got to get tough. Wanted to rob banks. Well, what's happened to him? He got killed. And Dick Galatas [who figured prominently in the Kansas City Massacre]—he's been getting heavy for a year or so. Running around with those big mugs and thinking he amounted to something. Why, they tell me he's even been carrying a gun. Can you tie that—a confidence man lugging artillery! What for? To tap wires with? Or deal seconds off a deck of cards? I'm telling you we've got to clean house! Got to throw out these people who are ruining our profession!"

The "Terrible Williamsons"

But Chicago had moved into its most violent criminal stages by that time, as had almost all other metropolitan areas, and the con clans no longer wielded power on a unified front. Five years after the hustlers'

Chicago convention, the last, and perhaps strangest, con clan became known to law officials. They operated in small towns, and on a door-to-door basis. They would be known for eighty years as the "Terrible Williamsons," and their members are active to this day throughout America.

Scottish by heritage, the first of the clan to immigrate to the United States was Robert Logan Williamson, who settled briefly in Brooklyn around 1895, raised a large family, and then moved off gypsy fashion, along with hundreds of his relatives, to fleece citizens by peddling phony goods. Before World War I the clan was firmly entrenched in American con, making Cincinnati their headquarters.

Like so many con men before and after them, the Williamsons concentrated on the gullibility of the American housewife. They sold her fake fur coats, at $100 a wrap, which would develop holes in a week; allegedly imported Persian rugs; Irish laces; English woolens all bearing impressive brand crests and guarantees—all of which were shoddy goods purchased in huge job lots from New York wholesale firms. A longtime supplier, Sweeney & Johnson, forwarded goods "c/o General Delivery" to the bilking area designated by the Williamsons. When asked about the conning practices of the clan, owner Patrick L. Sweeney tersely stated: "They're good customers, that's all. We don't claim the goods to be any different than it is. . . . What they do with it, how much they charge . . . [we] can't control."

The firm, however, functioned for years as a mailing address for Williamsons all over the country wanting to get in touch with other clan members. In 1933 owner Patrick Sweeney sent bail money to a cluster of Williamsons who had been arrested for peddling without a license.

Samuel Wiseman, operator of Eastern Woolens in Manhattan, was also a long-time benefactor of several Williamsons who sold his mail-order goods for absurdly inflated amounts. In 1955, when members of the clan invaded New England (an area known to hustlers as blue river land because it was so difficult to put across a scam there, Wiseman came to their aid. The chief of police in Littleton, New Hampshire, Stanley McIntyre, arrested Mrs. Katherine Williamson, her brother-in-law James Williamson, and a cousin, Mrs. Alexina Gregg. Not having the money to pay the $200 fine imposed by the state for peddling without a license, Mrs. Gregg asked if she could call a friend to help them out. She called Samuel Wiseman in New York while detectives listened in on another line.

"I'll wire the money," the lawmen heard Wiseman promise. "Pay the fines and get out of town." They did.

Tidal-Wave Con Clan

Williamsons have since dotted the land like daisies, preying upon both rural and urban suckers. Their number has reportedly increased to about 2,000 at this writing, with intrafamily marriages permitting first cousins to wed and thus perpetuate the close-knit fabric of the con clan. As a rule the Williamson travel in expensive cars—Cadillacs or Lincoln Continentals—live out of trailers and are constantly on the move. Patriarchs of the hustling brood for nearly half a decade were Uncle Isaac Williamson, known as "Two Thumbs," and his wife, "Black Queen Jennie," lifetime residents of Cincinnati. They ruled hosts of conning clan members with traditional Scottish and Sassenach names—McMillans, Stewarts, Greggs, Johnstons, Keiths, McDonalds, Reids. They received annual tribute for their expert advice on scams from their "families," sometimes as much as half of the take. Those members reluctant to kick back the proper shares were quickly collared by Isaac's three bully-boy sons, George ("Goose Neck"), Tom ("Texas"), and Alexander ("The Gopher"). The overall schemes perpetrated by this nomadic con clan was estimated to be $5 million a year.

Authorities first learned of the existence of the "Terrible Williamsons" in 1938 when one of their number, Charles Williamson, a law-abiding citizen horrified at the clan's activities, wrote to the Better Business Bureau in Pittsburgh, exposing his relatives.

He warned that fifty members of the clan were descending on one town to sell fake lightning rods (a painted stick or piece of rope for which members charged suckers as much as $300), paint sprays diluted with crankcase oil that would wash from the side of a building at the first rain, and cheap rugs and clothing. And then Charles Williamson added a note of terror to his letter: "Please, I beg you, please, don't reveal even where these letters were mailed from or they would kill my poor old wife and myself." Three of the clan were arrested, Charles Williamson's identity remained a secret, and the letters kept coming.

Through this plucky informant, as well as the periodic arrests (almost always on misdemeanor offenses), lawmen have a fairly accurate picture of the movement and migrations of the con clan. A running checklist of the clan's historical highlights:

1927. About 200 Williamsons descended upon Columbus, Ohio, fleecing hundreds of suckers with useless "prayer rugs" allegedly imported from Persia. This town still receives annual visits.

1935. An internecine war broke out between a band of Williamsons and their satellite family, the McMillans, in an Atlanta, Georgia, trailer park, with several members jailed after a free-for-all resulting from a dispute over which territory the factions controlled. The feud lasted for months and erupted again in another camp outside of Springfield, Pennsylvania.

1936. More than 100 Williamsons from the various subclans gathered in a sprawling trailer camp outside of Oklahoma City, under the command of matriarch Mrs. Jean Williamson. There they were involved in a con clan murder when Isaac Cotton Williamson was stabbed to death by George C. Williamson, the argument again over territorial rights. George attempted to commit suicide by drinking carbolic acid, but survived to turn himself in to police; he drew a two-year sentence for manslaughter, the strongest charge ever leveled at a Williamson to date. A glut of Williamsons in that same year invaded Omaha, Nebraska, bilking thousands of dollars from citizens by selling fake baby sealskin coats.

1948. A clan of Williamsons, almost 100 strong, swept through the state of Michigan in summer and gleaned $60,000 through phony paint-spraying offers.

1952. Scores of Williamsons were rounded up by police after members brawled themselves bloody in Miami Beach; again the fracas was over con spoils.

1954. Gangs of Williamsons took in more than $40,000 in two months from gullible Minnesota and Iowa farmers by installing fake lightning rods on houses and painting barns (the boards of which later warped from the application).

1955. Police in Hartford, Connecticut, raided a Williamson trailer camp and confiscated half a ton of cheap bolts of rayon the ring had been peddling as imported cloth from Heath, England; their average take in a five-week period was estimated to be $20,000. Other members of the con clan attacked suckers in Topeka, Kansas, late in this year, selling hundreds of rabbit-skin coats for $50 each; cost to the clan, $5 per.

1965. Donald Williamson headed a clan that bought a general store with an excellent credit rating in Flint, Michigan, and then began ordering thousands of expensive products on credit, selling the goods at reduced rates; the ring profited in the tens of thousands before being arrested. Donald Williamson got three years in prison.

1966. More than 600 members of the Terrible Williamsons invaded the Los Angeles area in what *Newsweek* described as "an annual migratory pursuit of that most gullible of all West Coast fish, the common California sucker." Their "guaranteed, aluminized" spray-painting jobs, fake roofing installments, and other bunco games gleaned the clan close to $500,000 in a few months. Two Williamsons, operating from a white pickup truck, conned one naïve old woman into giving them several blank checks, which she signed and thought to be payment for a new roof. They filled in amounts totaling $8,000 and cashed them.

The clan is still active, occasionally adding members to the con family resting place, Spring Grove Cemetary in Cincinnati, Ohio, while new generations of apprentice con men and women emergetically take the place of their gypsylike elders. This peculiar sub rosa society of con continues to this date, its members dedicated to a career of grift. A police official on the L.A. bunco squad who has been contending with this locust-like swarm of hustlers for years, shook his head and stated: "I think that, in their own mind, they don't think they're crooks. They do a job, after all. It goes back to this: You get what you pay for."

Packy Lennon and His Supreme Sucker

If there ever was a victim of a con clan who got nothing at all for what he paid out, except public humiliation and an enormous depletion of his bank account, it was the trusting industrialist Augustine Joseph Cunningham. The con clan that scored almost half a million dollars on him in one of the most unique schemes ever hatched waited twenty-two years to snare him.

Patrick Henry Lennon headed this Manhattan-based ring. Where the Williamsons are contented with nickel-dime profits accumulating into tens of thousands through group effort, Lennon and his cohorts would not settle for payments of less than five figures at each clip from Cunningham and other wealthy businessmen dupes. They were big-time bleeders all: Lennon, known as "Packy" in the world of con; Leo F. Hampton; Harold P. Odom; George V. Arlen; and a host of other ropers and scammers who had operated clan style for thirty years.

As early as 1930, Lennon was a proven stock sharper, his operations so notorious that the *New York Evening Journal* published his photo and beneath it warned its readers in a caption: "Don't let him sell you any stock." The reason for this journalistic blast was the $30-a-share Inter-City Radio & Telegraph Corporation, scandalously manipulated by Lennon and his cronies, which was discovered worthless in 1929. Lennon and others were indicted for stock fraud but not before they had bilked A. J. Cunningham out of more than $100,000; the industrialist from Rochester, New York, had been purchasing this stock for almost three years. The Lennon clan never forgot their most gullible victim.

Cunningham is perhaps the prime example of a sucker mulcted in a stock con, having invested blithely in a worthless firm since 1926. His financial empire was that of the genteel world of the nineteenth century, his grandfather a manufacturer of horse carriages as early as 1838. James Cunningham Son & Company moved on to produce the Cunningham automobile at the turn of the century, and during World War II the firm provided the military with tanks and planes. It went on to become a leader in producing electronic switches. (An occasional on-order Cunningham limousine was made for the Pope and reigning monarchs in Europe.)

The Inter-City Swindle

Lennon and his stock ring served prison terms for their various frauds after flimflamming Cunningham during the Jazz Age, and being the dedicated con men they were they kept up to date with, studied the movements of, and for years plotted against their wonderful sucker. In

1951, armed with complete profiles of Cunningham, the clan struck again. In February one of the clan showed up at Cunningham's Rochester mansion, explaining that he was a friend of one Harry Hoffman who had suffered great financial losses along with Cunningham when Inter-City collapsed those long, black years ago in 1929. It had come to his attention, the roper explained patiently, that Dr. Randolph Parker, who had been head of Inter-City, had died and left an extraordinary will in which he named the three largest investors in his company as inheritors of his patents. Cunningham and Hoffman were the first two, a man named J. Driscoll the other. The con man showed Cunningham a copy of the will. The industrialist got only a fleeting glance at the bogus document before the hustler again pocketed it. Cunningham was then told that the patents left to him and the other two had become quite valuable over the years, especially in the motion picture business, and that several Hollywood moguls, who had infringed upon them, were now willing to settle out of court to avoid publicity.

"What is the settlement?" Cunningham casually inquired.

"Oh, about sixty million dollars."

The industrialist didn't lift an eyebrow but asked to hear more details, and the con man promised to report back shortly. He returned some days later with Harry Hoffman in tow. Hoffman was Lennon. Cunningham not only failed to recognize the very hustler who had conned him into buying more than 8,000 shares of the worthless Inter-City stock twenty-two years before, but immediately took a liking to the congenial con man as they both bemoaned their 1929 losses. And true to his tight-lipped, close-to-the-vest attitude, Cunningham had not consulted with either his lawyer or banker to investigate the ridiculous Parker legacy. It was his business and no one else's. (Parker never did exist, neither did J. Driscoll—or Hoffman.)

Hoffman-Lennon explained that the $60 million in Hollywood settlements might have some snags. Other investors in the Inter-City deal would probably put forth claims against the three inheritors, not to mention the big block of shares held by the mysterious Mr. Driscoll. It might be necessary for both of them to buy off the troublemakers, but if it came to that, any appreciable amount would be quibbling compared with $60 million. Cunningham agreed to share the payments if necessary.

It was necessary. Two months later, Hoffman-Lennon called stating that a particularly annoying Inter-City investor could be bought off for a measly $3,200, Cunningham's payment being half. The Rochester industrialist dutifully sent along his check in the amount of $1,600, the first score in a series of nonstop payments that would accrue to a total of eighty-four checks. The payments were sent to a Manhattan office occupied by a friend of Lennon's, a disbarred lawyer.

Lennon's Ring Collects and Collects and Collects

Then began a regular courier service conducted by the con men traveling between Manhattan and Rochester. One time George Arlen, using another name, would appear to collect the payoff amounts from the duped Cunningham. Then it would be Harold Odom.

Payments had to be increased, Cunningham was informed, because certain Hollywood lawyers were demanding side money before allowing the settlement to take place. The industrialist paid out about $50,000, then got stubborn. Hoffman-Lennon called him and invited him to a meeting with the third heir, Driscoll, who had, surprisingly, arrived in town from Oklahoma and was staying at the Fifth Avenue Hotel. The trio met, Driscoll impersonated by an aging hustler named Knowles. The third heir launched into a diatribe against the Hollywood holdup artists to whom he claimed he had paid several hundred thousand dollars before Cunningham could voice his own discontent with the bogged-down proceedings. The conference ended with everyone making out more checks— Cunningham's the only one being valid—to pay off those huckstering Hollywood types.

The enterprising Lennon milked Cunningham for about $50,000 the following year through promises of getting partial payments from the West Coast moguls, at least $2 million. This didn't materialize, Lennon told Cunningham, because Driscoll had suddenly been killed in an auto accident and his widow was demanding instant payment. Cunningham again sent along a check for about $15,000. When things slowed down again, Lennon sent the ancient con man Leo Hampton to visit the Rochester businessman, and Hampton told the sucker that he had heard of the fantastic Parker will and had purchased an interest in Hoffman-Lennon's share for about $50,000. But there were all kinds of financial arrangements to be made, and more money was required. Hampton walked away with about $35,000 more of Cunningham's money.

It must have seemed to Packy Lennon that the bilking of Cunningham would never end. Throughout the next year, 1953, another $200,000 flowed into his clan's hands. On one occasion he called and told Cunningham that he needed $30,000 to put the deal through. He called a few days later and said that he had erred and that $50,000 was required. Cunningham, who was perhaps approaching senility by then, mistook the total amount for $80,000 and paid, to a Lennon courier in cash, incredibly, $30,000 more than what the con men had demanded.

The courier on this occasion was George Arlen (born Sidney Gottlieb), and when he discovered the overpayment, he conned the con clan by keeping the additional $30,000. He went into his own phony stock company, Lennon none the wiser and content to have his payment of $50,000.

Arlen's secret betrayal of the clan was duplicated with amazing ease by another Lennon emmissary named O'Brien, who collected a regular installment from Cunningham but returned two days later on his own and told the industrialist that another $14,000 was required and got that, too. O'Brien disappeared, and his scam over Lennon wasn't learned until the clan chieftan rang up his favorite mark and told him he again needed more money. Cunningham complained that he had given his secretary an additional $14,000 only days ago. Lennon gulped surprise and fumbled through some excuses about "mix-ups in our paperwork."

Delivering the Mythical Mother Lode

Early in 1954, Hoffman-Lennon rang up Cunningham and informed him that a new secretary named William Ryan would be handling the paperwork in New York. He, Lennon, was compelled to take to the road to tie up all the loose ends of the $60 million deal. The new secretary was Harold Odom, one-time race-track tout and dedicated con man. He bilked the industrialist for several weeks, and then Cunningham received a call from the erstwhile Hoffman-Lennon. The con man told him that they had won their expensive battle and that the Hollywood moguls had paid out $50 million in cash and this was on its way to New York inside an armored car.

Patrick H. "Packy" Lennon, one of the smoothest stock hustlers in the business for thirty years. (WIDE WORLD)

"All you have to do now, Mr. Cunningham," Lennon announced, "is sit by your window and watch for the truck to pull up. Your share is $28 million, and I would suggest locking this amount up in your safe when it is delivered and saying nothing about the whole affair."

Cunningham's vigil by the window was interrupted by another call from Lennon. Bad news. To shorten its route, the armored car had crossed into Canada, and when it reentered the United States the truck was searched and the $50 million impounded by federal agents. Legal funds were required to free the fortune from the grasp of the government. Cunningham sadly sent off another check.

After a nervous lapse of more than six months, Cunningham received another call from Lennon, stating that an additional $30,000 was desperately needed to pay off a stubborn customs official. The con man sent along another messenger, but this time the old man refused to pay. After several wheedling calls, all Lennon was able to extract from the gullible Cunningham was another $600. His mark, it seemed, was bilked out. When the loquacious Lennon did manage to convince Cunningham to dump another $10,000 into the scheme, the industrialist's bankers refused to extend him credit, having loaned Cunningham $325,000 in his zany, secretive deal. The businessman was in turn convinced by his bankers to investigate the affair, and postal inspectors were soon on Lennon's trail. Lennon's con clan had mulcted Cunningham for an amazing $423,771, but had kept their hands busy during 1951–55 by taking seven other wealthy men for more than $300,000.

Lennon, Odom, Arlen, and Hampton were picked up in early 1956, tried, and convicted. Lennon got five years, the others lesser sentences. Scores of other con men who worked in minor capacities for the Lennon con clan escaped. One of them called Cunningham some months after the ring was sent to prison and asked the industrialist to send him $10,000 for his children's education, since he was going to prison and the "little ones" would have no one to care for them. Before a postal inspector talked him out of it, Cunningham had his checkbook open and a pen poised.

Thirteen

Con International

PRAGUE-BORN HUSTLER Victor "The Count" Lustig, who was to make an almost revered name for himself among American con men, sat in a Paris cafe in 1922. No one looking over his elegant attire, including a diamond stickpin nestled beneath the knot of his tie, would think for a moment that his pockets were empty, save for the price of the glass of wine he was carefully sipping. As he read one of the Paris newspapers, Lustig's ever-alert eyes spotted a small notice that reported that the Eiffel Tower was in need of repairs.

A scheme of great and delicious proportions appeared before him, more attractive than any scam he had perpetrated since his con career was launched at age eighteen. The Count, as he preferred to be called, stood five foot seven, weighed 175 pounds, had large brown eyes, and thin blond hair, and wore a saber scar over his right eyebrow. He had been first arrested in Prague in 1908 and served two months in jail for petty theft. Fraud and embezzlement followed, with arrests and short prison terms in Vienna (1909), Klagenfurt (1910), Vienna (1911), and Zurich (1912). This highly cultivated sharper disappeared from the European world of grift during the Great War, but surfaced in France about 1920, becoming a roper for several gambling concerns in Paris. Misplacement of certain winnings caused the casino proprietors to request that Lustig depart or, as they politely put it, be found floating in the Seine.

The Count Sells the Pride of Paris

Right beyond Lustig's seat in the café loomed that masterpiece of early French engineering, pride of France and symbol of Paris, the Eiffel Tower, its iron spans and supports reaching majestically upward. He gazed at it, tore out the newspaper notice about its need for repairs, and walked immediately to a small printer, where he ordered, on credit, stationery emblazoned with the letterhead of the French Ministry of Posts and Telegraphs. Next he rented, also on credit, the spreading master conference room at the super-posh Hotel Crillon. Letters written on the new stationery were then hand-delivered by couriers to the six top businessmen dealing in scrap metal. They were invited, the letters announced, to attend a hush-hush conference of matters too delicate to be handled in government offices.

The scrap dealers lost no time in answering the Count's summons. Lustig, pretending to be a deputy director general of the Ministry of Posts and Telegraphs, addressed them in a curt and impatient manner. "Gentlemen, because of engineering faults, costly repairs, and political problems I cannot discuss, the tearing down of the Eiffel Tower has become mandatory. Immediate demolition would create a public crisis and perhaps bring down the cabinet. So we have decided to postpone dismantling the tower until receiving bids for the more than seven thousand tons of quality scrap iron in the structure." Once the government showed the public a quick profit, he explained, protest would be minimal.

The businessmen beamed, and Lustig selected one as the highest bidder —not that this man's bid was the best but he seemed to be the most susceptible sucker in the lot. To further allay this dealer's fears that he might not be talking with a bona-fide member of the French Government, Lustig complained about his miserable salary and that he could lose his job at any moment what with the instability and flux of French politics, which overturned cabinets for any kind of emotional reason.

This was the convincer. This dealer was long accustomed, as Lustig suspected, to bribing public officials to put across deals. He understood Lustig's plight, the scrap man said soothingly, and slipped him a handsome bundle of francs; the fact that Lustig took the money assured the dealer that he was palavering with a typical grafting government employee and that the Eiffel Tower deal was genuine. The two drew up an elaborate contract, the scrap dealer paid for the tower's iron—an estimated $50,000—and Lustig told him he would receive the official papers to proceed with demolition in a few days.

The con man did, indeed, send the dealer a official-looking ribbon-wrapped document that gave him the authority to tear down the French monument. He then fled to Vienna, scene of so many of his scams, and waited for the storm to break in the Paris press when the duped dealer arrived to claim his iron. Nothing occurred. Apparently, the Count reasoned, the businessman realized that he had been suckered and kept quiet out of an acute sense of shame and stupidity at being bilked.

So confident was Lustig of this particular bunco game that he returned to Paris six months later, and, manipulating four different scrap-iron dealers, pulled off the same con, this time for an estimated $75,000. With this stake, the international hustler traveled to America, where countless rubes awaited his inventive mulcting.

Victor "The Count" Lustig sold the Eiffel Tower several times and lived to enjoy the spoils. (UPI)

Mysterious Mr. Stavisky

Lustig only darted in and out of Paris, but a suave resident con man of that city, Serge Alexandre Stavisky, hustled the government directly in one of the most fantastic schemes ever hatched on the Continent, a scam that brought political chaos, death, and suicide to hundreds of distinguished Frenchmen.

Stavisky's life was something out of Eric Ambler. Born in Kiev, Russia, in 1886 of Russian-Jewish parents, Sacha, as he was nicknamed, was first arrested for fraud in 1908. Imprisoned for a short time, he embarked on a con man's career when released. Four years later, his second arrest so embarrassed his dentist father that the old man committed suicide. Stavisky migrated to Paris before the First World War and spent most of his time operating penny-ante scams. He dabbled in forgery, dope-peddling, even armed robbery. His true métier was con, however, and he specialized in disposing of stolen bonds. From this Stavisky graduated to a phony casting bureau and then a diagnostic clinic, where he treated hundreds of wealthy women to determine pregnancy through a crackpot device he called a matrascope. Through these women, Sacha developed strong political and financial contacts.

In a series of confidence games, Stavisky entangled gamblers, resort owners, ranking members of the secret police, the Sûreté Générale (for whom he spied, informing on fellow grifters and crooks), and even cabinet ministers. He was in company with the most influential French personages of the 1920s, escorting different mistresses to the most prestigious social gatherings.

His riches mounted through his various scams, while all the while his activities were cloaked and protected by the secret police of the Third Republic. Imprisoned in 1926 for bilking two suckers out of 7 million francs in one of his many bogus stock deals, Stavisky was arrested and given the finest cell in Paris's Santé Prison, apologies heavily extended to him by his police associates. Though he awaited trial for almost eighteen months, officials were either unable or unwilling to unscramble his mazelike operations, and he was released on provisional liberty in 1927, never to enter jail again.

Many reasons existed for this extraordinary courtesy on the part of the French Government. Georges Pressard, chief prosecutor for the Paris Parquet, also brother-in-law of then Premier Camille Chautemps, had postponed Sacha's trial nineteen times. Assisting in the delay was prosecutor Albert Prince. A judge of the Paris Appeals Court, along with Pressard, was later proved to have strong connections to Stavisky associates and possibly even be secret business partners in the many concerns the con man owned. Not the least of these were two Paris newspapers, *Liberté* and *Volonté* (one representing the rightist movement, the other the left, the hustler missing no bets in politically volatile France), several gambling salons, an impressive theater, and companies galore, many of them dummy operations. The Premier's brother Pierre acted as the lawyer for one of these firms. The French Government was up to its eyebrows in Stavisky's cons.

International con man Serge Alexandre Stavisky hustled French citizens out of $40 million before committing suicide in 1934. (UPI)

Bribes, Bonds, and Bunco

For six years Serge Stavisky paid out more than $3 million to French political and business leaders, keeping a careful record of those bribed in the form of "stock dividends." Through these men, Sacha had himself named as the agent for municipal bonds floated by several major French cities. His collateral for such bonds was stolen jewelry and elaborate and fake bookkeeping. He would then discount the bonds at a reputable bank and invest this money in one of his own firms. Seldom did he attempt to make good on the bonds, but in 1928, when officials of Orléans discovered that 10 million francs of municipal bonds were not accounted for by Stavisky, he scurried about, frantically tapping his illicit money sources, and made good before examiners looking over his records discovered his con.

When Premier Chautemps, through Albert Dalimier, Minister of Colonies, approved of investment in pawnshop securities, Stavisky moved in for the financial kill. He issued fraudulent bonds, using his usual fake jewelry as "backing," on the security of a municipal pawnshop in Bayonne for 239 million francs, and with the help of the local mayor, also on the con man's payroll, his scam went undetected until Christmas Eve, 1933. Police, incredibly not on Stavisky's payoff muster, arrested one of the hustler's confederates and he confessed all. More arrests followed, including two deputies of the chamber and Stavisky's editors, Albert Dubarry of *Volonté* and Camille Aymard of *Liberté*. Stavisky, who had been warned of the police pickups, disappeared.

The Minister of Colonies, Albert Dalimier, was then exposed by *L'Action Française* as the one responsible for recommending to investment firms, chiefly insurance companies, that they buy up Sacha's worthless municipal bonds in Bayonne. Dalimier immediately resigned from the French cabinet, and a mad incident then occured.

The Strange, Slow Death of Sacha

Furnished with a fake passport by the Sûreté Générale, Stavisky did not make for the border as his political sponsors expected. He merely retired to an exclusive resort at Chamonix to await results. The police found him first, and his suicide was announced a few days later on January 8, 1934.

The enraged French citizenry exploded over the con man's exploits and the corruption of those who allowed him to operate so brazenly. Nobody believed that Stavisky had committed suicide but thought that he had been exterminated to prevent his revealing the powers behind his far-reaching flimflam. More than a year later, a special committee investigating Sacha's death determined that Stavisky did, indeed, shoot himself, but that his death had been "somewhat forced." The hustler's aim had been poor, a flash response to police who broke down his door in an extremely unorthodox manner. Had he been rushed to a hospital he certainly would have recovered, the committee resolved, but police officers merely sat about watching him bleed to death on the floor of his room for an hour until he died. "This extraordinary negligence finished the task Stavisky had begun," the committee concluded.

The hustler's grand schemes ruined the government. His judicial confederate, Magistrate Prince, also disappeared for some time. His almost unrecognizable, mangled body was later found on the Dijon railroad line. Police prefect of Paris Jean Chiappe resigned his post, and Premier Chautemps was ultimately ruined, his ministry collapsing.

An ironic postscript to Stavisky's dark end and those countless civil servants entangled in his hustling web was provided by William L.

Shirer in *The Collapse of the Third Republic.* This marvelously astute journalist witnessed hordes of ex-servicemen wearing their old uniforms and medals, marching against the Chautemps government in protest over the roaring scandal. They were members of the Union Nationale des Combattants, commonly referred to as the UNC. He saw many signs being carried that read: "UNC. We want France to live in order and honesty." To that Shirer later wrote: "Probably few marchers knew that the national president of the UNC, Henry Rossignol, was on the board of a Stavisky company that had perpetrated one of the crook's last and most extravagant swindles."

Bilking the Baron

France has always been a hotbed of cloak-and-dagger swindles, its government leaders, as Stavisky knew so well, flamboyant, its secret dealings often romantically extralegal. A group of amazing international hustlers used this publicly accepted fact to fleece an equally amazing dupe, a nobleman at that, in one of the wackiest flimflams ever concocted, one that left the nation at large chuckling for years.

A staunch conservative, Baron Scipion du Roure de Beruyère feared mightily for himself, for his wife, and for France in the spring of 1950. Communists were active in the streets of Paris, marching with banners beneath the very windows of his swanky apartment. They were screaming the usual demands, and these included the breaking up the great estates, such as the baron's sprawling fiefdom at Bagnois-sur-Cêze and his two marvelous villas at Cap d'Antibes. The very thought of Communist deputies in the Chamber compelled the baron to eye his bank accounts more closely and think seriously of escaping the coming Russian invasion by emigrating with his attractive wife Eleonore (daughter of an ex-finance minister, Raymond Patenotre) to the verdant shores of America.

All of these fears the twenty-seven-year-old baron blurted one night to a Riviera acquaintance, Aimé Galliard, a dance-hall owner and hot-dog concession operator. Galliard listened attentively and was suddenly inspired with a scheme as ridiculous as the baron's obvious naïveté.

Galliard lost no time in introducing the patriotic baron to Inspector Raymond Alberto of the French Border Police. The swarthy thirty-five-year-old inspector and the baron shared a common bond; both were zealots eager to prevent the spread of communism across the smiling face of the free world. Alberto was to all appearances a stalwart defender of the Republic, his buttonhole bristling with ribbons of the Croix de Guerre and the Medal of the Resistance.

A Most Incredible Con Saga

Sitting in the baron's library in one of his Mediterranean villas, the inspector told the youthful patriot that through Galliard he had learned that he could be trusted with "state secrets," and he then proceeded to unravel a thriller. He was then in the process, he carefully explained, of smuggling uranium out of Germany for delivery to Franco's Spain, the last anti-Communist stronghold on the continent. The implication was all too clear—atomic weaponry for the West. This paramilitary operation, covertly backed by the French Secret Police, the Deuxième Bureau, meant that the uranium, at about $150 a gram, had to be privately purchased—the Secret Police could not ask the Chamber to finance such a hush-hush project without tipping its hand to the Communist members—at about 10 million francs. What was needed was a patriot with money—the baron, for instance, who would handle the transaction for the defenders of the Republic and make at least double his money when private payment from France could be arranged.

The wealthy du Roure was then introduced to the man in charge of this espionage operation, Lt. Col. Jean Berthier, whom Alberto confided was subchief of the French Counter Intelligence, whose members were working hand in dagger with the Deuxième Bureau. The colonel asked the baron if he would be willing to undertake the daring mission in transporting the priceless uranium part of the way and, in fact, as a private, patriotic citizen, would be willing to purchase the shipment both as a service to his country and as a business investment that would yield him, within a short time, double, perhaps triple his expenditures. The baron did not hesitate. Yes, he would be more than happy to aid his land against the perfidious Communist enemy. Within a few days du Roure had withdrawn 10 million francs from his account at the Worms Bank in Paris and turned it over to the inspector and colonel.

The pair arrived at du Roure's Paris apartment days later, sweating as they tugged at a large iron trunk, similar to an army foot locker, which was bedecked with colorful government seals and a blaring TOP SECRET stamp across the top, along with the warning: *"Danger! Do Not Open!"* They explained that the uranium recently smuggled from Berlin was inside. The baron was given top-secret orders to proceed by car, the uranium in the trunk of his Cadillac, to St.-Jean-de-Luz, a French resort close to the Spanish border, and there await Franco's emissary, a certain General Rodriguez.

Flight into Bamboozlement

The baron and his wife dutifully left on their delicate mission. No sooner had they checked into their resort rooms, and the uranium carefully tucked beneath their bed, than phone calls and wires announcing great apprehension over Communist detection arrived from Colonel Berthier and Inspector Alberto. Both men showed up in an army vehicle the following day, and the colonel, his face streaked with fear, explained that the Communists had been informed of their movements and that it was too risky to attempt the border crossing into Spain. They must place the uranium in a safe spot and await developments. The perfect hiding place, they thought, was one of the baron's villas. Du Roure agreed, and then began a hair-raising race from St.-Jean-de-Luz across the width of France to the Riviera. At times Alberto, who was accompanying the couple, spotted Russian agents following them, but they fortunately managed to evade their sinister pursuers, arriving at the villa quite ill. "Vapors" from the uranium, the baron explained, had given him headaches, and they had been compelled to make the entire journey with the car windows wide open, the result being that both the baron and his wife caught severe colds and were bedridden for several days. Foolishly, the baron thought later, he had placed the uranium in a bedroom closet. To protect against dangerous gamma rays and radiation, he donned an asbestos vest, which he wore at all times, including to bed.

To guarantee a night's rest, he and Alberto decided to bury the uranium in the garden, which they did, by moonlight, the baron and his wife digging while the fearless inspector stood guard with a sub-machine gun. New arrangements with Franco would have to be made, Alberto once again emphasized, and he disappeared for some months, his secret maneuverings on behalf of the Free World a mystery to the du Roures. Berthier finally called the baron and his wife to Paris, where he informed them that a second shipment of uranium was being sent from occupied Berlin. Would this honorable son of France agree to purchase and protect it as he had the previous valuable cargo? The price tag was 50 million francs. Du Roure nervously admitted that he hadn't that much cash on hand, but agreed to provide his wife's prized diamond necklace as security. It was worth about 65 million francs. Berthier reluctantly accepted the baubles. Three weeks later the inspector and the colonel arrived at the villa with another trunk, extremely heavy, and also marked DANGER. This, too, was buried in the baron's garden in the middle of the night.

More payments to the miserly Germans were needed to cover the shipments, Berthier informed the baron some weeks later, and du Roure tapped his Swiss bank account, draining it of gold and silver. He occupied much of his time, with Inspector Alberto's coaching, with writing letters of application to the "European Military Counter-Espionage School," letters the Inspector stated he would mail personally. (No such institution existed.)

The baron became restless and finally began asking Berthier and Alberto when he could expect his wife's necklace returned, when the delivery of the precious uranium and heavy water could be claimed by Franco, and when, especially when, would he see the profit so often promised him for the financial advances he had made on behalf of his beloved France for her atomic security. At this point his mind was conveniently occupied by a bizarre, gory event.

The Sinister Sharper

A dark stranger appeared one night at the baron's lavish villa, and speaking in whispers, asked the young nobleman for a private interview. Puzzled, du Roure showed him into his study, and there the man of mystery announced that he was an envoy of the Russian government, that he knew all about the uranium entrusted to the baron, and that his Soviet masters had authorized a payment of $1 million in exchange for the uranium. The patriotic du Roure bolted from his easy chair, glared angrily at the Communist spy, and pointed to the door. The baron dove for the phone after the spy disappeared and called Colonel Berthier.

The intelligence subchief and the trusty Inspector Alberto rushed to the baron's home, and there sat grim faced as du Roure detailed the stranger's visit.

"What did he look like?" Berthier asked sharply.

"Dark, like an Arab."

Alberto asked about scars, the man's height, color.

Exchanging furtive glances, Berthier and Alberto nodded as one. It was the Russian spy, all right. Both men stood up, walked to the door and assured the baron they would handle the intruder. Alberto patted a spot near his right armpit, the traditional place for a shoulder holster, as Berthier vowed: "We will have him before nightfall."

True to their word, the pair returned to the villa, solemnly picked up the baron and drove him to a deserted beach at La Garoupe. Behind some shrubbery, ceremoniously parted by the Inspector, lay the body of the dark stranger who had visited du Roure. Berthier flicked on a flashlight and jiggled the beam over the bloody face and bullet-rent body sprawled in the sand. "Is that the man?"

Du Roure gasped. "It's him, the spy!"

"He'll work no more for the Reds."

As the trio drove back to the villa, the baron was convinced once and for all that he was involved in The Most Dangerous Game and that the very life of his country was at stake. When Berthier asked for another $85,000 to finance more uranium shipments, the nobleman flinched not but borrowed and paid the sum almost immediately.

The operation had stretched on for almost three years, and when the baron again grew suspicious after he was told that Franco could not afford to buy the still-buried uranium, a new plot unfolded. The United States, through its State Department, would buy the precious uranium. It was only a matter of weeks before the deal could be made. And this time, the baron was informed, his profits would be ten times the amount of his original investment. A dignified, graying man, General Combaluzier, the chief of counterintelligence himself, showed up in the baron's Paris apartment to affirm the new transaction and to praise du Roure for his monumental service to France, adding that the baron was to receive the Legion of Honor medal, to be announced officially on December 31 of that year, 1952. The young man was ecstatic, so much so that he turned over to the general every franc he had left, about 5 million.

On December 31 the baron rushed out to buy the official bulletin that announced the new winners of the Legion of Honor, the one brilliant possession missing from his silver-spooned life. He nervously glanced down the list of recipients. His name was not there. Infuriated, he called his lawyer who, in turn, called the Deuxième Bureau. He was informed that there was no such person as General Combaluzier, no Colonel Berthier, and no Inspector Alberto. The nobleman had been mulcted out of the equivalent of $342,842, he realized, but he still had the uranium buried in his garden.

Faulty Uranium and Much Guffaw

Specialists arrived, dug up the trunks, and using Geiger counters, determined it safe to open the sealed boxes. Inside they found several casks of sand and some containers brimming with clear tap water—that was all. The scam was complete. The con men, however, made their whereabouts known, and police picked up Alberto, a one-time butcher who had, indeed, been a member of the police department in Nice (he had been fired for embezzling funds). Colonel Berthier was then arrested, and he proved to be a Corsican named Marius Carlicchi who had been imprisoned in 1947 for theft. The distinguished-looking General Combaluzier—he had taken his name from the trade name of an elevator, a manufacturer as popular in France as Otis is in America—

Three funny con men in a French court, 1953. (Left to right) Louis Gagliardoni, Marius Carlicchi, and Raymond Alberto; they flimflammed a nobleman out of millions in a wacky uranium scheme. (WIDE WORLD)

was Louis Gagliardoni who, like Carlicchi, was a Corsican with a long prison record for fencing stolen goods, black-marketeering, and theft. Then came the man who had made the absurd plot possible through his introductions, Galliard. He testified against the other three and was not tried. (The Russian secret agent was never found; he was a down-and-out actor hired for his one spy appearance and death scene.)

The trial was farcical. Paris guffawed. The magistrate hearing the trial could hardly contain his amusement over the bizarre con. Smiling, he told Alberto: "I congratulate you on your imagination. . . . How were you able to tell the baron such stupendous tales without ever laughing?"

Alberto blinked before the bench. "He just believed everything."

In June 1953 the "inspector" and the "colonel" each received four years in prison; the "general" got eighteen months. Weeks later Aimé Galliard told a reporter: "The baron was my pearl. I found him. And let me tell you, a man's got to crack a lot of oysters before he finds a pearl like that."

Abram Sykowski, Flimflammer with Finesse

Champion oyster cracker in Europe for several decades—he may still be at it now under any number of his endless *noms de guerres,* since he vowed to live to be one hundred—is a sly, lean man with a slender build and the eyes of a snake, Poland's contribution to international con, Abram Sykowski. Born in Radom, July 23, 1892, he immigrated to the United States as a boy. Sykowski learned his apprenticeship in con while struggling for survival in the Bowery slums. At sixteen he found he had the ability to throw his bones out of joint, and was featured as a vaudeville act called the "Human Frog." For those who goggled at his painful contortions, Sykowski held high contempt and an embryonic knowledge that Barnum's oft-quoted adage, "There's a sucker born every minute," was institutionally accurate and financially rewarding. (Mike McDonald, the political-gambling boss of nineteenth-century Chicago, is also credited with initiating the phrase.) In 1912, Sykowski traveled to what was then the most popular tourist trap for Americans, Havana, Cuba, and there fleeced vacationers in petty or short cons until he was arrested on June 15 and thrown into jail for a month. Upon his release he immediately began bilking marks, was again arrested, and this time given a three-month sentence. It was obvious to the fledgling hustler that he was not proficient at the short con. He would go after larger stakes or nothing the remainder of his days.

Forgery was not his métier either, having been convicted for two terms for such offenses. Sykowski attempted to sneak back into the United States under the name of Carlos Nunn in March 1921, but was apprehended and sentenced to three years for falsifying his passport. After serving two years, Sykowski drifted to Chicago and worked as a small-time enforcer for the Sheldon Gang, a Capone satellite. He was arrested again for stealing, served six years, and in 1929 was deported to Germany as an undesirable alien (he gave that country, rather than Poland, as his place of birth). During the upheavals of the shaky Weimar Republic, Sykowski bought and sold German arms, running these to any country on the verge of revolution, which, in the havoc created by the Versailles Peace Agreements, was just about anywhere on the Continent.

Sykowski dipped into cardsharping and smuggling, but became a full-fledged confidence man by 1934, mulcting dozens of wealthy refugees fleeing Russia and other countries on the promise to provide passports, none of which ever materialized. This scam netted him an estimated quarter of a million dollars, which he banked in Switzerland and used as his base of finance. Arrested in Madrid in 1934 on suspicion of dope smuggling, Sykowski was sent to Austria and was there ejected for using a phony passport.

Capone's Elusive Millions

Somewhere in between, according to Interpol, Sykowski developed a con that he would use as a mainstay throughout his known career as a hustler. In 1930, after losing heavily in the Zoppot Casino in Danzig, Sykowski confided to the owner that he had once worked for the billionaire gangster Al Capone, and that he, Sykowski, had several bootleg millions tied up in the United States. If the casino operator would help out by financing some payoffs to certain bank officials to release the money to him, he would not only pay his gambling debts but cut the owner in for a hefty percentage. The casino operator advanced Sykowski several thousand dollars, and somewhere amidst a flurry of cables to American bankers, the con man disappeared.

In 1936 Sykowski arrived in Rome, where he began to frequent the better nightclubs and casinos. In one club his roving eye caught a glimpse of a stunning woman, and he wangled an introduction to Clara Petacci, mistress to Italy's strong man Benito Mussolini. He glibly told her of his impounded bootleg millions in the United States, and wondered if her boyfriend, for a cut of the profits, would be willing to help. As Sykowski later boasted to police: "I was introduced to the Duce at the Royal Automobile Club by his girlfriend. . . . She . . . felt that the dictator might be able to help me. Mussolini saw there a splendid opportunity to acquire much-needed dollars, and at the same time play a trick on the U.S. government. He gave me seven million lira to let him in on the deal."

Gang czar Al Capone was conned by Victor "The Count" Lustig and never knew it. (UPI)

The Bogus Prince

Pocketing the money, Sykowski immediately decamped for Republican Spain with a huge shipment of arms he had purchased with Mussolini's money, selling the equipment to the very people against whom the Duce was then waging war. The gunrunning was profitable but too tedious, so Sykowski, using the name Carlos Ladenis, invited the police chief of Barcelona to his expensive hotel suite and conned him out of $35,000 with his Capone millions scheme. Sykowski was then off by steamer to Canada, where he took a suite of rooms in Montreal's Mount Royal Hotel, passing himself off as Count Alexander Novarro Fernandez, relative of the deceased Hapsburg King Alfonso XIII of Spain. One report has it that curious socialites wanted to stick pins in him to see if he was, indeed, a true hemophiliac, as befitting his ancestral line. He slapped away a hand and shouted: "Don't ever touch a person of royal blood!"

Using this front, Sykowski conned a group of businessmen into believing that, as a Hapsburg prince, he had years ago secreted more than $350 million in dozens of U.S. banks, and that for proper financing to arrange the intricate release of such staggering funds, he would give the group 10 percent of his fortune. They gave him $125,000 and the use of a private plane to leave the country. Sykowski gave them a code book that purported to reveal where his money was secreted and how to obtain it for him. It was, of course, a notebook of gibberish, but by the time the businessmen discovered that, Sykowski was dining, white-jacketed, on the terrace of a Venezuelan nightclub.

The globe-trotting con man sat out the war in South America, his swindles in that hemisphere shady but apparently yielding him more than half a million dollars by 1946. In September of that year he flew to Miami, where he was promptly arrested by FBI agents, J. Edgar Hoover announcing the capture of "Antonio Novarro Fernandez, a notorious international confidence man, wanted in connection with a $125,000 swindle."

King Farouk of Egypt, a hustler himself, fell to Abram Sykowski's $200,000 scam in 1952. (UPI)

The Trimming of Farouk

After much legal haggling, Sykowski received three years in prison, was paroled in 1949, and deported to Cuba. Somehow obtaining his long-hidden Swiss funds, Sykowski traveled to Paris in high style, arriving at the Hotel George V in a chauffeur-driven limousine and registering as Antonio Novarro, a Peruvian mine owner. (The con man spoke fluent Peruvian, as well as ten other languages.) He gave lavish fetes to which the cream of French society flocked. One party cost him an estimated $10,000. He then moved, his publicity of fabulous wealth preceding him, to the Riviera, to Cannes, where he gambled furiously on a night-and-day schedule, waging as much as $30,000 a hand. The playboy image was designed to entrap the one victim Sykowski had been after for months, Egypt's King Farouk, a con man of gigantic virtuosity in his own right. (Farouk had established his own casino in Cairo, the Auberge des Pyramides, which all but eliminated other gambling competitors; forced his subjects to buy oranges from his private groves at a higher cost than those imported; looted the treasury of his own government, and even stole the jeweled sword and other valuables from the coffin of the deposed Shah of Persia, Riza Khan Pahlavi, while the dead monarch's body, en route to Teheran, rested in a Persian plane refueling in Cairo.)

It was at the gambling tables that Sykowski met Farouk, challenging the florid-faced monarch to compete with him. The two men found each other entertaining, and Farouk listened in rapture as Sykowski spun off his tale of bootleg millions hidden in U.S. banks, this time raising the mythical fortune to $60 million. "I was known as Kid Tiger in those days," Sykowski-Novarro intoned. "It was up to me to send Canadian booze across the border, where Scarface's men picked it up."

For a promise of 10 percent of the fortune, Farouk reportedly gave Sykowski $200,000 in April 1952, with more to come if necessary. More never materialized, for in July 1952 the Egyptian king was overthrown and Farouk clutched his considerable assets like a drowning man.

Sykowski went back to small-time scams, specializing in black market money changes. He would promise to exchange $20,000 for black-market francs after the sucker had the sum deposited in his Swiss account, telling the mark that as soon as his bank notified him that the sum had been received, he would pay out the francs.

Victims found that Sykowski, once he had their money, either refused to pay them the inflated black-market value in francs or gave them only a token amount of what he had promised, knowing full well they would never go to authorities, at the risk of involving themselves in illegal affairs. Sykowski-Novarro failed, however, to meet his increasing gambling losses, and defaulted on creditors by skipping out of the Riviera in early 1953. His limousine was stopped at the Swiss border near Moelle-Salaz, and French police confined him to house arrest in a Paris suburb, pending a full investigation of his shadowy career. Sykowki attempted to escape with phony passports and aliases into Italy and San Marino, but was turned back. Then he went in the opposite direction and disappeared into West Germany. It was the last anyone ever saw of him, although rumors across the Rhine concerning his ongoing swindles abounded for a decade. As far as Interpol is concerned at this writing, the one-time contortionist and super continental hustler is still operating, working his guile and grift through the capitals of the Old World.

The Match King's Matchless Grift

Sweden's entry in international con holds the record for the most colossal flimflam in the world: more than $750 million. He was a cold, calculating man as sedate as the world bankers and stockmen he bilked. His name was Ivar Kreuger, and he is remembered in horror by the ruined millions who invested in his Kreuger & Toll, as "The Match King."

An enigma to his death, Kreuger was born in the small Swedish hamlet of Kalmar in 1880 and graduated as a mechanical engineer from the Stockholm Technical College. In 1900 he traveled to the United States. He sold real estate briefly in Chicago, then, beginning in 1902, as an engineer working for the Fuller Construction Company of New York, he helped build the Flatiron, Macy, and Metropolitan Life buildings and the St. Regis and Plaza hotels. He returned to Sweden in 1907, and in partnership with Paul Toll began the firm of Kreuger & Toll, centering his activities in construction. In a record number of years, Kreuger's buildings shot up all over Sweden. In 1913 he decided to go into the match business, and he consolidated all the independent match companies in the country, competing heavily with and finally absorbing in 1917 the monopolistic Jonkoping-Vulcan firm. Two years later, at age thirty-seven, Kreuger was one of the wealthiest men in Sweden.

Then something happened to the budding business tycoon. (Years later, some writers claimed that paresis of the brain, resulting from contact with a syphylitic prostitute in Vera Cruz, caused him to develop both megalomania and an insatiable desire for money and power.) Ivar Kreuger suddenly wanted to own the world. In 1919 the tycoon, who had just added 100,000 acres of prize timber to his holdings, went to the Scandinavian Credit Bank and the Swedish Commerce Bank in Stockholm and said: "I need sixty million kroner with which to expand the match business overseas. It shows a profit, but I need a big surplus to work with." Solely on his personal guarantee, Kreuger got his funds. He began to buy up match firms throughout Europe and the United States. Competition was, however, heavy, and he made little financial headway.

The Swedish Match King, Ivan Krueger, perhaps the greatest con man of them all. (UPI)

Ivar Kreuger Buys the World

It occurred to Kreuger that to eliminate competition and establish his match monopoly, he simply had to buy the countries. He accomplished this impossible feat by selling securities in his holding company of Kreuger & Toll. As security, Kreuger offered $100 million in Italian bonds, which he forged and kept from sight in a Stockholm vault. Bullish American stock buyers were his initial victims,, plunking down, through esteemed firms such as Manhattan's Lee, Higginson Co. (which floated on its own Kreuger bonds worth $60 million), more than $250 million by 1929. He floated another $500 million in European capitals, reusing the same worthless Italian bonds. He then embarked on an extraordinary policy of loaning huge amounts to countries whose treasuries had been depleted by World War I or had been devastated by crop failures, storms, or corrupt officials. He gave Greece a million pounds in 1926. He advanced $6 million to Poland in 1927, and in that same year $75 million to France. Ecuador got $2 million in 1928 and another $1 million the following year, the same year he doled out $36 million to Hungary, $22 million to Yugoslavia, $6 million to Latvia, and $30 million to Rumania. Even after the crash, he continued financing a depression-crippled world. In 1930 he pumped $6 million into Lithuania, $1 million into Danzig, $125 million into Germany, $2.5 million into Guatemala, $10 million to Turkey, and another $32 million to Poland. And all the while Kreuger & Toll, through its 225 subsidiaries, paid staggering dividends to stockholders, 25 percent paid annually between 1919 and 1928, 30 percent after that.

Of course, this most gigantic con of all time was simply a matter of Peter-to-Paul. What Kreuger took in from millions of duped investors in his hollow firm he merely fed back into the economies of dozens of countries. In return for "saving humanity," as one economist put it, he was granted exclusive monopolies in the making, distribution, and sale of matches until three out of every four matches available in the world were Kreuger's. His monopolies dominated every country in the world except Russia. (Kreuger hated the Soviets, whispering to confidants that they had marked him for death.)

His gigantic fraud seemed endless during the Jazz Age, and whenever in desperate need to shore up his trembling empire, he would dart off to Paris, London, or New York, where he maintained extravagant living quarters, and borrow more money, reselling over and over the same useless Italian bond forgeries. America was especially fanatic in its support of Kreuger. One of the Match King's company directors illustrated the free hand Kreuger enjoyed with his own firms when he told reporters: "Whenever Kreuger went to New York, the representatives of American banks were waiting for him on the landing stage, offering him all the money he needed without question. Kreuger came back and told us about it to illustrate the confidence he enjoyed over there. We could do nothing with him."

Bizarre Silence

The Match King would tolerate no criticism. Should a company director express worry about the soundness of Kreuger's activities, he was told to shut up. Many of Kreuger's company presidents were counts and barons; he enjoyed employing nobility and bossing them about. But Kreuger was no social lion. His private parties never exceeded a guest list of twenty, and were usually held on one of his six yachts anchored among the many islands near Stockholm, one of which he owned. A silent, stooped, short man, balding at forty-nine when he reached the zenith of his wealth, having a financial kingdom that on paper, at least, towered over any other private fortune on earth at the time, Kreuger was forever mysterious. His name never appeared on any passenger list or hotel register. He refused all interviews and was shy of cameras. He ignored invitations to large social affairs, even those sent by the King of Sweden.

On one rare occasion when he permitted an interview with Isaac F. Marcosson of the *Saturday Evening Post*, a praising personal profile, he stated: "Whatever success I have had may perhaps be attributable to three things: One is silence, the second is more silence, while the third is still more silence." And within that ghostly silence surrounding the world's richest man was his unbelievable swindle.

Kreuger's Stockholm offices reflected his devotion to eerie silence. Marcosson walked puzzled through the corridors of Kreuger's office building. "The entire home staff of the huge match organization consists of 150 persons, including secretaries. You scarcely ever see anyone as you move through the halls, and never hear a sound."

Kreuger's second-floor office was a long room decorated in soft brown color schemes. Old tapestries hung on the walls. Above his office door was a large carving of a torch, "symbolic of the match that has lighted the world." A bronze inkstand and a blotter were all that covered Kreuger's expansive mahogany desk. He was fond of showing select persons his collection of matchboxes, especially those distributed in Africa, pointing in amusement to the "kinky heads of African chieftans" adorning the label. "Do you know," he once pridefully stated, "that in many savage countries my matches, like salt and copper, are legal tender." And of much more value than the firms that produced them, he might have added.

Another prize was the statue of Diana dominating the square fronting Kreuger's main office. The tycoon con man would pose occasionally for a photo next to it, unsmiling, staring. Above his executive office, Kreuger had what he called "the silent room." He would retire there, for hours on end, locking the door behind him (only the janitor and he had keys to this inner sanctum). Kreuger would sit in the silent room and meditate. No doubt he had much to ponder over, since he had bought most of the world without ever having paid out a real cent, and would be in real trouble if he failed to build his bubble big enough by November 1931, when his phony Italian bonds fell due for repayment. Perhaps he worried not, for Ivar Kreuger was one of the strangest men in the annals of con. Nothing seemed to bother him. He was always calm, no matter what calamity arose. One report had it that he could not feel physical pain. "Dentists could work for hours on the most sensitive nerves in his mouth without giving him Novocain."

He was never ostentatious. He collected paintings, but only a few Rodins, some minor Dutch and Swedish works. He possessed a well-stocked library but was never seen to read. He entertained few female friends. One woman of mystery who made shadowy visits to his home once complained at the lack of roses in Stockholm because of the cold lingering into late spring. Before she arrived at his mansion, Kreuger ordered every rose in the city from florists and lined his driveway with the hastily replanted flowers. He maintained half an acre of strawberries behind his resplendent home and often picnicked there with this unknown woman, or sometimes with a few friends.

Curiously, though he smoked cigarettes nonstop, Ivar Kreuger never carried a match. When asked about it, he retorted, "a petty superstition."

It is apocryphal that Kreuger was the man who invented the superstition concerning "three on a match" being bad luck and therefore promoting the use of more matches. Yet such petty calculating would not be beyond this bogus titan of finance, a man T. G. Barman once called "the greatest constructive financial genius of our generation."

End of a Hustled Empire

Beginning with the stock market crash of 1929, Kreuger's genius seemed to evaporate. Inquiries were made into some of his dealings by government officials who, a decade before, would not have dared even to mention his name in a critical utterance. Repayment for the bogus Italian bonds Kreuger had put up as security for his financial kingdom a decade before came due in November 1931, and the Match King failed, inexplicably, to make good the $100 million. Months went by and Kreuger was suddenly unavailable. He flitted like a ghost betwen his lavish apartments in New York, London, and Paris. On March 12, 1933, Kreuger appeared in the City of Light, went to an exclusive gun shop, and purchased two antique pistols. He drove to his posh apartment on the Avenue Victor Emmanuel III and sat in seclusion for hours, thinking. There was no way out. The stock market crash of 1929 had cut off all American funding. He had bilked the world of $750 million and had no way of repaying the sum before being discovered.

Following a light dinner, the Match King stepped to the terrace of his apartment overlooking Paris, put one of the antique pistols to his temple, and squeezed the trigger. His empire collapsed with him to the floor. Weeks and months later scores of his business associates also committed suicide, and millions of investors were financially destroyed in the most mammoth swindle of all time.

When word of the Match King's suicide reached the ears of one victim, a powerful European financier, he broke down and wept openly. "Kreuger has ruined me and my banks," he sobbed. "But I cannot hate him. I still think he was a charming and lovable personality. As a delightful companion, I shall miss him to the end of my days." This gentleman was among a very small minority.

Fourteen

The Big Store

THE MOST REWARDING SWINDLE for the hustler is the big con or the big store, also known as "the wire," and "the joint." It has many variations, and the stakes are astronomical. To score in such a scam requires all of the artful dodging a con man can muster. Only the big-time hustlers played it, for it required a huge bankroll, unlimited self-confidence, and the kind of talent found only in a few masters.

Paper Collar Joe Taps a Line

Begun in the 1860s by such pioneering con men as Ben Mark's, the big store came into its heyday during the late 1890s and just after the turn of the century. Phony gambling dens and casinos were replaced by fake betting parlors, which were allegedly wired to receive instant news of racetrack, prize-fight, or other sporting results. The reputed originator of the wire was Joseph Kratalsky, better known as "Paper Collar Joe," who had been locked up on charges once a year, every year, for confidence games since he began his nefarious career in 1876, first bilking tourists at the Centennial Exposition. Paper Collar Joe was the first and only man to ever really wiretap race-track results, according to most reliable sources. Tiring of short cons, Kratalsky actually tapped a real telegraph wire in 1898, and, in league with other hustlers, held back the returns of a race at Long Branch until his associates placed bets on the winner, taking $35,000 from duped bookmakers. Kratalsky, realizing that the actual tapping of a wire was too dangerous and difficult, hit upon the idea of doing away with the real wiretapping and convincing the mark that he had received accurate advance information on the winner of a race or fight. It was Kratalsky who set up the first fake poolroom, peopling it with other con men pretending to be authentic gamblers and taking the lone sucker onto such a stage and bilking him. Paper Collar Joe died a millionaire on Park Avenue.

The Gondorf Brothers Make Good

By 1900 the big store was known as "the Gondorf game" because Fred and Charley Gondorf were its high practitioners, gleaning $15 million from wealthy dupes in fifteen years. One of Fred Gondorf's favorite big stores was the swanky gambling den. He and his brother and a few other associates would rent a posh suite of rooms at a fashionable New York address, attire themselves in tuxedos and disguise themselves to look like well-known rich men. A well-fixed sucker would then be inveigled into playing "a few hands" with such august company. The mark, always eager to ingratiate himself with titans of finance and to better his social standing, would lose without complaint in rigged poker games. In 1899 the Gondorf brothers hustled a St. Louis pawnbroker for more than $200,000 in just such a big store. The enterprising brothers bilked at least twenty victims like this every year.

Super grifters and kings of the big store, Fred and Charley Gondorf on trial in 1924. (UPI)

Wired for Profit

Charley Gondorf hit his stride in 1906 when he opened a permanent big store in Manhattan. For almost ten years he and a bevy of ropers and sidemen fleeced dozens of dupes each year. Gondorf specialized in the wire, and he and his brother netted half a million a year from this scam, after all their ropers, shills, and associates had been paid off. Gondorf, using several midtown Manhattan addresses, roped in suckers, leading them to what appeared to be a genuine bookmaking parlor, replete with cushiony chairs, a massive board giving the latest race results, busy parlor employees, and frenetic patrons heavily betting. Of course, the entire store was a fake right down to the employees and the patrons, all of whom were on the Gondorf payroll.

The mark was carefully selected according to his betting nature and the size of his wallet. He would be told that inside information could be obtained through an ex-telegraph employee, disgruntled over being fired. This man was usually passed off as a relative, thus bonding him to the grift through blood ties. He would simply tap the right wires and obtain racing results before they were flashed to the betting parlor, then pass these results to the man with the fix. The fixer would join with the mark in placing absurdly high bets. When both the tout and his mark lost, the sucker would be treated to a volatile outcry on the part of the tout that would shame the anger of Zeus. Thinking his loss only a small part of the overall betting in the fake parlor, the mark seldom complained, and would sometimes even allow himself to be roped once again into the same kind of flimflam.

Although Gondorf had been arrested numerous times for his big-store scams, he evaded conviction; the prosecuting witness always failed to show up, which is what Gondorf and his fellow con men counted on. A foreigner was to prove his undoing in 1914.

Foiled by a Foreigner

On a steamy July day of that year an Englishman named Eugene Adams arrived from London on the *St. Louis*. On the trip over, Adams was befriended by a genial fellow traveler named McDonald. The glib McDonald was really James W. Ryan, who had given up bank burglary in 1901 to take up the more lucrative pursuits of con and had earned himself, through various mail frauds, the sobriquet "The Postal Kid."

McDonald-Ryan convinced Adams that there were great riches to be made in New York in the betting parlors, that he had a friend who was a wiretapper and supplied him with race results before they were received by the bookmaker. No sooner was Adams cleared through customs than the Postal Kid steered him to Gondorf's posh betting room on West Forty-Ninth Street. In the frenzy of heavy betting, Adams lost $50. McDonald then produced the name of a winning horse at Belmont, sent along to him, he whispered, by his wiretapping friend. The tout then put up $5,000 and bet the amount on this horse. Adams, not having much cash on hand, wrote out a check for $10,000.

The betting parlor was pure bedlam, and what appeared to be tens of thousands of dollars crossed into the betting cages. The long shot Adams and McDonald picked wound up a winner. The proprietor of the parlor, Charley Gondorf, appeared and took Adams and McDonald into his private office. He pointed to several stacks of money on his desk. "There's your money, gentlemen. I suggest you count it." Adams sat down and counted out his winnings—$135,000.

The con moved abruptly to the payoff when Adams stood up, announced the figure right, and began to pocket the money.

"One moment," Gondorf said. "It's our policy never to accept checks as final payment. Before you take your winnings, you'll have to provide the $10,000 in cash."

"I guess that's only fair," McDonald put in, and Adams agreed to obtain the currency. He left the winnings with Gondorf and told the hustler that he would return on Monday, which he did. The betting parlor was then empty, and two of Gondorf's ropers, Jacob Cohn and Charles Carbonelli, met with the Englishman. Adams took out his wallet and showed the two men the $10,000 in five-pound notes. He then asked for his winnings. Just as the two con men were turning over a large sealed bag that allegedly contained Adams's winnings, an alarm went off in the parlor and loud banging on the door commenced.

Cohn threw open the door and held back two uniformed policemen (fakes), yelling to Adams and Carbonelli: "It's the cops! Run for it!"

"Your dough's on the table," Carbonelli shouted. "Every man for himself." With that the hustler grabbed the Englishman's wallet and ran out a side door. At this juncture the con man counts on the victim to be beside himself with fear of arrest and merely to pick up the package (which contained the perennial newspapers cut to currency size) and flee. Adams, however, perhaps because he was a foreigner and unfamiliar with Keystone Cop antics, did not act out the role expected of a fellow lawbreaker, and instead of picking up the package containing the alleged winnings, took off full speed after Carbonelli, screaming for the police as he bounded through heavy traffic in pursuit of the racing hustler.

Carbonelli was to be commended for his stamina, for he led a broken-field chase for ten blocks, leaving a trail of angrily sprawled pedestrians. At Columbus Avenue and Fifty-ninth Street, several policemen responded to Adams' rasping calls for help and tackled the con man moments after he had magnificently hurdled a large pink perambulator.

"Whatsa matter with you, you dumb sap!" Carbonelli shouted at Adams as he rushed up.

"Officers," Adams stated through heavy breathing. "This chap has stolen my wallet."

But there was no wallet. After a quick search, nothing was found on Carbonelli except a few dollars. He had handed the billfold off to Charley Gondorf, who had positioned himself in the crowd, a pre-arranged meet. The Englishman then broke another unwritten rule by gushing out the entire story of the betting parlor. Carbonelli was arrested and Jacob Cohn was rounded up at the Forty-ninth Street address.

To avoid having his star ropers imprisoned, Charley Gondorf, "King of the Wiretappers," then made one of the few mistakes he ever committed during his long career in hustling. He contacted Adams and arranged to meet with him, promising to return his wallet if the Englishman would get out of town.

New York police had long been plagued by Gondorf and his big-store associates, and assigned a special squad of detectives to follow Adams. He led them to Fifty-ninth Street and Broadway, where Charley Gondorf met him. Four detectives followed the pair onto a subway and rode uptown. Gondorf and Adams got off at 103rd and Broadway, and just as the hustler was handing Adams his money and a one-way ticket to Montreal, they closed in and arrested the con man.

"My name is John Jones," Gondorf stated indignantly as the cuffs were clicked over his wrists. "What's all this about?"

"You're Charles Gondorf," said a detective named Fennelly. "You run the biggest store in New York and this time you're going inside. Where's your brother Fred?"

"Nonsense, officers. My good friend Adams here and I were about to conclude a business transaction, which you've obviously misinterpreted as something shady . . . and I don't have a brother named Fred."

It did no good. Adams was far from friendly, and he vowed to testify against Gondorf and his ring. He did. The con man was sentenced to a long prison term in Sing Sing, following a quick trial.

Fred's Big Con Amuck

When Charley went to jail, Fred Gondorf took over the big-store operation, but his luck ran out, too, less than a year later. Gondorf, working the wire in a relocated big store, took $64,000 from Duncan S. Curry, ex-controller of Winnipeg, Canada, but Curry, like Adams, refused to take his bilking quietly. He went to the police. Gondorf was arrested and then released on $25,000 bail pending trial. Instead of fleeing, Gondorf remained in New York, believing his City Hall contacts would manage to quash the charges. He blithely went about fleeing another sucker, William O'Reilly, a wealthy building contractor from Toronto who was visiting the city.

A countrywide con man and experienced spieler, Roy Farrell worked for Blonger in Denver and Gondorf in New York.

Using the name Charley Douglas, Fred Gondorf befriended O'Reilly in a hotel and subtly explained that his brother Harry had recently been transferred from the Western Union office in Chicago to New York, that brother Harry could obtain racing results from half a dozen tracks before such information was sent to the bookmakers, and armed with such knowledge, the two of them could make a fortune. O'Reilly thought so, too, and the hustler accompanied the sucker to the Western Union Building and there met brother Harry, an aging roper whose real name was James Fitzgerald.

With considerable fanfare, the phony Western Union official tapped a few wires, or so it appeared, walking boldly through the Western Union work pools, in and out of private offices. O'Reilly won a small amount of money on the so-called advance information supplied by brother Harry. Thoroughly hooked, O'Reilly was then told that through the wiretapping brother he and Douglas-Gondorf could make a "killing," but considerable money was necessary. O'Reilly traveled to Toronto and back, retrieving $10,000.

Gondorf then escorted the mark to his big store, a fashionable rooming house run by Mrs. Robert D. Schrymer, who passed herself off as an amateur chemist, explaining the large crowds gathering in her posh upstairs parlor as visiting physicians and chemists. In reality, the groups infesting Mrs. Schrymer's parlor at 31 West Forty-seventh Street were all members of the Gondorf ring. O'Reilly and Gondorf rushed into the parlor, which was going full blast, with bettors throwing money about like party streamers (the phony players were the most accomplished con men in the business: John "Deafy" Morris, Henry Miller, and the Gondorf favorite, James Ryan, the Postal Kid.)

Putting up $10,000 for the "fixed" race, O'Reilly was surprised to see Douglas-Gondorf produce only $1,500. "It was all I could raise on such short notice," he told his sucker.

Naturally, the horse both men bet on lost. Then Gondorf went into his act, a wild oath-hurling tantrum. According to one report, "Douglas was nearly crazy with anger and grief. His brother must make good, he said. Something had slipped and they would try again."

O'Reilly was so thoroughly hooked that he again returned to Toronto and brought back another $7,400 in a matter of days. It, too, vanished behind the betting cage in the phony race-track parlor, but O'Reilly took his loss silently. After weeks of brooding about his incompetence as a gambler O'Reilly was convinced by relatives and a family priest that he had been bilked and that he should go to the police.

On June 4, 1915, O'Reilly entered the office of New York Police Inspector Faurot, explaining the flimflam. The enterprising inspector listened to the businessman's story with great interest. "That's the Gondorf game," he told O'Reilly. "We've been after that crowd for years. We got Charley Gondorf but it looks like you were conned by his brother Fred."

"He said his name was Douglas."

"He always has another name. It's the face that doesn't change."

That gave Faurot an idea. If O'Reilly could pick one of the flimflammers out of a crowd, make an identification, he would have a case. But the Gondorf hustlers would be on the lookout for victims. A disguise would be necessary.

Toronto businessman William O'Reilly emerged from Inspector Faurot's office with a new coat, bowler hat, and a luxuriant new black beard. From there he went to Times Square, several squads of detectives close on his heels. Faurot had instructed O'Reilly to stroll up and down Broadway and shake hands with the first member of the gang that he met. Their luck was superb. Within ten minutes, O'Reilly picked two men out of a crowd, and to their amazement, walked up to one of them and clasped his hand in a hearty manner, introducing himself as "Mannerheim . . . you remember me . . ."

"I'll be damned," the astonished Faurot said to a fellow cop, "it's Fred Gondorf." They closed in and arrested Gondorf and George Mitchell, known in the con world as "The Kentucky Gentleman," a hustler who sported a white mustache and goatee. After depositing his prisoners in a cell, Faurot led a raid on the Gondorf big store at 31 West Forty-seventh Street. A servant answered the door.

"Where's Mrs. Shrymer?" the inspector asked.

"The madam isn't in," he was told.

Faurot flashed his badge and bustled inside. He searched the large building with his men and found nothing. "Where is she?" he demanded, "and the rest of those conning rats?"

"Madam has been traveling abroad for several weeks now," the servant reported.

"Yes, I'm sure. Traveling ever since she helped to fleece a man named O'Reilly several weeks ago. When do you expect her to return?"

"Never," responded the servant.

"What do you mean, never?"

"Madam sailed on the *Lusitania*."

The O'Reilly caper was the last score the Gondorf brothers would pull off for several years. Fred pled guilty to bilking one William F. Davis while being tried for the Curry and O'Reilly cons. He expected a lesser sentence (he had bilked Davis out of only $8,000), but Judge Malone gave him one to ten years in Sing Sing.

As Gondorf awaited removal from the court, Judge Malone peered down at him and the victims of his big store. "There is little, the court thinks," he said, "to choose between the complainant and the defendant in point of morals or social decency. To all intents, both might be denominated not unfairly 'plain common swindlers,' for the defendant and the complainant were assuredly conspiring together, embarked as it seems, in a general swindling project. In the contest of wits the rogues who lose in such case invariably become the complainants and the prosecution's witnesses, while the rogue who wins becomes the prisoner at the bar. Fortunately, no honest man is affected injuriously by the conduct or acts of either. Under the circumstances, ordinarily, it might be thought that both the complainant and the defendant should be allowed to stew in their own grease, but our criminal machinery is not to be set in motion, or employed by the individual alone, but for the great body of the people of the state."

As Fred Gondorf was being led off to join his brother in prison, he turned and held up manacled hands, shouting to his victims: "You hear that, you fellows? You're a couple of crooks . . . just like me."

Charley Gondorf later admitted that "though we made millions as a group, it was the individual scores that counted." A lone con man, more or less renting a big store and its agile, hustling actors for approximately $2,500 for a few hours (as one would hire a catering service), could profit in the tens of thousands, depending upon the gullibility and wealth of his mark.

Some of the greatest scores in the big store provided the con man with enough money to retire on, but the urge to glean more suckers was always too strong to resist and the hustler went on and on. Eddie Jackson, pickpocket turned hustler, who saw the inside of his first prison cell at Joliet in 1909, and who was arrested "thousands of times" (therefore belying his monicker of "Eddie the Immune") scored as much as $100,000 in one big-store scam. Jackie French, in a wire game in 1922, took three Florida suckers for $345,000, the palmiest week of his life. Harry Lewiston, a noted Chicago con man, beat suckers out of $200,000 in big-store games in 1900; one of his victims was the house detective of the Dearborn Plaza Hotel. Hustler Plunk Drucker employed a fight store to mulct $200,000 out of a sucker from Cleveland. Charley Gondorf bilked almost $400,000 from a visiting Englishman in Manhattan. The all-time record, however, is held by Joseph "Yellow Kid" Weil, who according to Illinois officials, flimflammed in the summer of 1924, $500,000 from twenty victims, all suckered into big-store games in and about Chicago.

Joseph Weil Loved Banks

The Yellow Kid played the big store with all kinds of variations and with a touch of nobility. "Our victims were mostly big industrialists and bankers," the Kid told Senator Estes Kefauver at his famous 1956 crime hearings. "The old-time confidence man had a saying: 'Never send them to the river.' We never picked on poor people or cleaned them out completely. Taking the life savings from poor old women is just the same as putting a revolver to her head and pressing the trigger!"

Yes, the Kid mulcted with class and invention. One of his big-store routines, played with his erstwhile partner Fred "The Deacon" Buckminster, occurred in Chicago before the First World War. At the time, Weil was attempting to sell a well-known industrialist some worthless stock certificates in a copper mine. Weil, with the sucker listening in, received a phone call from the president of the Sheridan Trust and Savings Bank (Buckminster), stating that the certificates could be sold at the bank.

Weil, locking arms with his sucker, took a taxi to the bank and asked a man in shirtsleeves who appeared to be a bank employee (he was a Weil plant) where the president could be found. "He's downstairs in the vault," they were told.

With his mark anticipating the "special stock deal" that would make his fat wallet even more corpulent, Weil and the sucker descended to the safe-deposit vault. There, standing before an open box containing what seemed to be priceless stock certificates, stood the fake bank president, Buckminster. The hush-hush stock sale was made in the vault area, and useless certificates were soon bulging the inside pocket of the business-man's suit. The bank front was so impressive that Weil and Buckminster used it again and again, plying their con in a spot to which the public had access but was so impressive that it overpowered any suspicions each mark may have had. (Weil liked the looks of banks so much that he once rented a bank building in Muncie, Indiana, before its cages and offices were dismantled. He peopled the bank with a horde of con men and prostitutes, who dragged bags of money across the floor for deposit to impress marks who were brought in to be mulcted.)

Bank offices and vaults were favorite big store fronts for Joseph "Yellow Kid" Weil, shown here (left) en route to court in 1939 when things were getting a little too hot. (UPI)

A Phalanx of Fronts

Weil's inventive use of the big store knew no restrictions. He realized early that the front need not always be a phony gambling den or wire shop. Any building or office reasonably impressive would serve as a big store. He differed from most con men, also, in that he did not always play upon the sucker's dishonesty in making money through illicit or shady deals. A legitimate business deal that meant large profits would do.

The Kid once rented a deserted yacht club, fixed it up at a nominal cost, and then answered several ads placed by marks wanting to sell their yachts. In the impressive confines of the club, Weil bought the yachts with worthless stock certificates, then resold the ships for large profits. He used the same big-store concept in purchasing 50,000 gallons of olive oil and in selling a landscaping contract to a gardening company for a retirement home for broken-down jockeys, an institution that never existed outside of Weil's colorful imagination.

One of the most successful big stores the Kid worked was in St. Louis during the stock-mad 1920s. Here Weil rented three floors that had been vacant for some time and were available at a cheap rate, and set up a bustling brokerage office. To this beehive of rustling papers, shouted orders to buy and sell, sweating boardmen breaking chalk at a furious pace to write down the latest Wall Street returns, the Yellow Kid brought suckers by the herd. His pitch was that he could sell useless stock certificates for as much as $5 a share when he had paid but only $1 each. He demonstrated by selling hundreds of shares for instant cash in his own phony brokerage house. The mark would then buy up all the phony stock certificates from Weil for fabulous amounts a day later, rush to the stockbroker's office—and find it vacant. Weil would reopen the brokerage house weeks later and bring in another well-primed sucker.

Ideas gave blood to the Kid's fleshy big-store cons. As a reader of Nietzche and Herbert Spencer, a member in the early 1920s of Chicago's literary Dill Pickle Club, where he hobnobbed with Ben Hecht, Charles MacArthur, Sherwood Anderson, and other authors, Weil became a "thinker," and his thoughts constantly produced limitless tricks.

Banks remained his favorite workshops. He and Big John Worthington once purchased control of the American State Bank on Chicago's South

LaSalle Street for $70,000. Through this bank, Weil and his associates mulcted suckers out of $300,000 in a short time. When such bankrolling became too expensive, Weil merely borrowed the office of a legitimate bank president for an hour or so. Using fake identification, the Kid passed himself off as an important Wall Street millionaire, appearing in the banks of small towns whose presidents were desperately eager to please such powerful men and perhaps increase their accounts. Weil would ask to use the president's office for some pressing business and the banker was only too happy to comply. Next, a victim would arrive (the Kid's timing was always perfect) and ask for the bank president. He would be shown into the office Weil occupied, and the Kid, who had gained the confidence of the sucker beforehand, would then, in the role of bank mogul, bilk him out of a small fortune. He would thank the real bank president some minutes after the transaction had taken place and the mark had departed, and promise heady investments—which, of course, never materialized. On many occasions the bank presidents were sued for fraud.

John Henry Strosnider's Fatal Patsy

Weil's banking cons were so successful that John Henry Strosnider decided to imitate just such a big store, and in it he involved an innocent banker named Kirby, who was put on trial for embezzling funds, money Strosnider had bilked. The stern-faced Judge Kenesaw Mountain Landis heard Kirby's case in a federal court, and after the banker had undergone three days of severe cross-examination (while sitting in a wheelchair, such was his health), insisted on Kirby's guilt. "Where have you hidden the ninety thousand dollars that belongs to your depositors?" Landis demanded. "This court will not be satisfied until you have confessed the hiding place of the money that belongs to the poor people of your neighborhood." It was too much for the flimflammed Kirby. On the last day of the trial, cub reporter Ben Hecht watched as the banker "gave up the uneven debate and pitched dead out of the wheelchair."

A few months later police collared John Henry Strosnider, and he admitted perpetrating the big store for which banker Kirby paid with his life.

Stern-faced Judge Kenesaw Mountain Landis was severe with con men; one died on him in the witness chair and was later proved innocent. (UPI)

Such sinister doings were not for the Yellow Kid. He condemned the reckless operations of such hustlers like Strosnider. Weil prided himself on pulling big-store cons that "never cheated any honest men . . . only rascals."

The Kid, though master of the big store in the Midwest for decades, never seemed to hold onto the millions he scammed. His own business acumen was frail. He put most of his mulcted millions into the hands of real-estate men to invest, but earned nothing and subsequently went broke. According to writer Mort King, Weil "put as much confidence in the realtor as his suckers had put in him."

The Yellow Kid was not the total master of con, which one incident well proved. "The greatest confidence man of his day," as Saul Bellow once called Weil, was taken by a sweet-faced young lady when he was deep into grift and traveling to Europe on one of the more fashionable liners. It was a shipboard romance, and the attractive countess he adored sobbed against his shoulder one moon-flooded night as they strolled along the promenade deck. After much coaxing she admitted that she desperately needed $10,000 to cover some of her alcoholic father's debts. Weil forked it over, accepting as security her exquisite pearl necklace. She blew him a kiss from the gangplank when the ship docked, promising to meet him in a few hours. He never saw her again. The precious pearls, like the countess, were fake.

The Kid only shrugged at the memory of this expensive lost love, then squinted wisely and stated: "What a team we would have made!"

Fifteen

Impossible Imposters

THE GREATEST TOOL at the con man's disposal is the pose he presents to the mark and the world. His impersonation is only as convincing as his talent to act. The great actors among hustlers are the rarest of their breed and they know it, having chosen the most impossible roles to perform in setting up pigeons. Some were so good they came to believe they were actually the persons they were impersonating. Here are the stars of con.

The Advance Man Cometh

J. Bam Morrison was a pleasant, outgoing person whose florid face seemed forever split wide with a grin. A happy man was Mr. Morrison when, on a July day in 1950, he entered the Oklahoma hamlet of Wetumka (pop. 2,715), a quiet little town reeking of prosperity. Morrison pulled his car to the curb and studied the placid faces of the small-town folk, smiling and nodding to those who looked his way. Wetumka was swell, an untouched suckerland and a con man's paradise.

270

It didn't take Morrison long to convince Wetumka's patriarchs and storeowners that he represented Bohn's United Circus, which, he announced proudly, would be coming to town on July 24. At a special meeting of the Chamber of Commerce, Morrison told the eager citizens: "Why, it'll be the biggest thing that ever hit this sweet little burg. People will come from a dozen towns around here. Your business will zoom, so you better lay in those supplies, folks, yes, sir, lay in the goods."

J. Bam Morrison, the smooth-talking advance man for the big top, then outlined how, in return for advertising space on the circus grounds purchased by the local merchants, storeowners could provide the circus with everything from hot dogs to hay for the elephants. Their profits would be enormous. They agreed to a man and bought the advertising, Morrison pocketing a hefty roll of their cash. He then offered the merchants the use of the circus's sound truck. It would not only traverse every street and alley of Wetumka, but go through every neighboring town within fifty miles, bringing thousands of out-of-towners to the circus. More money for the use of the truck went into Morrison's pockets.

The townsfolk then got busy preparing for the circus. Julian Peixotto, the local grocer, put through an order for a hundred pounds of wieners. Argie Taylor, head of the farmers' exchange, ordered, C.O.D., tons of hay to feed the elephants. The manager of the small Meadors Hotel purchased twenty new mattresses to handle the overflow crowds sure to come. Restaurant owner Louis Charlton, who had been given a fat contract to feed the entire company of the circus, fed Morrison free for three days as the advance man ambled happily through Wetumka, selling more advertising space and sound-truck announcements. Even the local Boy Scouts were pressed into hurly-burly service through scoutmaster Charles Davis; they would be the official town sponsors of the circus. And everywhere J. Bam Morrison went, residents received from his pink, chubby hands free passes to the big top. Even the local doctor received tickets, and in return he treated the advance man free.

Burning the Whole Town

With much fanfare, Morrison suddenly told Wetumka's citizens that he must return to the circus. "Watch for us in a week, on the twenty-fourth.

You'll hear the band first way off in the distance—then the clowns, the aerialists, the horse acts, the tigers, the elephants. What a happy day!"

The good and trusting residents of Wetumka busied themselves for the great event, and on the appointed day hundreds of out-of-towners, responding to the town's own advertising and announcements, jammed Wetumka's main street. They waited for the toot of horns, and the throb of drums that would herald the circus. They peered anxiously up and down streets. They waited. Then somebody contacted Argie Taylor and told him there was a package for him at the post office. It was from the intrepid advance man. Taylor paid the 67 cents due and opened a small box full of hay. Inside was a card reading: "Regards, J. Bam Morrison."

"We've been had," C. A. McWilliams told his fellow Wetumkans. He had, as publisher of the local newspaper, published a full-page ad announcing the coming of the circus, and had printed and distributed hundreds of handbills. But McWilliams was a resourceful soul, and convinced Tom Smith, the mayor, that there was only one way of appeasing the expectant throng. Smith proclaimed the first annual Sucker Day. Merchants and businessmen then gave away the hot dogs, pop, and assorted goods they had stored for con man Morrison's mythical circus.

The response was so overwhelming that the storeowners did a booming business, and Sucker Day in Wetumka became an annual event. It worked out so well that hustler Morrison was forgiven, having inadvertently established a local tradition as well as enriched the residents. Statements were even published and circulated in which the townsfolk said they had no hard feelings toward Morrison, and that the genial con man was welcome in their humble hamlet any time.

Four years later the police chief of Warrensburg, Missouri, called Wetumka. He was holding J. Bam Morrison for the same con he had pulled in Oklahoma, and did anyone there wish to press charges? No, certainly not, the chief was told. Morrison was put on the phone, and a merchant asked him to be "the guest of honor at our next annual Sucker Day." The hustler would think about it. When set free in Missouri, the flimflammer called the merchant back, collect. He told the businessman that he would return to Wetumka if the merchant would be so kind as to send traveling money.

"That much a sucker I'm not," the wise Wetumkan replied, and hung up.

Casting Couch for Suckers

Morrison's role model was still very much in use when, in the summer of 1974, the advance man had changed to the movie man in the casual, beefy personage of Mel Greenberg, who roared into Lexington, Virginia, in a shiny new Matador and announced to one and all that Universal Studios was about to use the quaint southern town as the site of an epic motion picture. Naturally, it was to be a Civil War film, and Audrey Hepburn and Burt Lancaster would star. The problem was, Greenberg patiently explained to clusters of star-struck citizens, that extras and a few supporting players were sorely needed. These Greenberg, in his capacity of casting director, would cull from the ranks of the most talented local inhabitants.

Greenberg began assigning cavalrymen parts to horse riders; pedestrians would be foot soldiers. Others, extras, would appear in the immense banquet scene, where their ability to eat convincingly would bring them $34 a day (if they didn't eat and merely arrived at the shooting site, they would get, Greenberg promised, $22 a day).

The starlet part was sicky. Greenberg interviewed the town's prettiest girls, and some who were far from comely, for the part that would give the right young lady the big break. The lucky girl would receive $12,000 for her role, one that required her to appear in a nude bathing scene, a short take that called for "a sight of backside and left breast." To this end, Greenberg sat paunchily in his motel room and observed the town's female hopefuls as they paraded naked across the floor (a woman accomplice was present at all times). Greenberg seemed rather bored by the procedure, flinging out producer lines like: "Get rid of those tan marks."

Some suspicious types, however, thought Greenberg a sham, and they discovered, after calling Universal Studios, that no producer named Mel Greenberg was in their employ. Town prosecutor Eric Sisler called the movie man into his office and questioned him, but was soon convinced that he was genuine. Sisler, however ordered the would-be mogul to stop the nude tryouts.

Greenberg returned to his motel, packed his bags, cashed more checks with proprietor Norman Andersen and left Lexington with the gripe: "I'm fed up with this town."

The con man, of course, had stuck the motel owner for the bad checks and embarrassed the entire population of Lexington, especially when it was learned that he had been arrested trying to pull off the same con in Hillsboro, Ohio, a short time later. But to some residents the hustler was a memorable novelty, and one citizen told a *Newsweek* reporter: "We'd never seen a real con man before and we feel proud to have been in on this one. It was like a good load of moonshine coming to town."

Ross Potter Performing

Such rogues were not always as entertaining as the inimitable Mel Greenberg. In the grand tradition of Lord Gordon-Gordon, Ross Potter, born in Lancaster, Pennsylvania, dedicated himself, shortly after getting his college degree, to a career of con based upon magnificent impersonations. He worked for newspapers in Albany, New York, and Philadelphia in the early 1880s, but used his position to bilk suckers. Run out of Philadelphia, Potter, then known as Ross Raymond or James Sandy, traveled to Europe, where he assumed many disguises, among them Thomas Alva Edison. In this guise he handsomely fleeced French President Sadi Carnot. In England Potter became George W. Childs, American millionaire, and bilked dozens of dupes there until arrested and imprisoned.

A decade later, after having served almost ten years in European jails for fraud, Potter returned to the United States and became Alfred Parsons, Lord Rosse of Burr Coth, Ireland, a visiting lecturer. In this impressive capacity, Potter conned half a dozen college presidents into cashing worthless checks. Among his victims were Seth Low, president of Columbia University; Daniel C. Gilman, president of Johns Hopkins University; and General Thomas L. James, former U.S. Postmaster-General and president of the Lincoln Bank. When "Lord Rosse" was convicted once again of fraud in 1901, General James remarked: "He was altogether such a fine-appearing gentleman that I did not hesitate for a moment to accept his check."

An Engaging Lithuanian

At about the same time Lord Rosse was impersonating his way through academic scams, a shady Lithuanian named Lipman emerged in Dublin's intellectual society, claiming to be an undergraduate student at Trinity College. He was entertained by George Coffey and other leading literary lights in Ireland, and such was his imposing appearance as a weighty intellectual (though many of his sponsors privately admitted that they could not make out exactly what he was talking about), that the celebrated liberal T. W. Russell allowed Lipman free lodging in his Temperance Hotel.

Imposter Lipman was finally exposed and jailed. Upon his release he left Dublin and traveled to the United States, appearing in Boston as one Count Zuboff, a member of one of Russia's most distinguished families. In the words of James L. Ford: "The annals of social imposture reveal few careers as remarkable as that of Lipman, who leaped at one bound from a Dublin jail to a place in the most exalted intellectual society in the Modern Athens." In his role as Count Zuboff, Lipman bilked scores of social lions and lionesses. He gave huge parties in the mansions of others, and charged off the affairs to his duped sponsors.

At one of these fetes the actress Madame Modjeska addressed the imposter in Russian. He turned aside, shrugging his shoulders.

The actress was persistent, and again rattled off some Russian. Then she asked, puzzled, "But, Count Zuboff, why do you not respond in your own tongue?"

"You are speaking," he replied in English, "in a dialect impossible for me to understand, dear lady. There are hundreds of dialects in my country. That is why Russians do not understand each other."

Lipman's scam would have gone on indefinitely, but he became smitten with a Boston heiress and followed her to New York. Newspapermen there saw through the Count's act and exposed him. While awaiting trial for fraud in the Jefferson Market Jail, Lipman committed suicide.

Radzevil's Riotous Roles

Like Lipman and Gordon-Gordon, Luodovic Theodor Radzevil was ever mindful of presenting the figure of stern authority in convincing marks that his identity was real. An Austrian barber, Radzevil was two jumps ahead of a recruiting officer when he skipped to England some years before World War I. Finding himself stranded with two razors and ten shillings in his pockets, the Austrian con man decided that the White Star Line, through which he planned to reach America, urgently required an interpreter to handle the babbling rabble immigrating to the United States.

Radzevil's ability to translate languages was sketchy; his English, learned from the King James version of the Bible and a Jenkins' law book, was awkwardly alliterative and heavily underscored with fractured legalese. Entering the offices of the steamship company, the apprentice con man twirled the flowing ends of his ample mustache and addressed an official: "Does the honorable company the services of an upright and experienced interpreter require?"

"It just so happens we do," the official answered.

Radzevil then informed his potential employer that he was proficient in all European languages and the tongues of Africa and Asia as well.

"Fine," said the unbelieving official. "Make a few extemporaneous remarks in Chinese, if you will."

Radzevil beamed. "Let the honorable president of the company query me a question in Chinese, and I him will answer in the same speech."

Such strategy earned him the immediate position of interpreter. Payment, according to the Austrian's demand, consisted of $10 cash, one first-class cabin to the Promised Land, and a blue uniform with a lot of gold braid plus a naval cap with insignias. The following day, attired in this sartorial splendor, Radzevil entered the way-station area, where emigrants were crowded together as they awaited passage. He handed out cards, for which he had spent 4 shillings, emblazoned "Luodovic Theodor Radzevil, International Official Interpreter." Most of the foreigners couldn't read the cards but bowed low before the finely dressed Austrian, whom they took to be a British admiral.

Radzevil then walked across the street to a barbershop. The head barber greeted him with great respect. He, too, was awed by the strange uniform.

The imposter looked intently at the barber and spoke: "What for the shaving of the beard and furthermore and likewise the scissoring of the hair, is the price thereof?"

"Sixpence for each, sir." The barber threw in an obsequious nod of slavishness.

Drawing himself to his full height of six feet four, Radzevil held up his card and stated: "In the afterwards and hereafter, your price for whosoever bears a card like unto this one is two shillings for scissoring and one for shaving. Also and moreover, the half of these moneys will to me belong. Hire to you abundantly shavers and scissorers, for in fifteen minutes will arrive a multitude."

Marching back to the emigrant station, Radzevil held up a megaphone, and in four or five languages, shouted to the startled foreigners that the steamship company had ordered that every man and boy be shaved and shorn, or both. They were to hand his card to the barber and return it to him after they had gone under the scissors. The steamship company, he explained, refused to sail shaggy-haired foreigners to America.

Hundreds jumped up and grabbed Radzevil's cards and queued up across the street in front of the barbershop, its proprietor desperately sending out for every barber in Liverpool. For three days and nights, the emigrants shuttled under the flailing scissors. Then Radzevil showed up to collect his share. The barber attempted to short-change the enterprising Austrian, but the hustler produced the cards returned to him by the shorn immigrants and exacted his cut.

Employing the same approach, the con man visited a hardware store and then ordered the emigrants to purchase hunting knives with which to protect themselves against the fierce tribes of American Indians. The profit from the knives was also eye popping. And just as Radzevil was about to order each emigrant to take a Turkish bath and buy a new suit of clothes (transactions he had prearranged, again for a cut, with merchants), the steamship company ordered everybody on board the ship which sailed for America. Radzevil had taken the precaution, however, of stocking his first-class cabin with several barrels of apples. After two days of mediocre steerage food, the illustrious interpreter appeared and announced that the ship's captain had provided, through Radzevil's humanitarian offices, a fresh, luscious apple for each emigrant; one had to keep up standards of health. These would be sold for 2 shillings each. Radzevil sold out his supply within minutes.

When getting off the ship, the hustler carried new luggage, a new wardrobe, hundreds of dollars, and even more important, the names and addresses of more than 1,500 immigrants. In a few hours he secured an office in Manhattan and returned to the immigrants, who were awaiting clearance through customs. He addressed the throng, stating that he would continue to work for their well-being in America, mentioning somewhere in his babbled banter his long-standing friendship with the President of the United States. Should anyone care either to send or receive money from the Old Country or want exemption from military service in America, he would be only too happy to arrange matters.

The ship's captain, who witnessed Radzevil's diatribe, remarked to a junior officer: "You see that fellow? I predict one thing for him here. He will be lynched."

But Radzevil cleverly sidestepped the enactment of such prophecies. He opened opulent offices near the waterfront. Covering a solid three-story brick wall of his building was the imperial Austrian coat-of-arms, beneath which in gold lettering were the words: "Ludodovic Theodor Radzevil, Official Interpreter of the Austrian Empire and International Agent."

To the con man's offices flocked hundreds of immigrants seeking to avoid the compulsory military service that was the bugbear of Europe. None knew, of course, that there was at the time no draft in the United States, so when Radzevil told them that he would arrange matters with his good friend the President and they were not inducted into the army, grateful scores showered the hustler with money. He also provided services for sending and receiving money from Europe, but, oddly enough, these payments never materialized. Radzevil blamed the mails; avaricious postal employees were the culprits. He was keeping a minute record of each loss, however, and he would bring this up in one of his long-distance phone calls with the President when the time was opportune. (The con man's phone calls, allegedly made to the Chief Executive in Washington, D.C., would have been hilarious to anyone other than the badly informed immigrants sweating at deskside, the one-sided conversation a mixture of witless jokes, guffaws, and secret passwords spewed out in Radzevil's clumsy, unending stream of gobbledygook.)

The imposter lived lavishly for several years, banking a fortune in mulcted monies, taking a suite of rooms in a fashionable hotel, and driving through the Austrian communities of the city in a chauffeur-driven auto, each day's apparel different and decidedly field-marshal in rank. But the con man's dream world came to an abrupt end in 1913 when the Austrian consul got wind of his scam and informed postal authorities, who put a stop to his grandiose schemes.

Bunco Artist with a Badge

Aside from royalty or politicians and millionaires, a favorite target of impersonation for con men has been the detective business. George Austin, a notorious imposter at the turn of the century, conned thousands of dollars out of gullible saloon owners by pretending to be either a Manhattan detective or a director of one of the many vigilance committees, charging that bar men were breaking the excise laws and angrily threatening arrest. Hefty payoffs to the phony cop soothed his pious anger. Austin's act was interrupted when he took up the practice of visiting police precinct stations and ordering officers about while flashing a captain's badge. A wary desk sergeant called headquarters and found Austin to be a fake. He was thrown head first into a cell, and his badge confiscated.

A justice of the peace in Trenton, New Jersey, Peter Pollack, passed himself off as a captain of the "Federal Secret Service," and sold badges and other impressive documents of identification to any who had the $100 to become a "special agent." Convicted of everything from cruelty to animals to lewdness, imposter Pollack's favorite scam was to offer his expert services as a detective to firms seeking to recover stolen goods. After a company hired "Captain" Pollack, he would place a man in its warehouse who stole goods and brought them back to him. Pollack would then return the stolen goods to the company and merrily collect his bloated fee for the phony detective work.

The eccentric heiress Maud King (right), *whom Means bilked out of $150,000.* (UPI) (Left) *Gaston Bullock Means, shown here in 1935 as he entered the federal penitentiary at Atlanta.* (WIDE WORLD)

The Grifting Gumshoe

The man who carried the detective flimflam to its most absurd ends was a dimple-cheeked, heavyset con man who was actually employed as a special agent for the U.S. Bureau of Investigation, the indefatigable Gaston Bullock Means. Born into the genteel tradition of the Old South in 1880, Means spent most of his first thirty years in North Carolina as a cotton broker, school superintendent, and sometime lawyer. He joined the Burns Detective Agency in 1910 and was touted by his employer, William J. Burns, as "the greatest natural detective ever known." But Mr. Means was much more adept at con, and after five years with Burns, time spent mostly in using his position to mulct suckers impressed with badges, sleuth Gaston quit to manage the affairs of heiress Maude R. King.

Maude had married lumber millionaire James C. King in 1901. At the time she was twenty-four, and he fifty years her senior. She leaped from shopgirl to millionairess in four years. After her exhausted hubby quit the tribulations of this earth, she began a madcap tour through the Western world; she dropped wine bottles from the Eiffel Tower and exploded stink bombs in London's Parliament building. Gaston Means, his ever-alert eye watchful for such highly publicized zanies, felt it was his duty to safeguard the fortune of the witless, giddy Mrs. King. He conspired to meet her by hiring a thug to pretend to rob her and her chaperons on a Chicago street. Means strolled up during the so-called stickup, overpowered the thug, and became Mrs. King's hero.

From hero, Means became the manager of Maude King's affairs. He knew best which stocks to buy, which property to acquire. Maude turned over several hundred thousand dollars to his keeping, and by July 1917 he had bilked her out of more than $150,000. When she became curious about the manipulation of her fortune, Means suggested a hunting trip to his North Carolina homestead. He took her into the woods near Concord, she protesting, albeit feebly, that she knew nothing of hunting. Means convinced Maude that it was "fun."

Following a short hike in the damp woods, Means and Maude went off on their own to slake their thirst in a nearby pond. Other hunters in the party heard a shot and then saw Gaston stumble from the scrubby forest, gushing tears and belching sobs. "Oh, poor Mrs. King," he wailed. Maude King was no more, quite dead, and the distraught Means, her valiant protector, told a coroner's jury of local friends how the tragedy occurred.

"I had this twenty-five-caliber blue steel Colt automatic," his tear-streaked narrative ran, "and I put it in the crotch of a tree while I went to the spring to get a drink. Mrs. King insisted she wasn't thirsty, so I left her standing by the tree where the gun was while I went to the spring to quench my thirst." He looked back, he said, to see Maude giggling and twirling the automatic. "Mrs. King, poor soul, was very light headed. I shouted to her to put the gun back. Then I leaned down to get my drink and I heard this report." By the time the heavyset Means moved his considerable girth to the flighty woman's fallen body, she was dead. She had been shot behind the left ear and the coroner's jury concluded, country jakes that they were, that Maude King's death was accidental homicide, that the weapon had freakishly discharged when she dropped it.

A subsequent murder trial, studded with Means's gibberish about white supremacy before a jury dominated by Ku Klux Klanners, exonerated the con man and resulted in an incredible verdict of suicide. Means then had Mrs. King's remains cremated and moved on to his next scam, which was as improbable as Maude King's self-annihilation.

Mr. Means Goes to War

During World War I, Means conned British agents into believing he was not only a master detective but a master spy and hired out to them. His job was to keep them informed of German espionage activities in the United States. He then went to the Germans and offered his services to them. They paid him to "embarrass British commerce," according to the *New York Sun.* Cloak and dagger didn't pay too well, so Means added another client, the U.S. Army Intelligence Service. He offered to transport and guard top secret documents to wherever they had to be shipped.

According to the stories Means told about himself, he got the job and then, impersonating intelligence agents for three countries, did everything in his considerable powers to thoroughly confuse all of his employers. Don Whitehead relates how Means "had been battling spies, crooks and international thieves, all of whom seemed to be banded together to thwart his honest aims." Means ran the army ragged with his elaborate schemes, which smacked of espionage à la Charlie Chaplin. He told the army that he had recovered several trunks filled with defense secrets, but before he could deliver these safely to U.S. Intelligence officials, sinister secret agents, at least a platoon of them, jumped him from behind and stole the trunks. "The flaw in this story," Whitehead observed, "was that the trunks weighed the same when delivered without documents as they did when supposedly crammed with secret papers."

Means next appeared in Chicago in 1920, befriending a lawyer named Roy D. Keehn, for whom he did investigative leg work. When he learned that Keehn was expecting a $57,000 settlement on a case from the East, Means, stating that he was returning to his old homestead, volunteered to pick up the cash. After retrieving the money, Gaston Bullock Means simply mailed a package from his hometown of Concord, sending it through the Southeastern Express Company. Keehn received a block of wood neatly wrapped in brown paper. He sued Means. Means sued the express firm, claiming a clerk had substituted the block of wood for cash. The case was never tried, and Means went on a six-month binge with the loot from this score while he hazily plotted his next flimflam. He didn't have to tax the wellsprings of hustle, for his old employer, William J. Burns, called and told him that with Harding recently elected President, he, Burns, could be named head of the Bureau of Investigation, a post he very much desired and one that would certainly enhance his own detective agency. Means accepted a job to secure letters of recommendation for Burns to Harding from dozens of congressmen. He achieved his ends by merely digging up dirt on the lawmakers and blackmailing them into writing the letters.

When Burns took over the Bureau of Investigation, the immediate forerunner of today's FBI, he appointed Means as special investigator, much to the disgust of J. Edgar Hoover, then a lower official of the department. Means's job was that of a go-between for the Ohio Gang, the corrupt officials who moved to Washington with Harding and set up the notorious Teapot Dome. Blackmail and flimflamming were Means's chief avenue of income. He worked them with extraordinary agility, and soon moved his wife and young son into an expensive three-story white brick home in a fashionable district of Washington. His bank account blossomed.

Oiling the President's Mistake

The super sleuth got in over his hustling head, however, when he uncovered the extramarital affair between President Harding and an Ohio poetess, Nan Britton, ironically at the request of Mrs. Harding. He was sacked. He whiled away his time attempting to blackmail Harding and his wife for an alleged $50,000, but Harding died in office before Means could collect. (Some say he did collect $35,000 from Harding for his indiscretions before the President died mysteriously in San Francisco.) The con man then turned to literary pursuits and helped Nan Britton—he had stolen her diaries to make his scam against Harding—write a book entitled *The President's Daughter*, which claimed Harding had sired an illegitimate child. Means topped this notorious tome with an even more absurd book when he authored *The Strange Death of President Harding*, a scandalous best seller in which Gaston implied that Mrs. Harding had poisoned her husband.

The balance of the 1920s saw Means occupy himself with dozens of con games, all centering about his impersonation of a master detective. He shook down bootleggers, forged Andrew Mellon's signature to obtain bonded whiskey, sold fake protection to businessmen whose lives had been threatened through the mails (Means sent the letters), and even became a Communist subversive. Learning that Mrs. Finley Shepherd of Tarrytown, New York, had established a committee to fight Communism, he wrote her a letter that promised to wipe out her entire family and signed it "Agents from Moscow."

He then went to Mrs. Shepherd, an extremely wealthy woman, a member of the Gould family, and offered the services of the unbeatable detective, Gaston Bullock Means. She paid him handsomely to track down the would-be Communist killers. After having bilked her for thousands, Means began the same kind of operation on a nationwide basis, averaging from this bogus international threat about $1,000 a week.

Search for a Dead Child

Evalyn Walsh McLean, here wearing the fateful Hope Diamond, was mulcted out of $100,000 by Means in a zany search for the missing Lindbergh baby. (UPI)

Means crowned his impossible con career by fleecing copper-mine heiress and social gadfly Evalyn Walsh McLean, who was married to the publisher of the *Washington Post*. When the Lindbergh child was kidnapped in 1932, Mrs. McLean sent for the famous American Sherlock, whom she had met through the Hardings. She was desperate to do something to save the child. Though she knew Means was a con man, she felt that through his powerful underworld contacts (which never existed), he could locate the headquarters of the kidnapper where the police of a half dozen states had failed and restore to the Lindbergh family the only son of America's greatest hero. Means rolled up his sleeves, vowed vengeance on the filthy kidnappers, and went on his netherworld quest, a journey that occupied months of intrigue, clandestine meetings, and great moments in crime solving that always verged on, but never concluded in, the capturing of the kidnapper and the saving of the Lindbergh baby.

Through his herculean efforts he ultimately managed to track down the gang, he told Mrs. McLean, and if she would give him the $100,000 they demanded, plus $4,000 for his own expenses, he would deliver the Lindbergh child safe and sound. Mrs. McLean paid, and as usual the deal fell through. When Mrs. McLean's lawyers demanded the return of the $100,000, the con man replied, "Why, don't you have it? I gave it to a representative of your firm. Funny, too. When I demanded a receipt, he only shrugged. May I now have a receipt for the $100,000?" It was the old wood-block game. Means did not get the receipt, but instead received fifteen years in Leavenworth for fraud.

Visited by FBI men in 1938 after suffering a heart attack, Means was asked where he had buried the McLean money. He blinked wide eyes from his prison hospital bed, then died with a smile on his face.

Where Means enjoyed the pretense of being America's greatest detective, Joseph Levy, a con man who operated widely in the early 1950s, impersonated prison officials. His scam was that of passing bad checks. Levy would show up at a prison supply firm, place large orders for Sing Sing or other prisons, then ask to cash a personal check. So elated over the order, businessmen always provided the money. Sometimes Levy would impersonate prison wardens, parole officers, even U.S. states attorneys. Levy also passed bad checks while buying expensive items for famous people, pretending to be intimate with the high and mighty. In these purchases, he always made his checks larger than the sum the price tag called for, pocketed the difference, and skipped. In one weekly spurt of con, Levy purchased rare perfume for Mamie Eisenhower and a case of Scotch for the President. As with all of his "gifts" he wrote personal notes to his "friends." For Richard M. Nixon, then Vice-President, he purchased an expensive set of golf clubs and enclosed a note reading: "Dick, beat the boss."

The Yellow Kid was also a master impersonator, one of the best. In his long career of con, Weil posed as a doctor, a mining engineer, an emissary of the German Reichsbank, a famous geologist. Often times the Kid assumed the actual identities of world-known figures, such as the learned German chemist Rudolph Ruehl and the American money mogul J. P. Morgan.

Fraud for Fun and Money

Stanley Clifford Weyman gave Weil stiff competition in the impersonation con. Weyman, a Brooklyn-bred hustler, tired of the drab life of a clerk and took on impossible roles for decades, mostly to relieve his own

(Left) *FBI photo of Stanley Clifford Weyman, con man imposter, in 1943.* (Right) *Princess Fatima and retinue in Washington; Weyman (far right), is in disguise as a U.S. naval officer.* (UPI)

boredom. He was the U.S. consul delegate to Morocco, replete with purple uniform, and went to prison for charging meals, rooms, and store items to this mythical diplomat. He impersonated a military attaché from Serbia and a lieutenant in the U.S. Navy. He went to prison for those roles, too. After his release he became the Rumanian consul general and a commander in the Rumanian army. In this capacity he demanded to inspect the American battleship *Wyoming* and did, the ship's captain turning out his hundreds of men in their best whites while little Stanley Weyman strutted in review. Following each prison sentence, Weyman concocted a new role. In 1920 he became a prominent physician who was hired by a Manhattan development firm and sent to Peru to upgrade sanitary conditions in areas controlled by American interests.

A year later he was back in the United States in the role of an undersecretary of the State Department, and escorted Afghanistan's Princess Fatima about New York and Washington, bilking her of $10,000, which Weyman calmly stated was needed to buy gifts for State Department officials, mere protocol. Weyman carried out his ridiculous State Department guise to the limit, actually ushering the princess into the company of Secretary of State Charles Evans Hughes and President Harding. He was dressed in the uniform of a lieutenant commander of the U.S. Navy,

So convincing was Weyman's acting ability that Viennese Dr. Adolf Lorenz, celebrated for his bloodless surgery, took on "Dr. Weyman" as an assistant until his lack of basic medical knowledge became apparent. Weyman once showed up outside the walls of Sing Sing Prison claiming to be a prison reform expert, and gave a stirring interview against capital punishment to wide-eyed reporters as Warden Lewis Lawes looked on in a quandry. The height of Weyman's audacity was reached when he appeared at Middlesex University as a noted penal expert, addressing a throng at a dedication exercise. His harangue attacked psychiatrists who treated prison inmates, and the speech was entitled "Insanity: Its Defense in Crime." Dr. Weyman concluded his hectoring talk with: "To be specific, gentlemen, I think that the average alienist should himself be subjected to a searching mental examination."

The Con Man at Stage Center

At the pinnacle of such grift was the personable hustler Frederick Emerson Peters, who writer Robert Yoder once called "one of the elite of the imposters," and crime historian Beverly Smith, Jr., who knew him, termed Peters "the crook everyone liked."

Born to middle-class Ohio parents in 1885, Peters began his con career by cashing a bad check in 1902, impersonating someone else. He was so successful that authorities did not apprehend him until 1915. His technique was always the same. He would purchase a store item, usually from expensive, specialized shops, carry on an impressive and intellectual conversation with the clerk, outlining his considerable military, academic, or diplomatic background, and then pay for his purchase with a check written out for more than the cost, pocketing the extra money. It was the extra amount he was after; the gift, to be sent on to his university or club, was always returned.

Peters was really a small-time con man, taking only what he needed out of each bad check. His career was interrupted in 1915 when he was sent to the federal penitentiary in Atlanta for ten years. Through the intervention of Newton D. Baker, Secretary of War and an old friend of

FBI mugshots (here and on facing page) of the intellectual con man and imposter Frederick Emerson Peters.

his father's, Peters was released from Atlanta by order of President Wilson in 1920. By then such clemency was lost on him, and he was soon hanging paper by the ton.

The hustler had read extensively while in prison—in fact, jail served as his college—and he broadened and deepened an already gifted mind with a plethora of knowledge in history, military affairs, politics, and specialized academic studies. When he was let loose on the streets in May 1920, he added to this weighty intelligence the postures of famous men. In cashing checks he became Franklin Delano Roosevelt, Theodore Roosevelt, Jr., Gifford Pinchot II, Booth Tarkington, and later, having a determined literary taste, Philip Wylie.

He didn't last long. Peters was back in prison in 1924 at the federal penitentiary on McNeil Island. Finding the prison library practically nonexistent, Peters convinced Warden Finch Archer that it was disgraceful not to provide inmates with a method by which to improve their minds. More books were needed, sure, the Warden agreed, but the prison budget prohibited purchase. Peters solved that problem. With the warden's blessing, he wrote impassioned letters to every major American book publisher, imploring them to send all their new titles to the prison to enrich the minds of the unfortunate wretches therein. Hearing of Peters's request, Mary Roberts Rinehart urged publishers to supply him with books.

Tomes by the trunks arrived, a library of more than 15,000 books covering science, biography, fiction, the best American publishers had to offer. Peters indexed and cataloged the books himself. But the avid readers of the prison population failed to appear at the library doors, which is what Peters knew would happen. The books, as he had planned all along, were for himself, and they would serve as a form of instruction in how to better his impossible impersonations once he was set free. In 1931 an academic giant among con men was released, and his scams went into full throttle.

The roles Peters played were so intense that he actually came to believe that he, indeed, was the individual he was portraying. He spoke with such sincerity and knowledge that everyone else believed him, too. One time he was R. A. Coleman of the American Peace Society. In purchasing a silver chalice that the society wanted to donate to a Washington church, Peters explained the entire history of the group dating back to

1828. The clerk was enthralled with the con man's erudite conversation and was more than happy to cash Peters's check, which considerably exceeded the cost of the chalice. Other times Peters would be Dr. J. J. Morton of the University of Kansas or from Yale, purchasing some rare article to be sent on to the campus.

For fifty years the hustler entertained his victims with performances worthy of a Paul Muni or a Fredric March. His remarkable career was studded with prison sentences, but these always served as academic intervals in which Peters would go back to the books to immerse himself in a field he had chosen to represent once he was released, a master imposter rehearsing as would an actor, at the expense of the government.

By 1952 the con man was an aging flimflammer who had lost none of his charm or wit. In that year a sharp-eyed detective spotted him lounging in the foyer of Washington's Lafayette Hotel and thought he recognized the then much-wanted hustler. Approaching the white-haired gentleman, the detective inquired: "You're Frederick Emerson Peters, aren't you?"

The con man blinked quizzically. "No," came his confident response. "I'm Paul Carpenter. I'm publicity agent for the Montevideo Music Festival." By then Peters had so retreated into his bogus personalities that he was totally convinced that he was Paul Carpenter or whomever he said he was and that Peters hardly existed any more, that his real identity as he later explained, "seemed only vaguely familiar to me—perhaps someone I had known long ago."

The detective was not to be put off. He suggested that the elderly fellow accompany him to the police station, where his story could be checked. On the way, Peters clung innocently to his role as Paul Carpenter, insisted that a mistake was being made. He was still Paul Carpenter when he was fingerprinted and while he awaited the results of the police check. Not until the truth had been learned did he seem to slip back into his own identity.

Watching as the con man was led down a long hall past a row of cells, the detective, years on Peters's trail, smiled at the hustler's amazing gall and stubborn performance. Frederick Emerson Peters then turned, looked up at the detective, and before stepping into a cell, smiled back and said in a pleasant voice: "It's been a lot of fun, hasn't it?"

A Chronology of Con

Beginning in 1800, the following is a timetable of confidence men and games throughout the world, chiefly in the United States, which is designed to include all those notorious hustlers and their specific scams which make up the curiosities and landmarks of grift. Chapter numbers follow those hustlers and games treated extensively in the general narrative.

1800

American countryside is inundated with wonder drugs sold by fake nostrum peddlers such as Dr. John Tennant of Virginia, who promotes Rattlesnake Root which guarantees to cure pleurisy (IV). . . . First phony mail-order cons appear, such as Perkins's Metallic Tractors, which claims to cure any disease through "electrical currents" (IV).

1811

Edward Tinker, captain of a commercial vessel, scuttles his ship off Roanoke Island, and then puts in a fake insurance claims (one of the first such swindles attempted in the United States) for the ship and lost cargo. When one member of the crew, a seaman named Edwards, refuses to support his false story, Tinker kills him. He is quickly apprehended, tried, and convicted, being hanged at Cateret, North Carolina, in September.

1815

Future stock manipulator Daniel Drew mulcts several wealthy New York State cattlemen, including Henry Astor, into purchasing bone-thin herds, which he cleverly fattens by watering shortly before sales are made (I).

1818

Operators of the New York Lottery are exposed as swindlers by arranging for certain numbers to win and receiving kickbacks from the rigged winners. Says Charles N. Baldwin, editor of the *Republican Chronicle*: "It is a fact that in this city [New York] there is SWINDLING in the management. A certain gentleman in town received intimation that a number named would be drawn on Friday last and it was drawn that day! This number was insured high in several different places. A similar thing had happened once before in this same lottery; and on examination of the managers' files the number appeared soiled as if it had been in the pocket several days . . . " Baldwin is sued for libel and one of the complainants, John H. Sickles, is revealed by the New York Select Committee, on the following April 6, 1819, to be a secret contractor of the lottery and guilty of providing political friends with advance information on winning numbers. Baldwin is acquitted.

1820

Samuel Shirley opens his crooked gambling den in Washington, D.C., bilking suckers with his rigged faro games.

1823

Thousands of participants in the Grand National Lottery, authorized by Congress for the benefit of Washington, are bilked by the contractor, a hustler named Gillespie, when he refuses to pay winners and skips with about $300,000.

1830

The first notorious card flimflammer, Elijah Skaggs, appears in Nashville, Tennessee, to trim suckers in faro. In twenty years Skaggs will be a millionaire, operating principally in the plush, giant Mississippi riverboats, fleecing marks at a profit of $100,000 a month. . . . "Umbrella Jim" Miner begins operating his blatant shell game along the Mississippi (II). . . . Jonathan H. Green, later known as the "Reformed Gambler," reveals to Louisville police the existence of "The Secret Band of Brothers," a New Orleans-based enclave of card sharpers and con men numbering 1,000 members, who work suckers in assorted teams and scams, splitting all income from their collective games. Green insists that this con clan was first organized by a hustler named Goodrich at Hanging Rock, Virginia, in 1798.

1832

Col. J. J. Bryant opens his fixed gambling saloon in Vicksburg, roping suckers to rigged banco, faro, and roulette tables.

1834

The rebirth of fake remedies such as Moore's Essence of Life, which promises cures of all ailments, suckers thousands into outlandish health-scare purchases (IV).

1835

Irate citizens of Vicksburg, Mississippi, formed into a law-and-order faction called the "Volunteers," and disgusted by the gangs of con men and hustlers infesting their town, break into a gambling den and tavern operated by sharper John North. He, Sam Smith, Dutch Bill, D. Hullum, and a flimflammer named McCall are hanged July 6. . . . The Drake inheritance con game begins in the United States after centuries of being operated in Europe (V). . . . Eighteen-year-old hustler Charles Cora fleeces every crooked faro table in Natchez for $50,000 in one week. . . . James Ashby, a wizard at card cheating, begins to prey upon his fellow con artists on the Mississippi paddle-wheelers, preferring to sting sharpers rather than suckers. According to one account, he "usually worked with a partner who was disguised as a gawky young backwoodsman, en route home after selling a drove of hogs. Ashby impersonated the young man's fiddle-playing old Pappy who didn't have all his buttons and was forever playing snatches of tunes on his fiddle, especially after the young backwoodsman had been inveigled into a card game. Not for a long time did the gamblers learn that the tunes were signals. . . ."

1839

Allen Jones, a wealthy saddler and devout card player, is trimmed by Col. J. J. Bryant in Huntsville, Alabama. Bryant plays a slow come-on, letting Jones win and then forcing a showdown for every cent each man has, dealing Jones four kings to his four aces and winning all. So impressed is Jones with the hustler's dexterity that he begs to apprentice with Bryant. After learning every flimflam the experienced Colonel knows, Jones sets off on his own, soon to become one of the most accomplished con artists in the country.

1840

Charles Legate ("Charley Black Eyes") begins his notorious swindling career along the Mississippi River towns and on board steamboats, "disguised variously as a planter, a banker, a merchant."

1841

A bevy of sharpers led by John Powell (including Jimmy Fitzgerald, Henry Perritt, Allen Jones, Price McGrath, John Lawler, Gabe Foster,

Tom Wicks, Ben Burnish, and Johnny Chamberlin) take suites in the new, elegantly-styled Planters Hotel in St. Louis, using this as a confidence game and cardsharping headquarters.

1842

Scores of gambling dens in Chicago run by King Cole Conant, George C. Rhodes, Walt Winchester, Cole Martin, and others serve as headquarters for the most prominent con men of the era. The con ring sector, a series of old, wooden one-story buildings jutting out into Lake Michigan on wobbly piers, is known as "The Sands." Faro, banco, three-card monte, and shell games abound here until Mayor Long John Wentworth burns down the section in 1857.

1843

Confidence man and cardsharper Martin Curtis opens his faro game hall in Milwaukee, Wisconsin, and dominates con games and crooked gambling in this city for the next decade. Using his fabulous mulcted winnings, Curtis finances the town's first real hotel, the 136-room Kirby House, named after the city's mayor, Abner Kirby, which will open in 1845.

1849

The gold-brick con is begun during the California Gold Rush.

1850

William Jones, better known as "Canada Bill," along with a host of other sharpers—George Devol, Tom Brown, Holly Chappell—invade the Mississippi riverboats, stinging suckers with three-card monte, one of the most durable con games of the nineteenth century (II).

1854

Robert Schuyler, grandson of the revolutionary general and president of the New York and New Haven Railroad, issues huge blocks of fake stock on his firm, pockets tens of thousands of dollars, and escapes to Europe before his gigantic swindle is exposed.

1856

Charles Cora, who had joined the California Gold Rush and fleeced miners for several years as one of the wiliest con men in the business, shoots and kills General W. H. Richardson, who is also a U.S. marshal, over a woman. The San Francisco Vigilance Committee storms the jail that houses Cora and he is hanged on May 20.

1859

Cuban con man Julian Cinquez appears in New York high society, freely bilking social lions and matrons under the alias of Colonel Novena. It is Cinquez who inaugurates the first large real-estate scams in the U.S. (I).

1862

One-time roper and capper for a skinning house on Hairtrigger Block in Chicago, George Trussell operates in partnership with Old Bill Leonard and Otis Randall, almost all the rigged gambling dens in the city. One report has it that "to bring victims into their houses, Trussell and his partners employed a gang of ropers whose tactics caused much ill feeling among the keepers of the few honest games. It was the custom of these slickers to sneak into the hallway of a square house and turn out the gas, and then when a sucker came along tell him that the place had been

closed and steer him to a den controlled by Trussell's syndicate." . . .
Sophie Lyons begins her con career in New York.

1863

Ben Marks, a pioneer con man, opens the first big store in Denver,
Colorado, fleecing suckers in rigged horse and foot races (XIV).

1864

"Hungry Joe" Lewis and others begin bilking marks in banco and other
con games in New York City (I).

1866

James "King" McNally is credited with starting the green-goods game
and becoming its most adept sharper at this time (II). . . . John Flanagan
organizes a bevy of sharpers in Minneapolis, opening two notorious
gambling dens that feature banco, faro, three-card monte, even the old
shell game. These wolf traps operate at Hennepin and Nicollet avenues
for two decades, Flanagan retiring in the late 1880s with an estimated
fortune of $1 million.

1867

Super con man Daniel Drew appoints two upcoming sharpers, Jay
Gould and Jim Fisk, directors of the Erie Railroad, a firm they immediately proceed to secretly gut through phony stock manipulations (I).

1868

Georgia farm boy James Addison Reavis, a small-time real estate man in
St. Louis, begins to forge charters and land grants alleging that hundreds
of miles of Arizona territory belong to one Miguel de Peralta, a Spanish

nobleman of his own invention; Reavis, in years to come, will lay claim to these lands in one of the most giant swindles in U.S. history. . . . International swindler "Lord Glencairn" first appears in Edinburgh, Scotland, to fleece reputable jewelers (I). . . . Jeanette Villiers, a matrimonial con lady, surfaces in Baltimore to inveigle a rich widow into giving her large portions of her inheritance (VIII).

1869

Fisk and Gould move to corner the American gold market, netting millions in their colossal scam (I).

1870

Flimflammer, gambler, and political fixer Mike McDonald begins his career in Chicago; he will establish a budding colony of con men in the Windy City that will rule supreme through police payoffs and political clout for almost three decades. . . . Elijah Skaggs, who had made millions in con games, dies in Texas in an alcoholic stupor, without a dime in his pockets. . . . "The Crying Kid," one of the great ropers of his time, starts operating in New York (I).

1871

"Lord Gordon-Gordon" begins one of the most fabulous con games in history, culminating with the stinging of Jay Gould the following year for half a million dollars (I). . . . John Slack and Philip Arnold set in motion their fantastic diamond mine scam in San Francisco (VI).

1872

Jim Fisk is shot to death by a rival for the affections of his mistress, January 6. . . . The first fake energy-producing machine is offered to the world by con man John E. W. Keely (IX).

1873

Daniel Drew goes broke and pawns his household goods. . . . William Udderzook, who attempted to defraud insurance firms through arson in Baltimore, is hanged for the murder of his brother-in-law, W. S. Goss, whom Udderzook murdered to make the claim appear genuine.

1874

Con man Ross Saulsbury kills a Chicago saloon owner and escapes with a mild prison sentence through Mike McDonald's influence (XII).

1876

Get-rich-quick ads, placed by hustlers to bilk suckers out of tens of thousands of dollars, appear in record numbers. . . . "Paper Collar Joe" Kratalsky begins his con career by bilking tourists at New York's Centennial Exposition. . . . First Peter-to-Paul scam offering astronomical returns on invested monies is inaugurated by Dona Baldomera Larra in Spain.

1877

Joseph "Yellow Kid" Weil born in Chicago (for archane reasons Weil insists his birthday was in 1875, but records state otherwise). . . . William "Canada Bill" Jones dies in the Charity Hospital in Reading, Pennsylvania. . . . Therese Dauignac begins the Humbert swindle in Paris, France, a scam that will bring her $14 million before its exposure in 1902 (I).

1880

Gaston Bullock Means is born in North Carolina. . . . Middle-aged Ellen Peck embarks on her incredible con career by bilking a New York millionaire (VIII). . . . Ivar Kreuger born in Sweden. . . . French-Canadian con artist Lou Blonger moves to Denver and establishes himself as con chief of a flimflamming ring that will reign for forty-some years (XII). . . . Reed Waddell, a college boy from Illinois, sells his first gold brick in New York, becoming the leading sharper in this game (II). . . . Con man Al Burgess from Galesburg, Illinois, begins his carrer as a steerer in Mc-Tague's Saloon, a notorious Kansas City sharper's den; Burgess will enjoy a forty-year run as one of the leading hustlers in eight-dice cloth.

1882

"Hungry Joe" Lewis and others fleece poet Oscar Wilde who is touring the U.S. (I) . . . Sucker lists are born in mail-order bucket shops in New York City.

1884

Herbert H. Edwards of Cleveland begins his Edwards Inheritance scam.

1885

Frederick Emerson Peters, who will become one of the world's greatest imposters of con, is born in Ohio (XV).

1886

Serge Stavisky is born in Russia. . . . Con inventor Harry Holland bilks the city of Chicago by painting the court house with his magical "preserving fluid" (IX).

1890

Elizabeth Fitzgerald (Madam Zingara), begins one of the first spiritual con games in Harlem, N.Y. (X). . . . American Ross Potter, using various aliases, mulcts leading figures in Europe (XV). . . . The first great public stock swindle occurs in Chicago, when a phalanx of sharpers united under the banner of Flemming and Merriam's Mutual Cooperative Fund bilks thousands out of $2 million of invested funds in a few months, promising ridiculous profits on shares. One of the firm's brochures, freely distributed before the company is raided and closed down, reads in part: "The great fortunes of the kings of the pit have been built up because these men had capital enough to swing the market their way; there has been no guesswork, no chance, no gamble about it, for they had the ready money with which to back their gigantic deals. It is time the common people, the small speculators, learned this trick of the captains of industry. Your available money, added to that of thousands and tens of thousands of other small investors, will form a centralized fund of proportions which will dwarf the available money of the biggest speculator who ever operated on the Board of Exchange. . . ."

1892

International-con-man-to-be Abram Sykowski is born in Poland.

1893

Roper extraordinaire Tom O'Brien takes suckers for half a million dollars at the World's Fair in Chicago.

1894

Engineer W. C. Crosby takes up con in Philadelphia as an inventor of a host of bogus machines (IX).

1895

Gold-brick artist Reed Waddell is shot and killed in Paris by Tom O'Brien. . . . James Addison Reavis is tried in Santa Fe and found guilty of perpetrating the enormous Peralta land grant fraud in Arizona; he had collected tremendous fees from railroads such as the Southern Pacific, which traversed the lands his forged titles claimed, and payments from every mining company, such as the lucrative Silver King Mine, to mine his land. Reavis is found guilty of swindling and sent to prison for six years . . . . The notorious Williamsons con clan emmigrates from Scotland and settles in Brooklyn (XII).

1896

Leopold Balbach perpetrates the $5 million stock swindle known as the "E. S. Dean Safe System of Speculation." Balbach suckers his marks with what he claims to be a foolproof method of "beating the market," and offers 300 to 400 percent interest per annum (similar to the Fund W. scheme of 1890). More than 10,000 persons sent in 26,000 separate sums of money at a rate of $25,000 a day. When fraud orders are issued the following year, Balbach flees. He is never apprehended.

1897

Connecticut con man Prescott Ford Jernegan bilks investors out of more than $350,000 with his "gold accumulator" invention (IX). . . . William Elmer Mead, inventor of the magic-wallet con games, is first arrested in California for bilking a sucker (III).

1898

"Paper Collar Joe" Kratalsky, a telephone lineman, actually taps the first wire to obtain racing results in advance to bilk bookmakers, the real beginning of the wire, a big-store game (XIV). . . . Christ Tracy, a New York sharper and friend of Kratalsky, sets up the first big store in Manhattan.

1899

William Franklin Miller, who is to be known as "520 Percent Miller," begins his business investment con, the Franklin Syndicate, promising 10 percent return per week, dollar-for-dollar, every week of the year for invested monies (XI). . . . The Gondorf brothers hustle a St. Louis pawn-broker in a big-store game for $200,000. . . . Con man George Smith operates a phony insurance-claim con in Manhattan, making as much as $50,000 per claim from transportation firms in faked accidents. He was described as "a human wreck. His right leg was bruised and twisted; his right arm was as crooked as his character was subsequently found to be; he had four newly healed wounds distributed about his head; the index finger of his right hand was missing; he was minus several teeth and he said his spine was badly strained and twisted. He was a living demand for damages—a permanent, hobbling, pitiful protest and testimony against the recklessness and cruelty of a heartless and giant corporation." . . . Hotel swindler Alonzo J. Whitman, former senator from Minnesota, is arrested as leader of a confidence ring in Manhattan. Whitman will be found guilty of using phony credit to secure loans and then writing bad checks, defrauding for large amounts such hotels as the Bartholdi in New York, the Parker House in Boston, the Grand Pacific in Chicago, and the Isleworth Hotel in Atlantic City. . . . Henry Allen and Julius Price, leading con men in New York bucket shops, are convicted, after long careers, of selling fake Rapid Transit shares.

1900

"Yellow Kid" Weil embarks on a series of short cons (VII). . . . Con man Buck Boatright invents the smack (VII). . . . Medicine flimflammer J. H. Kelly makes $1 million with his bogus mental healing con (IV). . . . The marrying bluebeard of con, Sigmund Engel, bilks the first of scores of gullible women in Vienna, Austria (VIII). . . . "Yellow Kid" Weil and Bob Collins sell phony race-track park concessions at $5,000 a clip.

1901

Green goods hustler George Lehman, alias Nigger Baker, is found guilty of fraud in the notorious New York City case exposed by reformer Anthony Comstock (II). . . . Intellectual con man Count Zuboff (real name Lipman) begins his impersonations in bilking literary and social figures in Ireland (XV).

1902

George Gray, known as "The Professional Fit-Thrower," is arrested in Manhattan after mulcting suckers through his ability to induce epileptic seizures (VII). . . . A spate of spiritual and witch-doctor cons surfaces across the country. . . . The Baker inheritance con begins in Pittsburgh, Pennsylvania (V). . . . Jim Roofer opens the first wire store in Chicago.

1903

The colorful Poillon sisters of New York, towering, rotund marriage swindlers, begin their carrer when Katherine Poillon sues wealthy William G. Brokaw of Manhattan for $250,000 for breach of promise (he settles out of court for $170,000). . . . Edgar Zug, specializing in one of the wierdest witchcraft cons known, is convicted of fraud (X). . . . The first fight store (a big-con or big-store game) is established in Colorado Springs. . . . Con woman Sophie Beck swindles the Story Cotton Company of Philadelphia out of $2 million.

The flimflamming sisters Katherine (above) and Charlotte Poillon, experts in the matrimonial swindle. (UPI)

1904

Cassie Chadwick (born Elizabeth Bigley) is arrested for pretending to be the illegitimate daughter of Andrew Carnegie. This amazing con woman pretends to visit the multimillionaire at his New York mansion (talking only to the housekeeper) while a distinguished lawyer from her home town of Cleveland waits outside in a carriage. When returning to the carriage, Cassie "accidentally" drops a promissory note allegedly signed by Carnegie (which she has forged) and made out in her name for $2 million. The astounded lawyer is thus duped into believing her story that she is Carnegie's born-out-of-wedlock daughter and that she possesses half a dozen or so notes, which she keeps in a drawer at home. The lawyer, as Cassie knows he will, wastes no time in going to his banking friends in Cleveland, convincing them to make Cassie fabulous loans, which they do, charging exorbitant interests in the belief that when Carnegie dies, their profits will be enormous. The fraud is stymied by Carnegie himself, who issues a statement that he "does not know Mrs. Chadwick." Cassie is arrested and jailed after a quick trial, but not before she has enjoyed the many millions duped bankers have showered upon her, buying diamonds by the carton and giving $100,000 dinners. It requires the entire Cleveland police force to hold back the crowds clamoring for a look at the con woman when she arrives in custody from New York after her conviction. . . . Lou Blonger, head of the powerful con clan in Denver, takes a full-time partner, "Kid Duffy," to control his immense con empire (XII).

An early photo of super con lady Cassie Chadwick (née Bigley), who flimflammed millions by pretending to be Andrew Carnegie's illegitimate daughter. (WIDE WORLD)

1905

Charles Ponzi, who will use William Miller's Peter-to-Paul con to create soaring profits in fifteen years, is arrested in Montreal, Quebec, for forgery.

1906

Charley Gondorf opens a permanent big store in Manhattan (XIV). . . . First big stores are opened by other sharpers in Oakland, Spokane, Salt Lake City, and Seattle. . . . Dr. Theodore White, dealer of black and white magic in Baltimore, is convicted of defrauding his "students" of enormous sums (X). . . . Stock promotor and con man George H. Munroe hustles a worthless stock—Montreal and Boston Consolidated Copper Company—into millions, giving $20,000 banquets and taking big investors to British Columbia in the private car of railroad magnate James J. Hill to view vast mining property (which belongs to another firm). It is one of the largest stock scams in history; Munroe skips with the loot.

1907

Hustler Edward Pape who employs his broken neck to make fortunes in claims against public transportation firms is arrested in New York (VII). . . . Future grand stock manipulator Lowell MacAfee Birrell is born.

1908

International con man Victor "The Count" Lustig, a master of the money box, is first arrested in Prague, Czechoslovakia (XIII). . . . "Yellow Kid" Weil gleans thousands of dollars from saloon keepers by borrowing money against a real diamond ring, then selling a phony imitation ring. . . . Chicago's king of the confidence men Mike McDonald dies. . . . Charles Ponzi is arrested in Atlanta, Georgia, for smuggling aliens into the United States.

1909

Big-store operator Eddie Jackson goes to prison for confidence games in Illinois (XIV). . . . Philip Musica, who will bleed white the firm of Mc-Kessen and Robbins decades later, is first arrested and jailed for one year with a $5,000 fine for bribing officials and failing to pay customs duties on Italian foodstuffs. . . . A flurry of cons begin in Tin Pan Alley that offer to publish music of novice composers for extravagant "expenses"; police arrest scores of hustlers in this racket.

1910

Operating out of gorgeous offices in the Flatiron Building, Eugene and Shelton Burr sell wholesale lots of fake stock crudely printed on lithograph paper. Their scam is exposed the following year, and they are arrested after operating for a decade and netting approximately $50 million, according to post office inspectors. . . . William Elmer Mead promotes Halley's Comet and the end of the world through his magic-wallet scam (III). . . . New York con man Cam Spear reaps a fortune in selling sucker lists to bucket shops. . . . A. L. "Dead Man" Hicks invents most of the

scams that will become traditional con games in "selling stiffs" (VII).
. . . W. T. Wintemute, one of the sleaziest stock swindlers of the era, is
arrested in his New York offices. He has sold bogus stock since 1906 (under the name of Norman W. McCloud and Company; Norman McCloud
is Wintemute's clerk), charging as much as $100 a share and then resell-
ing the stock for 25¢ a share, working from a prime sucker list of approximately 12,000 names, most of whom are supplied by Wintemute's London
representative, Herman Warszawiak. (This individual, arrested in London the same time Wintemute is apprehended in New York, published an
oddball periodical called *The Jewish Christian* and ran a mission for
converting Jews to Christianity. One report stated: "Besides being dismissed from the Presbyterian Church while studying for the ministry on
charges of gambling and immorality, Warszawiak put his paper into
bankruptcy after collecting much money to convert the Jews.") Wintemute, who netted $1,300,000 in his ten-year-long fraud, is undone by
two English women, Lady Tankerville and Miss Henrietta Elout, who
purchase through Warszawiak about $45,000 of his worthless stock. Miss
Elout sends Wintemute $2,500 in additional funds by mistake and de-
mands by letter the return of her money. The stock hustler replies
(according to a letter found by postal inspectors who raided his luxurious
offices): "I am aware that sometimes a misunderstanding engenders dis-
trust unjustly and consequently might mislead to misjudge the motive
which prompted me at Mr. Warszawiak's suggestion to grant you the
addition 2,500 shares. But let me assure you, Miss Elout, that but for the
dividends which are imminent, you could not possibly have secured this
allotment." Wintemute, following a long trial, goes to jail.

1911

A banner year for con men working the U.S. mails. According to post
office officials, hustlers take in $77 million through phony mail schemes . . .
Future oil-lease con man Seymour Ernest J. Cox is arrested and convicted
of fraud in Michigan (XI). . . . Train tycoon E. H. Harriman is stung by
a flimflamming art broker into buying worthless paintings, paying out
hefty but undisclosed sums. Says Harriman after the con is exposed:
"I'll leave picture buying to someone who knows pictures. I'll stick to

railroads." . . . Cardenio F. King publishes a weekly newspaper of stock tips, all of them promoting fraudulent stocks. He is arrested and sent to Charlestown Penitentiary in Boston. . . . An enormous fight store opens in Baltimore and takes scores of suckers for $100,000 a week

Louise Musica, her face bloodied after brawling with police in her attempted escape to Honduras with other members of her hustling family, is taken into custody in 1912; her brother Philip was to rise to million-dollar frauds in following decades. (UPI)

1912

Using the title Avalon Oil Lands (after the then-popular song), Gustav Aufrecht, Sam Biddison and other hustlers begin selling phony stock in mining concerns long deserted, pinpointing their pitch to those in booming real-estate areas. . . . Hustler Alvin Clarence Thomas, a passenger on board the ill-fated *Titanic,* survives the sinking of the luxury liner and turns con man by putting in phony insurance claims, thus earning the monicker "Titanic Thompson" (VII). . . . Real-estate con artist Clarence D. Hillman takes in a young fortune for phony land promotions in California. One report describes how he "paints broken-lown, ebb-tide dump cars with shiny red paint. Then he sketches large white letters on the car side, reading: 'Boston Harbor Railroad.' He puts down a few railroad ties on the main street of the somnolent village of Boston Harbor, installs a lone wheel scraper, and leaves the outfit to stand there peacefully rusting and crumbling and slumbering on the ties, while he sells building lots on the sure success of a lightning express railway system, steaming through the section. This financier of the Golden West has salted down over $2 million in other ways as catchy as the Lightning Express that never budged." . . . The trial of George Munroe for bilking investors out of hundreds of thousands of dollars in fake Marconi Wireless stock (he later surfaced to promote the United Shoe Shining Company) ends in his conviction at age thirty-six. . . . Philip Musica is jailed for three years following his conviction of swindling several banks of $500,000, using fake export shipments and equally false shipping invoices.

1913

Ivar Kreuger enters the match-making business in Sweden, a move that will lead him into the largest business swindle in history. . . . The hilarious imposter Luodovic Radzevil cons his fellow immigrants to the United States in a series of ridiculous but highly profitable flimflams (XV).

1914

Charley Gondorf's big store in Manhattan is raided and Gondorf is arrested and sent to jail (XIV). . . . Postal inspectors break into the offices of James W. Ryan, alias "The Postal Kid," and unearth his neatly penciled card catalog of suckers, all of whom are among Manhattan's social elite. One card reads: "Interested in welfare schemes. Will contribute to any kind of fund for social betterment." A second card explains: "Prides himself on his knowledge of art. Will buy any kind of picture if you flatter him into believing he knows all about it." A third card specifies: "Strong on uplift. Will contribute to sociological schemes of all kinds." A fourth: "Immensely vain and easy to land for flattering stuff. Likes to have histories of his family written. Easiest lead is to talk genealogy." . . . Thomas "Mournful" Meeker, one of the shrewdest hustlers in short death cons, is arrested and imprisoned at the wake of a wealthy New Yorker (VII). . . . Millionaire sex medicine promoter Edward Hayes is tried and fined $5,000 for fraud in April (IV). . . . Marcus Garvey arrives in Harlem and sets up his black-confederation scams (XI).

1915

Joseph "Yellow Kid" Weil and his long-time confederate, Fred "Deacon" Buckminster open a big store in Chicago, hustling bogus stocks for about $200,000. . . . Katherine and Charlotte Poillon are arrested in New York for bilking an elderly businessman who paid for their "favors." . . . Fred Gondorf's big store is closed by police and Gondorf joins his brother Charley in Sing Sing following his conviction of mulcting three suckers for large amounts of money (XIV).

1916

Con inventor Louis Enricht defrauds manufacturing tycoons with his scheme to change water into gasoline (IX).

1917

Self-proclaimed super sleuth Gaston Bullock Means bilks heiress Maude King out of $150,000 in July (XV). . . . A Forth Worth, Texas, barber, J. W. Carruth, who calls himself "Hog Creek Curruts," swindles tens of thousands of dollars out of eager investors clamoring to participate in the Oklahoma and Texas oil booms. One of his fraudulent mailers reads: "Hog Creek Carruts. The name that will live through-out the ages as the name of the man who toiled single-handed for seven long years to prove up his belief and attain his goal—who traced an oil structure twenty miles across the ranges from Strawn to Desdemona—who conceived and organized the famous Hog Creek Oil Company—who drilled the discovery well of the great Desdemona field, at one time called the richest spot on earth—who transformed a desert into a fountain of liquid gold—who built a city of 30,000 souls from a village of 200 people and who paid every person who held shares of stock in his renowned Hog Creek Company $10,135.00 for every $100 invested." The one well Carruth did drill turned up a duster; he will be exposed the following year as a con man and put out of business. . . . William Elmer Mead stings a Cheyenne lady rancher for $35,000 with his magic-wallet scam (III).

1918

The *Oklahoma City News* launches a campaign against oil-leasing swindlers and compels police raids and subsequent arrests in Oklahoma City. . . . Medical quack Charles Aycock perpetrates his fake cure of TB, "Tuberclecide" (IV). . . . Gaston Means cons British, German, and American agents into paying him staggering fees for spying on all of them (XV).

1919

Two sharpers, Mrs. Sudie Whiteaker and Milo F. Lewis, con the Hartzell family in Iowa with the ancient Drake inheritance flimflam, a hustle that leads Oscar Hartzell into developing the scam on a broader base than ever before (IV).... William Allan Pinkerton warns that a horde of bad-check hustlers have unleashed a nationwide campaign to bilk bankers.... Boston con man Charles Ponzi makes his move by inaugurating William Miller's old Peter-to-Paul swindle in Boston. In June, Ponzi opens offices and tells all would-be investors that he will double their money by merely purchasing postal coupons in foreign countries, where they sell at depressed rates, and redeem them in the United States, where they can be converted at a higher rate, which will bring enormous profits; he promises to double investors' money within 90 days and does so, paying out to early investors money received from later investors. Thousands flock to his offices in Boston and New York, and Ponzi, a one-time clerk for the import-export firm of J. P. Poole, is suddenly a millionaire, taking in $200,000 a day. The money pours in so fast that Ponzi reduces his due date to 45 days and the result is a deluge of investments from suckers. He is hailed by his clients as "the greatest Italian of them all," because he "discovered money." ... Ivar Kreuger decides to set up his world monopoly of matchmaking and distribution and launches his colossal swindle by floating immense loans on phony Italian Bonds (XV).

Boston flimflammer Charles Ponzi, whose Peter-to-Paul swindle brought him millions in 1919. (UPI)

1920

Philip Musica is arrested for peddling alcohol to bootleggers through a fake hair-tonic firm (his product is called Dandrofuge), but is released when he turns state's evidence against his partner Joseph Brandino, who is sent to prison.... Joseph "Yellow Kid" Weil and John Worthington buy the American State Bank in Chicago and bilk creditors out of $300,000 through cleverly manufactured letters of credit (XIV).... The Cook family tree swindle is begun.... A. C. Bidwell organizes his phony auto club, the Automobile League, and reaps millions (IV).... Jean Pierre Lafitte, who claims descendency from the pirate brothers, begins his long career in con (VI).... Celedonia Sevilla enters the Spanish prisoner game (II).... Con imposter Stanley Clifford Weyman poses as a physician and is hired by a development firm and sent to aid natives in Peru (XV).... Joe Furey and four others, a subgang of con men working under Lou Blonger's protective umbrella out of Denver, swindle a Texan named J. Frank Norfleet in Fort Worth out of $45,000, touching off one of the greatest manhunts in the annals of con (XII). . . . The "Yellow Kid" and Sam Banks con scores of suckers with a fake medium setup, using a microphone, hidden in the mystic's turban, through which personal information about the mark is transmitted and subsequently relayed to the victim. Their take is never less than $1,000 a session. . . . Gaston Means buncos a Chicago lawyer for $57,000 (XV). . . . Stock booster S. C. Pandolfo, through the Commercial Club of St. Cloud, bilks residents of St. Cloud, Minnesota, by selling $4,750,000 in his Pan Motor Company, setting the stock at twice its par value. He will later go to jail for ten years, sentenced by Kenesaw Mountain Landis. . . . Charles Ponzi's fabulous Peter-to-Paul swindle of returning dollar for dollar on invested monies within 45 days is exposed by the *Boston Globe*, creating, on August 13, a run on his company. He pays off $15 million of the $20 million he took in during his year of operation and is then arrested and sent to Plymouth Prison for four years.

1921

Marcus Garvey, self-appointed head of the Negro Improvement Association and African Communities League, levies an additional $1 duty on members, gleaning millions. Garvey, one of the most influential con men of his day, also addresses the League of Nations in this year as one of the alleged leading blacks in the world (XI). . . . The "Yellow Kid" and others unload useless land touted as oil-rich real estate to the wealthy Albright sisters for $180,000. . . . Elmer Mead stings a rich Jacksonville, Florida, resident with his magic wallet for $11,600, but is identified and postal inspectors sent on his trail (III). . . . Polish-born con man Abram Sykowski apprehended while entering the United States with a fake passport under an alias; he receives three years in prison (XIV).

1922

Victor "The Count" Lustig swindles $10,000 from the American Savings Bank of Springfield, Missouri, while using the alias Robert Duval. Lustig accomplishes this deft con merely by switching envelopes with an un-witting bank official while negotiating a real-estate deal by trading Liberty Bonds for cash (he gets the bonds, too). . . . Lou Blonger's con clan in Denver swells to more than 500 flimflammers on or indirectly associated with his payroll (XI). . . . Peter Pollack establishes fake "Federal Secret Service" in Trenton, New Jersey, to bilk businessmen (XV). . . . Con man Jackie French takes three Florida businessmen in a wire game for $345,000, one of the biggest scores ever in a big-store operation. . . . A Manhattan magic-wallet ring led by William Kent is trapped by police after a long profit-taking run (III). . . . A group of New York sharpers scoop up tens of thousands of dollars from gullible blacks who contribute from weekly wages to the Mutual Burial Society so that they can be "buried in a royal robe and planted to the strains of a brass band." . . . Giovanni Mogavec Minneci, alias Minnec, sells in-surance at a rate of $1 a month, all of his coverage useless. The con man pockets tens of thousands of dollars and protects himself through a "small print" flimflam. One report states: "There was no examination so the old, the ill and the feeble-minded were easy prey. In large type Minnec's company promised thousands of dollars in case all conditions were met. These conditions were set forth laboriously in type literally so small that it could not be read without a magnifying glass. The tiny type named the diseases which were not covered by the policy and mentioned every disease known except the contagious. It was a statistically proven fact that 97 percent of all who died between the ages of forty and eighty died of an illness mentioned in the small type." Minnec turns down one claim of a man killed when run over by a tractor, pointing out that the death certificate mentions "crushed lungs" and his policy does not cover "lung trouble." He will eventually go to jail for four years, but not before suing Postmaster General James Farley for $1 million (the suit will be thrown out, Farley the object of Minnec's wrath since it is the postal inspectors who trap him). . . . Leo Koretz, Chicago real estate and oil-leasing flimflammer, stings a host of millionaires in his phony oil-lands swindles (XI). . . . Alberto Santos Guimaries, a handsome gigolo and con artist, uses showgirl Dot King to fleece a Boston banker. Guimares is to figure prominently in the murder of Miss King the following year and that of wealthy Washington socialite Mrs. Aurelia Drefus, whom he also bilks for large sums before she "accidentally" falls to her death from the

Alberto Santos Guimares under arrest in 1922 under suspicion of killing his sweetheart, showgirl Dot King. (UPI)

balcony of her mansion. . . . After serving a year in Sing Sing for fraud, con inventor Louis Enricht is pardoned (IX). . . . William Elmer Mead is captured after fleecing a Colorado sucker and is sent to prison for ten years in the Canon City Penitentiary (III).

1923

Philip Musica, using the alias F. (Frank) Donald Coster, establishes an amorphous firm, Girard and Company, in Mount Vernon, New York, purchasing large amounts of alcohol allegedly to produce hair tonic, but sells it instead to bootleggers, and with his profits buys the giant firm McKesson and Robbins in four years, using this company as a front for other illegal operations. . . . Dr. Frederick A. Cook, claimant of North Pole discovery; Seymour Ernest J. Cox; and others are convicted of fraud in selling Texas oil leases and sent to prison (XI). . . . Durrell Gregory & Co. bilks millions out of gullible stock investors, buying for its clients only about 10 percent of legitimate stock promised and pocketing the balance. At the trial of R. H. and John M. Gregory, one witness states that R. H. Gregory had warned him to stay on as the firm's salesman and to forget branching out on his own. Gregory, according to this testimony, addressed several discontented salesmen, saying: "Why, boys, if you attempt to go into business for yourselves, you will be in jail inside of a month. . . . Do you know why it is that firms like ourselves don't go to jail? It is because we reserve one third of our profits to handle the 'kicks.' "
. . . Victim of a magic-wallet scheme, J. Frank Norfleet completes a three-year-long quest for those who bilked him, tracking down the five con men through a dozen states and countries and apprehending some of them single handed (XII).

1924

Manipulator of the Drake inheritance swindle, Oscar Hartzell leaves Iowa, after organizing a far-flung ring of ropers in his scheme, for London under the pretext of locating the real Drake heir; he is promptly flim-flammed himself by a crafty English medium (V). . . . A con ring in Chicago compels prostitutes to deliver sucker lists for future scams. . . . Lee T. Brooks, a notorious stock flimflammer, is arrested in New York and turned over to New Jersey authorities, where he is convicted and imprisoned for receiving phony stocks from stock racketeers and listing them on the exchange. . . . Ohio, Michigan, Iowa, and Kentucky are swamped with worthless stocks, more than $150 million worth, which are foisted upon the public by con men duping country bankers to put through promissory notes for the initial purchase of such stock and then reselling the certificates to suckers. . . . Sharpers sting two Gramercy Park matrons and socialites, Mrs. Van Hilt and Miss Holden, spinsters living alone, for $60,000 in bogus stock (Moose Creek Mine Corporation), which leaves the elderly women homeless. . . . "Yellow Kid" Weil takes $500,000 from twenty suckers in Chicago in big-store games (XIV). . . . In November, Alves Reis starts to duplicate the official currency of Portugal upon the discovery that the Bank of Portugal does not keep an inventory of serial numbers of old currency before it is destroyed. . . . Marcus Garvey goes to the Atlanta Penitentiary for five years for fraud (XI).

Con man on the run, Charles Schwartz added murder to his elaborate insurance swindle in 1925. (UPI)

1925

Out on appeal, Charles Ponzi is arrested in Florida while attempting to swindle real estate investors. . . . San Franciscan Charles Schwartz attempts to collect insurance on his so-called synthetic silk-making plant and his own life insurance by torching his warehouse and killing a look-alike to take his place. Police, with the help of master criminologist Edward O. Heinrich, finally trap Schwartz in an Oakland hideout, and the con man commits suicide before they break down the door. . . . In February Portuguese con man Alves Reis convinces the official printers of Portuguese currency, Waterlow and Sons, Ltd., of London, to print huge sums of new currency for him on their belief that he is an operative of the Bank of Portugal (he tells them the currency is to be used exclusively in the Portuguese colony of Angola, thus redirecting through this circuitous route the monies into his own accounts). . . . International con man Victor "The Count" Lustig stings gangster Al Capone in Chicago on a simple investment scam (VII). . . . One of the largest bucket shops in New York history is raided and closed. Police arrest super dynamiters Charles Greehaus, Sigmund Levy, Edward Rosenberg, and Louis Manes, all directors of the bogus stock company, J. F. Townsend and Company . . . Con woman Lulu Cummings arrives in Chicago to dine with Clarence Darrow and bilk scores of gullible social lions (VIII). . . . In December the Bank of Portugal discovers five genuine banknotes of the 500-escudos type with duplicate numbers and series, which leads officials to track down tens of thousands of other duplicate notes, revealing Reis's gigantic swindle; the con man has obtained 580,000 banknotes and passed notes in the amount of $200 million, exchanging them for genuine Portuguese notes, gold, silver, jewels, land, and buildings.

1926

Patrick Henry Lennon, one of the sharpest stock swindlers in U.S. history, inveigles tycoon A. J. Cunningham in the first of a series of cons that will stretch over three decades (XII). . . . New Yorkers lose an estimated $500 million in the operations of crooked promoters, bogus brokers, and fake security salesmen. . . . Rearrested in Florida after serving a year in jail for fake real-estate cons, Charles Ponzi is sent to Massachusetts to serve out another nine-year sentence connected to his massive Peter-to-Paul scam of 1919–1920.

1927

German-born sharper Walter Hohenau appears in Houston, Texas, and stings investors there for huge amounts, which are put up to develop the claptrap energizer machine he claims will turn water into gasoline (taking a page from Louis Enricht's book of grift). He then flees to Mexico when his scam is uncovered (IX). . . . Hugh Garland begins his bogus pyramid of companies, inflating the worth of his Automatic Signal Company to $32.5 million, thousands of times its real value. . . . From London Oscar Hartzell demands by endless cables that his representatives in the United States increase investment monies being sent to him to hasten the settlement of the nonexistent Drake inheritance (V). . . . Scores of the "Terrible Williamsons" con clan invade Columbus, Ohio, to bilk residents (XII). . . . Released after serving a year in the Paris prison, Serge Stavisky puts top French leaders on his enormous payroll and continues his con career (XIV). . . . Marcus Garvey is released from prison and deported to Jamaica (XI). . . . Hugh B. Monjar becomes a millionaire by setting up his fraudulent Mantle Clubs (IV). . . . Philadelphia sharper Robert Boltz begins a Peter-to-Paul investment scam that is to make him millions and last for thirteen years (XI).

1928

Serge Stavisky, through his contacts in the French government, monopolizes the pawnshop securities with the aid of Premier Chautemps, reaping millions of dollars while using fake collateral and stolen jewelry to obtain certificates (XIII).

1929

Peddlers of phony securities have their greatest field day of selling worthless stock prior to the stock market crash. . . . Philip Musica (alias F. Donald Coster) issues thousands of inventory invoices against a subsidiary of McKesson & Robbins, to shore up $640,000 in losses he personally incurs from company funds in wild Wall Street speculations. . . . Con man Robert Arthur Tourbillon is released from the New Jersey State Prison after serving long sentences for scores of flimflams; he disappears forever. . . . Oscar Hartzell cables his thousands of Drake inheritance dupes that President Hoover has caused the stock market crash to prevent billions in settlement dollars from being released to them, a gamble for more time to perpetrate his fraud (V). . . . Born in St. Peters-

Using the name F. Donald Coster, con man Philip Musica took over control of the gigantic firm McKesson & Robbins, using its funds to cover his staggering stock losses. (UPI)

burg, the son of a banker under the czars, Serge Rubinstein, in exile in Paris with his family, takes a job as a clerk in Banque Franco-Asiatique in Paris. He is the bank manager in two months, and immediately staffs the institution with White Russian emigrés whom he feels he can trust. Rubinstein then confiscates $60,000 of the depositors' money and buys control of a restaurant chain worth $450,000, which he promptly loots.

1930

In early May Alves Reis's trial begins, the major charge being the fraud and forgery involved in the 580,000 duplicate Portuguese bank notes he caused to be printed by Waterlow and Sons (the scam left the firm disgraced and near bankruptcy). Reis is found guilty and sentenced to eight years in prison followed by twelve years in exile. . . . France deports Serge Rubinstein for wild manipulation of francs. . . . Mississippi hustler Odie Moore begins his Choctaw Indian settlement scam (V). . . . Victor "The Count" Lustig abandons his money-box con for counterfeiting (VII). . . . The *New York Evening Journal* warns its readers about buying stock from Patrick Henry "Packy" Lennon (XII). . . . Abram Sykowski fleeces casino owners in Danzig, Poland, with a tale of having control of Capone's millions in American banks and requiring additional monies to bribe officials to release funds to him, a con he will use for twenty-five years (XIII).

1931

Hundreds of conmen attempt to mulct a Manhattan youth, Edward F. Dougherty who is widely publicized as having received a $150,000 windfall (IV). . . . A ring of sharpers pass off a construction site in Yonkers, New York, as a newly developed gold mine and sell $135,000 in fake stock certificates (VI).

1932

Gaston Means bilks Evalyn Walsh McLean in phony detective hunt for the missing Lindbergh baby. His con is revealed and he is sent to Leavenworth for fifteen years (XV). . . . Employing his magic-wallet routine, Elmer Mead stings a sucker in Missouri for a staggering $200,000 and another mark in Massachusetts for $59,000 (III). . . . William P. Hunt takes up Mead's magic-wallet con and is arrested after a long run of scores (III).

1933

A con artist's convention takes place in Chicago, flimflammers being enraged at the inroads organized crime is making into their ranks and scams (XII). . . . Joseph Harriman, whose father was railroad magnate E. H. Harriman, bilks his own bank, the Harriman National Bank, in order to rig the market in the bank's stock. He is sent to prison for two years. . . . An enterprising con man drives into every gas station in Poughkeepsie, New York, and orders his gas tank filled with water. He then makes a great show of dropping into the tank what he calls his "100-mile pill," claiming it converts water into gas (his car has a dummy gas tank which he empties when out of sight). He sells hundreds of pills, at $13.50 each, to astonished gas-station owners. . . . Learning that he has no more time to repay $500 million in loans against forged Italian bonds he has been using as collateral to inflate his gigantic financial empire (the largest scam on record), "Match King" Ivar Kreuger commits suicide in Paris (XIII). . . . Sacha Stavisky's national scams in France are exposed and scores of his representatives and political and police associates are placed under arrest; the con man flees into hiding (XIII). . . . Oscar Hartzell is extradited from England and is convicted of fraud in his Drake swindle, entering Leavenworth in November (V).

1934

Stavisky is found in early January, commits suicide while police officials stand by. His nine-year looting of government securities with politicians in high places causes the downfall of the Chautemps cabinet (XIII). . . . "Yellow Kid" Weil takes a wealthy investor for $50,000 while posing as a bank president in an office borrowed from the legitimate president. . . . Mail order flimflammer William J. Cressy begins to make his millions by offering fake Indian head pennies (IV). . . . Abram Sykowski fleeces refugees from Russia and other countries by selling fake passports; he is later in the year arrested in Vienna for smuggling dope (XIII).

Turkish con artist Sülün Osman poses jauntily on the Galata Bridge, which spans the Golden Horn in Istanbul; Osman sold this bridge for $2,000 to a gullible merchant, and the Orient Express for much more. (WIDE WORLD)

1935

"Yellow Kid" Weil, Richard Hampton, and Harris Norris pose as geologists in Manhattan, conning well-to-do Warren Edmunds into investing in nonexistent properties for large amounts. . . . An intrafamily feud breaks out among the "Terrible Williamsons," which spreads from Georgia to Pennsylvania (XII). . . . Ralph Marshall Wilby (alias James W. Ralston) is first picked up for embezzlement in Norfolk, Virginia. . . . Oscar Hartzell's confederates in the United States, including Lester Kirkendall, Joseph Hauber, and Delmar Short, are arrested in the Drake offices in Chicago, face trial, and go to prison for fraud (V). . . . "Yellow Kid" Weil bilks several pigeons for heavy scores with the story that he is going to Europe to get Adolf Hitler to invest in mythical copper mines. . . . Victor "The Count" Lustig is arrested for counterfeiting and sent to Leavenworth (VII). . . . William Elmer Mead is apprehended and sent to prison for fraud.

1936

Turkish con man Sülün Osman sells the *Orient Express* to a fellow country man for $75,000 and receives two years in prison. . . . After being dormant since 1902, the Baker inheritance con is expanded in Pennsylvania by William Cameron Morrow Smith, who is arrested and sent to prison months later (V). . . . Serge Rubinstein buys 173,000 shares of the Chosen Corporation from a swindler facing jail. He inflates the stock of the mining company, sets up six dummy companies under it, and sells off millions of shares through his French associates. Rubinstein makes millions and drastically deflates the yen. . . . Abram Sykowski cons dictator Mussolini into advancing funds to free his mythical Capone millions in the United States. He uses the same scam to con Barcelona's chief of police later in the year (XIII). . . . "The Frisco Kid" sells memberships in his bogus nationwide patriotic clubs, which he claims will create a "far-flung society to foster and encourage Americanism." Branch managerships are available from the Kid at $300 each.

1937

Serge Rubinstein, in company with his current paramour (he usually travels with *three* attractive women), the self-appointed Countess Natasha, arrives in Japan and sells off his Korean-based Chosen mine property, all of which is gutted, but is stymied by the Japanese, who have passed laws forbidding any of their currency to leave the country. Rubinstein manages to smuggle out $3.5 million yen wrapped in a huge lot of obis (an obi being the seven-yard-long waist garment worn by Japanese women). Rubinstein then dumps the yen on the open market and reaps millions; the Japanese currency falls to the disaster level, not regaining its strength for years. . . . "Yellow Kid" Weil makes one of his biggest scores by selling phony stock in hair mattresses, $300,000 by his own estimate. . . . Pyramid builder Wallace G. Garland goes to prison for a $4.5 million swindle.

1938

Authorities first learn of the existence of the Williamson con clan in America when a rare law-abiding member of the group secretly informs Pittsburgh officials of the clan's activities (XII). . . . The maze of swindles worked by Philip Musica (alias Coster) under the McKesson and Robbins umbrella is finally examined, and two U.S. marshals go to the con man's mansion to arrest him. The hustler sees them arrive, quickly gulps down a shot of whiskey, runs upstairs and locks himself in a bathroom, and then shoots himself, falling neatly into the bathtub so as not to stain an imported carpet with his blood. For hours his widow paces the floor below wailing and shrieking: "My God, Daddy, why did you do it?" . . . Wall Street shortly produces one of its more cornball epitaphs for the hustler who had bilked dozens of legitimate companies out of $8 million: "He couldn't face the Musica." . . . Gaston Bullock Means dies with a smile on his lips in Leavenworth as FBI men grill him at bedside as to the whereabouts of the large amounts of money he had mulcted from Mrs. McLean (XV).

1939

Authorities crack down on con games across the country, sending Manhattan's "High-Ass Kid" to prison for a stretch after he is caught working a short con. . . . Payoff store grifters James McKay and William Graham are arrested in Reno and receive nine years and heavy fines. . . . Swindler Ralph Wilby, using the alias of James W. Ralston, is arrested in Colton, California, for fraud.

1940

Con man George Ashley begins his lonelyhearts club, through which he works a multitude of swindles (VIII). . . . John Weiss sells large sections of track belonging to the Long Island Railroad to junk dealers for huge amounts of money. Junk dealer Michael Palermo, one of Weiss's suckers, and three others are arrested days later as they begin tearing up the Long Island's tracks. . . . Juan Barrena and Camilo Lopez Vasques are tried and convicted in San Francisco for running one of the most notorious Spanish prisoner swindles in this century (II).

1941

Immigration authorities begin seven-year investigation of Serge Rubinstein's questionable entry into the United States in 1938 (he openly brags of entering the country with a fake passport. . . . Henry Ford swindle begins when Marie Fuller tells interested investors that the car mogul is about to break up his financial empire and is willing to sell off his shares of stocks at vastly reduced rates to avoid inheritance taxes. Mrs. Fuller, to convince suckers to purchase her fake Ford Stock, impersonates a baritone "Benson" Ford over the telephone in folksy chats with her victims. Her take in nine years will be more than $200,000.

1942

Washington con woman Mildred Hill begins her nationwide matrimonial con, passing herself off to would-be suitors as her own daughter (VIII). . . . Ralph Wilby, in the role of a traveling auditor, embezzles almost $400,000 out of the national firm, William T. Knott Company, a department store corporation, before being apprehended after fleeing to Canada. He will be given five to seven years in Sing Sing.

1944

Hustler Ralph M. Wilby, who swindled his employer out of $400,000 in a three-year span; he is shown here while he was the happy auditor of his victim, the William T. Knott Company. (WIDE WORLD)

Lowell McAfee Birrell, through the efforts of the dying millionaire broker Cecil B. Stewart, obtains directorships of many of Stewart's firms. Using these as collateral, the con man takes out huge loans to buy more firms, emptying the treasuries of these firms to pay back initial loans. His pyramiding soars for another decade (XI). . . . Bebe and Carl Thomas Patten arrive in Oakland; C. Thomas immediately launches a campaign to build up his evangelistic scam (X).

1945

Money-box con artist Joseph Esposito stings Providence, Rhode Island, grocer Joseph Tutalo for $15,000. Tutalo states that Esposito "out of friendship offered to triple" his investment "by inserting bills and blank paper into a pressing device and producing $100 bills." In return for his $15,000, the sucker was given "a package containing a single $100 bill bound on top of a packet of plain paper." . . . Matrimonial swindler

Mildred Hill is apprehended by Chicago police while attempting to con another victim (VIII). . . . Francis Gross of Utica, New York, is found guilty in June of "selling stiffs" and is sentenced to one year and a day in prison. Gross obtained money from the relatives of sailors lost at sea during World War II after he informed them he would forward their personal effects (VII). . . . Norman D. Harris, a Cleveland sharper, sells hundreds of six-room houses for deposits ranging from $100 to $1,500 and promises completion within 90 days. Harris never turns a shovel of dirt for months, stalls irate customers with complaints about bad weather and unfair competition, further mulcting as much as $30,000 from individuals to expedite construction. He is arrested and sentenced to nine years in prison. . . . Canadian con men, 272 in all, using the mails to sell phony mining stock, reap $1 million a week, according to one estimate.

1946

Serge Rubinstein, using his flimflammed millions from Europe and the Orient, invests in American firms and gleans another $5 million, first juggling each company's stock and then looting the firm. Government investigators attempt to prove fraud against him, but Rubinstein, represented by the finest legal minds available, evades conviction. . . . Flying into the United States from South America, Abram Sykowski is arrested by the FBI and jailed for fraud while posing as "Antonio Novarro Fernandez" (XIII). . . . Dr. Walter Bromberg and Dr. Sylvan Keiser release their five-year psychiatric study of con men. They discovered that these swindlers were "well groomed men of the world, superficially cultured and often affecting an air of social eminence. Many went in for 'stylish' clothes, had foppish manners and gave an intimation of effeminacy. Others wore the garb of the sporting world. All were found to be intelligent, suave, glib and companionable. The swindlers commonly showed deviation in their sexual life, suffered from reduced libido, were unmarried by choice and led nomadic lives." The psychiatrists conclude that those hustlers they studied possess "moral perversion without intellectual disturbance," and were "fantastic liars without an inner ethical sense." . . . Three times jailed for con games, Samuel Mussman (who walks on a peg leg as a result of a World War I wound) using the alias

Mason, stings Boston businessman Joseph Bennett by allegedly serving as his Washington representative. Mussman was to steer government contracts his way but no contracts were forthcoming, only a $22,765 bill for the con man's expenses. Mussman also takes Bohdan Katamay for $37,000 in Philadelphia on the promise that he can deliver hundreds of government buildings that will soon be vacant, and these Katamay, editor of a Ukrainian-language newspaper, can rent out and make millions on. The reason, Mussman explains, is simple. The government, which expects an atomic attack at any moment, is going underground, a top secret confided to the con man by his powerful White House friends, and that vacated government office buildings and warehouses will be leased for $1 a year. The $37,000 Katamay gives Mussman is "sewer money to take care of people who decide on those things." . . . Robert L. Knetzer opens a mammoth car agency through which he supplies brand-new cars, then not readily available in the postwar car boom. Operating out of Edwardsville, Illinois, Knetzer purchases the few showroom cars then available from other dealers and uses this Peter-to-Paul method to convince customers he has an unending supply of new autos from Detroit, sending some of his autos as far as California. Most of his customers deposit large amounts of money and never receive their autos. . . . Expert hustlers in the construction scam, Charles Richman and Howard Clements bilk hundreds of blacks in Philadelphia out of $150,000 for houses that never go beyond the drawing board. Both men will be caught the following year and sent to jail for a year. . . . Robert Lyman Seibert, alias Paul J. Black, cons suckers through the mails from New Orleans to buy nylons at 35 percent discount, collecting an average of $11,000 a week. . . . Returning veterans are mulcted in a host of scams. A con man named Brown opens his U.S. Employment Service in Brooklyn, promising jobs to vets for deposits that bring him thousands of dollars. He has no jobs. One veteran is conned into buying a thriving restaurant from a flimflammer in Chicago only to discover that the patrons mobbing the establishment when he first inspects it are enticed to the diner through an offer of free meals.

1947

Victor "The Count" Lustig dies in Leavenworth (VII). . . . Serge Rubinstein, who gives three lavish parties in the United States each year (estimated cost per party, $200,000) openly brags about his ability in evading the draft during the war (he always dresses as Napoleon at his parties—"Napoleon does not go and fight wars, he directs them"). His boast incurs the wrath of the entire country and, in particular, the draft board, inspectors for which mount a case against the hustling businessman. Rubinstein spends $500,000 in legal battles and more to bribe officials. He points out that he had purchased an aircraft factory and was its chief executive, a man vital to war production. Publicity, the enemy of all con men, ruins him and he is convicted of draft evasion and sent to prison for two years. . . . Spiritual con man C. Thomas Patten takes in almost $1 million in his evangelistic scams in Oakland, further lining his pockets by selling, unknown to his rabid followers, the church property and buildings he has promised his congregation forever to the Loyal Order of the Moose for $450,000 (X). . . . The con combination of Charles Richman and Howard Clements splits up after both bilk blacks in Philadelphia with phony housing projects. Richman befriends a black deacon and through him mulcts a dozen black church pastors of $28,000 on promises to build inexpensive cathedrals for them. He is arrested and gets a year in prison plus another year for the phony housing projects. Clements bilks black leaders in the Dominican Republic for $100,000 in a wild scheme to build vast housing complexes by "pouring concrete over large, inflated balloons." Clements joins Richman in jail for a year after his arrest in Miami Beach.

1948

A group of merchants turned con men in Houston increases the weight of their turkeys and chickens by injecting them with hypodermic needles filled with water just before they are sold. . . . Oakland's district attorney launches a full-scale investigation of the money-grabbing evangelists Bebe and C. Thomas Patten (X). . . . The Los Angeles Better Business

Bureau uncovers fraud in a medical rebate scheme that mulcts the invalid and elderly by hiking by 50 percent the cost of x-rays, eyeglasses, and elaborate testing. . . . The Kaadt brothers of Indiana bilk hundreds and make millions with their phony cure for diabetes (XIII). . . . Undertakers in Norfolk, Virginia, hustle flowers at funerals for a 20 percent increase after promising to deliver the posies at wholesale prices. . . . Jake Max Landau, a Middlewest con man who specializes in "selling stiffs," offers to reveal hidden insurance policies on the deceased to relatives for exorbitant fees (VII). . . . A Boston con ring cleans up with a scam of selling rare tropical plants that, after purchase, disintegrate in water. . . . The furnace and roof scams begin. Repairmen, checking furnaces for a charge of $5 each, discover the need for expensive repairs to furnaces and roofs (after tearing them apart with crowbars). . . . A huge faction of the "Terrible Williamsons" invade Michigan, taking in tens of thousands of dollars from suckers (XII). . . . Used-car scams blossom, the chief con being the arbitrary tacking on of additional costs (as high as $300 a car) in fine-print contracts on the excuse of required insurance fees. . . . Ruth Bourjaily, leader of a hustling mob in Chicago, is tried for her widespread directory racket. Miss Bourjaily, or a confederate, would call the personnel manager of a company and read off a help-wanted ad the firm was currently running in a newspaper and ask if the wording was all right. The duped manager would unhesitatingly approve, then receive in the mails, days later, a huge bill (some ranging upward to $5,000) from the "verification firm." These bills were almost always paid.

1949

A host of carnival cons become widespread—milk bottles to be knocked over for a prize feature two aluminum bottles with lead bottoms; hoops to be thrown around blocks can only be throw correctly from the back (which the barker smilingly demonstrates to show the sucker how easy it is), baseballs to be thrown into a bucket, three in all—the first ball generally goes in and stays, but this ball affects a mechanism in the bucket that forces the other two balls to bounce out.

1950

C. Thomas Patten (he says the "C" stands for "cash") goes on trial in February, and following sensational displays by the Pattens and their zealot disciples, climaxes in the evangelistic con man's conviction on five counts of grand theft; he receives a five to fifty-year prison sentence (X). . . . Black con men perfect the pigeon-drop hustle, the most successful being Oakey Jackson, Emmet Cobb, and "Boss" Harvey Caldwell (V). . . . J. Bam Morrison makes a sucker out of an entire Oklahoma town (XV). . . . Joseph Levy, who specializes in impersonations, pretends to be a prison official, places large orders with supply firms, and writing out bad checks with surplus amounts, which he pockets (XV). . . . Grandmother Marie Fuller is arrested for her Henry Ford swindle. Police find in her apartment boxes of fake Ford Motor stock certificates, spurious Ford Motor stationery and records revealing her various takes in the scheme amounting to more than $200,000. The former beauty parlor operator, her husband, and three other men are arrested and tried for fraud. Says con woman Fuller: "I've lived in terror the last two years . . . my life has been a hell."

Con woman Marie Fuller hustled a fortune in her fabulous Henry Ford swindle; "It's been hell for me," she sobbed to photographer. (WIDE WORLD)

1951

Washington hustler Samuel Mussman bilks the Order of St. Basil the Great (Greek Orthodox) out of $200,000 by promising to delivery 99-year leases on all government buildings in New York, which they can then sublease. Mussman drives two of the church's representatives (who carry valises full of $100 bills at his instructions) about Washington, promising to introduce them to General Marshall and President Truman. Instead, he takes them to the "engineers" building, where he allegedly delivers the church money to "spread about in the right places to make sure of those 99-year leases." Mussman's gigantic scam is learned, and the con man is called before a special investigating committee headed up by Senator Clyde Hoey. Hoey asks him if he has paid any income tax on his flimflamming profits. An excerpt of incredible testimony:

MUSSMAN: I don't think there was any income left.

HOEY: Did you ever stuff any money into your artificial leg?

MUSSMAN: Only once, senator. That was in 1925 when I needed cash for a stock market deal. [He told no one about it at the time.] You only got to let one person know and you got no leg and you got no money.

Mussman is turned over to the IRS to face income-tax evasion charges. . . . Patrick Henry "Packy" Lennon and his stock-market con clan begin their four-year-long mulcting of millionaire A. J. Cunningham, which will net them $439,121 (XII).

1952

Abram Sykowski bilks the double-dealing King Farouk of Egypt for an estimated $200,000 on the French Riviera (XIII). . . . The "Terrible Williamsons" con clan is exposed in Miami Beach when an internecine brawl breaks out and squads of police are required to quell the near riot (XII).

Playboy Robert Schlesinger hustled fraudulent investments. (WIDE WORLD)

1953

The trial of three French con men ends as a laughing Paris magistrate hands down gentle sentences for their three-year-long uranium fraud, perpetrated against a gullible French nobleman (XIII). . . . Two of Lowell Birrell's business associates in high con, Virgil David Dardi and Alexander Guterma, receive stiff prison sentences for their mulcting activities (XI). . . . Playboy hustler Robert Schlesinger (whose mother is Countess Mona Bismarck, remarried widow of utilities magnate Harrison Williams, and whose father is H. J. Schlesinger, a retired Milwaukee industrialist) purchases $132,000 in jewels from Van Cleef and Arpels for actress Linda Christian, the estranged wife of actor Tyrone Power. Schlesinger makes out a phony check, and to cover it develops an elaborate con, according to Manhattan's district attorney Frank Hogan. Working as a business drummer for Glore, Forgan and Company, Schlesinger contacts his bosses and tells them his mother is investing, on the sly, about $500,000 in secret Louisiana oil fields and he can arrange for their participation. After fake phone calls allegedly from his mother's financial adviser, Paul Preger, Schlesinger mulcts more than $150,000 from his employers. He sends a check made out to him by power-saw tycoon Robert P. McCulloch to the jewelry firm of Van Cleef and Arpels but McCulloch, growing suspicious, calls Preger in St. Louis and learns the Louisiana oil deal is a phony and stops payment on his check. Schlesinger is indicted on eight counts of fraud, but the playboy con man is nowhere to be found, rumored to have fled to South America. . . . Abram Sykowski vanishes from the custody of French police, who have him under house arrest pending the completion of an exhaustive investigation into his thirty-year con career. He is never found again (XIII). . . . Evangelistic flimflammer C. Thomas Patten is paroled on the condition that he can never again take up collections in his wife's revivalist church (X). . . . Matrimonial con man Nathaniel Herbert Wheeler stings his 150th female mark.

1954

The "Paddy hustle" exercised against gullible armed forces personnel, becomes rampant. In one week in San Francisco, this con game brings sharpers $40,000. The scheme is a simple one. A soldier or sailor is led to a small hotel, where he is told that an attractive girl awaits him in such-and-such room. The hotel manager convinces the soldier to leave his valuables in the hotel safe. When the soldier finds the hotel room empty he goes to the manager's office to demand the return of his wallet and watch, only to discover that the real manager knows nothing of the tryst or the valuables. . . . Gangs of the "Terrible Williamsons" move into Minnesota and Iowa, stinging farmers for large amounts in various scams (XII). . . . Millionaire con man Serge Rubinstein, paroled from prison for draft evasion in 1949, finds, despite his millions, that he has been ostracized in high society.

1955

On January 27 super hustler Rubinstein is found strangled to death on the satin-canopied bed of his posh Manhattan apartment. The forty-six-year-old hustler is discovered with tape across his mouth and curtain cord binding his hands and feet. His apartment has been torn apart as if the murderer or murderers had been searching for something. Police find an address book containing 2,000 names, listing bankers, politicians, and call girls. Says one detective, who believes the killer is somewhere in the 2,000 names, "where do you start with such a man?" Rubinstein's murderer is never found. . . . Patrick Henry Lennon and his phony stock-market con ring are rounded up after their four-year-long mulcting of industrialist A. J. Cunningham (XII).

1956

Sharpers promote the Great Sweet Grass stock through boiler-room tactics (distribution controlled by Milton J. Shuck) until the public is bilked out of $12 million for stock, which later drops for a 5¢-a-bid share, to a total worth of $84,583. The stock is removed from the Stock Exchange. . . . N. James Elliott, a con man with a long record, attempts to promote his bogus American Silver Mine stock by employing twenty top film stars to drive a truck, loaded down with ten tons of silver, in relays from Panamint (allegedly where the mine is located) to Wall Street, where the silver will be dumped while press photographers take photos of the gleaming pile. It will then, according to Elliott, be shoveled back into the truck and driven onto the main floor of the main ballroom of the Waldorf Astoria Hotel, at which time a mammoth party will be given for the movie stars buying stock and a select 1,000 East Coast investors. All others attending would have to pay a $10 entrance fee to view the silver load. Responding by wire to the wild scheme were only two actors, Ben Blue and Rod Cameron. Errol Flynn's representative, A. R. Blum, sends a wire reading: "Errol too ill at present to make trans-continental trip. Furthermore he advises me that he knows nothing about

Wonder boy of finance, Earle Belle strolling along the beach in Rio de Janeiro after fleeing the United States, following a grand mulcting of their Pittsburgh firm. (WIDE WORLD)

it." Elliott persists in his scam, but a reporter for the *New York Journal American*, Donald R. Hassell, who has become one of Elliott's aides as part of his investigation, exposes the scheme before it is completely hatched (where Elliott was to obtain the ten tons of silver remains a mystery).

1958

Earl Belle, once considered the boy wonder of high finance and head of Cornucopia Gold Mines, flees to Rio de Janeiro, Brazil, after he and a partner mulct their company through various bank loans of an estimated $2 million. The twenty-six-year-old Pittsburgh sharper was once interviewed by Mike Wallace, saying: "If you claw your way up to success, you never have to ask anyone for anything. It's a terrible feeling to have to call on anybody for help." From Rio, Belle admits that his books were "falsified and quite incomplete. . . . I am deeply sorry for all the people who have been misled and for the wrongs done . . . I imagine a permanent exile [for himself] is punishment enough." . . . Billie Sol Estes, wheeler-dealer from Pecos, Texas sells hundreds of nonexistent anhydrous ammonia tanks to fertilize cotton, leasing the tanks for the same amount as the sums farmers agreed to pay by contract. These contracts are then mortgaged by Estes, a method by which he generates close to $15 million in credit.

1959

Evangelistic con man C. Thomas Patten dies in California, his religious scams remaining the biggest of their kind on record (X).

1962

Billie Sol Estes's massive cotton scams in Texas, Oklahoma, Georgia, and Alabama are exposed. He has engineered mortgages and loans from dozens of banks and other financial institutions to cover the purchases of his fertilizing and leasing systems from farmers for more than $22 million, all of which is still outstanding. On March 29 Estes is charged with transporting fraudulent mortgages on the anhydrous ammonia tanks across a state line. Strange deaths surround the Estes scams. One of the con man's many accountants, George Krutilek, is found dead in his car in El Paso, a hose leading from the auto's exhaust to the closed car. Henry Marshall, who is in charge of cotton allotments in Texas and has been connected to Estes's many cotton fields, is also found dead in a pasture next to his parked truck in June. Five .22-caliber bullets from a bolt-action rifle are found in his abdomen. Incredibly, the death is ruled a suicide. The elaborate cons perpetrated by Estes are largely due to the cotton price supports and grain-storage fees paid for by taxpayers. Without these programs, one report states, "there would have been no inviting storage business for him to get into, no cotton allotments to obtain by fraud."

1963

Anthony "Tino" DeAngelis, following about fifteen years of methodical planning and scheming, has brought about a crafty $219 million swindle known now as the "Great Salad Oil Swindle." DeAngelis simply faked, through false-bottomed tanks, the amounts of salad oil he had on hand, and with the receipts given him by independent storage firms who housed his oils, borrowed huge amounts of money to corner the cottonseed and soybean markets on the commodities exchange. Myriad other methods were employed by warehouse workers bribed by DeAngelis to fake the contents of his oil tanks. Sometimes officials would measure from the top of the tanks to the point where the oil rested in the tank and include this amount as being present, many millions of pounds of oil over that which was really on hand. Fake inventories and forged receipts are finally unearthed, and DeAngelis's fantastic swindle is exposed.

1965

DeAngelis is sentenced to twenty years in prison for his Great Salad Oil Swindle, $1 million from the colossal swindle never recovered. . . . Donald Williamson, a leader of the Williamson clan, pulls off a massive credit swindle in Flint, Michigan, after buying a department store (XII).

1966

Two real-estate con men sell a retired school teacher the ghost town of Death Valley Junction. She plans to use the site as a future senior citizen's community. The con men camouflage the broken-down town with Hollywood-type facades and she pays them $200,000. . . . Hundreds of the "Terrible Williamsons" invade Los Angeles to pull off dozens of high-priced cons (XII). . . . Bunco operator Willard Talbot grosses more than $1.5 million in a con taken almost literally from "The Music Man." He sells more than 4,000 parents each a $489 music package of cheap instruments and accordian lessons, verbally promising that all the children will play in a Rose Bowl concert featuring an all-accordian band.

1968

Real-estate swindles become widespread, particularly in Texas and New Mexico. A group of sharpers selling undeveloped property in these two states throw a huge fete in Renton, Washington, stinging suckers who invest in the worthless land for tens of thousands of dollars. The scheme involves marks putting up part payments, considerable sums, for the land, upon which the company promises to erect apartment buildings. The rents from these apartments will defray the mortgage payments for the land. Of course the buildings are never constructed, and the suckers are stuck with barren tracts of land. . . . Italian wine inspectors discover that millions of quarts of Vino Ferrari have been made from banana paste, seaweed, tar acid, and other weird ingredients in a mammoth exporting swindle.

1970

The lost-wallet con becomes rampant in New York and Chicago (VII). . . . Prior to the announcement of its bankruptcy, fifteen officers of the Penn Central Railroad sell off more than 40,000 shares of the firm; 2 million more shares are dumped on the market by banks and other large-block holders, who work surreptitiously from inside information just days before the railroad becomes officially broke. . . . Glenn Turner's dubious distributorship schemes, such as Koskot for "Kosmetics for the Kommunities of Tomorrow" and "Dare-to-be-Great," become widespread.

1971

A group of sharpers take advantage of the success of the McCulloch Corporation's land development at Lake Havasu City, Arizona. They shovel up a few dirt roads in a spot they call Lake Havasu Estates and peddle expensive lots in the undeveloped desert. This ring, according to the testimony of some victims, lead them "to believe that we were dealing with the McCulloch Corporation, and that Lake Havasu Estates was responsible for bringing London Bridge to Arizona." (It was the McCulloch organization that bought the bridge and reerected it in their development site along the Colorado River.)

1972

Anthony "Tino" DeAngelis, perpetrator of the "Great Salad Oil Swindle," is released from prison, after serving seven years of a twenty-year sentence. He begins to write his memoirs and launches a crusade against con men like himself . . . Hustler Charles Geotis, using the alias Endicott, sells at public auctions and high prices vast areas of "lovely Maine woodland." The con man is arrested for postal and credit-card fraud and is sentenced for two years in prison, entering jail in September.

1973

A group of Bordeaux wine merchants and brokers perpetrate a giant wine fraud by mislabeling Bordeaux wines really made of a cheap red-and-white wine mixture from another province of France. The $800,000 exporting swindle will eventually lead to the indictment of eighteen of the country's most distinguished wine merchants, including Lionel Cruse, head of the 155-year-old company, Cruse et Fils Frères. The world press dubs the scam as "Winegate."

Con man Anthony DeAngeles, who brought about the "Great Salad Oil Swindle," is released from the federal penitentiary at Lewisburg, Pennsylvania, after serving seven years. (WIDE WORLD)

1974

Robert S. Trippet, about to face charges of fraud in his $100,000,000 Home-Stake promotions. (UPI)

Robert Dale Johnson, a former telephone employee of McClean, Virginia, allegedly puts together a $26 million fraud by telling investors that he will use their money to corner the market for European industrial wines used in salad dressing. Johnson, reportedly using the old Miller and Ponzi Peter-to-Paul con game, promises to return 30 to 100 percent of their investments after only nine months. The company never exists, and, according to reports, Johnson pays early investors with money coming from later investors until he is exposed. One duped businessman, Joseph Holt, Jr., comments: "I never went so far as to check out [the] business. You don't rock the boat when you're getting returns of 30 to 100 percent." . . . The Securities and Exchange Commission charges Home-Stake Production Company, founded and operated by a brilliant Oklahoma lawyer, Robert S. Trippet, with operating a con game, a soft-sell Ponzi scheme that paid investors reasonable returns on their money. Begun by Trippet in the late 1950s, the firm does not flag-wave dividends, which avoids publicity, and is ostensibly geared to providing tax breaks for those in high-income brackets, using all of the tax shelters inherent in oil digging. But the oil digging is a sham, accordng to reports. The firm allegedly installs pumps in Santa Maria, California, that appear to be working but do nothing; one farmer is gulled into allowing the company to paint his irrigation lines to appear as oil pipes. By this year, the alleged fraud approaches the $130 million mark. An early breakthrough to high-rolling suckers was made by Trippet, reports state, when he convinced two dozen top executives of GE, including Fred J. Borch, later GE's chairman, to invest more than $3.7 million over a decade in the scam. Top talent agent Martin Bregman, producer of *Serpico,* subsequently invested $50,000 and "opened the door" to a mob of Hollywood investors eager to escape heavy tax bites. These include, according to the *Wall Street Journal,* Liza Minnelli, $231,000; Barbra Streisand, $28,500; Andy Williams, $538,000; Bob Dylan, $78,000; and TV's Barbara Walters, $28,500. Politicians snared in the scam include South Carolina Senator Ernest F. Hollings, $19,000 and New York Senator Jacob K. Javits, $28,500. Javits tells reporters: "I have not [previously] deducted it from my income tax. . . . But I'm sure I will . . ." One of the biggest losers in the alleged Home-Stake flimflam is tight-wad comedian Jack Benny who receives the news from *Chicago Sun-Times* columnist Irv Kupcinet, who emphasizes that his phone call was not collect.

"Ever hear of the Home-Stake Production Company?" Kup asks him.

"Never," Benny responds.

"Then I've got some good news and some bad news for you."

Says Benny: "Give me the good news first."

"Your picture is on practically every page one in the country."

"Hey, that's great. What's the bad news?"

"You lost $300,000."

Comes the wail: "Whaaaaat?"

1975

Con man and rubber check artist Dale Otto Remling escapes the world's largest walled prison at Jackson, Michigan, being taken from the prison yard by a swooping helicopter in the charge of a confederate, similar to the escape depicted in the picture *Breakout*. He is recaptured thirty hours later in the small town of Leslie, thirteen miles away from the prison. Remling, a native of Hooker, Oklahoma, has escaped from two other prisons in California and has a career in con through most of his adult life. He once bilked a farmer in Hooper, Nebraska out of 260 hogs, and using the alias of Jimmy Mangan (he found a wallet with identification papers for James L. Mangan in 1951), hustled the town of Sidney, Michigan, for $35,000 in bad checks after marrying the daughter of the village's wealthiest resident. It was on the latter charge that Remling was sent to the Jackson prison. Of the charming con man, one Sidney citizen remarks: "You won't find anybody who'll say a bad word about him. . . . He was a very nice fellow and everyone liked him, even the littlest child loved him."

Grinning con man Dale Remling, recaptured following his helicopter breakout from Southern Michigan Prison. (UPI)

Glossary

Ace—Having "the ace"—to be assured that legal authorities will not interfere with a confidence game after they have been suitably bribed; also, "the fix."

Angle—A type of approach con men use when attempting to bilk a victim.

Apple—Victim of a con man.

Autograph—A confidence game in which a victim is persuaded to autograph a piece of paper, the signature later used to forge a check.

Backup Man—A con man's closest confederate, who operates in the role of a steerer or capper (*q.v.*).

Banco—Pioneer con game in which cards or dice are employed.

Bat—The gold-brick confidence game.

Bates—Victim of a con man.

Beef—When a victim of a con game complains after losing his money.

Big Con.—*See* Big Store.

Big Mitt—A confidence game involving fraud in a card game in a big-store operation.

Big Store—Any confidence game requiring a fake front, such as an office, bank, gambling den, bookmaking parlor; also called "joint," "the store," or "the big con."

Bilk—To victimize in a con game.

Bill-wrapper—*Arch.*, confidence man who wrapped currency inside soap or candy packages and sold the products to victims hoping to win the small sums of money. (Only confederates in the crowds actually received the currency.) *See also* Soap scam.

Blowoff—The last move in a confidence game.

Blue River Land—Any geographical area where confidence men find it difficult to perpetrate their frauds.

Blute—Newspaper clippings employed in the big-store cons.

Boiler room—*See* Bucket shop.

Boob—Victim of a con man.

Boodle—Money taken in a confidence game.

Boost—A shill for con games.

Brace game—A crooked faro game.

Broads—Three-card monte.

Broad work—*Arch.*, three-card monte.

Bubble—Giant speculation, usually in real estate, operated under fraudulent conditions such as that perpetrated by John Law.

Bucket shop—A secret room in which confidence men pretending to be legitimate stockbrokers sell nonexistent or bankrupt stock to duped investors; also, "boiler room."

Bucking the tiger—Playing faro.

Build-up—That aspect of a confidence game which implants trust in the victim.

Bunco—To bilk, mulct. Now, general term for con games. (From banco, buncombe, bunkum.)

Button—The stage in the big-store game when con men impersonating detectives raid a phony gambling den and pretend to arrest the owner of the store, thus effecting the con man's escape from his victim, who is on hand.

Cannon—*Arch.*, to victimize in a con game.

Capper—A confederate of a con man operating a confidence game who lures a victim into the game, or is already present at the game and pretends to win large amounts from the game to convince the victim of its genuineness. Also, "roper," "steerer."

Chump—Victim of a con man.

Come-on—*Arch.*, victim of a con man. Also, any device or method employed by confidence men to entice a victim into a confidence game.

C.O.D.—In short death cons, whereby various exorbitantly priced items such as Bibles, pens, etc., are sent to the deceased in expectation of the survivors paying cash on delivery, or "collect on death."

Con—Confidence game.

Con man—A confidence man.

Convincer—Method by which a victim is lured into continuing with a confidence game, usually when he is allowed to win money.

Cool—To appease any victim disgruntled over being fleeced.

Country send—That part of any confidence game involving farmers or rural residents when the victim is sent home to obtain money to invest in the intended swindle.

Cush—Money.

Customer—Victim of a con man.

Depot worker—A confidence man who works the plane, train, and bus stations.

Drag game—The pigeon-drop confidence game.

Dropping the leather—The pigeon-drop confidence game.

Drop-the-poke—The pigeon-drop confidence game.

Duke—A confidence game using cards.

Dukeman—A card cheat.

Dupe—A gullible victim who is thoroughly indoctrinated in a con game by a confidence man.

Easy mark—Victim of a con man.

Envelope switch—That aspect of a confidence game in which an envelope containing money is deftly exchanged for one containing nothing more than newspaper clippings cut to currency size.

Fight store—A big-store con game using phony or fixed prize fights. Also, "wrestle" or "foot race stores."

Fish—Victim of a con man.

Fix—To set up immunity for a criminal facing charges. *See also* Ace.

Fixer—One who sets up immunity for criminals.

Fleece—To con.

Flimflam—To victimize in a con game.

Flimflammer—A confidence man.

Flyflat—*Arch.*, victim of a con man.

Foot race—A confidence game involving a runner who defrauds a bettor in cooperation with a confidence man.

Foot race store—*See* Fight store.

Gaff—Three-card monte, used only in gambling dens. Also, a "big store."

Get-rich-quick scheme—Any confidence game to which a victim is lured through the use of advertisements and the mails; any con game in which the victim is promised great wealth in an overnight transaction.

Gimmick—Three-card monte.

Glim-drop—A confidence game in which an artificial eye is employed. Worked like the pigeon-drop game (*q.v.*).

Gold brick—A confidence game in which a normal brick is disguised as one of solid gold and sold to a victim; swindles and frauds of a general nature, especially archaic confidence games.

Gouge—Three-card monte.

Greek—A professional cardsharp.

Green—An extremely naïve victim, also a "greenhorn."

Green goods—A confidence game in which a victim exchanges real money for what he thinks to be perfect counterfeit money (prior to 1880 for various state currency then available). *Also,* "the spud."

Greenhorn—*See* Green.

Grift—Any type of confidence game.

Grifter—A confidence man.

Gull—To victimize a sucker.

Gullery—A huge number of victims involved in a single fraud.

Gypsy blessing game—A confidence game in which a fake gypsy pretends to bring good fortune to a victim for a high price.

Hang paper—To write out and cash fraudulent checks.

Hawk—To sell a victim on the idea of participating in a confidence game.

Heat—Police or legal action brought about by a victim of a confidence game.

Hot seat—A confidence game, similar to the green-goods game, whereby a victim believes he is delivering money (newspapers cut to currency size) while the real money he has posted is taken by con men. Also, "the wipe."

Hurrah—That point in a confidence game where the victim has committed himself to plunge ahead, the point in time where he is trapped, as it were, into putting all his money into the scheme out of fear that he will lose enormous, illicit profits should he hesitate.

Hush money—The money paid by a victim to a confidence man, which takes the form of blackmail and is demanded of a usually prominent victim to safeguard against his gullibility being made public.

Hustle—Any confidence game.

Hustler—A confidence man.

Hype—A confidence game using short change.

Inside man—A confidence man to whom ropers bring a victim.

Jake—Victim of a con man.

John—Victim of a con man.

Joint—*See* Big store.

Jug—A bank.

Juggins—*Arch.*, victim of a con man.

King Con—Name criminals gave to the most accomplished confidence men. In this century only two men held this sobriquet: Victor "The Count" Lustig and "Yellow Kid" Weil.

Lemon—A confidence game in which flimflammers work in collusion against a victim in betting.

Lookout—In con games involving cards, one who works secretly with the dealer, watching the other players.

Lost-and-found wallet—*See* Magic wallet.

Lugger—An outside man in a big store game.

Magic wallet—A big-con game in which the victim is induced into investing money in a "private deal." Invented by William Elmer Mead. Also, "lost-and-found wallet."

Make—To recognize, particulary when a victim identifies a con man who has taken his money in a confidence game.

Mark—Victim of a con man.

Match—A confidence game in which coins are matched. Also, "smack."

Matrimonial con—Any confidence game in which the victim is promised marriage once money has been turned over to the confidence man.

Money box—A confidence game in which a box purporting to make money is employed.

Monkey—Victim of a con man.

Mr. Goodman—Victim of a con man.

Mr. Wright—Victim of a con man.

Mush—A short confidence game whereby a con man on a rainy day takes bets at a race track and then disappears under an open umbrella, merging into a crowd thick with umbrellas.

Never send them to the river—A saying among the more genteel confidence men which means that they should never bilk a victim to the point of suicide; originated with "Yellow Kid" Weil.

Nut—Amount of money take in a con game.

One-liner—Con parlance for the short con.

Opening—Initial verbal approach used by a con man, usually with rural victims.

Outside man—A member of a con ring who befriends a victim and sets him up for a con.

Paper—A negotiable check, usually one that is fraudulent.

Parlay—To promote a victim into a larger, more elaborate swindle than the con game into which he was originally lured.

Passer—A member of a confidence or counterfeit ring who passes packages alleged to contain money or counterfeit currency.

Payoff—An involved con game which includes the wire and the fight (*q.v.*) and is always connected with the big con or big store (*q.v.*).

Peter-to-Paul—A big-store confidence game in which a host of victims receive huge profits in a short amount of time, monies paid to them from the deposits of later investors. Begun in the United States by William Franklin Miller and successfully duplicated by Charles Ponzi.

Phony—Fraudulent, fake.

Pigeon—Victim of a con man (originated c. 1600).

Pigeon-drop—A confidence game where the victim, in company with hustlers, who "accidentally" meet, discovers a bag or wallet containing a large amount of money. The victim is then convinced to hold the handbag and money for a short period to allow the owner to claim it before the money is divided. The victim is then persuaded to provide the con man with earnest money during the time the found money is being held. Obtaining this, the con man then switches bags or slips the found money into his pockets and departs.

Pitch—The verbal approach a con man uses when enticing a victim into a confidence game.

Point-out—That stage of the con game when a member of a con ring is singled out and described as a person of influence and high status.

Pow-wowers—*Arch.*, nineteenth-century confidence women who bilked victims in fraudulent seances.

Prime—To encourage a victim to participate in a fraud, usually a short con.

Queer—Counterfeit money.

Queer "the deal"—An event or person who interrupts a confidence game and frightens off the victim.

Rag—A big-store game in which the mark thinks he is participating in the financial breaking of a bucket shop in league with a supposedly legitimate broker. He wins and is then sent for more money, sometimes as much as $500,000, which he suddenly loses in a fixed stock swindle. The same as the payoff which involves beating bookmakers on racing results.

Red-inking—The threat of a confidence man to eliminate a victim from an elaborate swindle to frighten him into continued participation. Employed extensively by Oscar Hartzell in his Drake inheritance fraud.

Rig—To establish a big store or fake gambling den with crooked games before the arrival of the victim(s).

Roper—*See* Capper.

Rube—Victim of a con man.

Salt a mine—To place real gems or gold in an otherwise panned-out mine or field and thus convince victims to invest in working the mine.

Sap—Victim of a con man.

Scam—A con game.

Score—Succesful completion of a con game, particularly one bringing sizable profit.

Selling stiffs—Any confidence game involving dead persons.

Send—The stage of a con game when the victim is sent home to obtain money.

Sharper—A confidence man.

Shell game—A confidence game in which a victim tries to guess under which of three shells a pea or nut is hidden.

Shift—A swift substitution, such as employed in the green-goods game (*q.v.*), when the con man quickly distracts the victim's attention, placing a bag full of paper cut to currency size into the place of a similar bag containing money.

Shill—One who lures a victim to a con game.

Shillaber—*Arch.,* a member of a con ring who lures a victim to a confidence game.

Short con—Any con game requiring a short amount of time and usually one in which the con man settles for the amount of money the victim is carrying.

Smack—*See* Match.

Soap—to bribe a high official, who in turn allows a confidence game to operate.

Soap scam—An old con game invented by Jefferson Randolph "Soapy" Smith, in which a sharper pretends to wrap $5 bills around bars of soap. Shills in the crowd buy the bars of soap around which the $5 bills are wrapped and thereby induce a number of victims to purchase the items without money wrapped inside. *See also* Bill-wrapper.

Spanish handkerchief—A variation of the Spanish prisoner game (*q.v.*) in which the victim's money is switched inside a bound handkerchief. Also, "the wipe."

Spanish prisoner—An elaborate confidence game in which a victim is convinced that a jailed person, unjustly imprisoned, will reveal his hidden money or treasure on the victim's promise to care for relatives and sometimes secure legal aid for the prisoner.

Spud—*See* green goods con game.

Squeeze—Any crooked wheel games such as roulette, prize wheel, or the spindle.

Stake-player—In gambling dens where the games are crooked, a cardsharp who cheats, raising high antes and splitting his winnings with the house.

Stall—That point in a confidence game when the victim is delayed or momentarily prevented from participating in rewards in order to accelerate his desire to invest.

Steer—To direct a victim to a con game.

Steerer—*See* Capper.

Sting—To complete a con game, successfully victimizing a sucker for a sizable amount of money. The actual taking of the money.

Stingaree—Any con game for short money.

Stock-reloading—A stock con in which victims are convinced to sell shares in bankrupt stock for equally worthless stock.

Sucker—Victim of a con man.

Switch—To exchange real money for a parcel usually containing cut newspapers. An integral stage of the green goods game (*q.v.*).

Tat—A short-con game worked in nightclubs and with crooked dice.

Tear-up—The act of tearing up a victim's check by a con man who tells the victim he apparently did not understand the game, a measure used only when the victim suspects fraud. The check torn up is a copy of the original, which is quickly cashed.

Three-card monte—Classic American confidence game in which three cards, usually two aces and a queen, are employed. The victim must pick out the "lady" after the dealer quickly rotates the cards face down with two hands. Con men first "accidentally" bend up the corner of the queen and allow a roper who has befriended the victim or the victim to win a few rounds before deftly bending back the corner of the queen and bending up the corner of one of the aces to mislead the victim into selecting the wrong card. Also, "broad," "broad work," "gaff," "gimmick," "gouge."

Tiger—Faro (*q.v.*). Early, c. 1830s, top-notch gamblers carried mahogany cases about with them that contained their faro outfit. Upon the box was a painting of a tiger, which soon became the symbol of the game.

Touch—Money bilked from a victim.

Tout—To promote or encourage a victime to participate in a confidence game.

Watered-down company—A near-bankrupt firm promoted by con men as one of wealth.

Wipe—A condicence game, a version of the Spanish handkerchief (*q.v.*), by which a victim is persuaded to place his money into a handkerchief, which is knotted and then switched with another containing cut newspaper.

Wire—A big-store game in which a con ring pretends to have advance racing results and is thus able to place bets with bookmakers and win "sure things." Sometimes the ruse is accomplished by an inside man posing as an official of Western Union or as a wiretapper. Originated by "Paper Collar Joe" Kratalsky and The Christ Kid.

Wise guy—Victim of a con man.

Wrestle store—*See* Fight store.

Bibliography

The research for this book was done in a score of libraries, city archives, and newspaper offices, and includes interviews with con men and police and postal officials. Following are some of the most helpful published sources:

BOOKS

ADAMS, SAMUEL HOPKINS. *Incredible Era, The Life and Times of Warren Gamaliel Harding.* Boston: Houghton Mifflin Co., 1939.

ALLEN, FREDERICK LEWIS. *Only Yesterday, An Informal History of the Nineteen Twenties.* New York: Harper & Bros., 1931.

———. *The Lords of Creation.* New York: Harper & Bros., 1935.

ALLEN, L. B. *Brief Considerations on the Present State of the Police of the Metropolis.* New York: n.p., 1821.

Anonymous. *Snares of New York, or Tricks and Traps at the Great Metropolis, Being a Complete, Vivid and Truthful Exposure of the Swindles, Humbugs and Pitfalls of the Great City.* New York: n.p., 1879.

ASBURY, HERBERT. *The Gangs of New York.* New York: Alfred A. Knopf, 1927.

———. *Sucker's Progress.* New York: Dodd, Mead & Co., 1938.

———. *Gem of the Prairie.* New York: Alfred A. Knopf, 1940.

AYDELOTTE, FRANK. *Elizabethan Rogues and Vaagabonds.* Oxford Historical and Literary Studies. Oxford: At the Clarendon Press, 1913.

BAKER, GENERAL L. C. *History of the United States Secret Service.* Philadelphia: J. E. Potter & Co., 1889.

BARNES, DAVID. *The Metropolitan Police.* New York: Baker & Goodwin, 1863.

BENTON, ROGER. *Where Do I Go from Here?* New York: Lee Furman, 1936.

BERGER, MEYER. *The Eight Million.* New York: Simon & Schuster, 1942.

BIGELOW, L. J. *Bench and Bar.* New York: Harper & Bros., 1871.

BLOOM, MURRAY TEIGH. *The Man Who Stole Portugal.* New York: Charles Scribner's Sons, 1953.

BLUM, RICHARD H. *Deceivers and Deceived.* Springfield, Ill.: Charles C. Thomas, 1972.

BOOTH, ERNEST. *Stealing Through Life.* New York: Alfred A. Knopf, 1929.

BOTKIN, BENJAMIN A. *The Treasury of American Folklore.* New York: Crown Publishers, 1951.

BRACE, CHARLES LORING. *The Dangerous Classes of New York.* New York: Wynkoop & Hallenbeck, 1880.

BRANNON, WILLIAM T. *The Fabulous Drake Swindle.* New York: Mercury Press, Inc., 1955.

BRITTON, NAN. *The President's Daughter.* New York: Elizabeth Ann Guild, 1927.

BROLASKI, HARRY. *Easy Money.* Cleveland: Searchlight Press, 1911.

BROWN, HENRY COLLINS. *Brownstone Fronts and Saratoga Trunks.* New York: E. P. Dutton & Co., 1935.

———— (ed.), *Valentine's Manual of Old New York.* New York: Valentine's Manual Inc., 1919.

BUSEY, SAMUEL C., M.D. *Pictures of the City of Washington in the Past.* Washington: Ballantyne & Sons, 1898.

BUTLER, RICHARD J., and DRISCOLL, JOSEPH. *Dock Walloper.* New York: G. P. Putnam's Sons, 1933.

BUTTERFIELD, ROGER. *The American Past.* New York: Simon & Schuster, 1947.

BYRNES, CLARA. *Block Sketches of New York City.* New York: Radbridge Co., Inc., 1918.

BYRNES, INSPECTOR THOMAS. *Professional Criminals of America.* New York: Chelsea House, 1969.

CAMPBELL, HELEN. *Darkness and Daylight.* Hartford, Conn.: A. D. Worthington & Co., 1892.

CANFIELD, KID. *Gambling and Card-Sharper's Tricks Exposed.* New York: n.p., n.d.

CARPENTER, MARY. *Our Convicts.* London: W. & F. G. Cash, 1864.

CARRINGTON, HEREWARD. *Gamblers' Crooked Tricks: A Complete Exposure of Their Methods.* Girard, Kan.: Haldeman-Julius Co., 1928.

CHAEFETZ, HENRY. *Play the Devil.* New York: Clarkson N. Potter, 1960.

CHANDLER, FRANK W. *The Literature of Roguery.* 2 vols. Boston: Houghton Mifflin Co., 1907.

CHURCHILL, ALLEN. *A Pictorial History of American Crime.* New York: Holt, Rinehart & Winston, 1964.

CLARK, CHARLES L. and EUBANK, EARLE E. *Lockstep and Corridor.* Cincinnati: University of Cincinnati Press, 1927.

CLARKE, DONALD HENDERSON. *In the Reign of Rothstein.* New York: Vanguard Press, 1929.

CLEWS, HENRY. *Fifty Years in Wall Street.* New York: n.p., n.d.

COLLIER, WILLIAM ROSS and WESTRATE, EDWIN VICTOR. *The Reign of Soapy Smith, Monarch of Misrule.* Garden City, N.Y.: Doubleday, Doran & Co., 1935.

COMSTOCK, ANTHONY. *Frauds Exposed; or How the People are Deceived and Robbed, and Youth Corrupted.* New York: J. Howard Brown, 1880.

COOPER, COURTNEY RYLEY. *Ten Thousand Public Enemies.* Boston: Little, Brown & Co., 1935.

COX, JAMES. *My Native Land.* St. Louis: Blair Publishing Co., 1895.

CRAPSEY, EDWARD. *The Nether Side of New York, or The Vice, Crime and Poverty of the Great Metropolis.* New York: Sheldon & Co., 1872.

DANFORTH, HAROLD R., and HORAN, JAMES D. *The D.A.'s Man.* New York: Crown Publishers, 1957.

DEUTSCH, ALBERT. *The Trouble with Cops.* New York: Crown Publishers, 1954.

DEVOL, GEORGE. *Forty Years a Gambler on the Mississippi.* New York: H. Holt & Co., 1926.

DODGE, HARRY P. *Fifty Years at the Card Table, The Autobiography of an Old Sport.* Syracuse, N.Y.: n.p., 1885.

DOLAN, J. R. *The Yankee Peddlers of Early America.* New York: Clarkson N. Potter, 1964.

DULLES, FOSTER RHEA. *The United States Since 1865.* Ann Arbor: University of Michigan Press, 1959.

DUNBAR, SEYMOUR. *History of Travel in America.* Indianapolis: Bobbs-Merrill Co., 1915

DWIGHT, TIMOTHY. *Travels in New England and New York.* London: W. Baynes & Sons, 1823.

EARLE, ALICE MORSE. *Stage Coach and Tavern Days.* London: Macmillan Co., 1927.

EDWARDS, EUGENE. *Jack Pots, Stories of the Great American Game.* Chicago: Jamieson-Higgins Co., 1900.

EDWARDS, MONROE. *The Life and Adventures of the Accomplished Forger and Swindler, Colonel Monroe Edwards.* New York: n.p., 1848.

ELDRIDGE, BENJAMIN P., and WATTS, WILLIAM B. *Our Rival the Rascal.* Boston: Pemberton Pub. Co., 1897.

ELLISON, E. JEROME, and BROCK, FRANK W. *The Run for Your Money.* New York: Dodge Publishing Co., 1935.

FARMER, JOHN STEPHEN, and HENLEY, W. E. *A Dictionary of Slang and Colloquial English.* New York: E. P. Dutton & Co., 1905.

FINK, ARTHUR E. *Causes of Crime.* Philadelphia: University of Pennsylvania Press, 1938.

FISHBEIN, MORRIS. *Fads and Quackery in Healing*. New York: Covici, Friede, 1932.

FLINN, JOHN T. *History of the Chicago Police from the Settlement of the Community to the Present Time*. Chicago: Police Book Fund, 1887.

FOSDICK, RAYMOND B. *American Police Systems*. New York: Century Co., 1920.

FULKERSON, H. S. *Random Recollections of Early Days in Mississippi*. Vicksburg, Miss.: Vicksburg Publishing Co., 1885.

FULLER, ROBERT H. *Jubilee Jim*. New York: Macmillan Co., 1928.

GIBNEY, FRANK. *The Operators*. New York: Harper & Bros., 1960.

GOLDEN, HYMAN E.; O'LEARY, FRANK; and LIPSIUS, MORRIS, eds. *Dictionary of American Underworld Lingo*. New York: Citadel Press, 1962.

GOULD, LESLIE. *The Manipulators*. New York: David McKay Co., 1966.

GREEN, J. H. *Gambling Unmasked! or The Personal Experiences of J. H. Green, the Reformed Gambler*. Philadelphia: Privately published, 1847.

————. *Report of Gambling in New York*. New York: Privately published, 1851.

GREENE, LAURENCE. *America Goes to Press, The News of Yesterday*. Indianapolis: Bobbs-Merrill Co., 1936.

————. *The Era of Wonderful Nonsense, A Casebook of the Twenties*. Indianapolis: Bobbs-Merrill Co., 1939.

GUERIN, EDDIE. *I Was a Bandit*. Garden City, N.Y.: Doubleday, Doran & Co., 1929.

HAMBLY, CHARLES R. *Hold Your Money: A Sucker's Handbook—Con Games Exposed*. Los Angeles: Monitor Publishing Co., 1932.

HANDY, ISAAC W. K., D.D. *United States Bonds, or Duress by Federal Authorities*. Baltimore: Turnbull Bros., 1874.

HAPGOOD, HUTCHINS. *Autobiography of a Thief*. New York: Fox, Duffield & Co., 1903.

HARDING, THOMAS SWANN. *Aren't Men Rascals?* New York: Dial Press, 1930.

————. *Fads, Frauds and Physicians*. New York: Dial Press, 1930.

————. *The Popular Practice of Fraud*. New York: Longmans, Green & Co., 1935.

HARPENDING, ASBURY. *The Great Diamond Hoax*. San Francisco: James Barry Co., 1913.

HARRISON, LEONARD V. *Police Administration in Boston*. Cambridge, Mass.: Harvard University Press, 1934.

HART, SMITH. *The New Yorkers*. New York: Sheridan House, 1938.

HAYWARD, ARTHUR L., ed. *A Complete History of the Lives and Robberies of the Most Notorious Highwaymen, Footpads, Shoplifts, and Cheats of Both Sexes*. London: G. Routledge & Sons, 1926.

HECHT, BEN. *A Child of the Century.* New York: Simon & Schuster, 1954.

———. *Gaily, Gaily.* Garden City, N.Y.: Doubleday & Co., 1963.

HIBBERT, CHRISTOPHER. *The Roots of Evil.* Boston: Little, Brown & Co., 1963.

HILL, ELWIN C. *The American Scene.* New York: M. Witmark & Sons, 1933.

HOLBROOK, STEWART. *The Age of Moguls.* Garden City, N.Y.: Doubleday & Co., 1954.

HOOVER, J. EDGAR. *Persons in Hiding.* Boston: Little, Brown & Co., 1938.

HOPKINS, ERNEST JEROME. *Our Lawless Police.* New York: Viking Press, 1931.

HORAN, JAMES D. *The Pinkertons: The Detective Dynasty That Made History.* New York: Crown Publishers, 1967.

HYND, ALAN. *Con Man.* New York: Paperback Library, 1961.

IRVING, HENRY BRODRIBB. *A Book of Remarkable Criminals.* New York: George H. Doran Co., 1918.

IRWIN, INEZ HAYNES. *Angels and Amazons, a Hundred Years of American Women.* Garden City, N.Y.: Doubleday, Doran & Co., 1934.

IRWIN, WILL. *Confessions of a Con Man.* New York: B. W. Heubsch, 1909.

JAMES, H. K. *The Destruction of Mephisto's Greatest Web; or All Grafts Laid Bare.* Salt Lake City: Raleigh Publishing Co., 1914.

JOHNSTON, ALVA. *The Legendary Mizners.* New York: Farrar, Straus & Young, 1942.

JOHNSTON, JAMES P. *Grafters I Have Met: The Author's Personal Experiences with Sharpers, Gamblers, Agents, and Their Many Schemes.* Chicago: Thompson & Thomas, 1906.

JONES, WILLOUGHBY. *Weighed and Found Wanting, The Stupendous Schemes and Enterprises that Make Rich Men Poor and Poor Men Rich in a Day.* Philadelphia: W. Flint, 1872.

JOSEPHSON, MATTHEW. *The Robber Barons.* New York: Harcourt Brace & Co., 1934.

JUDGES, A. V. *The Elizabethan Underworld.* London: G. Routledge & Sons, 1930.

KAHN, SAMUEL. *Sing Sing Criminals.* Philadelphia: Dorrance & Co., 1936.

KARPMAN, BEN. *Case Studies in the Psychopathology of Crime.* Washington, D.C.: Mimeotorm Press, 1933.

———. *The Individual Criminal.* Washington, D.C.: Nervous & Mental Diseases Publishing Co., 1935.

KLEIN, ALEXANDER, ed., *Grand Deception.* Philadelphia and New York: J. B. Lippincott & Co., 1955.

———. *Double Dealers.* Philadelphia and New York: J. B. Lippincott & Co., 1958.

KNOWLES, HORACE, ed. *Gentlemen, Scholars and Scoundrels.* New York: Harper & Bros., 1959.

KRAUS, MICHAEL. *The United States to 1865.* Ann Arbor: University of Michigan Press, 1959.

KWITNEY, JONATHAN. *The Fountain Pen Conspiracy.* New York: Alfred A. Knopf, 1973.

LAMB, RUTH deFOREST. *American Chamber of Horrors.* New York: Farrar & Rinehart, 1936.

LANE, WHEATON J. *Commodore Vanderbilt, An Epic of the Steam Age.* New York: Alfred A. Knopf, 1942.

LAVINE, SIGMUND. *Allan Pinkerton, America's First Private Eye.* New York: Dodd, Mead & Co., 1963.

LENING, GUSTAV. *The Dark Side of New York Life.* New York: F. Gerhard, 1873.

LEWIS, JERRY D. *Crusade Against Crime.* New York: Bernard Geis Associates, 1962.

LEWIS, LLOYD, and SMITH, HENRY JUSTIN. *Chicago, the History of Its Reputation.* New York: Harcourt, Brace & Co., 1929.

LOFTS, NORAH, and WEINER, MARGERY. *Eternal France.* Garden City, N.Y.: Doubleday & Co., 1968.

LOWENTHAL, MAX. *The Federal Bureau of Investigation.* New York: William Sloane Associates, 1950.

MacDONALD, ARTHUR. *Criminology.* New York: Funk & Wagnalls, 1893.

MacDOUGALL, CURTIS D. *Hoaxes.* New York: Dover Publications, 1958.

MacDOUGALL, MICHAEL, and FURNAS, F. C. *Gamblers Don't Gamble.* New York: Greystone Press, 1939.

MACE, WILLIAM H. *American History.* Skokie, Ill.: Rand McNally, 1925.

MACKAY, CHARLES. *Extraordinary Popular Delusions and the Madness of Crowds.* London: G. Routledge & Sons, 1841.

MARKS, HARRY H. *Small Change, or Lights and Shadows of New York.* New York: Standard Publ. Co., 1882.

MARTI-IBÁÑEZ, FELIX, M.D. *The Epic of Medicine.* New York: Clarkson N. Potter, 1962.

MASKELYN, JOHN NEVIL. *Sharps and Flats, A Complete Revelation of the Secrets of Cheating at Games of Chance and Skill.* New York: Longmans, Green & Co., 1894.

MAURER, DAVID W. *The Big Con.* New York: Bobbs-Merrill Co., 1940.

McADOO, WILLIAM. *Guarding a Great City.* New York: Harper & Bros., 1906.

McHUGH, HUGH [GEORGE VERE HOBART]. *You Can Search Me.* New York: G. W. Dillingham Co., 1905.

McMASTER, JOHN BACH. *History of the People of the United States.* New York: D. Appleton, 1891.

McWATTERS, GEORGE S. *Knots Untied, or Ways and Byways in the Hidden Life of American Detectives.* Hartford, Conn.: J. B. Burr & Hyde, 1871.

————. *Detectives of Europe and America, or Life in the Secret Service.* Chicago: Laird & Lee, 1892.

————. *Forgers and Confidence Men, or The Secrets of the Detective Service Divulged.* Chicago: Laird & Lee, 1892.

————. *The Gambler's Wax Finger and Other Startling Detective Experiences.* Chicago: Laird & Lee, 1892.

MEANS, GASTON B. *The Strange Death of President Harding.* New York: Gold Label Books, 1930.

MEEK, VICTOR. *Cops and Robbers.* London: G. Duckworth, 1962.

————. *Private Enquiries: A Handbook for Detectives.* London: G. Duckworth, 1967.

MERRIAM, CHARLES E. *Chicago.* Chicago: University of Chicago Press, 1929.

MIZNER, ADDISON. *The Many Mizners.* New York: Sears Publishing Co., 1932.

MOLEY, RAYMOND. *Tribunes of the People.* New Haven, Conn.: Yale University Press, 1932.

MOONEY, MARTIN. *Crime, Incorporated.* New York: Whittlesey House, 1935.

MOORE, DAN TYLER. *Wolves, Widows and Orphans.* New York: World Publishing Co., 1967.

MOORE, LANGDON W. *His Own Story of His Eventful Life.* Boston: L. W. Moore, 1893.

MOORE, MAURICE E. *Frauds and Swindles.* London: Gee & Co., 1933.

MOREAU, WILLIAM B. *Swindling Exposed: Methods of the Crooks Exposed.* Syracuse, N.Y.: n.p., 1907.

MORRIS, JOHN (JOHN O'CONNOR). *Wanderings of A Vagabond.* New York: Published by the author, 1873.

MORRIS, LLOYD R. *Not So Long Ago.* New York: Random House, 1949.

NASH, JAY ROBERT. *Citizen Hoover.* Chicago: Nelson-Hall Co., 1972.

————. *Bloodletters and Badmen, A Narrative Encyclopedia of American Criminals from the Pilgrims to the Present.* New York: M. Evans and Co., 1973.

NELSON, VICTOR. *Prison Days and Nights.* Boston: Little, Brown & Co., 1933.

NORFLEET, J. FRANK. *Norfleet: The Actual Experiences of a Texas Rancher's 30,000-Mile Transcontinental Chase after Five Confidence Men.* Fort Worth: W. F. White, 1924.

————. *The Amazing Experiences of An Intrepid Texas Rancher With an International Swindling Ring* (as told to Gordon Hines). Sugar Land, Tex.: Imperial Press, 1927.

NORTHRUP, W. B., and NORTHRUP, J. B. *Insolence of Office: The Story of the Seabury Investigation.* New York: n.p., 1932.

O'CONNOR, HARRY. *The Astors.* New York: Alfred A. Knopf, 1941.

O'CONNOR, JOHN J. *Broadway Racketeers.* New York: Liveright Publishing Corp., 1928.

OSTERBERG, JAMES W. *The Crime Laboratory*. Bloomington, Ind.: Indiana University Press, 1968.

PARKER, TONY, and ALLERTON, ROBERT. *The Courage of His Convictions*. New York: W. W. Norton, 1962.

PARKHURST, CHARLES H. *My Forty Years in New York*. New York: Macmillan Co., 1923.

PARTRIDGE, ERIC. *A Dictionary of the Underworld, British and American*. London: Routledge & Kegan Paul, 1949.

PATTERSON, ROBERT T. *The Great Boom and Panic, 1921–1929*. Chicago: Henry Regnery Co., 1965.

PIERCE, BESSIE L. *A History of Chicago*. New York: Alfred A. Knopf, 1937.

PINKERTON, ALLAN. *Criminal Reminiscences and Detective Sketches*. New York: G. W. Dillingham Co, 1878.

POORE, BEN. PERLEY, *Perley's Reminiscences of Sixty Years in the National Metropolis*. 2 vols. Philadelphia: Hubbard Brothers, 1886.

PRINGLE, PATRICK. *Hue and Cry*. New York: William Morrow & Co., 1956.

PROAL, LOUIS. *Political Crime*. New York: n.p., 1898.

QUINN, JOHN PHILIP. *Fools of Fortune, or Gambling and Gamblers*. Chicago: W. B. Conkey, 1890.

RICE, GEORGE G. *My Adventure with Your Money*. Boston: R. G. Badger Company, 1913.

RICHARDSON, ALBERT D. *Beyond the Mississippi*. Hartford, Conn.: American Publishing Co., 1867.

RIDER, FREMONT. *Rider's New York City*. New York: Macmillan Co., 1924

RIIS, JACOB AUGUST. *How the Other Half Lives*. New York: Charles Scribner's Sons, 1890.

———. *The Children of the Poor*. New York: Charles Scribner's Sons, 1892.

———. *The Battle With the Slum*. New York: Macmillan Co., 1902.

ROBERTSON, FRANK C., and HARRIS, BETH KAY. *Soapy Smith, King of the Frontier Con Men*. New York: Hastings House, 1961.

ROEBURT, JOHN. *Tough Cop*. New York: Simon & Schuster, 1949.

ROSEFSKY, ROBERT S., *Frauds, Swindles, and Rackets*. Chicago: Follett Publishing Co., 1973.

ROVERE, RICHARD. *Howe and Hummel: Their True and Scandalous History*. New York: Farrar, Straus, 1947.

ROWAN, RICHARD WILMER. *The Pinkertons, A Detective Dynasty*. Boston: Little, Brown & Co., 1931.

ROYAL, H. W. *Gambling and Confidence Games Exposed: Showing How the Proprietors of Gambling Houses and the Players Can be Cheated*. Chicago: H. W. Royal, 1896.

SHAW, CLIFFORD R. *The Jackroller*. Chicago: University of Chicago Press, 1930.

———. *Brothers in Crime*. Chicago: University of Chicago Press, 1938.

SHEPARD, ODELL. *Connecticut, Past and Present*. London: Alfred A. Knopf, 1939.

SHIRER, WILLIAM L. *The Collapse of the Third Republic*. New York: Simon & Schuster, 1969.

SINCLAIRE, ANDREW. *Prohibition*. Boston: Little, Brown & Co., 1962.

———. *The Available Man*. New York: Macmillan Co., 1965.

SMITH, MATTHEW HALE. *Sunshine and Shadow in New York*. Hartford, Conn.: J. B. Burr & Co., 1868.

STANLEY, LEO. *Men at Their Worst*. New York: Appleton-Century Co., 1940.

STODDARD, WILLIAM L. *Financial Racketeering and How To Stop It*. New York: Harper & Bros., 1931.

SULLIVAN, EDWARD DEAN. *The Fabulous Wilson Mizner*. New York: Henkle Co., 1935.

SUTHERLAND, EDWIN H., ed. *The Professional Thief*. Chicago: University of Chicago Press, 1973.

———. *White Collar Crime*. New York: Holt, Rinehart & Winston, 1949.

SWANBERG, W. A. *Jim Fisk, the Career of an Improbable Rascal*. New York: Charles Scribner's Sons, 1959.

TALMAGE, T. DeWITT. *The Abominations of Modern Society*. New York: Adams, Victor & Co., 1872.

———. *The Masque Torn Off*. Chicago: J. Fairbanks & Co., 1880.

TAYLOR, BAYARD. *Eldorado, or Adventures in the Path of Empire*. New York: G. P. Putnam, 1850.

THOMPSON, BASIL. *The Criminal*. London: Hodder & Stoughton, 1925.

TOZER, BASIL. *Confidence Crooks and Blackmailers*. Boston: Stratford Co., 1930.

TRAIN, ARTHUR. *True Stories of Crime*. New York: Century Co., 1908.

TROLLOPE, FRANCES. *Domestic Manners of the Americans*. New York: Alfred A. Knopf, 1949.

———. *Great Crimes and Criminals in America*. New York: R. K. Fox, 1881.

TRUMBLE, ALFRED. *Crooked Life in New York, The Mysteries of Metropolitan Crime and Criminals Unveiled!* New York: R. K. Fox, 1882.

———. *Faro Exposed, or The Gambler and His Prey*. New York: R. K. Fox, 1882.

———. *The Female Sharpers of New York, Their Haunts and Habits, Their Wiles and Their Victims*. New York: R. K. Fox, 1882.

———. *Famous Frauds: Or the Sharks of Society*. New York: R. K. Fox, 1883.

TULLY, ANDREW. *Era of Elegance*. New York: Funk & Wagnalls Co., 1947.

VAN CISE, P. S. *Fighting the Underworld*. New York: Houghton Mifflin Co., 1936.

VAN RENSSELAER, MRS. JOHN KING. *The Devil's Picture Books*. New York: Dodd, Mead & Co., 1890.

WAGNER, WALTER. *The Golden Fleecers*. Garden City, N.Y.: Doubleday & Co., 1966.

WALLING, GEORGE W. *Recollections of a New York Chief of Police*. New York: Caxton Books Concern, 1887.

WEIL, JOSEPH. *"Yellow Kid" Weil* (as told to W. T. Brannon). Chicago: Ziff-Davis Publishing Co., 1948.

WENTWORTH, HAROLD, and FLEXNER, STUART BERG. *Dictionary of American Slang*. New York: Thomas Y. Crowell Co., 1967.

WHITEHEAD, DON. *The FBI Story*. New York: Random House, 1956.

WHITE, GEORGE M. *From Boniface to Bank Burglar*. New York: Seaboard Publishing Co., 1907.

WILLARD, JOSIAH FLYNT. *Tramping with Tramps*. New York: Century Co., 1899.

———. *Notes of an Itinerant Policeman*. Boston: L. C. Page & Co., 1900.

———. *The World of Graft*. New York: McClure, Phillips & Co., 1901.

———. *My Life*. New York: Outing Publishing Co., 1908.

WILSON, RUFUS ROCKWELL. *New York: Old and New*. Philadelphia: J. B. Lippincott Co., 1902.

WINWAR, FRANCES. *Oscar Wilde and the Yellow Nineties*. New York: Harper & Bros., 1941.

WOLFF, ANTHONY. *Unreal Estate*. Los Angeles: Sierra Club, 1974.

WRIGHT, RICHARDSON. *Hawkers and Walkers in Early America*. New York: J. B. Lippincott Co., 1927.

YOUNG, JAMES HARVEY. *The Medical Messiahs*. Princeton, N. J.: Princeton University Press, 1967.

PERIODICALS

"American Credulity." *The Outlook*, December 3, 1910.

"Another Device of the Dynamiter." *Literary Digest*, September 27, 1924.

ASBURY, HERBERT. "The Great Diamond Swindle." *American Mercury*, May 1932.

BAARSLAG, KARL. "Old Poison, Nemesis of the Con Men." *American Mercury*, September 1956.

———. "The Great Estate Swindle." *American Mercury*, October 1956.

"Back Home in Handcuffs." *Newsweek*, May 4, 1964.

"Bad Seed." *Newsweek*, October 8, 1956.

"Bamboozling The Baron." *Time*, June 15, 1953.

BARFOD, EINAR. "Avoid this Fellow! The Fake Stock Swindler Has a New Bag of Tricks." *Collier's*, January 2, 1926.

BARMAN, T. G. "Ivar Kreuger: His Life and Work." *Atlantic Monthly*, August 1932

BARNES, JOHN K. "Reloading and Dynamiting Financial Dupes." *World's Work,* January 1923.

————. "An Arabian Night's Tale of High Finance." *World's Work,* February 1923.

————. "Fighting the Fakers in Finance." *World's Work,* October 1925.

"Battling the Biggest Fraud." *Time,* July 16, 1973.

BELLOW, SAUL. "A Talk with the Yellow Kid." *Reporter,* September 6, 1956.

BERNARD, ALLEN. "The Fabulous Uranium Swindle." *Coronet,* April 1960.

————. "The Count's Money Making Machine." *Coronet,* May 1960.

"Beyond the Dream of Avarice." *Blackwood's Magazine,* January 1908.

"Big Operator Billie Sol." *New Republic,* May 28, 1962.

"Billie Sol: The Scandal Grows." *Newsweek,* May 21, 1962.

"Billy Boy from Pecos." *New Republic,* May 14, 1962.

BINGHAM, T. A. "The Organized Criminals of New York." *McClure's Magazine,* November 1909.

"The Birrell Break." *Newsweek,* June 28, 1965.

"Birrell's Day in Court." *Newsweek,* December 18, 1967.

"Birrell Verdict." *Newsweek,* January 8, 1968.

BLACK, JACK. "A Burglar Looks at Laws and Codes." *Harper's Magazine,* February 1930.

"The Boy Wonder." *Time,* August 4, 1958.

"Boy Wonder's 'Justice'." *Newsweek,* August 4, 1958.

BREAN, HERBERT. "A Master Rogue Unmasked." *Life,* July 20, 1959.

BROCK, FRANK, and LEE, HENRY. "Rackets from Door to Door." *Coronet,* November 1951.

BROWN, CARLTON. "Confidence Games." *Life,* August 12, 1946.

BULGER, BOZEMAN. "The Psychology of the Sucker." *Saturday Evening Post,* March 15, 1922.

BURNS, SHIRLEY. "Male Vampires." *Forum,* February 1917.

BURNS, WILLAM J. "The Trail of the Bank Swindler." *Saturday Evening Post,* January 13, 1925.

"Cash-and-Carry Evangelism." *Newsweek,* June 26, 1950.

"Caveat Emptor." *Time,* January 17, 1964.

CHAMBERLAIN, HENRY B. "Some Observations Concerning Organized Crime." *Journal of Criminal Law and Criminology,* January 1932.

CHASEN, WILL. "The Old Con Game." *New York Times Magazine,* February 5, 1958.

COFFEY, JOHN. "The Autobiography of an Ex-Thief." *Outlook,* March 12, 1930.

COLLINS, J. H. "If Anyone Leaves You Money—Beware!" *Pictorial Review,* January 1927.

CRAPSEY, EDWARD. "Our Criminal Population." *Galaxy* 7 (1869).

CROSBY, W. C., and SMITH, EDWARD H. "Con." *Saturday Evening Post,* January 24, 31, 1920; February 7, 14, 1920; March 15, 1920.

CROWLEY, KARL A. "How Gullible Is the Public?" *Scribner's Magazine,* August 1935.

DAVENPORT, WALTER, and BURGESS, AL. "Dirty Work at the Crossroads." *Collier's,* March 8, 1930.

————. "Relieving the Farmer." *Collier's,* May 3, 1930.

————. "Helping Hands." *Collier's,* August 13, 1932.

"Decline & Fall." *Time,* May 25, 1962.

"Deep in the Heart of Texas." *Nation,* May 12, 1962.

DEMPSEY, DAVID, and HERR, DAN. "Beware of Gyp Jewelers." *Saturday Evening Post,* July 31, 1948.

DIES, JEROME. "The Fine Art of Catching the 'Sucker.'" *Outlook,* March 28, April 4, April 11, 1923.

DOUGHERTY, GEORGE S. "The Public the Criminal's Partner." *Outlook,* August 23, 1913.

"Downfall of an Old Smoothie." *Time,* July 4, 1949.

"Dr. Cook's New Usefullness." *Literary Digest,* December 8, 1923.

DUNKIN, LESLIE E. "How to Outwit the Gyps." *American Mercury,* March 1957.

"Dupes & Drake." *Time,* December 3, 1935.

"Earl Belle, Boy Wonder." *Newsweek,* July 21, 1958.

EDSON, LEE. "The GI's Friend in San Francisco." *Coronet,* April 1954.

ELLISON, E. JEROME, and BROCK, FRANK W. "Racket Smashers." *Reader's Digest,* May 1936.

————, "Fabulous Frauds." *Reader's Digest,* September 1936.

ESCHER, FRANKLYN. "The Get-Rich-Quick Promoter: His Methods and His Victims." *Literary Digest,* June 29, 1912.

"Exposing the Frauds and Swindles." *Literary Digest,* January 9, 1937.

"Filmland Fleecing." *Newsweek,* May 8, 1950.

"The $5,000,000 Swindle." *Time,* March 15, 1963.

"Fleecing the Wise." *Literary Digest,* May 16, 1936.

"Fooling the People." *Outlook,* February 3, 1912.

FORD, JAMES L. "The Professional Russian." *Century Magazine,* January 1926.

FRAZER, ELIZABETH. "The Widows Mite." *Saturday Evening Post,* September 6, 1924.

————. "The Dynamiters." *Saturday Evening Post,* November 17, 1928.

FRIGGENS, PAUL. "Land Swindles: A Con Game to Beware Of." *Reader's Digest,* May 1973.

"Gips and the Gip Game." *Literary Digest,* June 27, 1925.

GLEASON, ARTHUR H. "Promoters and Their Spending Money." *Collier's,* March 2, 1912.

"Golden Age Fraud." *Time,* January 1, 1973.

"Gourmet Pirate." *Time,* December 19, 1969.

"The Great Ford Swindle." *Time*, October 9, 1950.

GREGG, ALBERT SIDNEY. "Pinkerton Tells How We Make It Easy for Swindlers." *American Magazine*, September 1919.

GREGORY, JOHN R. "The Three Per Cent Loan Swindle." *World's Work*, September 1923.

GRIMSTAD, LUDWIG F. "Hotel Room Prowlers, Connivers, and Sneak Thieves." *Saturday Evening Post*, June 30, 1934.

"The Gyp's Dirty Dozen." *Literary Digest*, January 30, 1926.

HADLEY, GRACE TALBOT. "Man Lives, Loves, Laughs." *Overland Monthly*, May 1930.

HARTWELL, DICKSON. "A Sucker's Best Friend." *Collier's*, October 30, 1948.

"Heirs' Still Claiming Philadelphia." *Literary Digest*, December 26, 1936.

"The Henry Ford Swindle." *Life*, October 9, 1950.

HERALD, GEORGE. "Dean of Con Men." *Coronet*, February 1957.

HOOVER, J. EDGAR, and COOPER, COURTNEY RYLEY. "The Man With the Magic Wallet." *American Magazine*, March 1937.

"How Many Say Amen?" *Time*, July 10, 1950.

"How Women are Swindled in Music." *The Ladies Home Journal*, March, 1909.

HOWARD, TONI. "The Great Uranium Hoax." *Saturday Evening Post*, November 21, 1953.

HUNGERFORD, EDWARD. "Street Railway Companies." *Harper's Weekly*, September 14, 1907.

"A Hush-Hush Deal." *Time*, June 13, 1955.

HYND, ALAN. "The Pied Piper of Boston." *True, The Man's Magazine.* May 1956.

———. "Philadelphia's Robin Hood Swindler." *Cosmopolitan*, October 1959.

"I'll Gyp You Every Time." *Saturday Evening Post*, September 17, 1949.

"Imaginative Crooks." *Literary Digest*, February 7, 1914.

JARMAN, RUFUS. "How the Spanish Prisoner Swindle Works." *Saturday Evening Post*, November 8, 1952.

KAHN, E. J., JR. "An Obstacle or Two." *New Yorker*, April 11, 1959.

KEYS, C. M. "The Get-Rich-Quick Game." *World's Work*, March 1911.

KEY, V. O. "Police Graft." *American Journal of Sociology*, March 1935.

KING, MORT. "The Secrets of Yellow Kid Weil." *Real Detective Tales*, January 1931, February 1931.

———. "The Terrible Williamsons." *Saturday Evening Post*, October 27, 1956.

KOBLER, JOHN. "The Worst Swindle." *Saturday Evening Post*, June 8, 1957.

———. "Beware the Advance-Fee Racket." *Saturday Evening Post*, December 20, 1958.

KRILL, JOHN. "Suckers' Celebration." *Coronet*, April 1957.

LANDESCO, JOHN. "The Criminal Underworld of Chicago in the Eighties and

Nineties." *Journal of Criminal Law and Criminology*, September 1934, March 1935.

————. "The Woman and the Underworld." *Journal of Criminal Law and Criminology*, March 1936.

LAWRENCE, EDWIN W. "Swindling Through the Post Office." *Outlook*, January 14, 1905.

LEE, HENRY. "The Worst Racket of All." *Coronet*, July 1953.

"Let the Seller Beware." *Saturday Evening Post*, May 13, 1933.

LEVY, NEWMAN. "Easy Money." *Collier's*, May 2, 1925.

LIEBLING, A. J. "The American Golconda." *New Yorker*, November 16, 1940.

LOCHRIDGE, PATRICIA. "Vultures on the Home Front." *Woman's Home Companion*, July 25, 1944.

"A Long History of Hoaxes." *Time*, March 4, 1974.

LOTH, DAVID. "A Look at Famous Swindlers." *American Legion Magazine*, August 1969.

"Lover on Trial." *Life*, November 7, 1949.

"Lubrication Expert." *Time*, March 20, 1950.

MABLEY, JOHN, and BALLANCE, BILL. "King of the Con Men." *American Mercury*, June 1941.

MacCRACKEN, BROOKS W. "The Case of the Anonymous Corpse." *American Heritage*, June 1968.

"Mail Racket." *Newsweek*, November 22, 1937.

MANDEVILLE, ERNEST W. "Some Very Secret Service." *Outlook*, October 20, 1926.

MARCOSSON, ISAAC F. "The 'Easy' Rich." *Collier's*, April 16, 1914.

————. "The Match King." *Saturday Evening Post*, October 12, 1929.

McWILLIAMS, CARREY. "God Will Slap You Cockeyed." *Nation*, August 19, 1950.

MEHLING, HAROLD. "The Man with the Green Magic." *Coronet*, March 1956.

————. "The Fantastic Swindle of 520% Miller." *Coronet*, May 1959.

MILLER, KEN. "Where They Celebrate a Swindle." *Saturday Evening Post*, June 16, 1951.

"Millions Cost in Fake Enterprises." *Outlook*, April 13, 1912.

"Monopolist." *Time*, October 28, 1929.

MORRIS, ALEX. "Swindlers on the Turnpike." *Saturday Evening Post*, June 30, 1956.

NATHAN, GEORGE JEAN. "The 'Mermaid' and the Farmer." *Harper's Weekly*, May 29, 1911.

"The New Crop of Swindlers." *Literary Digest*, February 15, 1922.

"New York State's Declaration of War on Fake Stock Promoters." *Literary Digest*, June 25, 1921.

NUGENT, LEE. "Here's How I Gyp You." *Saturday Evening Post*, June 29, 1957.

O'CONNER, T. P. "Criminals I Have Known." *Harper's Weekly*, January 10, 1914.

O'DONNELL, JACK. "We Boys and Easy Money." *Collier's*, December 26, 1925.

OLIPHANT, H. N. "Ghouls Who Prey on Our War Dead's Next-of-Kin." *Readers Digest*, May 1947.

"Once More the 'Spanish Prisoner' Flourishes." *Literary Digest*, November 14, 1925.

"One for the Record." *Time*, March 7, 1955.

OSKISON, J. M. "The Round-Up of the Financial Swindlers." *Collier's*, December 31, 1910.

"Our Knights of the Fleece." *The Literary Digest*, January 4, 1913.

PALMER, JAMES. "Multi-Million-Dollar Talent Racket." *Cosmopolitan*, November 1959.

"The Passing of the Wireless Wire-Tappers." *Outlook*, February 16, 1916.

PHILLIPS, H. I. "I'm Still on the Sucker List But I Don't Bite Any More." *American Magazine*, July 1925.

PORTER, LAURA SPENCER. "On the Benefits of Being Flimflammed." *Delineator*, February 1922.

POSEY, BUFORD W. "Green Supremacy." *Nation*, April 23, 1955.

PRATT, FLETCHER. "The Grift Goes Legit." *Harper's Magazine*, June 1955.

PRICE, WARWICK JAMES. "How Some Folks Are Easily Swindled." *Ladies Home Journal*, August 1908.

"Queen for a Day." *Newsweek*, July 1, 1974.

"Radio-Fakers." *Literary Digest*, August 7, 1926.

"Return of the Naive." *Time*, November 9, 1962.

"Romeo." *Newsweek*, July 4, 1949.

ROSS, IRWIN. "Mr. Hard-to-Catch." *Reader's Digest*, February 1951.

SCOVILLE, SAMUEL, JR. "Trappers of Men." *Lippincott's Magazine*, December 1913, January 1914, February 1914.

———. "Trappers of Women." *Ladies Home Journal*, January 1920.

SELIG, TREBOR. "The Financial Tout." *Overland Monthly*, December 1928.

SHIVELY, CARLTON A. "The Hatry Affair." *Outlook and Independent*. October 23, 1929.

SIDENER, MERLE. "Patrolling the Avenues of Publicity." *World's Week*, April 1918.

SIMMONS, E. H. H. "What the Swindler Steals Besides Money." *Collier's*, May 16, 1925.

SIMMONS, RUSH D. "These Swindlers Trap Thousands of Suckers Every Year." *American Magazine*, January 1924.

"Sleight of Hand." *Newsweek*, July 20, 1959.

"Sleuthing the Scammers." *Newsweek*, November 1, 1965.

SLOCUM, WILLIAM J. "Sucker Traps: Plain and Fancy." *Collier's*, January 28, 1950.

SMITH, BEVERLY, JR. "The Crook Everyone Liked." *Saturday Evening Post,* December 12, 1959.

SMITH, EDWARD H. "Profit in Loss." *Saturday Evening Post,* February 5, 1921.

————. "Fool's Gold." *Collier's,* December 3, 1921.

————. "Land Pirates Too." *Collier's,* December 10, 1921.

————. "Grift." *Collier's,* April 8, 1922.

————. "The Credit Trimmers." *Saturday Evening Post,* May 13, 1922.

————. "With a Patent Hook." *Collier's,* December 31, 1931.

SMITH, MARSHALL. "Larceny on the Links." *Life,* March 1, 1956.

SONTHEIMER, MORTON. "The Meanest Crooks on Earth." *Collier's,* December 11, 1948.

SPARKES, BOYDEN. "Highway Robbers." *Saturday Evening Post,* October 2, 1926.

————. "New Styles in Swindles." *World's Work,* January 1928.

————. "Flying Kites." *Saturday Evening Post,* October 19, 1929.

"Swindling by Mail." *Newsweek,* September 26, 1938.

"Swindling the Charitable." *Outlook,* May 24, 1916.

TAPER, BERNARD. "Somebody Is Going to Get Hit." *New Yorker,* January 17, 1959.

"Ten Thousand for Everybody." *Saturday Evening Post,* March 15, 1924.

"The Thief Asleep in Everyman," *Saturday Evening Post,* January 27, 1923.

THOMPSON, CRAIG. "America's Boldest Swindle." *Saturday Evening Post,* February 28, 1953.

"Too Good to Be True." *Literary Digest,* March 23, 1929.

"The Tribe of Barnum." *Nation,* March 20, 1913.

TULLY, JIM. "Yeggs." *American Mercury,* April 1933.

TURNER, G. K. "The City of Chicago." *McClure's Magazine,* April 1907.

"Uncle Sam Harpooning the Oil Sharks." *Literary Digest,* April 14, 1923.

VANDERWATER, FREDERICK F. "City Slicker." *Saturday Evening Post,* October 10, 1925, November 7, 1925.

VELIE, LESTER. "Swindler's Paradise." *Collier's,* July 21, 1945.

————. "Life and Death of a Twisted Genius." *Reader's Digest,* June 1956.

"War on the White-Collar Bandits." *Literary Digest,* March 6, 1926.

"Washington Waltz." *Newsweek,* July 30, 1951.

WEISS, DAVID A. "The Great Norfleet Manhunt." *Coronet,* September 1955.

WENDT, LLOYD. "The Seductive Widow from Natchez." *Coronet,* December 1951.

WHARTON, DON. "Four Frauds to Beware of This Christmas." *Reader's Digest,* December 1968.

WHITE, FRANK M. "New York's Ten Thousand Thieves." *Harper's Weekly,* December 29, 1906.

WISEHART, M. K., "How Swindlers Fleece Women." *Pictorial Review,* June 1931.

WILSON, HARRY B. "The Suckers Came Running!" *Saturday Evening Post,* February 10, 1951.

WINTER, KEYES. "Parasites of Finance." *North American,* November 1927.

WITTEN, GEORGE. "Mrs. Van Hilt Receives a Caller." *Outlook,* October 15, 1924.

————. "Felix! You Show 'Em!" *Outlook,* January 21, 1925.

————. "To Suit Any Situation." *Outlook,* May 6, 1925.

"The Yellow Kid Returns." *Newsweek,* December 24, 1956.

YODER, ROBERT M. "A Way with Women." *Saturday Evening Post,* May 7, 1955.

DOCUMENTS, PAMPHLETS, AND REPORTS

Annual Report No. 2 of the New York Association for the Suppression of Gambling. New York, 1852.

Better Business Bureau. *Beware the War Gyps.* Indianapolis, Ind., 1942.

Illinois Crime Survey. Chicago, 1929.

LANDESCO, JOHN. "Organized Crime," *Report of Illinois Commission on Criminal Justice.* Chicago, 1929.

New York State. *Report of Senate Committee on the Police Department of the City of New York* (Lexow Committee). Albany, N.Y., 1895.

————. *Report of Committee on the Government of the City of New York* (Seabury Committee). New York, 1932.

Reports of the Chicago Crime Commission. Chicago, 1919–1974.

Report of the City Council Committee on Crime. Chicago, 1915.

Report of the New York Crime Commission, New York, 1928.

Report of the Senate Select Committee on Improper Activities, Washington, D.C., 1958.

Seabury, Samuel. *Final Report in the Matter of the Investigation of the Magistrates' Court in the First Judicial Departments.* New York, 1932.

NEWSPAPERS

Extensive use of newspapers and related files prohibit the listing of specific dates. Those most helpful include: *Boston Globe, Chicago Daily News,*

Chicago Sun-Times, Chicago Tribune, Connecticut Courant, Denver Post, Indianapolis Star, Kansas City Star, London Times, Los Angeles Times, Montreal Star, New Orleans Picayune, New York Evening Journal, New York Sun, New York Times, New York Tribune, Philadelphia Daily News, St. Louis Post-Dispatch, San Francisco Chronicle, Toronto Star, Washington Post.

Index

Adam and Eve Root, 192, 194
Adams, Eugene, 259-61
Adams Express, 198
Adams, Red, 222
Adler, Polly, 127
Adolph, Anderson, 148
Adrian of Hollywood, 186
Agnew, John G., 199
Albany Hotel, 215
Alberto, Raymond, 240-45
Alfonso XIII, 248
Allen, Henry, 303
AMA (American Medical Association), 208
American Peace Society, 288
American Savings Bank, 312
American Silver Mine, 331
American State Bank, 267-68, 311
American Stone and Brick Preserving Company, 162
Ammon, Robert Adams, 199-202
Anderson, Norman, 273
Anderson, Sherwood, 267
Angelus Temple, 180
Archer, Warden Finch, 288
Arlen, George V. (Sidney Gottlieb), 228, 230, 231, 232
Arnold, Philip, 96, 98-108, 298
Asbury, Herbert, 103
Ashby, James, 294
Ashley, George (M. George Fauyer), 149-50, 322
Associated Advertising Clubs, 75
Astor, Henry, 5-6
Astor House, 36
Astor, John Jacob, 5
Atlantic Hotel, 114, 115
Auburn Prison, 137, 140
Aufrecht, Gustav, 308
Automatic Signal Company, 317
Automobile Club of America, 167, 311
Austin, George, 279
Avalon Oil Lands, 308

Aycock, Charles, 62, 310
Aymard, Camille, 238

Babbit, T., 135-36
Baby Typewriter, 72
Baker, Col. Jacob, 93
Baker, Newton D., 287
Balbach, Leopold, 301
Baldwin, Charles N., 292
Balsam of Life, 60
Bank Général, 2
Bank of California, 99, 104, 107
Bank of Portugal, 316-17
Banks, Sam, 312
Banque Franco-Asiatique, 318
Barker gang, 223
Barlow, Gen. Samuel L., 104
Barman, T. G., 255
Barnard, Tom, 84
Barnett, "Big Joseph," 34
Barrena, Juan, 29-30, 322
Bartholdi Hotel, 303
"The Battle Hymn of the Cooks," 96
Baughman, U. E., 121
Beck, Sophie, 133, 304
Belmont, August, 104
Belle, Earl, 211-12, 332
Belmont Race Track, 259
Bellow, Saul, 269
Bennett, Joseph, 325
Bennett, Mrs. May Jennings, 176-77
Berthier, Lt. Co. Jean (Marius Carlicchi), 240-45
Better Business Bureau, 150, 225, 326-27
Bezoar Stone, 59
Biddison, Sam, 308
Biddle, C. C., 81
Bidwell, A. C., 75, 311
Birrell, Lowell McAfee, 208-212, 306, 323, 329
Bismarck, Countess Mona, 329
Bismarck, Otto, Furst von, 12
"Black-Eyed Johnny," 222

Blackstone Hotel, 155
Blackwell, James, 37-39
Blake, E. C., 198-99
Blonger, Lou, 43, 214-17, 221, 300, 305, 311, 313
Blue, Ben, 331
Blum, A. R., 331
Boatright, Buck, 20, 115-117, 303
Boltz, Robert, 199, 317
Borch, Fred J., 336
Borchardt, Mrs. Freda, 188
Boston Globe, 312
Borden, Victor E., 29
Bourjaily, Ruth, 327
Bowen, Betty (Madame Jumel), 133
Brabezon, Sarah J., 174-75
Brandino, Joseph, 311
Brandreth's Pills, 60
Breakout, 337
Bregman, Martin, 336
Brisbane, Arthur, 213
Britton, Nan, 283
Brokaw, William G., 304
Bromberg, Dr. Walter, 324
Brooks, L. T., 315
Brown, Tom, 23
Brush, Billy, 222
Bryant, Col. J. J., 293, 294
Buchanan, President James, 17
Buckminster, Fred "The Deacon," 113-115, 217, 265-66, 309
Burdick, Rep. Usher, 95
Bureau of Investigation (forerunner to the FBI), 218, 283
Burgess, Al, 300
Burnish, Ben, 295
Burns Detective Agency, 280
Burns, Mollie E., 173-74
Burns, William J., 218, 280, 282, 283
Burr, Eugene, 221, 306
Burr, Shelton, 221, 306
Busch, Harry J., 156
Butler, Gen. Benjamin, 104
Byrnes, Inspector Thomas, 33, 133-34, 138, 141

Cadwalader, Wickersham and Taft, 208
Cagliostro, Alessandro Conte (Joseph Balsamo), 172
Caldwell, "Boss" Harvey, 57, 328
Calles, Plutarco Elias, 170
Cameron, Rod, 331
Canot, Sadi, 274
Canyon City Penitentiary, 50, 314
Capone, Alphonse ("Scarface"), 117-18, 223, 246, 247, 250, 316, 318, 321
Carbonelli, Charles, 260
Carnegie, Andrew, 4, 133, 304-05
Carruth, J. W. ("Hog Creek Curruts"), 310
Central American Oil, 213
Chadwick, Cassie, 4, 133, 304-05
Chamberlin, 295
Chappell, Holly, 23
Charlestown Penitentiary, 308
Charlton, Louis, 271
Chautemps, Pierre, 236
Chautemps, Premier Camille, 236, 238, 317
Chiappe, Jean, 238
Chicago Board of Trade, 126
Chosen Corporation, 321
Christian, James, 51-52
Christian, Linda, 329
Christman, Earl, 223
City Club, 182, 183
Clark, Horace, 14
Clements, Howard, 325, 326
Cobb, Emmet, 57, 328
Cochran, A. L., 81
Coffey, George, 275
Cohen, Jacob, 260
Collapse of the Third Republic, The, 239
Collins, Bob, 303
Colton, David, 101, 102, 105, 108
Columbani, Julius, 138
Combaluzier, General (Louis Gagliardoni), 244-45
Commercial Club of St. Cloud, 312
Comstock, Anthony, 34-35, 304
Conant, King Cole, 295
Confidence Games Practiced Art, 307

(Confidence Games, Con't.)
Baker inheritance con, 93-94, 304, 320-21
Banco, 19, 35-36, 295, 296, 297
Banks, 247, 248, 250, 308, 311, 312-13, 315-16, 318, 319
Begging, 122-23
Big stores, 257-69, 302, 304, 305, 306, 308, 309, 313
Bonds, 251-55, 300, 308, 311, 313, 319
Buildings, 325, 328
Carnival, 327
Check cashing, 274, 287-89, 311, 337
Circus, 271
Clairvoyant, 178
Club memberships, 321
Coins, 320
Construction, 324-26
Corporations, 208-12
Country send ("California euchre"), 43
Credit, 227
Death, 127-32, 306-07, 309, 324, 327
Detective, 135-36, 279-85, 313, 319
Dog con, 113
Drake inheritance con, 77-93, 293, 310-11, 315, 316, 317, 319
Edwards inheritance con, 94-95, 300
Eiffel Tower, 233-35
Envelope switch, 218, 313
Farm, 126, 330, 332
Fit-throwing con, 123-25, 304
Food, 326
Foot races, 42, 217, 297
Furnaces, 327
Gambling, 292, 293, 294, 295, 296, 300
Gas, 319
Get-rich-quick schemes, 66-71, 299
Gold brick, 36-39, 295, 300, 301
Golfing, 126-27
Gordon-Gordon con, 9-15
Green goods, 32-35, 297, 304
Horse-race, 20, 297, 303
Hotels, 143-44, 303
Humbert swindle, 4-5
Impersonations, 4, 133,

(Confidence Games, Con't.)
270-89, 304-05, 311, 327
Inheritance, 298, 318
Insurance, 125, 291, 299, 303, 306, 313, 315
Invention, 160-71, 291, 298, 301, 302, 309, 316
Jewelry, 9, 137-38, 298, 306, 329-30
Junk, 322
Lightning rods, 225, 226
Loans, 136
Lost wallet, 334
Lottery, 292
Magazine-and-spectacles con, 113
Magic wallet, 44-55, 217, 306, 310, 312-14, 318
Mail-order, 59-76, 122, 291, 300, 307
Matrimonial, 144-59, 303, 304, 309, 322, 323, 324, 330
Medical, 59-62, 112, 221, 236, 291, 293, 303, 309, 310, 327
Merchandise, 224, 225, 226, 227, 325
Migration, 203-05, 276-78, 308, 309
Mississippi bubble, 2-3
Money box, 118-21, 306, 318, 323
Motion pictures, 273
Music, 306
Musical instruments, 334
Oil, 205-07, 307, 310, 314, 336
Paints, 162-63, 225, 226, 227, 300
Passports, 246, 312, 320
Patents, 229-32
Pawnshop securities, 237
Personnel service, 327
Peter-to-Paul, 195-203, 251-55, 299, 303, 305, 311, 316, 317, 325, 336
Pigeon-drop ("the dray game"), 55-57, 328
Plants, 327
Real estate, 17-18, 138-40, 296, 297-98, 302, 308, 312, 320, 334, 335
Religious, 179-94, 323, 326, 328, 330
Roofing, 227, 327
Salad oil, 333
Salting mines, 97-109, 298

(Confidence Games, Con't.)
Shell game, 21-22, 293, 295, 297
Shipboard, 111, 308
Smack, 115-16, 303
Soapgame, 215
South Sea bubble, 3
Spanish handkerchief, 24-25
Spanish prisoner, 26-32, 311, 322
Spirit, 172-75, 176-77, 300, 305, 312
Stocks, 6-8, 138, 212-13, 228, 236-37, 296, 297, 301, 302, 303, 305, 306, 307, 308, 312, 313, 314, 315, 316, 317, 318, 321, 322, 323, 325, 328, 329, 331, 332, 336, 337
Three-card monte, 22-24, 295, 297
Uranium, 240-245, 329
Watering livestock, 5-6, 292
Wine, 334, 335
Witchdoctors, 175-76, 304
Cook, Dr. Frederick A., 206-07, 209, 314
Cooper, Courtney Riley, 223
Cora, Charles, 294, 296
Cornucopia Gold Mines, 332
"Correspondence College of Science," 191
Corrigan, Mrs. Resada, 154, 155, 156-57, 158
Coster, F. Donald, see Philip Musica
Coughlan, "Bathhouse" John, 112
Cowing, Judge, 137
Cox, Seymour Ernest J., 205-06, 209, 307, 314
Crawford, Robert Henry, 4
Cressy, William J., 74, 320
Crosby, W. C., 20, 160-62, 301
Crown Point Jail, 119
Cruse, Lionel, 335
"The Crying Kid," 19-20, 298
Cummings, LuLu, 143-45, 316
Cunningham, Augustine Joseph, 227-32, 316, 329, 331
Curry, Duncan S., 261, 264
Curtis, Martin, 295

Dalimier, Albert, 237
Dancing Rabbit Treaty, 95

Dandrofuge, 311
Dannemora Prison, 158
Dardi, Virgil David, 210, 211, 329
Darrow, Clarence, 144, 316
Dauignac, Emile (Humbert clan), 4
Dauignac, Romaine (Humbert clan), 4
Dauignac, Therese (See Therese Humbert)
Davis, Charles, 271
Davis, William F., 264
Dean, E. S. Company, 199
DeAngelis, Anthony "Tino," 333, 335
Dearborn, Plaza Hotel, 265
Defiance, 77
Delaney, Police Chief Mike, 216
Delavigne, Theodore, 167
Deuxieme Bureau, 240, 241, 242, 244
Devol, George, 23-24
Diamond Drill Company, 100
Dillinger, John Herbert, 119
Dill Pickle Club, 267
Dodge, Gen. George M., 102, 104, 105, 107
Doeskin Products, Inc., 210
Dorothea De la Vere Peaches-and-Cream Complexion Beautifier, 70
Dougherty, Edward F., 76, 318
Drake, Edward Thomas T., 89
Drake, Ernest, 80, 81
Drake Hotel, 92
Drake, Sir Francis, 26, (inheritance con), 77-93
Drake, Thomas, 89
Drefus, Mrs. Aurelia, 313-14
Drew, Daniel, 5-8, 292, 297, 299
Drew Seminary, 5
Drucker, Charley, 20, 222
Dubarry, Albert, 238
Ducker, Plunk, 265
Duff, Adolph W. ("Kid Duffy"), 214, 216-17, 221, 305
Duke of Orleans (Philippe II), 2-3
Du Roure de Beruyere, Baron Scipion, 239-44
DuRoure, Eleonore, 239
Durrell Gregory & Company, 314

Dutch Bill, 222, 293
Dylan, Bob, 336

Earp, Wyatt, 221
Edwards, Dr. Herbert H., 94-95, 300
Edwards Heirs Association, 94
Edwards, Robert, 94-95
Eiffel Tower, 233, 234, 235, 280
Eiman, Maurico, 24-25
Einstein, Milton, 124
Eisenhower, Mamie, 285
Elizabeth, Queen (I), 77, 80
Elliott, N. James, 331
Elm Tabernacle, 181
Elout, Henrietta, 307
Emmons, S. F., 107
Engel, Sigmund ("Carl Arthur Laemmle, Jr."), 151-59, 303
Enricht, Louis, 165-68, 169, 309, 314, 317
Enricht Peat Corporation, 170
Erie Railroad, 6-8, 11, 12, 13, 14, 297
"Erie War," 7-8
Esposito, Joseph, 323
Estes, Billie Sol, 332, 333

Fair, James, 100
Farley, James, 313
Farouk I, 249-50, 329
Fatima, Princess, 286
Faurot, Inspector, 263
Fawcet, George, 98
Fay, James, 222
FBI (Federal Bureau of Investigation), 145, 146, 248, 283, 285, 324
FCC (Federal Communications Commission), 187
Feldman, Dora, 223
Fennelly, Detective, 261
Field, David Dudley, 14
Fifth Avenue Hotel, 230
First National Bank of Cincinnati, 212
Fisher, Charles E., 162
Fisk, James, 6-8, 297, 298
Fisk, Lucy, 8
Fitzgerald, D. F., 173
Fitzgerald, Elizabeth (Madam Singara), 172-74, 300
Fitzgerald, "Red Jimmy," 222, 263, 294
Flanagan, John, 297

Flannery's Hotel, 34
Flatiron Building, 251, 306
Flemming and Merriam's Mutual Cooperative Fund, 301
Fletcher, John, 87
Flynn, Errol, 331
Ford, Henry, 167-68, 323
Ford, James L., 275
Ford Motor Company, 323, 328
Fortney, James, 51-52
Foster, Gabe, 294
Franco, Gen. Francisco, 240, 241, 242, 244
Franklin Syndicate, 3, 196-203
Freas, Dr. Thomas, 166
Fremont, Gen. John C., 17
French Counter Intelligence, 240
French, Jackie, 265, 313
"Frisco Kate" ("Klondike Kate"), 41
"The Frisco Kid," 321
Fuller Construction Company, 251
Fuller, Marie, 323, 328
Fund W, 302
Fundamental Ministerial Association, 181
Furey, Joe, 47, 214, 217, 218, 219, 220, 221, 311

Galatas, Dick, 223
Galliard, Aime, 239-40, 245
Gansl, A., 103
Garden of the Gods, 217
Garfield, President James A., 63
Garfield, Samuel, 210
Garland, Hugh, 317, 321
Garvey, Marcus Aurelius, 203-05, 309, 312, 315, 317
Genovese, Vito, 108
Geotis, Charles, 335
Gerber, Charles, 217, 218
"Gift Family," 176
Gilman, Daniel, 274
Girard and Company, 314
Giroux, Sam, 98
Given, Howard, 203
Glore, Forgan and Company, 329
Goddard, Judge Henry, 129
Gold Accumulator Company, 162
Golden Fleece Mining, 221
Gondorff Brothers, 117, 303
Gondorff, Charles, 20, 222,

257-61, 263, 264, 265, 305, 309
Gondorf, Fred, 222, 257-64, 309
Gordon-Gordon, Lord ("Lord Glencairn"), 9-15, 274, 276, 298, 299
Goss, W. S., 299
Gould, Jay, 6-15, 136, 297, 298, 299
Grady, John D., 137
Graham, Billy, 179
Graham, William, 322
Grand National Lottery, 292
Grand Opera House (New York), 8
Grand Pacific Hotel, 303
Grant, President Ulysses Simpson, 8
Gray, George, 123-25, 304
Greater New York Breweries, 208
"Great Salad Oil Swindle," 333
Great Sweet Grass Co., 331
Greeley, Horace, 11, 12, 104
Green, Jonathan H., 293
Greenberg, Mel, 273-74
Greenhaus, Charles, 316
Gregg, Mrs. Alexina, 224-25
Gregory, John M., 314
Gregory, R. H., 314
Griffiths, Maj. Arthur, 33
Grosch, "Gas," 163
Gross, Francis, 129, 324
Guerin, Webster, 223
Guimaries, Alberto Santos, 313
Guterma, Alexander, 210, 211, 329

Hagen, Marion, 154
Hall, Austin C., 92
Halley's Comet, 44, 45, 306
Halliott, Henry, 142-43
Hamlin, Reno, 217, 219
Hames, Byron, 217
Hampton, Leo, 228, 230-31, 232
Hampton, Richard, 320
Handridge Oil Company, 210
Hansen, Adm. Johann Carll, 136
Harding, President Warren G., 282, 283, 286
Harib, Peter, 154-55, 156, 157
Harriman, E. H., 307-08, 319
Harriman, Joseph, 319

Harriman National Bank, 319
Harris, Norman D., 324
Harley, Robert (Earl of Oxford and Mortimer), 3
Harlow, Edward T., 174
Harpending, Asbury, 102, 103, 105, 107
Hartzell, Canfield, 78, 81, 82, 88, 92
Hartzell, Merrill Oscar ("Premier Duke of Buckland"), 76, 78-93, 310-11, 315, 316, 317, 319, 320
"Hashhouse Kid," 126
Hassell, Donald R., 332
Hauber, Joseph, 91, 92, 320
Hawksworth, Alfred T., 93
Hayes, Edward, 61, 309
Hecht, Ben, 267, 268
Hearst, George, 100
Hearst, William Randolph, 213
Hearth and Home, 113
Heinrich, Edward O., 315
Hell Gate Bridge, 76
Henry, Patrick, 168
Hepburn, Audrey, 273
Hess, Edward J., 92
Hicks, A. L. ("Dead Man"), 128, 306-07
"High-Ass Kid," 322
Hill, James J., 305
Hill, Mildred, 146-47, 323, 324
Hillman, Clarence D., 308
Hindenberg, Paul von, 171
Hitler, Adolf, 320
Hoey, Sen. Clyde, 328-29
Hoffman, Joseph, 35
Hogan, Frank, 211, 329
"Hogan's Alley," 112
Hog Creek Oil Company, 310
Hohenau, Walter (Frederick Jonas), 165, 169-71, 316
Holland, Harry S., 162-63, 300
Holland Tunnel, 76
Hollings, Sen. Ernest F., 336
Holsinger, Maurice Paul, 150-51
Holt, Joseph, Jr., 336
Home-Stake Production Company, 326
"The Honeygrove Kid," 20
"Hoosier Harry," 126
Hoover, J. Edgar, 248, 283

Hoover, President Herbert, 86, 317
Hotel Brunswick, 19
Hotel Cecil, 174
Hotel Crillon, 234
Hotel de Soissons, 3
Hotel George V, 249
Hotel Windsor, 219
Hotel Woodward, 51
How to Sell Your Business and Beat the Con Men, 75
Huebler, Mrs. Vivien, 157
Hughes, Charles D., 199
Hughes, Charles Evans, 286
Hullum, D., 293
Humbert, Frederick, 4
Humbert, Therese (Therese Dauignac), 4-5, 299
Hunt, William P. (William P. Thompson), 52-55, 319
Hutchinson, Ruth, 193
Hydro Production Company, 170

"Indiana Harry," 126
Inter-City Radio & Telegraph Corporation, 228, 229
International Automobile League, 75
Interpol, 247, 250
Irwin, Will, 41
Isleworth Hotel, 303

Jackson, Eddie ("Eddie the Immune"), 264-65, 306
Jackson, Oakey, 57, 327
James Cunningham Son & Company, 228
James, Gen. Thomas L., 274
Janin, Henry, 105, 106, 108
Javits, Sen. Jacob, 336
Jefferson Market Jail, 275
Jelke, Mickey, 209
Jernegan, Prescott Ford, 160, 302
Jewish Christian, 307
John Hampton's Vital Restorative, 60
Johnson, Leonard, 144
Johnson, Mrs. Lyndon Baines, 109
Johnson, President Andrew, 17
Johnson, Robert Dale, 336
Johnston, Alua, 111
Jones, Allen, 294
Jones, William ("Canada Bill"), 23-24, 295, 299

Jonkoping-Vulcan Company, 251

Kaadt Brothers, 221, 327
Kansas City Massacre, 223
Katamay, Bohdan, 325
Keehn, Roy D., 282
Keely, John E. W., 164-65, 298
Keely Motor Company, 164
Kefauver, Sen. Estes, 265
Keiser, Dr. Sylvan, 324
Kelly, J. H., 60-61, 303
Kent, William, 51-52, 313
Keyes, Asa, 180
"Kid Duffy" (see Adolph W. Duff)
"Kid Miller," 222
Killits, Judge John M., 208
King, Cardenio F., 308
King, Clarence, 107
King, Dot, 313
King, James C., 280
King, Maude R., 280-81, 310
King, Mort, 269
Kirby, Abner, 295
Kirby House, 295
Kirkendall, Lester, 91
Klein, R., 62
Knetzer, Robert L., 325
Knight, Billy, 20
Kobler, John, 55
Koretz, Leo, 212-13, 313
Kratalsky, Joseph ("Paper Collar Joe"), 256-57, 299, 302
Kreuger & Toll, 251, 252
Kreuger, Ivan ("The Match King"), 251-55, 300, 308, 311, 319
Kruger, Irving L., 156
Krutilek, George, 333
Kubiak, Mrs. Ann, 157
Ku Klux Klan, 281
Kupcinet, Irving, 337

L'Action Francaise, 238
Lafayette Hotel, 289
Lafitte, Jean Pierre, 108, 109, 311
Lake Havasu Estates, 335
Lancaster, Burt, 273
Landau, Jake Max, 130, 327
Landis, Judge Kenesaw Mountain, 269, 312
Langton, Mrs. Pauline D., 157, 158
Larra, Donna Baldomera, 199, 299
LaRue, Mrs. M., 178
Law, John, 2-3

Lawes, Warden Lewis, 287
Lawler, John, 294
League of Nations, 204, 312
Leazenbec, Walter, 124
Lee, Higginson Co., 252
Lee, Richard E., 75
Legate, Charles ("Charley Black Eyes"), 294
Lehman, "Dutchy," 222
Lehman, George ("Nigger Baker"), 34-35, 304
Lennon, Patrick Henry ("Packy" Henry Hoffman), 227-32, 316, 318, 329, 331
Lent, William, 102, 103, 105, 107, 108
Leonard, David, 38
Leonard, "Old George," 296
Levy, Joseph, 151, 285, 328
Levy, Sigmund, 316
Lewis, George, 188
Lewis, "Hungry Joe," 18-19, 297, 300
Lewis, Milo F., 78, 79, 80, 81, 82, 310
Lewiston, Harry, 265
Lexington Hotel, 53
Liberte, 236, 237
Liebling, A. J., 105
Life's Estate, Ltd., 149-50
Lincoln Bank, 274
Lincoln, President Abraham, 49
Lincoln, Robert Todd, 78
Lindbergh, Charles A., Jr., 284, 319
Lipman, V., 275, 276, 304
Loeterie, William, 52-55
Loftus, Willie ("The Sleepy Kid"), 20
London Times, 107
Long Branch Race Track, 257
Long, Huey, 86
Long Island Railroad, 322
Loomis, Col. John S., 10, 11
Loomis, Ralph, 109
Lord Cave, 85
"Lord Glencairn," See Gordon-Gordon
Lorenz, Dr. Adolf, 287
Lott, Dr. Christopher, 136-37
Louis XV, 2
Louisiana Lottery, 3
Low, Seth, 274
Lowther, Edgar Allan, 29
Loyal Order of the Moose, 187, 326
Ludlum, Lou, 222

Lusitania, 264
Lustig, Victor "The Count," 98, 117-121, 233-35, 306, 312-13, 316, 318, 320, 326
Lyon & Co., 62
Lyons, Ned, 18
Lyons, Sophie, 18, 133, 297

Mabray gang, 217
MacArthur, Charles, 267
MacDonald, Joe, 20
MacMahon, Will, 67-70
Macy Building, 251
Madone, William John, 75
Magnetic School, 61
Malloy, "Snapper Johnny," 222
Malone, Judge, 264
Mandelbaum, Fredericka ("Marm"), 18
Manes, Louis, 316
Mangan, James L., 337
Man Medicine, 61
Mansfield, Josie, 8
Mantle Clubs, 74, 317
Marconi Wireless Co., 308
Marcosson, Isaac F., 253
Marks, Ben, 20, 23, 24, 256, 297
Marks, Dr. Jason, 136
Marmola, 61
Marshall and Son Jewelers, 9, 10, 15
Marshall, Gen. George, 328
Marshall, Henry, 333
Martin, Cole, 295
Martinique Restaurant, 154
Mason, Hugh, 139, 140
Maxim Munitions Corporation, 167
Mayer, Franz, 139-40
McArthur, Allen (Ashur McAvoy), 147-49
McBride, Mrs. William, 175-76
McClellan, Gen. George B., 104
McCloud, Norman, 307
McCulloch Corporation, 335
McCulloch, Robert P., 330
McDonald, Mike, 162-63, 222-23, 246, 298, 299, 306
McGarigle, William J., 163
McGrath, Price, 294
McIntyre, Stanley, 224
McKay, James, 322
McKeithen, Gov. John, 109
McKessen and Robbins, 306, 314, 316, 321

McLean, Evalyn Walsh, 284-85, 319, 322
McManus, William "Hump," 127
McNally, James "King," 33, 222, 297
McPherson, Sister Aimee Semple, 179-80, 181
McTague's Saloon, 300
McViccor, Jimmy, 20
McWalters, George S., 16
McWilliams, C. A., 272
McWilliams, Carey, 185
Mead, William Elmer ("The Christ Kid" "The Christian Kid"), 39, 40-51, 52, 55, 56, 217, 302, 306, 310, 312, 314, 319, 320
Meadors Hotel, 271
Means, Gaston Bullock, 280-85, 299, 310, 312, 319, 322
Meeker, Thomas "Mournful," 130-32, 309
Mellon, Andrew, 86, 383
Meriwether's Elixir, 112
Metallic Tractors, 59, 291
Metropolitan Hotel, 10
Metropolitan Life Building, 251
Middlesex University, 287
Mike Ryan Gang, 35
Miller, Charles P., 19, 36
Miller, Henry, 262
Miller, O. R., 120-21
Miller, William Franklin, 3, 195-203, 303, 311
Millicent Montressor Magic Hair Auxiliator, 70
Mills, Darius, 100
Miner, Jim ("Umbrella Jim"), 21-22, 293
Ministry of Posts and Telegraphs, 234
Minneci, Giovanni Mogavec (Minnec), 313
Minelli, Liza, 336
Mississippi Company, 2-3
Mitchell, George ("The Kentucky Gentleman"), 263
Mizener, Addison, 3-4, 110, 128
Mizener, Wilson, 3, 110-111, 128
Modjeska, Helena, 275
Momsen, Jennings B., 74
Monjar, Hugh B., 74, 75, 317
Montague, Miss St. John, 84

Montevideo Music Festival, 289
Montezuma Mining and Smelting, 221
Montreal and Boston Consolidated Copper Company, 305
Moore, Odie, 95-96, 318
Moore, Timothy (J. E. Breen), 33-34
Moore's Essence of Life, 59-60, 293
Moose Creek Mine Corporation, 315
Moran, Chappie, 98
Morgan, Henry, 62-63
Morgan, J. P., 285
Mormon Bishop Pills, 60
Morris, John, 3
Morris, John "Deafy," 262
Morris, Lloyd, 180
Morrison, J. Bam, 270-72, 273, 328
Morrison, Prince Bil, 75-76
Mosbacher, Miss Cecil, 189
Mount Royal Hotel, 248
Munroe, George H., 305, 308
Murphy, M. J., 174
Musica, Philip (F. Donald Coster), 306, 308, 311, 314, 317, 321-22
Mussman, Samuel, 324-25, 328-29
Mussolini, Benito, 171, 247, 248, 321
Mutual Burial Society, 313

The Nation, 185
National Power Motor Company, Inc., 168
Neptune, Esther, 155
New Haven Railroad, 296
New Jersey State Prison, 317
Newsweek, 186, 227, 275
New York Centenial Exposition, 256, 299
New York Central Railroad, 7
New York Evening Journal, 228, 318
New York Journal-American, 332
New York Stock Exchange, 6, 7, 209, 331
New York Sun, 282
New York Times, 198, 221
New York Transit System, 125
Nixon, President Richard M., 285

Norfleet, J. Frank, 217-221, 321, 314
Norfleet, Mrs. Mattie, 218
Norman W. McCloud and Company, 307
Normand, Wilson and Schubert, 140
Norris, Harris, 320
North, John, 293
Northern Pacific Railroad, 10, 11
Novena, Colonel M. (Julian Cinquez), 16-18, 296

Oakland Council of Churches, 187
Oakland Women's City Club, 182
O'Brien, Tom, 19, 37, 222, 301
Odom, Harold P., 228, 230, 231, 232
Ohio gang, 283
Ohmart, Lester, 92
Oklahoma City News, 310
Old Brewery, 5
Order of St. Basil the Great, 328
O'Reilly, William, 261-63, 264
Orient Express, 320
Ormiston, Kenneth, 180
Osborne, Harry, 81
Osman, Sulan, 320

Pahlavi, Riza Khan (Shah of Persia), 249
Palermo, Michael, 322
Palm Grove Inn, 154
Pandolfo, S. C., 312
Pan Motor Company, 312
Pape, Edward, 125, 306
Paper Moon, 128
Park Avenue Hotel, 52
Parker House, 303
Park National Bank, 19
Parro, Mrs. Genevieve C., 154
Pasternak, Irving, 210
Patenotre, Raymond, 239
Patten, Bebe (Bebe Harrison), 181-90, 323
Patten, Carl Thomas, 181-90, 323, 326, 328, 330, 332
Peary, Robert, 206
Peck, Ellen (Nellie Crosby), 133-141, 299-300
Peck, Richard W., 134, 137, 141
Peikotto, Julian, 271

Penn Central Railroad, 334
Perritt, Henry, 294
Perry, Mrs. Corrine, 153, 157
Petacci, Clara, 247
Peters, Frederick Emerson, 287-89, 300
Pinkerton Detective Agency, 18, 142, 143, 213
Pinkerton, William Allan, 311
Pittsford, Wilson, 121
Planters Hotel, 295
Plaza Hotel, 251
Plimsoll Club, 109
Plymouth Prison, 312
Poillon, Charlotte, 304, 309
Poillon, Katherine, 304, 309
Pole, George, 20
Pollack, Peter, 279, 313
Ponzi, Charles, 3, 196, 202, 305, 306, 311, 312, 315, 316
Post, George W., 222
Potter, Ross, 274, 300
Powell, Willis B., 71
Power, Tyrone, 329
Preger, Paul, 330
Prendergast, Police Commissioner, 157
President's Daughter, The, 283
Pressard, Georges, 236
Preuss, Carl A., 201
Price, Julius, 303
Prince, Albert, 236, 238

Radio Opposer, 164
Radzevil, Luodovic Radzevil, 276-79, 309
Ralston, William C., 99, 100, 101, 102, 103, 104, 105, 106, 107, 108
Randall, Otis, 296
Rattlesnake Root, 59
Rawhide Tarantula, 221
Raymond, "Nigger Nate," 127
Reavis, James Addison ("The Baron of Arizona"), 297-98, 301-02
Reis, Alves, 315-16, 318
Remling, Dale Otto, 337
Republican Chronicle, 292
Reynolds, Carrie, 174-75
Rhodes, George, 295
Richardson, Gen. W. H., 296
Richman, Charles, 325, 326
Rinehart, Mary Roberts, 288
Rio Grande Steamboat Line, 23

Roberts, George, 99, 101, 103
Rochel, Emil, 92
Roofer, James, 304
Roosevelt, President Franklin D., 86, 288
Roosevelt, President Theodore, 139, 288
Root, Elihu, 14
Rosenberg, Edward, 316
Rosenberg, J., 201
Rossignol, Henry, 239
Rothschild, Baron Lionel Nathande, 103
Rothstein, Arnold, 127
Rowlett, George D., 126
Rubery, Alfred, 105, 107
Rubinstein, Serge, 209, 318, 321, 322-23, 324, 326, 330-31
Ruehl, Rudolph, 285
Ruse, "Boss," 222
Russell, T. W., 275
Ryan, James W. ("The Postal Kid"), 259-60, 262, 309

St. Louis, 259
St. Louis and San Francisco Railroad, 167
St. Regis Hotel, 251
San Francisco and New York Mining and Commercial Company, 107
San Quentin Prison, 41
Sante Prison, 236
Saturday Evening Post, 253
Saulsbury, Ross, 222, 299
Scandinavian Credit Bank, 251
Schlesinger, Edward, 199
Schlesinger, H. J., 329
Schlesinger, Robert, 329-30
Schrymer, Mrs. Robert D., 262, 263-64
Schuyler, Robert, 296
Schwartz, Charles, 315
Scott, Col. Thomas A., 11
Seal, Jessie B., 139, 140
"Secret Band of Brothers," 293
SEC (Securities and Exchange Commission), 109, 208, 209, 211, 326
Seibert, Robert Lyman, 325
Selassie, Haile, 126
Seligman, Henry, 104
Serpico, 336
Sevilla, Celedonio, 30-31, 311
Seward, William Henry, 17

Shea, Nellie, 137
Sheldon gang, 246
Shepherd, Ada (Drake), 87
Shepherd, Mrs. Finley, 284
Shepherd, W. A., 87
Sherman, David, 51-52
Sheridan Trust and Savings Bank, 265
Shinburn, Mark ("Baron"), 18
Shirer, William L., 239
Shirley, Samuel, 292
Shiro, Mayor Victor, 109
Shuck, Milton J., 331
Short, Delmar, 91, 92, 320
Sickles, Gen. Daniel, 14
Sickles, John H., 292
Silver King Mine, 302
Simmons, John Leonard, 151
Sing Sing Prison, 285, 287, 309, 314, 323
Sir Francis Drake Association, 80
Sisler, Eric, 273
Skaggs, Elijah, 292, 298
Slack, John, 96, 98-107, 298
Smith, Beverly, Jr., 287
Smith, George, 303
Smith, Gipsy, 179
Smith, Frank (Cameron Bostetter, "Red Adams," "Big Charlie" White), 37-39
Smith, Jefferson Randolph ("Soapy"), 215
Smith, Sam, 293
Smith, Thomas, 15
Smith, William Cameron Morrow, 93-94, 321
"Snitzer the Kid," 222
Snively, F. M., 34
Soezy Sewing Machine, 73-74
Sokolowski, George, 98
Southern Pacific Railroad, 302
Southeastern Express Company, 282
South Sea Company, 3
Spanish Armada, 26
Speake, Inspector James E., 29
Spear, Cam, 306
Spencer, Richard, 122
Spencer, W. B., 217, 219, 221
Spring Grove Cemetery, 227
Stambaugh, Mrs. Susan, 175-76
Stanley, Marie, 145-46
Stavisky, Serge Alexandre

("Sacha"), 235-38, 300, 317, 319, 320
Stewart, Cecil P., 208-09, 323
Stewart, W. J., 83
Sting, The, 20
Stockholm Technical College, 251
Stokes, Edward S. ("Ned"), 8
Storey Cotton Company, 133
Strange Death of President Harding, The, 283
Straus, Henry, 174
Strauss, Jesse, 124
Streisand, Barbra, 336
Strosnider, John Henry, 20, 268, 269
Strunk, H. D., 201
Summerfield, Larry, 98
Sunday, Billy, 180
Sûreté Générale, 236, 238
Swain, Denver S., 184
Swan-Finch Oil Co., 209
Swedish Commerce Bank, 251
Sweeney & Johnson, 224
Sweeney, Patrick, 224
Sykowski, Abram, 246-50, 301, 312, 318, 320, 321, 324, 329, 330
Syracuse University, 208

Talbot, Willard, 334
Taney, Roger Brooke, 17
Tankerville, Lady, 307
Taper, Bernard, 183
Tarkington, Booth, 288
Taylor, Augie, 271, 272
Teapot Dome, 283
Temperance Hotel, 275
Tennant, Dr. John, 59, 291
Thole, A. H., 65-66
Thompson, "Titanic" (Alvin Clarence Thomas), 126-27, 308
Tiffany, Charles Lewis, 103, 104, 108
Tinker, Edward, 291
Titanic, 126
Tourbillon, Robert Arthur, 317
Town, Richard, 2
Townsend and Company, 316
Tracy, Christ, 302
Trinity College, 275
Trippet, Robert S., 326
Truman, President Harry, 328
Trussel, George, 296

Tuberclecide, 62
Turley, "Big Joe," 20
Turlington's Original Balsam, 60
Turner, Dick, 215
Turner, Glenn, 325
Turner, John (Hank Davis), 222-23
Tuscarora Rice, 60
Tutalo, Joseph, 323
Tweed, Boss Mary, 8

Udderzook, William, 299
Uhlig, H. M., 201
Union National des Combattants, 239
Union Pacific Railroad, 8, 101
United Dye and Chemical Corporation, 210
United Shoe Shining Company, 308
U.S. Federal Penitentiary-Alcatraz, 121
U.S. Federal Penitentiary-Atlanta, 205, 287, 288, 315
U.S. Federal Penitentiary-Leavenworth, 90, 121, 285, 319, 320
U.S. Federal Penitentiary-McNeil Island, 288
Universal Studios, 273
University of California, 184
University of Kansas, 289
University of Michigan Law School, 208

Van Cleef and Arpels Jewelers, 329-330
Vanderbilt, Commodore Cornelius, 6-8
Van Zand, George N., 139, 140
Vasquez, Camilo Lopez, 29-30, 322
Victoria, Queen, 12
Villiers, Elizabeth (Countess of Orkney), 2
Villiers, Jeanette, 141-43, 298
Volonte, 236, 238

"Waco Kid," 217
Waddell, Reed, 19, 32, 37, 300, 301
Waldorf Astoria Hotel, 331
Wallace, John, 222
Wallace, Mike, 332
Wallace, Tom, 222
Wall Street Journal, 336

Walters, Barbara, 336
Ward, E. J., 217, 218
Ward, Pat, 209
Warszawiak, Herman, 307
Washington Post, 284
Washington Syndicate, 199
Waterlow & Sons, 318
Watts, William, 121
Webb City gang, 217
Weber, August, 201
Weil, Joseph ("Yellow Kid"), 24, 112-115, 117, 128, 157, 217, 223, 265-68, 269, 285, 299, 303, 306, 309, 311, 312, 315, 320, 321
Weinstein, Frank, 201
Weinstein, I., 72
Weiss, John, 322
Wentworth, Mayor "Long John," 295
Westchester Depot Gang, 35
Western Union, 8, 219, 262
Weyman, Stanley Clifford, 285-87, 311
Wheeler, Nathaniel Herbert, 151, 330
White, Dr. Theodore, 191-94, 305
Whiteaker, Mrs. Sudie, 78, 79, 80, 81, 82, 310

Whitehead, Don, 282
White Star Steamship Co., 276
Whitman, Alonzo J., 303
Whyland, Charles D., 222
Wicks, Tom, 295
Wilby, Ralph Marshall (James W. Ralston), 320, 322, 323
Wilde, Oscar, 18-19, 300
Williams, Andy, 336
Williams, Harrison, 329
Williams, J. P., 34
Williamson, Alexander ("The Gopher"), 225
Williamson, Charles, 225-26
Williamson, Donald, 227, 333
Williamson, George ("Goose Neck"), 225
Williamson, George C., 226
Williamson, Isaac Cotton, 226
Williamson, Isaac ("Two Thumbs"), 225
Williamson, James, 224
Williamson, Mrs. Jean, 226
Williamson, Jennie ("Black Queen"), 225
Williamson, Mrs. Katherine, 224

Williamson, Robert Logan, 224
Williamson, Tom ("Texas"), 225
Williamsons, the "Terrible," 223-27, 228, 317, 320, 321, 327, 329, 330, 334
Wilson, Allen D., 107
Wilson, "Beau," 2
Wilson, President Woodrow, 48, 50, 85, 288
Winchester, Walt, 295
Wintemute, W. T., 307
Wiseman, Samuel, 224-25
Wood, Robert, 29
Worms Bank, 241
Worth, Adam, 18
Worthington, "Big John," 267, 311
Wyatt, Judge Inzer B., 213
Wylie, Philip, 288
Wyoming, U.S.S., 286

Yale University, 289
Yant, Otto, 81, 91, 92
Yoakum, Benjamin F., 167, 168
Yoder, Robert, 287

Zoppot Casino, 247
Zug, Edgar, 175-76, 304